Ancient Mesoamerican Warfare

Ancient Mesoamerican Warfare

Edited by

M. Kathryn Brown
Travis W. Stanton

ALTAMIRA
PRESS
A Division of
ROWMAN & LITTLEFIELD PUBLISHERS, INC.
Walnut Creek • Lanham • New York • Oxford

AltaMira Press
A Division of Rowman & Littlefield Publishers, Inc.
1630 North Main Street, #367
Walnut Creek, CA 94596
www.altamirapress.com

Rowman & Littlefield Publishers, Inc.
A Member of the Rowman & Littlefield Publishing Group
4501 Forbes Blvd., Suite 200
Lanham, MD 20706

PO Box 317
Oxford
OX2 9RU, UK

British Library Cataloguing in Publication Information Available

Library of Congress Cataloging-in-Publication Data

Ancient Mesoamerican warfare / edited by M. Kathryn Brown & Travis W. Stanton.
    p. cm.
    Includes bibliographical references and index.
    ISBN 0–7591–0282–1 (hardback)—ISBN 0–7591–0283-X (pbk.)
  1. Indians of Mexico—Warfare.   2. Indians of Central America—Warfare.   3. Indians of Mexico—Antiquities.   4. Indians of Central America—Antiquities.   5. Archaeology—Methodology.   6. Mexico—Antiquities.   7. Central America—Antiquities.   I. Brown, M. Kathryn, 1965–   II. Stanton, Travis W., 1971–
    F1219.3.M55A43   2003
    972′.01—dc21
                                    2002154153

Printed in the United States of America

♾ ™ The paper used in this publication meets the minimum requirements of American National Standard for Information Sciences—Permanence of Paper for Printed Library Materials, ANSI/NISO Z39.48–1992.

Contents

List of Figures and Tables

Figures

Table

Chapter One

Studying Warfare in Ancient Mesoamerica

Travis W. Stanton and M. Kathryn Brown

From the first encounters between Spanish conquistadores and the indigenous populations of Mesoamerica, the Western world has known that the civilizations of Middle America, like all complex societies, engaged in violent conflict. Bernal Díaz del Castillo's (1956) incredible account of the first three Spanish expeditions to Yucatán and Mexico, culminating in the conquest of Tenochtitlán by Hernán Cortés, contains numerous descriptions of indigenous military tactics, arms, and fortifications as well as factional, alliance, and tribute relationships. Although written from the Spanish perspective, we know from such ethnohistoric accounts that the Aztecs, Totonacs, Maya, and Tlaxcalans, among other groups, were well versed in the arts of violent aggression. Yet our understanding of the nature, extent, and variability of pre-Columbian warfare, especially from early periods, remains limited. This volume is an attempt to broaden both our understanding of the diverse nature of pre-Columbian warfare and violent conflict in ancient Mesoamerica and address approaches to the study of warfare in the archaeological record.

The topic of warfare has received sustained attention from Meso-american archaeologists over the past few decades (Carlson 1991; Conrad and Demarest 1984; Demarest 1978, 1997a, 1997b; Fox 1987;

Freidel 1986a, 1992; Hassig 1988, 1992a, 1992b; Inomata 1997; Marcus and Flannery 1996; Pohl and Pohl 1994; Schele and Freidel 1990; Schele and Miller 1986; Webster 1975, 1976a, 1976b, 1976c, 1977, 1993, 1998), yet our understanding of the range, nature, and variability of warfare remains underdeveloped. This volume was conceived as a forum to develop basic criteria to identify the material patterns of warfare and better contextualize these activities in the broader cultural system. Since this is the first comprehensive edited volume on warfare in Meso-america, a variety of methodological approaches have been included to showcase the diverse ways that Mesoamerican researchers are iden-tifying and interpreting the material remains of warfare. This volume provides a number of productive strategies toward a greater under-standing of these issues and for interpreting data related to warfare and other forms of violent conflict.

Definitional Issues

Although we have charged the contributors to this volume with exploring the nature of warfare in ancient Mesoamerica, the term *warfare* itself invites discussion. What is warfare? Terms used to denote forms of violent aggression are notoriously ill defined (see Ferguson 1984, 1990; Fried et al. 1968; Givens and Nettleship 1976; LeVine and Campbell 1972; Nettleship 1975). The lack of consensus is due to a variety of reasons, including arguments regarding the "causes" of various forms of aggression, whether aggression is part of "human nature," and scales of aggression. This list is not inclusive but identi-fies some key conceptual differences among scholars studying the issue. A further problem concerns the use of classificatory systems that construct analytical boundaries between types of aggression. Dis-tinguishing between behaviors such as raiding and war can be as dif-ficult as placing societies in neoevolutionary categories, such as bands, tribes, chiefdoms, and states (see McIntosh 1999; Yoffee 1993, 1994). Categories are difficult to distinguish because of the diversity of human behavior. Furthermore, as chapter 10 in this volume illustrates, our etic categories of aggression may not match the emic typologies of the people we study. In this volume, we are concerned not so much with a focus on a type of violent aggression as with expressions of its diversity in the archaeological record of Mesoamerica. Thus, we have adopted two rather general terms for participants to use: *warfare* and *conflict*.

Although used interchangeably with terms such as *war, violence, aggression,* and *conflict* by archaeologists, *warfare* is defined quite broadly. Divale and Harris (cited in Riches 1991:290; see also Monks and Osgood 2000:6) define *warfare* as follows: "Warfare means all organized forms of inter-group homicide involving combat teams of two or more persons, [and] explicitly includes highly localized and small-scale incidents which would be more usually described as skirmishes, raids, or feuds." *Conflict* is similarly defined broadly. This term can be used to denote small-scale disagreements between individuals, large-scale war between nation-states, and situations ambiguously described as being "disharmonious." We chose such general terms because our intentions are to explore the diversity of material remains related to violent aggression in ancient Mesoamerica. Thus, the scale, nature, and causes of such behavior have been left to the discretion of the authors.

Organization and Introduction

This volume is organized into four thematic sections followed by a comparative chapter and a summary view. The four sections are 1) warfare, spatial boundaries, and the material record; 2) warfare and ritual; 3) epigraphic and iconographic approaches to warfare; and 4) ethnohistoric and ethnographic approaches to warfare. Following the four thematic sections, a comparative study from the American Southwest covers issues related to the study of warfare in both regions. Payson Sheets then follows with a summary view.

The contributions in the volume have built on previous scholarly work. In this introduction, we briefly summarize and critique several key studies of warfare and conflict in ancient Mesoamerica. It is not our intention, however, to synthesize the entire corpus of literature on Mesoamerican warfare and conflict, as space constraints will certainly not allow us to do so. Instead, we provide an overview of the major themes addressed by the following chapters.

Warfare, Spatial Boundaries, and the Material Record

The first section of this volume addresses settlement pattern data, boundary maintenance, and the impact of conflict on material culture. Although sometimes studied apart, these three facets of archaeological inquiry are often studied in tandem to investigate the nature of intergroup conflict. For example, settlement pattern data, such as the presence of fortifications, the defensible (or nondefensible) location of sites, and access to routes of communication and transportation, have been examined as indicators of conflict (Armillas 1944, 1948, 1951; Demarest et al. 1997; Freidel 1992; Gorenstein 1973; Hassig 1988, 1992a; Hirth 1989, 1995; Litvak King 1971; Sanders et al. 1979:104–5; Webster 1975, 1976a, 1977b, 1977c, 1979, 1980). Settlement pattern data, combined with evidence for changes in material culture, however, have also been used to support models of warfare and conflict. Mesoamerican archaeologists have identified changes in ceramics and other material categories as evidence for invasions or migrations. Notable examples include Sabloff and Willey's (1967; see also Adams 1973; Ball 1974; Fox 1978, 1981, 1987; Thompson 1970) fine-orange invasion, the proposed conquest of Kaminaljuyú and other areas by warriors from Teotihuacan (Hirth 1978; Hirth and Angulo V. 1981; Kidder et al. 1946:225), the imperialistic tendencies of Monte Albán (Marcus and Flannery 1996; Redmond 1983; Spencer 1982), and various Epiclassic migration hypotheses that equate ethnohistoric accounts with changes in material culture (Nicholson 1960; see also Chadwick 1966; Jiménez M. 1966; McCafferty, chapter 12 in this volume). Additionally, boundaries between styles of material culture are often interpreted as ethnic or polity boundaries characterized by varying degrees of conflict. For example, in a settlement pattern study of the Texcoco region, Parsons (1971:202–8) suggested that the virtual abandonment of the central portion of this region may have been a result of conflict between the Epiclassic centers of Tula and Cholula. Parsons (1971), on the basis of the known distribution of settlements and ceramics types, hypothesized that the northern Tula polity was associated with Mazapan ceramics and that the southern Cholula polity was associated with Aztec I ceramics. The apparent vacant space in the Texcoco region between these two ceramic spheres was postulated to be a no-man's-land between these two competing polities. Similar arguments have been proposed for polities in other regions as well (Andrews and Robles C. 1985; Freidel 1992). In this section, Bey, Golden, and Joyce discuss ancient Mesoamerican warfare and conflict in light of these data sets.

In chapter 2, Bey examines the use of ceramics in archaeological models of warfare. Ceramics are extremely important in Mesoamerica and elsewhere because they are so ubiquitous and can shed light on various behaviors related to social, economic, and political interaction. Archaeologists consistently use this artifact class to understand both chronology and the spatial scale of interactions. Most current models of warfare based on ceramic data, however, assume a great deal about ceramic production, distribution, use, and discard. As Bey illustrates with three examples from the Maya lowlands, such assumptions are common in archaeological interpretations of Mesoamerican warfare (Ball 1993; Davies 1977; Foias and Bishop 1997; Sabloff and Willey 1967).

Some studies suggest that ceramics were impacted by conflict. Bey points to a study by Foias and Bishop (1997) indicating that increasing conflict in the Petexbatun area of the Maya lowlands resulted in the "balkanization" of some ceramic attributes. Other studies not covered by Bey also suggest that conflict impacts ceramic production and distribution. In a ceramic study of the "hegemonic" states of the early Aztec period, Minc et al. (1994) suggested that the economy of a conquered community could be greatly affected by its absorption into new political spheres. They cite the mid-thirteenth-century conquest of Culhuacan by Coatlinchan. This conquest appears to have affected the distribution of Black/Orange ceramics and subsequent exchange interactions in Central Mexico. The potters of Culhuacan may have realigned their ceramics to meet the demands of the consumers from the Coatlinchan area. Similarly, Redmond and Spencer (Redmond 1983; Redmond and Spencer 1983; Spencer 1982) argued that ceramic changes in the Cuicatlán Cañada during Monte Albán period II, combined with other evidence such as shifts in settlement, evidence of destruction, the creation of a buffer zone, and the construction of a fortress, suggest a military takeover by the Zapotecs (see also Joyce 1993a and chapter 4 in this volume; Zeitlin 1990; Zeitlin and Joyce 1999). While these studies suggest that warfare could impact the production and distribution of ceramics, they neither adequately address the complex links between ceramic distribution in the material record and conflict nor explain how or why ceramic production and distribution is variably impacted by conflict. The diverse ways in which people create and consume style (see Carr and Neitzel 1995; Conkey and Hastorf 1990; Dietler and Herbich 1989) and use technology (see Dobres 1995) are seldom articulated. The fact that Aztec ceramics are rarely found at centers conquered by the Aztec suggests that using ceramics alone to infer patterns of warfare and conflict is problematic (see Berdan et al. 1996).

A central question that Bey addresses is how ceramic production and distribution systems articulate with sociopolitical interactions including warfare and conquest. This question is difficult to answer but is important for constructing methodologies that rely heavily on ceramic data. Bey argues convincingly that we must consider the social agency of potters and those who may influence their behavior to gain a better understanding about how material culture and style are used by people (see also Arnold 1999). His argument could be productively used to reevaluate other classes of data as well (such as art and architectural styles).

Turning to conjunctive approaches using both settlement and ceramic data, Joyce and Golden analyze evidence for warfare and conflict in Oaxaca and the Maya lowlands, respectively. Both studies address issues of boundary maintenance and polity integration. In chapter 3, Golden examines the issue of lowland Maya warfare at La Pasadita, a secondary center located on the boundary between the two nearby competing polities of Yaxchilán and Piedras Negras in the Usumacinta Basin. Golden addresses sociopolitical organization and boundary development during the Late Classic period, when a limited historical sequence focusing on alliance and warfare was recorded by the elite of Yaxchilán, Piedras Negras, and several secondary centers, including La Pasadita. Examining various data classes, he suggests that elites actively participated in social negotiations that determined boundaries between hostile polities. Through analysis of such boundaries, we can better understand the dynamics of interpolity conflict.

In chapter 4, Joyce examines settlement patterns and various classes of material culture in the Río Verde Valley of Oaxaca to approach the question of military imperial expansion. Joyce concludes that, contrary to traditional reconstructions by Marcus and Flannery (1996; Marcus 1976, 1983, 1992a), archaeological sites in the lower Río Verde do not suggest Zapotec imperialism and military conquest. Although there appear to be cultural ties between the two areas, the evidence does not suggest conquest warfare, as can be seen in the Cuicatlán Cañada, where Redmond and Spencer (1983; Redmond 1983; Spencer 1982) documented strong evidence for Zapotec military involvement. In fact, Joyce suggests that the best evidence indicating a conquest of the lower Río Verde implicates Teotihuacan, a site that numerous Mesoamericanists have speculated was a center of imperial power based on the distribution of stylistic attributes. This chapter highlights the methodological intricacies for identifying imperial expansion.

Bey, Golden, and Joyce not only lead us to reexamine how we use artifactual and settlement data to reconstruct patterns of warfare and conflict but also implicitly lead us to rethink how we conceptualize boundaries. Boundaries can be artificially imposed as archaeologists attempt to draw arbitrary lines around "culture areas" and time periods by using material culture to reconstruct polities and ethnicities. As numerous scholars have pointed out (Barth 1969; Carr and Neitzel 1995), equating such variables can be problematic. Further, even historically documented and apparently clear-cut boundaries marked by fortifications, such as the Tarascan/Aztec border (see Brundage 1972; Gorenstein and Pollard 1991; Hyslop 1976; Pollard 1994; Stanislawski 1947), were complex places. People often crossed these boundaries on a daily basis to engage in a variety of social interactions. While violent conflict is an important aspect of all complex societies, we should remain cognizant that daily life continues even during some of the most extreme forms of conflict and that people often ignore the boundaries imposed by elites and combatants. Our notion of conflict and boundaries may need revision as the fluid nature of some boundaries becomes more apparent.

Warfare and Ritual

Ritual behavior has received much attention by scholars in Mesoamerica since the inception of systematic archaeological investigations in the 1800s. This is largely due to the popular appeal of ceremonial structures and the elaborate nature of many ritual deposits. Rituals have been discussed recently in relation to violent activities such as sacrifice and war (Boone 1984; Freidel 1986a; Schele and Miller 1986). An example is the Postclassic Central Mexican practice of *xochiyaoyotl*, or the so-called Flowery Wars, that some scholars argue were battles fought for the sole purpose of taking captives for ritual sacrifice (see Bray 1968; Brundage 1972; Conrad and Demarest 1984; Davies 1974; Hassig 1988; Hicks 1979; Isaac 1983a, 1983b; Monjarás-Ruiz 1976; Soustelle 1970; Valliant 1941). Although the ties between ritual and conflict are complex, the chapters in this section focus on only one aspect: a particular pattern of material destruction that has been recently ascribed to rituals associated with violent conflict (Mock 1998a, 1998b; Suhler and Freidel 1998). These rituals are called desecratory termination rituals. The interpretations of certain deposits as the remains of such rituals, however, have become the subjects of debate, especially among lowland Maya archaeologists. For this reason, the focus of the chapters in this section is on clarifying the nature of termination deposits and their possible relation to violent conflict.

Warfare in prehistoric societies could result not only in death but also in the destruction of material culture. Behavior such as raiding or conquest could include captive taking; sacrifice, burning, and destruction of architecture; destruction of monuments and material culture; and the desecration of important burials (Roper 1975; Tarlow 1997). Yet destruction of material culture can occur for a variety of other reasons, including accidental fires, natural disasters, reoccupation, and a variety of postabandonment activities. The problem of equifinality complicates the process of interpretation. For example, Stirling's (1940:334) interpretation that Olmec monument mutilation was a result of defeat in war has recently been questioned (Grove 1981). Porter (1989, 1990) has argued that some "mutilation" was the result of recarving. Even the destruction recorded by Acosta (1956–1957) at Tula has been debated (Davies 1977; Diehl 1983). Thus, an understanding of archaeological evidence for material destruction needs to rely on careful contextual analyses of the material remains. In Mesoamerica, the issue is complex, as some scholars now distinguish between warfare-related destruction associated with behaviors such as sacking, which involve a set of rituals themselves, and carefully proscribed ritual behaviors, called termination rituals, designed to symbolically "kill" people, places, and objects.

The identification of termination rituals in Mesoamerica stems from a recent understanding that Mesoamerican peoples had an ideology that included beliefs that the world was animate. Power derived from sacred landscapes, material objects (mirrors, jade ornaments, and so on), or deceased ancestors could be ritually manipulated by social agents within ideological systems. Ritual behavior focused on imbuing or charging these sources of power with life is well known from ethnographic sources as well as in the archaeological record (Pendergast 1998). Caching behavior is a prime example of ritual offerings placed in buildings to imbue them with life. Yet there also appear to be rituals associated with discharging and the destruction of symbolic life forces as well. These are referred to as termination rituals. Evidence suggests that at least some of these rituals, desecratory termination rituals, were related to violent conflict.

Analysis of ritual deposits and evidence of destruction relating to warfare began in the Maya area when members of the University of Pennsylvania Piedras Negras Project suggested that patterns of intentional destruction at this Usumacinta site were the result of "hostile intent" (Satterthwaite 1958). Coe (1959:94–95) identified some deposits at Piedras Negras as "terminal deposits" linking the archaeological remains with ritual behavior (see also Wauchope 1948:25). Subsequent research at Tikal identified similar patterns. Researchers working at this site, however, ascribed the destruction to squatter activity and peasant revolt, interpretations advanced by J. E. S. Thompson (Shook 1958:19). Two decades later in the Maya highlands, researchers began to equate evidence for destruction with violent conflict returning to the original ideas of Stirling (1940) and Acosta (1956–1957). Lowe (1977) cited evidence of Formative monument destruction in Chiapas and highland Guatemala as suggestive of strife and violence, an argument that continues to be used to support the idea of a violent lowland Maya expansion during the rise of El Mirador, the largest center in Petén during the Late Formative. Similarly, Brown (1977:263) cited evidence for destruction at Late Classic Kaminaljuyú as evidence for conflict. Yet it was not until the 1980s that patterns of destruction in the archaeological record were equated directly with ritual behavior. Work at Cerros revealed complex deposits associated with the burning and destruction of facades and elite artifacts (Freidel 1986b; Garber 1986; Reese 1996). These termination deposits were first identified as the remains of reverential destruction, but further research at other lowland sites has indicated that similar deposits may indeed be related to warfare activity (Freidel et al. 1998; Mock 1998b; Suhler and Freidel 1998).

Chapter 5, by Pagliaro, Garber, and Stanton, addresses the problems associated with identifying different types of termination ritual deposits. To better understand ritual behavior associated with material destruction, we must continue to develop rigorous methodologies for identifying a range of material patterning and eschew prior assumptions concerning what evidence for destruction means. Pagliaro and his colleagues examine material patterns and propose a preliminary trait list for identifying desecratory termination deposits. This study illustrates the complexity of these deposits and calls for more detailed contextual studies of evidence for destruction in the material record.

Chapters 6 and 7 are case studies that explore evidence for destruction in the Maya lowlands, the area where most of the current research for termination rituals is being conducted. In chapter 6, Brown and Garber examine evidence for desecratory termination rituals and warfare in the Middle Formative at the site of Blackman Eddy, Belize. Although this is the earliest proposed evidence for warfare in the Maya lowlands (for other areas of Mesoamerica, see Bernal 1969; Coe 1965a, 1965b, 1967, 1968; Coe and Diehl 1980; Marcus and Flannery 1996; Reilly and Garber, chapter 8 in this volume), we should expect warfare at this early date, as it is typically present in incipient complex societies worldwide. Brown and Garber examine the Maya creation myth, the Popol Vuh, and compare certain aspects of the story to patterns found in the archaeological record. They suggest that warfare was both important and prevalent during the early stages of Maya complexity and was therefore emphasized in the Maya creation myth. In essence, the volatile nature of the prestate society helped shape the Maya creation myth, and in turn, the Maya creation myth both legitimized and perpetuated warfare within the society.

In chapter 7, Ambrosino, Ardren, and Stanton examine evidence for desecratory termination deposits at the site of Yaxuná, Yucatán, Mexico, from the Early Classic through the Terminal Classic. They discuss four episodes of destruction encountered in stratigraphic sequences of elite architecture. Interestingly, some of these episodes correlate with major transitions in ceramics, architecture, settlement patterns, and mortuary patterns. The last event is even marked by the hasty construction of defensive walls around an acropolis. Ambrosino and his colleagues outline and evaluate the evidence for warfare in each of these episodes and discuss the implications for understanding the ancient sociopolitical landscape of the northern Maya lowlands. They propose that the analysis of such deposits may shed light on the dynamic interactions of cooperation and competition at the interpolity level.

Although studies of desecratory termination rituals are limited primarily to the Maya lowlands, patterns of material destruction are common in other regions of Mesoamerica. Examples of material destruction are numerous, including Teotihuacan (Armillas 1950; R. Millon 1981, 1988; Sugiyama 1998), La Quemada (Nelson et al. 1992), the Cuicatlán Cañada (Redmond 1983; Spencer 1982; Spencer and Redmond 2001), the Oaxaca Valley (Marcus and Flannery 1996), Cholula (McCafferty, chapter 12 in this volume), and Tula (Acosta 1956–1957; Healan et al. 1989:247). Comparable patterns of material destruction associated with warfare can be found in other societies outside Mesoamerica as well, including the American Southwest (see LeBlanc, chapter 14 in this volume) and the American Southeast (Shelby 1993). Careful contextual analyses of such deposits may provide clues to the nature of the social action that produced them and in some cases may better elucidate patterns of conflict and warfare in the past.

Epigraphic and Iconographic Approaches to Warfare

The third section of the volume focuses on epigraphic and iconographic evidence for warfare. Iconographic evidence of warfare is widespread in Mesoamerica but also extremely variable. Warfare is quite explicit in many cases, such as the Bonampak and Cacaxtla murals (Foncerrada de Molina 1980; López de Molina and Molina F. 1986; Miller 1986; Robertson 1985; Ruppert et al. 1955). In other cases, the iconography of war can be implicit, as the people of ancient Mesoamerica often represented such concepts in abstract forms, such as in star and Venus iconography (Baird 1989; Carlson 1991; Schele and Freidel 1990). The first two chapters in this section address warfare iconography in abstract forms, while the latter two focus on more explicit representations of warfare in the iconographic and epigraphic record.

In chapter 8, Reilly and Garber examine evidence for warfare among the Formative Olmec. They suggest that jaguarian imagery was an abstract form of visually representing institutionalized warfare during the Middle Formative. Such imagery was tied to a complex panoply of themes, including not only warfare but also sacrifice and fertility. Other Mesoamericanists have postulated the presence of warfare in Olmec society (Coe 1967, 1968; Coe and Diehl 1980; Stirling 1940), but many researchers remain skeptical of the evidence that has been presented (such as Grove 1981). The question of early Mesoamerican warfare is important given the role warfare appears to play in the rise of complexity (Carneiro 1970; Webster 1975). Reilly and Garber successfully demonstrate that the iconographic record can be used to elucidate patterns of warfare in Olmec society.

Moving ahead in time to the Classic period, iconographic evidence of warfare from the city Teotihuacan has been a major focus of both art historians and archaeologists for some time. The warfare-related art and iconography suggest that Teotihuacan was not a pacific society (Berlo 1983, 1984, 1992; Langley 1986; C. Millon 1973, 1988; Sugiyama 1992; von Winning 1948). In chapter 9, Headrick argues that the abstract images of butterflies, found throughout the iconography of Teotihuacan, were used by the elite as a propagandistic tool to promote the institution of warfare. It was a symbol of state ideology that closely resembled the concept of jihad, or holy war, from historical Middle Eastern societies.

The last two chapters in this section focus on explicit references to warfare in iconographic and epigraphic texts in the Maya area, where explicit data are widely available (Reilly and Garber, chapter 8 in this volume). The iconography of violent conflict is quite common in the Maya lowlands; however, it was often minimized or ignored for some time because of an adherence to the romantic belief that the Classic Maya were peaceful (Webster 1993). Spinden (1916) recognized the violent content of some Classic period lowland Maya monuments early in the twentieth century; however, publications by Maudslay (Maudslay and Maudslay 1899), Morley (1946), and Thompson (1954) perpetuated the romantic mystique of the peaceful Maya for over half a century (see Miller 1986; Webster 1993). Conflict, in the form of a peasant revolt, was only invoked as an explanation for the Classic Maya collapse (Altshuler 1958) or restricted to the Postclassic northern Maya lowlands (Tozzer 1957). The idea of the peaceful Maya was challenged with the discovery of the Bonampak murals. Although the graphic scenes were originally interpreted as an insignificant raid (Ruppert et al. 1955), some scholars could no longer ignore the evidence (Armillas 1951:78; Rands 1952). After the classic study of defensive features at the site of Becán by Webster (1976a, 1976b), the idea of the peaceful Maya began to wane, and in-depth studies of warfare and sacrifice using iconographic and epigraphic data became more prevalent (Schele and Miller 1986). Toward the end of the 1970s, the decipherment of Maya hieroglyphs began to have an impact on the study of Maya politics and warfare. These data provided a unique insight into Mesoamerican warfare and precipitated increased attention to this subject matter, which has endured to the present (Miller 1993). Of particular importance was the decipherment of the shell/star glyph. Ian Graham (1967) was the first to suggest that this glyph was of a military nature, but it was not until 1978 that Peter Mathews accurately deciphered its meaning as a verb signifying an act of war (cited in Sosa and Reents 1980; see also Riese 1984). The use of the shell/star glyph has been termed as "star-war" events by Linda Schele and David Freidel (1990). Coupled with the increasing iconographic studies of captives and sacrifice in Maya art (Baudez and Mathews 1978; Marcus 1974; Miller 1986; Proskouriakoff 1963; Schele 1984; Schele and Miller 1986), the presence of star-war events was used as evidence to support the hypothesis that a primary function of Maya warfare was to obtain sacrificial victims. Chapter 10, by Chase and Chase, and chapter 11, by Freidel, MacLeod, and Suhler, continue to expand our understanding of Maya warfare using explicit representations.

In chapter 10, Chase and Chase explore epigraphic texts related to warfare events at Caracol, Belize. The epigraphic record can provide a large amount of data pertaining to warfare, including different types of warfare. Chase and Chase continue the study of warfare glyphs by exploring the meanings of warfare texts at Caracol and comparing their use with archaeological data. They identify four different glyphs used by the ancient Maya to denote different forms of warfare and conflict.

In chapter 11, Freidel, MacLeod, and Suhler attempt an ambitious contextualization of violent factional competition at Tikal by studying the individual social actors in the elite texts and iconography in conjunction with complex stratigraphic deposits in the site center. They focus on the recently revived idea that Teotihuacan conquered Tikal during the Early Classic period. Freidel and his colleagues attribute Teotihuacan-style influence at Tikal not as a result of conquest but as a complex factor in the process of internal factional competition. Reading epigraphy, iconography, and the built environment of the Tikal central core as "texts" (cf. Hodder 1991), they argue that Maya rulers and their internal adversaries manipulated the impressive ritual stages of site centers in order to legitimize their claim to power. The Tikal case is impressive because some of the important social agents involved in the factional competition can be identified with their monuments.

Ethnohistoric and Ethnographic Approaches to Warfare

The fourth section of the volume illustrates ethnohistoric and ethnographic approaches to the study of ancient Mesoamerican warfare. We are fortunate to have rich ethnohistoric sources in Mesoamerica (Ixtliltxochitl 1975–1977; Alvarado Tezozomoc 1975; Durán 1967; Roys 1933; Sahagún 1950–1982; Torquemada 1975; Tozzer 1941). These range from conquest and colonial accounts written by the Spanish and indigenous peoples to postcontact documentation of native texts and oral traditions. Many scholars have taken advantage of these data in studying ancient conflict. For example, some scholars, drawing on ethnohistoric documents, have noted the patterns of warfare and shifting alliances that crosscut ethnic groups in Oaxaca during the Postclassic

(Byland and Pohl 1990, 1994; Flannery and Marcus 1983a; Gonzalez L. and Marquez M. 1995; Pohl 1991; Spores 1967; Whitecotton 1977). An emphasis has been placed on comparing archaeological data with these documents. In his study of Huitzo and Guiengola, Flannery (1983a) discussed the problems of archaeologically identifying battles from the ethnohistories. Although Flannery (1983a) cited intrusive burials and tombs from these communities as evidence, he concluded that there was very little data implicating these events. Despite initial problems outlined by Flannery, research into identifying ethnohistorically known warfare in the archaeological record has continued in Oaxaca and other areas of Mesoamerica. For example, Byland and Pohl (1994) have compared archaeological evidence for warfare against data from the Mixtec codices. They suggested that the defeat of the Red and White Bundle faction by the rulers of Tilantongo and Suchixtlan could be identified by the abandonment of the area held by the former faction around A.D. 1100. These works demonstrate the applicability of ethnohistoric materials in archaeological models of warfare and conflict.

Ethnohistoric and ethnographic data, however, should not be taken at face value. Pre-Columbian cultures were transformed shortly after the first Spanish expedition set foot in Mesoamerica. Problems can arise when comparing textual and archaeological data from different periods. Furthermore, we must remain acutely aware that each ethnohistoric and ethnographic document we use was written from only one point of view and that for each view of reality there are many others. These same problems apply to iconography and hieroglyphic texts.

In chapter 12, McCafferty compares the extensive ethnohistoric evidence for warfare with archaeological data at the site of Cholula. This Central Mexican site was a major center from the times of Teotihuacan through the Spanish conquest, and, as McCafferty notes, indigenous and Spanish ethnohistories record a series of military defeats. Native accounts discuss the migrations and conquests of Epiclassic period and Early Postclassic groups known as the Olmeca-Xicallanca and Tolteca-Chichimeca, respectively. Using these examples and that of the infamous Cholula Massacre carried out by Cortés's troops and recorded by the Spanish, McCafferty demonstrates the lack of congruence between archaeological evidence for conquest and the ethnohistoric documents. In short, the political agendas of both the native and Spanish authors of these documents do not seem to be based accurately in real-world events.

In contrast with McCafferty's ethnohistoric evaluation, Mock utilizes ethnographic data in conjunction with ethnohistoric and archaeological evidence in chapter 13. She contextualizes ancient Mesoamerican values about conflict by making a link between Classic period trickster complexes and modern Day of the Dead festivals. Mock argues that the macabre humor in modern-day ceremonies of conflict has its roots as far back in time as the Classic period. Her study is an innovative cognitive approach toward a better understanding of the ethos of conflict and warfare in ancient Mesoamerica.

Comparison and Summary

The final section begins with a comparative analysis of the study of warfare in Mesoamerica and the American Southwest. In chapter 14, LeBlanc compares evidence for warfare in these two areas and provides an excellent outside viewpoint illustrating the need for more communication and knowledge exchange between scholars working on similar issues in different regions. It is necessary to understand the standards used to identify patterns of warfare in other cultural areas in order to effectively establish our own criteria to recognize patterns related to warfare and conflict. A recent emphasis on warfare in the archaeology of the American Southwest provides for interesting parallels with the development of archaeological ideas and perceptions about warfare in Mesoamerica. LeBlanc illustrates well how the divergence and convergence of ideas in both areas can point scholars in each area in productive directions. Further, given that the Southwest has been conceived by some as the northern frontier of Mesoamerica (Phillips 1989), LeBlanc's comparison increases our understanding of the nature and variability of warfare and conflict among cultures to the north of those focused in this volume.

In chapter 15, Sheets provides an excellent overview of the history of Mesoamerican warfare studies. He also examines the current status of warfare research and provides twelve categories of evidence that may reflect warfare. Briefly highlighting accomplishments from each chapter, Sheets suggests productive strategies for future work. He stresses the importance of incorporating the research of cultural anthropologists, which will broaden both our ideas and our perspectives on the subject of warfare. This, we feel, cannot be emphasized enough. Sheets challenges Mesoamerican researchers to continue scholarly debate on the subject of warfare and to "cast a wider net" to enlarge our approaches to the analysis of this subject matter. We hope that this volume is a step in this direction.

Acknowledgments

We thank Tara Bond, George Cowgill, James Garber, Arthur Joyce, Kit Nelson, Payson Sheets, and two anonymous reviewers for their comments on this chapter. We maintain full responsibility for the final version.

Part I

WARFARE, SPATIAL BOUNDARIES, AND THE MATERIAL RECORD

Chapter Two

The Role of Ceramics in the Study of Conflict in Maya Archaeology

George J. Bey III

Interpretations of the role and nature of conflict in Mesoamerica are built on our understanding of a wide variety of archaeological data. One of the most important of these lines of data is ceramics. Unfortunately, while ceramics are commonly utilized in discussions of conquest throughout Mesoamerica (see Ambrosino et al., chapter 7, and Joyce, chapter 4 in this volume), archaeologists have made little effort to systematically examine their use in the interpretation of conflict. This chapter is an effort to move studies in that direction by considering how Maya archaeologists have used ceramics in discussing conflict during the Late and Terminal Classic periods (A.D. 600–1050). Although this analysis is a consideration of Maya research, it also has wider implications for conflict studies in Mesoamerica. It begins to satisfy the need in Mesoamerican archaeology for explicitly evaluating the role ceramics play in the arguments we offer about the nature of conflict in the past.

This chapter is a preliminary assessment of the subject that focuses on two levels of analysis—one obvious, the other perhaps less so. The first examines the ways in which Maya archaeologists have incorporated ceramic data and ceramic analysis into their arguments on conflict, primarily as ways of supporting a particular model. The second addresses the types of assumptions that this use of ceramic data makes about the nature of ceramic production and distribution systems. Such a study provides insights into the relationships that archaeologists argue exist between ceramic economics and Maya power and politics. It examines, to quote Ball (1993), "the socio-behavioral correlates assumed but rarely made explicit by Mayanist archaeologists in utilizing such constructs as the ceramic group, complex, and sphere" (243). If correct, their arguments have implications for understanding how the Maya used ceramics in their efforts to successfully manage conflict.

In this chapter, I explore the assumptions about the nature of ceramic production and distribution that are implicit in the way ceramics are utilized to interpret conflict and avoid a critique of the archaeological methodology of the studies that are discussed. Clearly, the validity of the relationships established by archaeologists between models of conflict and the ceramic data are crucial, but that evaluation will have to wait until another time.

All the cases considered here are Late to Terminal Classic and thus date roughly from A.D. 600 to 1050. In terms of the ceramic units employed, they range from specific types to complexes and spheres. The ceramic units are discussed in different dimensions of conflict, highlighting the fact that ceramics play a role in supporting a wide variety of conflict interpretations in Late/Terminal Classic Maya archaeology. Ceramics are used to support more or less microscale models of internal and external conflict as well as more macroscale models that address pan-Maya phenomena.

The Yaxuná Case: Ceramics and External Conflict

The first case deals with the nature of warfare and conquest during the Late Classic at the site of Yaxuná in northeastern Yucatán (see Ambrosino et al., chapter 7, and Freidel et al., chapter 11 in this volume). Yaxuná has been studied since 1986 by a project under the direction of David Freidel, who, with his associates, has defined a 2-square-kilometer central core settlement and a sequence based on ceramic analysis of five occupation phases spanning the Formative through Postclassic periods (Suhler et al. 1998). On the basis of excavation and analysis, they have proposed a "long complex history of dynastic succession, warfare, and territorial expansion comparable to the known histories of many southern lowland cities" (Suhler et al. 1998:167). Their analysis indicates that at the end of the Early Classic, Yaxuná was "in a weakened or vulnerable state" (Ardren et al. 1998). Around A.D. 600, the eastern city of Cobá, which was flourishing, took advantage of this vulnerability and conquered Yaxuná. In the words of Ardren et al. (1998:1), "The 150 years of A.D. 600–750 were a period of subordination through imposed rule from which Yaxuná would never fully recover." This interpretation is based on architectural and archaeological data. In the first category is the construction of the 100-kilometer-long, hastily built Yaxuná-Cobá *sacbe* (causeway) and associated ramparts (Villa Rojas 1934), Structure 6F-8, several additions made to existing residential architecture, and a number of burials that are dated to this period. In the second category are several carved panels of captives and the ceramics.

The replacement of ceramic complexes is the most significant artifactual data for the conquest of Yaxuná. The ceramic evidence comes from burials, domestic refuse, and architectural fill. Four of the five burials associated with this period have Arena Red vessels in them. This ceramic type is identified as the signature of Cobá's power at Yaxuná during the Late Classic period (Suhler et al. 1998). Arena Red is common at this time at Cobá, its east coast ports such as Tancah and Xelhá, and along the *sacbe* to Yaxuná (Robles 1990:149). It is, however, virtually unknown in the western peninsula or at the site of Ek Balam, which would have been booming at this time. At the domestic level, the entire Early Classic ceramic complex is replaced by one from Cobá, but with only about 50 percent of the types present at Cobá during this time period.

The Yaxuná project members suggest that Yaxuná was "a tightly controlled population" and that Cobá used ceramics as a crucial element of this model of conquest and subjugation. The significant underlying assumption of this model is that the conquerors replace ceramic complexes. This model assumes that the Yaxuná ceramic production and distribution system was shut down by the Cobá invaders and replaced by a completely new one from Cobá. If so, they would have had to do one of three things: 1) import all domestic pottery from Cobá and make everyone use it, 2) force all local producers to stop producing one complex and start producing another, or 3) replace all local Yaxuná potters with new producers from Cobá. Any of these scenarios suggest that household ceramic inventories were a crucial link in the identity of Classic Maya political power. To state that such a model presupposes a very close relationship between domestic ceramic production and distribution and the government is an under-statement. It argues that the Cobá polity saw conquest and identity hooked to domestic ceramic inventories and practiced a policy of conquest that included replacing the domestic pottery of the people of Yaxuná. This strategy, if true, stands in sharp contrast to the common assumption made in the study of Late Classic Maya pottery production and distribution that political centers did not exert any major influence on the economics of domestic pottery (Ball 1993:245).

The Petexbatun Case: Ceramics and Internal Conflict

In contrast, the conclusions reached by Foias and Bishop (1997) in their study of Petexbatun domestic pottery do support the idea that there is a lack of control by the elites of domestic pottery production and distribution. The Petexbatun region is a subarea of the larger Pasión Valley located in Guatemala. Results of the project, begun in the mid-1980s under the direction of Arthur Demarest, indicate occupation of the region from the Formative through Late Classic periods. The Vanderbilt Petexbatun Project was designed from its beginning to focus on issues of warfare and collapse, and the region indeed has produced striking evidence of an epoch of endemic warfare between A.D. 760 and 830, followed by a tremendous demographic collapse. Foias and Bishop (1997) have explicitly studied ceramics from the Petexbatun region as a way of understanding conflict, in this case as it relates to collapse in the Petexbatun. In particular, the Foias and Bishop study looks at how conflict might have impacted the production and distribution system. They are interested in determining which model of collapse is best supported by the changes in ceramics in the Petexbatun pottery assemblage from the Late Classic Naciemiento phase to the Terminal Classic Sepens phase. They focus on identifying shifts in the pottery manufacture and production system and comparing their findings to three of the major theories "used to explain the Classic Maya collapse: (1) the foreign-invasion theory; (2) the internal warfare theory; and (3) the commercialization theory" (Foias and Bishop 1997:275). The analysis is based on a standardization study of the most common domestic types as well as a neuron activation analysis study "of a large sample of monochrome, polychrome, and fine-paste pottery . . . used to model changes in intraregional production and exchange and in interregional exchange" (Foias and Bishop 1997:275).

The results of the analysis supported the second theory: internal warfare. It was assumed that internal warfare would produce three effects on the pottery production and distribution system that could be measured through their study: "(1) Because warfare would period- ically disrupt exchange, pottery production would become more local- ized, and exchange would decrease; (2) if production became more localized, there would be more potters producing less for a smaller area; and (3) more producers would lead to a decrease in the stan- dardization of the pottery" (Foias and Bishop 1997:285). And this is what they find, based on the fact that their standardization study reveals small decreases in the standardization of monochromes and polychromes and that their paste study reveals decreased amounts of paste variation within and increased amounts of paste variation between sites.

Perhaps the more powerful finding of their study was how minor these changes were. The patterns are clear but not nearly as dramatic as one might have thought given the social upheaval taking place in the region during this period. For Foias and Bishop, this indicates the resiliency of the nonelite class (which produced nonglyphic pottery) and the lack of integration of the economic system with the political system. Despite the increasingly intense level of conflict assumed for the region, potters kept producing a complex that in most ways was the same as that produced during the period of political stability. Their chemical analysis also indicates the original system of produc- tion and distribution of domestic wares to have been at the polity level. There was no panregional distribution system that broke down with the onset of the conflict that wracked the area.

North versus South: Identity and Conflict

The third case is drawn from Ball (1993). This seminal work presents what might be inferred about pottery economics and its relation to other interlinked subsystems during the Late Classic based on current archaeological knowledge. As part of his analysis Ball uses ceramics in a panregional look at conflict, focusing on large-scale changes and differences between the southern and northern lowlands at the sphere level. In the northern lowlands, "from the Chenes subregion on the southwest to the northwestern Caribbean coast, the single most impor- tant ceramic development of the eighth century was the appearance and spread of the slateware ceramic tradition. . . . By the close of the century—essentially the start of the full Late Classic florescence in the north—these low-gloss, 'soapy' wares of the Cehpech sphere completely dominated the northern assemblages. Local variations likely correlating with local producer communities are present, but the overriding impression conveyed by the Cehpech is of a monolithic production tradition" (Ball 1993:257). He contrasts this phenomenon with the southern lowlands, where he notes the increasing regionalization of ceramics and assemblages during this period, culminating in a mosaic of subregional spheres. He also notes similar parallels in the fine-ware systems, contrasting the growth of palace schools of production in the south with the decline of painted ware in the north.

Ball hypothesizes that these differences are due to variations in the level and nature of conflict in the two regions. The differences are not due to the direct result of conflict or to the impositions of the political systems but rather are reflections of the conflict. The ceramic changes in the south "bespeaks something far more deeply and seriously wrong with the basic fabric of southern Maya society than mere political fragmentation and the collapse of individual political units. What were becoming increasingly alienated in the south were not just rulers and ruling families, elites and their cohorts, but individuals and communities at all levels of society" (Ball 1993:257). Their existence and the dendritic networks of the distribution of the numerous palace schools "imply a highly fragmented sociopolitical landscape characterized by a great need to symbolize local identities and signify formal ties of relation" (Ball 1993:263). The lack of this development in the north conversely "may correlate with a lesser need for self-signification on the part of individual polities and centers than existed in the south" (Ball 1993:263).

The assumption is that ceramic production and distribution at the sphere level or at the panregional level geographically are impacted by conflict in specific ways. Increased levels of social instability and alienation between political units result in increased regionalism in the kinds of pottery produced and consumed by the masses as well as by the elites. Though it is not forcefully asserted, it is clear that Ball is suggesting that the sphere pattern reflects the kinds of social conflict that lead to collapse in the south and continued prosperity in the north at the end of the eighth century. An even deeper assumption is that domestic and elite producers were responding to populations' feelings of alienation and need for increased local self-identification in the south and populations' desire to emphasize social and cultural unity and downplay self-signification in the north. This model suggests a powerful role for domestic and elite potters and distributors in reinforcing patterns of conflict versus social harmony.

It is important to remember that Ball is offering this idea despite the fact that he argues against the economy of production and distribution being controlled by the political structure of Maya society. Thus, we have to ask, are the decisions being made by northern- and southern-sphere producers to follow separate routes (regionalization versus monoregionality) being made by the producers as a way to meet the cultural identity needs of consumers? Or are these responses a by-product of the particular forces of conflict at work in the two regions? For example, is regionalism a natural result of decreased contact due to increased conflict? And do these indirect forces, causing the changes in ceramic production and distribution, in turn serve to reinforce the different concepts of cultural identity that emerge in the north and south?

Conclusions

Ceramics are important elements in the discussion of conflict by Maya archaeologists studying the Late and Terminal Classic. They are used in different levels of analysis (interregional, intraregional, and panregional) and at different analytical levels, including those of variety, type, complex, and sphere. In addition, they are used to support different forms of conflict, including specific forms of conflict, such as invasion and internal warfare, as well as the broader forces of conflict that lead to widespread social disintegration.

This study also reveals a number of interesting assumptions about how Maya archaeologists view ceramic production and distribution. In the Petexbatun case, the fact that the ceramic evidence did not indicate any major reorganization of the economy during the period of collapse suggests to Foias and Bishop a lack of control by the elite and that elite power was not economic. The polities of the Petexbatun region did not use pottery for politics and power. This contrasts with the assumptions of the Yaxuná case, where the invasion and conquest by Cobá resulted in the replacement of the domestic production and distribution system. The interpretation offered by Ardren, Suhler, and Johnstone and more fully developed by Justine Shaw (personal communication, 1998) assumes a very tight control of production and distribution by the Cobá polity and the explicit use of domestic pottery for political purposes. Pottery is power in the Cobá case.

Given these different assumptions about the relationship between power and pottery, how can both analyses be correct? One solution would be that power and pottery were more closely integrated in some areas than in others and that we cannot assume a pan-Maya economic system during the Late and Terminal Classic. An alternative would be that polities used pottery for power differently in different types of conflicts. In other words, domestic pottery was not an important tool in the internal conflicts carried out by the elite of a region where complexes were basically similar to begin with but were a powerful political tool in the politics between regions where complexes were distinct.

Finally, Ball's panregional case assumes that though political systems did not control production and distribution systems, processes of conflict still have significant impacts on the production and distribution of pottery, even at the sphere level. The fact that the Petexbatun case does not seem to reflect Ball's ideas is interesting, though here again we may be dealing with issues of scale. Perhaps the definition of identity through pottery in response to the conflict that Ball sees in the south works in units larger than that encompassed by the Petexbatun region. This idea should be testable, and the implications for understanding Maya concepts of cultural identity would be fascinating. In addition, though Ball's assumptions also conflict with the Yaxuná case, there may be some common ground in the area of cultural identity. Assuming that pottery reflects self-identification in the ways Ball suggests, is it that unlikely that in specific types of conflict, such as the Yaxuná case, Maya polities would assume more active control of it? If you want to make people identify with Cobá, you impose a Cobá identity on them.

Ball's ideas, however, also open the door for a further possibility in the Yaxuná case. If the people of Yaxuná saw themselves as part of the Cobá polity, perhaps they would have wanted to use the Cobá ceramic complex. In other words, can the process of change at Yaxuná in the Late Classic be explained only in terms of subjugation and conquest imposed by state control of ceramic production and distribution? Could not the changes have resulted to some degree from an active desire on the part of the indigenous population to acquire this pottery and use it to identify themselves with the Cobá polity?

Other cases need to be examined to develop a full understanding of how Mayanists are using ceramics in the study of conflict during the Late and Terminal Classic. The most common use I think will turn out to be similar to that presented in the Yaxuná case (for example, the appearance of new types in the ceramic record of a site or region being considered as evidence of conquest or conflict). Two further examples of this line of reasoning are the ceramic changes associated with the ninth-century transformations at Seibal (Sabloff 1973) and the appearance of the Sotuta complex associated with the Chichén Itzá polity (see Andrews and Robles C. 1985).

The Seibal case differs from the Yaxuná one in that the conquest of Seibal by Chontal Maya or Putún is associated only with selective changes in the ceramic complex (Sabloff 1973). A set of elite and ceremonial types appears in the ceramics of the Bayal phase (A.D. 830–930); however, the domestic pottery found throughout the site during this Terminal Classic phase remained unchanged from that of the previous Tepejilote. The introduction of the new suite of elite and ceremonial pottery types, in conjunction with architectural and iconographic evidence during the Bayal phase, is thought to be the result of conquest. These conquerors, unlike those of Cobá, had no interest in imposing changes on domestic pottery. The association between politics and ceramic economics appears to be focused on changing access to imported ceramics and new types of ritual behavior and changes in ideology. If so, ceramics are being used in yet a different model of politics, conflict, and pottery economics.

In the case of Chichén Itzá, the association of the Sotuta complex with the better-known architectural remains and iconography were first thought to represent evidence of outside invaders (Brainerd 1958), who in essence brought about the cessation of the preceding Cehpech sphere. With the present understanding supporting a temporal overlap between the Sotuta sphere and the Cehpech sphere, archaeologists have shifted to using ceramics to determine the extent of Chichén Itzá's power. Sotuta ceramics are equated with Chichén Itzá control, and their distribution is evidence of Chichén Itzá's success in carving out a state in the northern Maya lowlands. Deposits of Sotuta pottery found in otherwise Cehpech sites, particularly when associated with architecture that has been interpreted as purposefully destroyed, is used as evidence of specific acts of Chichén Itzá directed violence (see Ambrosino 1997; Stanton 1999; Suhler et al. 1998). Conversely, the absence of Sotuta ceramics, such as at the nearby center of Ek Balam, has been used in conjunction with architectural and obsidian evidence to argue a lack of Chichén Itzá control.

A closer examination reveals the situation to be much more complex than an either-or-nothing scenario. First, the Sotuta complex represents a modification of a traditional northern Maya lowland complex with the addition of new types and forms of domestic pottery as well as the introduction of a particular set of elite pottery, including fine paste wares and plumbate. In other words, the Sotuta complex involves the development of a regional version of a Cehpech sphere complex with new elite wares. Work by Kepecs (1998) supports this hypothesis. Her analysis of ceramics in the Chikinchel region of north-central Yucatán found little indication of a pre-Sotuta Late Classic Cehpech sphere complex prior to the appearance of Sotuta. Kepecs argues that much of the Sotuta complex's distribution was a result of in situ evolution rather than displacement of a competing Cehpech sphere complex. An in situ evolution of the complex, combined with the addition of a subcomplex of trade wares, if evidence of conflict, would suggest a model for the spread of the Itzá polity quite different regarding the assumed relationship between politics and ceramic economies.

Second, in some cases, such as at Ichmul de Morley, located between Chichén Itzá and Ek Balam, Late and Terminal Classic inhabitants used a largely Cehpech sphere ceramic complex like Ek Balam but with a significant proportion of Sotuta pottery (Bond et al. 1999; Smith 1998). In addition, it appears that some potters were manufacturing Sotuta forms with Cehpech complex types. This pattern, like the one mentioned previously, does not fit nicely into the prevailing conflict model and may represent the result of behaviors other than direct conflict. For example, the Ichmul situation may be the result of efforts to avoid conflict and to develop ways to manage the community's interactions with the two competing polities. The incorporation of new ceramic types or even complexes may be due to the efforts by a polity or region to avoid conflict rather than evidence of it. Perhaps the presence of Sotuta complex material is not always due to conquest but in some cases may have been part of a strategy for maintaining autonomy. If so, this means that ceramic change even at a significant level cannot automatically be equated with conquest.

Finally, there is a situation in the northern lowlands that in some ways parallels the work of Foias and Bishop. Just as the Petexbatun region underwent dramatic stress without a major impact on the domestic ceramic production and distribution system, the decline of the major Puuc centers and the Ek Balam polity in the northern lowlands was not initially associated with a major change in their ceramic complexes (Bey et al. 1997). The architectural evidence suggests that there was a clearly defined postmonumental occupation at such sites as Ek Balam, Uxmal, Sayil, and Labná when the polities were no longer able to undertake major construction and existing monumental buildings had started to fall apart. This evidence has been taken to reflect major sociopolitical disintegration at the end of the Late Classic. Ceramically, however, at the gross level of the complex, the ceramic production and distribution system remained intact. Potters continue to manufacture Cehpech sphere ceramics during this period of decline. Although not directly parallel, the evidence suggests, as in the case presented by Foias and Bishop, a significant degree of resiliency in domestic ceramic production and distribution in the face of major social transformation.

In this chapter, I have highlighted how important ceramics are in the study of conflict in Maya archaeology. It should be noted that this same role is found not only in the Maya area but throughout Mesoamerica as well. In many cases, conflict is defined on the basis of assumptions of how ceramic economics interfaced with political structure. Yet many of these arguments do not make fully explicit the way they assume that ceramic production and distribution systems operated in these ancient societies. This is a problem that must be addressed if we intend to construct powerful interpretations of the role and nature of conflict in Mesoamerica. By examining the assumed underlying interrelationships between ceramics and other parts of culture, we refine the validity of interpretations on the basis of these assumptions. As we move forward in our examination, it will lead to a significant reassessment of the logic of some of our long-held, but usually implicit, beliefs of how the past worked. The end result of this reassessment will be a more rigorously constructed understanding of both how conflict was carried out in Mesoamerica and its impact on the larger society.

Chapter Three

The Politics of Warfare in the Usumacinta Basin: La Pasadita and the Realm of Bird Jaguar

Charles W. Golden

Research into the origin and nature of Maya warfare has focused primarily on the economic and ritual aspects involved (for example Culbert 1991a, 1995; Freidel 1992; Schele and Freidel 1990; Schele and Mathews 1991; Schele and Miller 1986; Webster 1975, 1976a, 1976b). If we are to fully understand warfare in the Maya lowlands, however, we must begin to situate it within the broader range of sociopolitical interactions that bind together people and places (Webster 1998). While I do not deny the role of religious or economic influences, warfare must also be examined as a political action that occurs when and where authority is lacking. Warfare is an act intended either to extend the boundaries of political authority or to eliminate threats and thereby maintain those boundaries. These frontiers fluctuate, as they represent the variable limits of consensual versus coercive force (Reyna 1994a; see also Beekman 1996). As an interpolity activity, it is the relationships between ruler and ruled and between core and periphery within a polity that structure the resources of material and manpower available to wage war (Cohen 1984). One way, therefore, to begin to understand the complexities of warfare is to investigate the nature of the political boundaries across which warfare was conducted.

I argue that in the Usumacinta River Basin of the eighth century A.D., the rulers of Yaxchilán sought to consolidate the boundaries of their authority through the use of subordinate nobility at frontier sites such as La Pasadita, Guatemala. Warfare played an important intrapolity role in this process, as it offered an arena of mutual benefit for both ruler and ruled. Nonroyal nobility might achieve prestige through their association with monarchs in return for the continued assurance of political support and security.

Royal Power and Negotiated Authority

Though it is true that some individuals are capable of initiating warfare, these events are most often systemic and not a symptom of social disorder (Wolf 1999:5). Rulers wage war conscious of the needs of those who provide them with support in such endeavors, or they put their own position at risk. Though Maya rulers based some measure of their authority on their divine nature, as Wolf states,

> [it is] unlikely that ultimate sacred propositions remain in place by virtue of their own ineffable qualities. It is more probable that their very ambiguity will invite challenges and threaten destabilization, unless they can be made secure through adequate means of domination. Such means usually combine outright force with hegemonic powers of persuasion. (Wolf 1999:285)

Mesoamerican rulers, then, were in some sense embodiments of fundamental powers, but their roles were nonetheless negotiated (Houston and Stuart 1996, 2001). Warfare played a pivotal role in the use of both force and persuasion in Classic Maya polities.

An increasing number of noble titles appeared in the inscriptions of the Late Classic (A.D. 600–800), even as texts dealing explicitly with warfare events make their first appearance (Chase and Chase, chapter 10 in this volume; Child 1999; Houston and Stuart 2001).[1] This is not a coincidence, for the two are inextricably linked. It is significant that evidence throughout the Maya lowlands suggests that the position of monarchs was increasingly unstable over the course of the Classic period, even as the subordinate nobility of Maya polities entered into the historical record (Fash 1989; Fash and Sharer 1991; Fash and Stuart 1991; Houston 1993; Villela 1993). Though an increasing number of titles apparent in the epigraphic record may reflect an increase in the number of titled personages within Maya polities during the Late Classic, there is no reason to believe that many such individuals were not present in Early Classic society. In turn, an increasing number of texts dealing with warfare are not necessarily indicative of increased warfare activities (Child 1999; Stuart 1993). Textual references must be understood as social acts related to, but independent of, the sociopolitical import of the warfare itself. Their significance is not simply the recording of the act of warfare. Such inscriptions are imbued with social meaning defined by the needs of those who controlled the recording of such events.

I contend that an increasing focus on warfare and a proliferation of noble titles in the texts, especially pronounced in the Usumacinta River Basin, is associated with increasingly direct control over the governors and populations of the secondary centers that straddled the frontiers of authority between Maya polities. The creation of these texts, particularly those dealing with the governors of subsidiary political centers, was ultimately aimed at tying the ruler and his subordinate nobility more securely together. This process was made material through the directed growth of secondary centers whose governors acted to regulate access and trade, thereby helping maintain the boundaries of regal authority through activities such as warfare.

A Case Study: La Pasadita, Guatemala

La Pasadita was a secondary political center governed during the eighth century A.D. by a *sajal*[2] named Tilo:m, who was loyal to the ruler of Yaxchilán (figure 3.1). Located within the modern borders of Guatemala, approximately 17 kilometers to the northwest of Yaxchilán, La Pasadita is situated just south of a narrowing in the valley that runs between Yaxchilán and Piedras Negras. This same valley represents the most direct portage route around the series of rapids that punctuate the Usumacinta between Yaxchilán and the Boca del Cerro, to the north of Piedras Negras. Approximately 20 kilometers to the north of La Pasadita, on the western bank of the river, is El Cayo, Chiapas, whose governors were subordinate to the rulers of Piedras Negras. Somewhere in the space between these two secondary centers lay the ancient frontier between the Piedras Negras and Yaxchilán polities. La Pasadita was ideally placed to maintain control of the only overland access routes between those two polity centers and to serve as a staging point for attacks against, or defense from, the enemies of the lords of Yaxchilán (Webster 1998:331).

Epigraphic evidence suggests that the frontier between Yaxchilán and Piedras Negras was not always a peaceful one. Piedras Negras

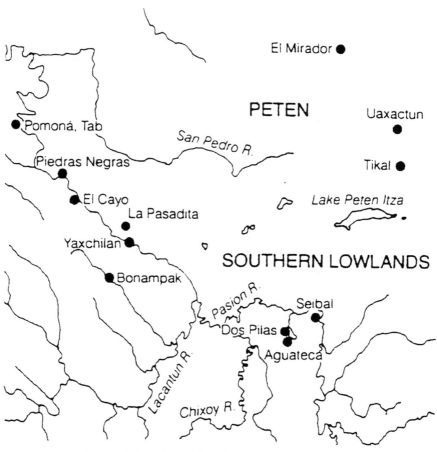

Figure 3.1   Map of the Usumacinta River Basin
(after Schele and Miller 1986:8)

Panel 12 depicts a captive Yaxchilán *ajaw,* while Stela 8 shows a captive *sajal* from Yaxchilán. Furthermore, Lintel 10 from Yaxchilán appears to record the capture of the last known king of Piedras Negras, Ruler 7, in A.D. 808 (Stuart 1998a). Excavations conducted in the 1930s by the University of Pennsylvania Museum of Archaeology and Anthropology seem to indicate a violent episode of destruction in the royal palace of that site contemporaneous with the reign of Ruler 7 (Holley 1983:157).

Conflict between Yaxchilán and Piedras Negras did not take place in a political vacuum, however. The rulers of these two centers, along with their subordinates at sites such as La Pasadita, were politically involved with each other over a period of centuries. Inscriptions on monuments from both sites record the history of marriages, royal and noble visitations, and warfare events that bound the centers of the Usumacinta together in a dynamic process of political interaction (Mathews 1988; Schele 1991a; Schele and Mathews 1991).

Geography and Settlement at La Pasadita

The landscape in and around La Pasadita is dramatic, with high cliffs rising from low hills and narrow valleys, all surrounding a small, deep lake. Settlement in the valleys around this lake is sparse. Those few structures located on the valley floor tend to take advantage of lower hill slopes or low rises that were leveled out with small terraces. Small platforms, which almost certainly held perishable superstructures, were constructed atop these terraces but only occasionally exceed 1 meter in height (figure 3.2a). There are notable exceptions to this pattern, including a large vaulted structure (now collapsed) associated with several caves (figure 3.2b). There is little evidence for intensive agriculture, such as terracing, in the immediate vicinity of La Pasadita.

It is clear that the inhabitants of La Pasadita preferred to construct their residences on hilltops, where by far the majority of settlement is located. Every hilltop in the area with suitable space for occupation contained at least one structure. Patio groups seem to be organized around the constraints imposed by the natural landscape. Some structures were built along the edges of deep chasms and sheer cliff faces. The Main Group is the most dramatic example of this, overlooking a vertical drop of at least 40 meters (figure 3.3). In contrast to occupation on the valley floor, platforms on hilltops tend to be larger, commonly with mounds up to 2 meters in height.

Access to these hilltop structures is severely restricted. At present, most can be reached only after a short climb up a vertical rock face, and there is no evidence that the Maya constructed staircases or other access routes. Though much of the settlement thus appears naturally defensible, there were no obvious artificial defenses at La Pasadita (see Demarest et al. 1997; Webster 1976a, 1976c, 1979 for comparison). Low, short, linear, rubble mounds were visible along the flanks of

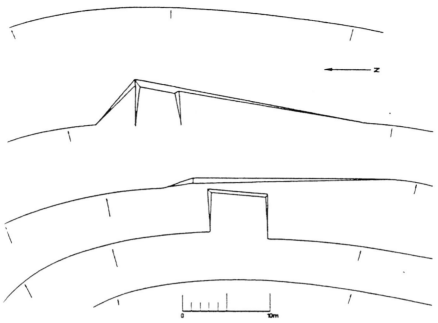

Figure 3.2a   Structures built on the lower slopes of a hill

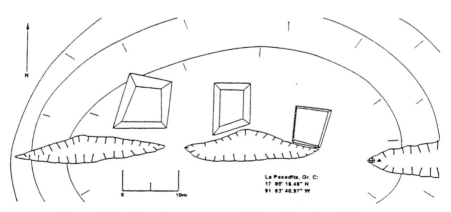

Figure 3.2b   Structures arranged along the edge of chasms

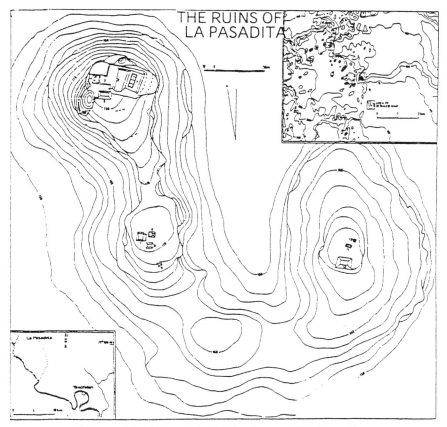

Figure 3.3   Map of the Main Group of La Pasadita
(mapped and drawn by Ian Graham)

several hills, but without excavations it is impossible to say whether
these are ancient, modern, or natural features.

Although the topography is similar, the settlement patterns contrast markedly with settlement to the south of La Pasadita as well as
in the periphery of Piedras Negras. To the south of La Pasadita, the
remains of settlement are abundant along the 14 kilometers of valley
floor leading to Yaxchilán. This occupation of low-lying areas clearly
differentiates the region from La Pasadita proper. Survey in the
southern periphery of Piedras Negras indicates that settlement there
is restricted largely to low hills and the lower slopes of hillsides
(David Webster and Amy Kovak, personal communication, 1999). To

my knowledge, settlement data for Yaxchilán and its periphery have not been published, making comparisons with that site impossible.

The only site in the region of which I am aware with planning similar to that of La Pasadita lies near El Cayo. Just to the south of El Cayo, on the Guatemalan side of the river, are two Usumacinta tributaries known as the Arroyo Macabilero and the Arroyo Casadora. The small valleys through which these flow provide the only other easy access to the valley within which both La Pasadita and Piedras Negras lie. On the hilltop between these two arroyos, Shook (1998) reported a group of structures surrounded by deep chasms and cliff faces to which he had some trouble gaining access.

My own reconnaissance of this area in 2000 revealed a settlement pattern wherein patio groups facing the Usumacinta River were built on hilltops, as far as possible from the riverbank. Other patio groups shielded from the Usumacinta by hills were built on the lower slopes of those hills, as close as possible to the feeder streams that provided potable water. I believe that structures at Macabilero, like those of La Pasadita, were positioned with defense in mind and acted to dominate the entrance to the La Pasadita/Piedras Negras Valley, limiting access from the Usumacinta. It is impossible to say at present whether the inhabitants of these structures were subject to the governor of El Cayo and therefore within the domain of the ruler of Piedras Negras or whether they were under the authority of the ruler of Yaxchilán.

Material Chronology

Our primary source of chronological information for the La Pasadita area comes from ceramic material collected from three caves, designated Yax Ik, Zac Ik, and Tepescuintle. In Zac Ik, a number of sherds representing types generally associated with the Late Formative and Protoclassic periods were identified. Occupation of the valley, then, can be postulated to extend back into at least the Late Formative (400 B.C.–A.D. 250), though no structures can be assigned to that period.

Though this sample is not representative, these data do allow me to begin to address an important issue: Is there material evidence for a frontier between La Pasadita and Piedras Negras, and, if so, is La Pasadita more closely associated with Yaxchilán? Many ceramic types common at both Piedras Negras and La Pasadita express very different modes at La Pasadita, from at least the Early Classic on. Vessel forms approximate those that are common at Piedras Negras, while their surface decoration varies. This divergence in style broadens into the Late Classic. Unfortunately, data pertaining to the ceramic assemblage of Yaxchilán remain largely unpublished, and therefore it is not possible at present to postulate an artifactual connection between La Pasadita and Yaxchilán (but see Lopez V. 1989). This pattern appears to substantiate the epigraphic evidence that La Pasadita did not fall under the sociopolitical dominance of Piedras Negras (Ball 1993). It should be noted that though ceramic boundaries may not always reflect political boundaries, Ball (1993) does suggest that polities never extend beyond one ceramic sphere (see also Bey, chapter 2 in this volume).

La Pasadita has been heavily looted, and the sadly abundant looters' pits and trenches provide stratigraphic data for the site. Only two phases of construction are in evidence within the Main Group, indicating a burst of construction at La Pasadita during the Late Classic. In fact, no more than a single phase of construction was apparent in any looters' pit outside the Main Group. Epigraphic evidence would seem to indicate that this flurry of construction of monumental architecture took place during the second half of the eighth century A.D., coincident with the reign of Tilo:m, under the sponsorship of his overlord at Yaxchilán.

The Politics of Warfare in the Eighth-Century Yaxchilán Polity

Warfare in a society such as the one that existed in the Maya lowlands of the eighth century A.D. (often referred to as "state" level) cannot necessarily be equated with warfare as it is conducted under other forms of political organization. Sociopolitical leaders of such complex organizations are not unusual in their ability simply to make war but rather "in the control they wield over warmaking" (Ferguson 1990:50; see also Cohen 1984). The reasons why the ruler of a Maya polity chose to go to war may not have been within the realm of the economic, social, or religious interests of the populace as a whole. The ruler's interests may, in fact, have been drastically different from the interests that inspired people to follow him into battle (Carneiro 1994). Furthermore, it is increasingly clear that each Maya polity had its own unique historical and political trajectory (Sharer 1991). Given this situation, if we are to understand warfare and its associated phenomena within a particular polity, it is ideal to be able to achieve some understanding of the individual history of the ruler.

It is possible to achieve a preliminary understanding of the nature of the relationship between the rulers of La Pasadita and Yaxchilán using the inscriptions on a number of monuments from Yaxchilán, La Pasadita, and several other as-yet-unidentified secondary centers. Yaxchilán experienced an interregnum of ten years between the reigns of Shield Jaguar I and Bird Jaguar IV, from A.D. 742 to 752 (Mathews 1988; Schele and Freidel 1990:271). When Bird Jaguar finally emerged as the *k'uhul ajaw* ("holy lord") of Yaxchilán, he initiated a dynamic program of monument production unequaled at that site, dedicated to the glorification of himself, his parents, his heir, and the chosen few of his subordinate nobility.

The quantity of monuments dedicated to Bird Jaguar may be the result of his struggle for the throne, with impediments to his accession coming both from within and without his future domain. Lintel 3 from Piedras Negras, for instance, describes an event that occurred during Yaxchilán's interregnum, witnessed by an individual identified as the *k'uhul ajaw* of Yaxchilán. This individual is unknown at Yaxchilán and may represent a pretender to the throne in competition with Bird Jaguar and supported by the rulers of Piedras Negras (Stephen Houston, personal communication, 1998; Stuart 1998a).

Once Bird Jaguar was enthroned as the *k'uhul ajaw* of Yaxchilán, it would have been necessary for him to do two things: publicly validate his rule and ensure the stability of his domain. The first of these goals was addressed through public rituals that included the creation and placement of numerous stelae and lintels at Yaxchilán. The second helps explain the abundance of monuments from secondary centers. These monuments elevated the status of a loyal noble through the monumental depiction of the subject, often alongside his lord, and established exactly who was the lord and who was the subject.

Additionally, such actions aided in the development of a defensible frontier between the limits of Bird Jaguar's authority and that of his rivals at centers such as Piedras Negras. Bird Jaguar depicted himself with *sajal* both at home and abroad, often in scenes depicting war captives (Mathews 1988; Schele and Freidel 1990:295). There are at least fourteen such monuments from centers subsidiary to Yaxchilán, including La Pasadita, and two unlocated sites, known as Site R and Laxtunich. In fact, artisans from Yaxchilán created many of these monuments at secondary centers.[3] Of the monuments associated with Tilo:m, La Pasadita Lintel 1 (dated A.D. 759) depicts Bird Jaguar receiving captives from Tilo:m and another individual (figure 3.4). Lintel 2 (figure 3.5) depicts the celebration by Bird Jaguar and Tilo:m

Tilo:m Sajal   Bird Jaguar IV

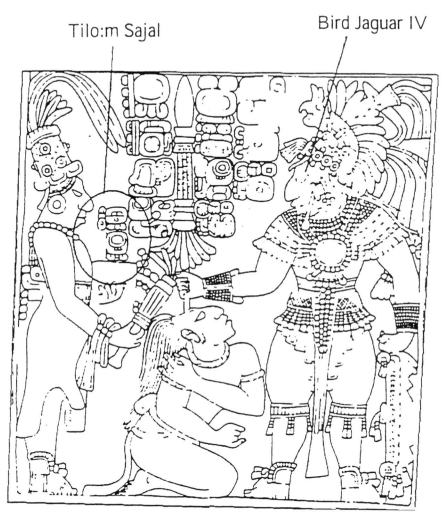

Figure 3.4   La Pasadita Lintel 1 (after Schele and Freidel 1990:302)

of the 9.16.15.0.0 (A.D. 766) period ending. Lintel 3 depicts Tilo:m and Shield Jaguar II, while a fourth lintel depicts Tilo:m without his over-lord.

Participation with the ruler in activities such as warfare provided an important source of prestige and political power for subordinate nobility such as Tilo:m. Subordinate nobles acted as military allies and

Tilo:m

Figure 3.5   La Pasadita Lintel 2 (after Schele and Freidel 1990:302)

acquired captives for the *k'uhul ajaw*. At times, *k'uhul ajaw* are depicted receiving such captives from their subordinates (such as La Pasadita Lintel 1 and Piedras Negras Stela 12), and it is often not clear that these "holy lords" participated in the warfare events so recorded (Houston and Stuart 2001; Schele and Matthews 1991). In addition, *sajal* would have acted to guard the frontiers of the polity and help regulate trade access. In return for their services, *sajal* received the benefits of status ascribed through textual and iconographic representation on monuments, carved by scribes whose work was controlled by, and the prerogative of, the ruler.

It was, therefore, performance in acts such as warfare that shaped the roles and privileges of titleholders such as Tilo:m (Houston and Stuart 2001; Inomata 2001). Such a pattern of alliance development and advancement of subordinates through service to the political leader typifies warfare in many societies, both modern and ancient (Ferguson 1994). By linking *sajal* more tightly into a network of exchange that benefited both ruler and ruled, Bird Jaguar and other *k'uhul ajaw* of the Usumacinta Basin acted to stabilize and perhaps extend their political domain and the boundaries of consensual force. Where they were unable to do so, warfare played yet another role as a show of coercive force across boundaries.

Ritual and Economic Considerations

Though I have predicated my argument on the basis of the political-historical record from the Usumacinta region, it is often impossible to separate the concept of political authority from the economic and ritual aspects involved in warfare (Reyna 1994b). In the Maya area, warfare-associated rituals were evidently quite elaborate and involved combatants in a process that included dressing for battle, fighting, and the presentation, mutilation, and sacrifice of prisoners. The murals of Bonampak contain the most elaborate depictions of such activities (see Miller 2001). Many carved monuments also portray the treatment of captives, perhaps most famously Piedras Negras Stela 12 with its elaborate scene depicting the presentation of prisoners to the *k'uhul ajaw*.

It also seems that rituals associated with warfare extended beyond the treatment of people to include buildings. Evidence for ritual destruction of buildings following the conquest of Maya sites is increasingly abundant and spans the Maya lowlands (see Ambrosino et al., chapter 7, and Brown and Garber, chapter 6 in this volume), though it remains difficult to differentiate reverential burning and destruction from desecration (see Pagliaro et al., chapter 5 in this volume; Stuart 1998b). In one example from the Usumacinta region, it appears that the conquest of Piedras Negras, probably by the last known ruler of Yaxchilán (Houston et al. 1998; Stuart 1998a), was followed by the destruction of all human figures on the architectural facades of that site's acropolis. In addition, the royal throne of Piedras Negras was smashed and scattered across the throne room, and the faces of the individuals depicted thereon were completely destroyed or carried away. Rituals, though, are associated with warfare in almost all societies. Rather than the causative factor of the killing, whether enacted before or after a battle such rituals are better understood as an activity that in some sense normalizes warfare and makes it a socially purposeful and acceptable behavior (Ferguson 1990:46; 1994:100–1).

For their part, the economics of Classic period Maya polities are poorly understood at best (McAnany 1992). It is difficult to say with any certainty what constituted the full range of materials that were traded across political boundaries along the lengths of the Usumacinta River. A broad spectrum of luxury goods, in addition to necessities such as salt, were traded over long distances in late preconquest Yucatán (Roys 1943), and there is no reason to doubt that trade during the Classic period was any less vigorous.

The nobility and especially the royalty of Maya polities were the recipients of trade goods that formed many of the most obvious markers of their status (for example, quetzal feathers, jade, and spondylus). The very nature of such elite trade goods, of course, is that they are not readily reproduced within the consumer's domain. Such goods are continually removed from use, whether through breakage or through ritual disposal (for example, burials and caches). Moreover, an increasingly conspicuous secondary elite, represented by individuals such as Tilo:m, would have siphoned off a greater percentage of these limited resources as time passed in return for their continued service to their overlord.

While locally produced versions of status markers may very well have increased in frequency during the Late Classic (Rathje 1973) in order to fill some of the demand, some items could simply not be replicated. In a society where the display of power as embodied by such items as jade and feather-worked costumes was essential to the authority of the ruler, maintaining a steady supply was imperative. To use the example of late preconquest Yucatán once more, trade often continued to flow unabated across the boundaries of warring areas. In fact, the cessation of trade between regions did, at times, provide the basis for the initiation of warfare (Roys 1943). In considering the Usumacinta River Basin, such an embargo would have represented a threat to the authority of the *k'uhul ajaw*, and force may often have been required to ensure that traders and their wares could pass unhindered through areas accessible to the nobility of Yaxchilán and their agents.

In practice, the effects of warfare on economic processes are often ambivalent (see Bey, chapter 2, and Chase and Chase, chapter 10 in this volume). There does exist the potential of economic benefit for both king and polity, as warring may accumulate both coercive and consensual force through the acquisition of resources, territory, and subjects that could be redistributed as wealth. It builds alliances and brings in tribute (Ferguson 1994; Reyna 1994b:149). Warfare, though, is also expensive in terms of people and materials, and the cost may far outstrip any material gain (Cohen 1984:353).

Ultimately, even warfare couched explicitly in economic terms is intrinsically a question of authority. All-out destruction of the enemy may be expensive in the short term but reduce the need for warfare in the long term by eliminating threats to royal power (see Ambrosino et al., chapter 7 in this volume). Even small-scale "inexpensive" raids can serve to reinforce boundaries. Political actions intended to control trade routes and territorial access, such as warfare and the construction of defensive sites such as La Pasadita, act to ensure royal authority in general if they are successful. It is impossible to say whether the construction of sites such as La Pasadita was successful in regulating trade as it passed northward through the territory of the Yaxchilán polity. If, however, it allowed a military advantage in the region (the potential for more successfully applied coercive force), then it would have functioned as a physical statement of the authority of the *k'uhul ajaw* of Yaxchilán over such trade in his kingdom.

A General Consideration of Maya Polities and Political Structure

This process of competition for, and consolidation of, power by Bird Jaguar has important implications for our understanding of Classic Maya political organization in general. Most recent models of Maya polities are built on modified versions of the segmentary state (Fox 1987; Sanders and Webster 1988), galactic polity, or theater state (Demarest 1992). Those characteristics of "weak states" that the Yaxchilán polity does exhibit, such as intraelite tension and conflict (Tambiah 1977), are present in most if not all forms of political organization.

In segmentary states and galactic polities, political functions and functionaries are replicated at most if not all levels of social organization (Fox 1977; Southall 1988; Tambiah 1977). This is demonstrably not true among the Maya, where both epigraphic and archaeological evidence support the concept that the upper echelons of Late Classic society represented an exclusive hierarchy of political figures. Though a few *sajal* may have achieved the title of *ajaw,* the role of the *k'uhul ajaw* was never replicated and performed by the *sajal* (Houston and Stuart 2001). *Ajaw* and *sajal* title bearers might be further subdivided by the addition of the *ba-* ("head") prefix, ranking those individuals within a polity who were the head-*sajal* above all others holding the *sajal* title by itself (Houston and Stuart 2001). The great range of titles recorded during the Late Classic and the exclusion of some titleholders from the possession of other titles indicate that the Maya elite were not interchangeable political building blocks.

Finally, there is the question of frontiers. Weak states, by definition, have highly variable frontiers defined only by the authority, charisma, and ritual efficacy of the king (Demarest 1992; Geertz 1980; Tambiah 1977). In such political organizations, subsidiary elite and the centers they govern are not locked into a stable political hierarchy. As suggested by those monuments related to warfare, however, this does not appear to be the case among the Late Classic Maya. As seen on monuments such as La Pasadita Lintel 1 and Piedras Negras Stela 12, the role played by the *k'uhul ajaw* depicted in the acquisition of the captives is unknown. Subordinate nobility apparently delivered their prisoners as tribute not because their overlords as individuals were the most capable warriors but because *k'uhul ajaw* controlled and distributed artisans, resources, and titles that helped define the social position of individuals such as *sajal*. Secondary nobility were actively engaged in the exchange of allegiance, in activities such as warfare and defense of territorial boundaries, in return for status markers such as inscriptions. This made the maintenance of the polity's frontiers socially meaningful to *sajal* in terms of the political position of *k'uhul ajaw* and the prerogatives available to that position apart from the personal performance of the ruler.

Conclusions

I can at present offer several observations about La Pasadita, Yaxchilán, and the nature of warfare in the eighth-century A.D. Usumacinta Basin. First, though occupation and use of the valley continued from Late Formative times through to the Late Classic, construction of La Pasadita's monumental architecture appears to have been limited to the Late Classic. It is almost certain that La Pasadita and Tilo:m owed this florescence to the patronship of Bird Jaguar IV of Yaxchilán. Second, areas to the south of La Pasadita and in the near periphery of Piedras Negras exhibit a greater level of occupation oriented around lower hill slopes and valley floors. Occupation at La Pasadita was clearly focused on construction atop hills bounded by cliff faces. La Pasadita is a defensible site, and its placement would have functioned to help its inhabitants guard the ancient frontier, controlling access through the valley between Yaxchilán and Piedras Negras and providing a staging point for both offensive and defensive military actions. Certainly, La Pasadita Lintel 1 would indicate that Tilo:m was personally involved in some of the warfare events involving Bird Jaguar and the Yaxchilán polity. Finally, though I cannot securely associate La Pasadita materially with Yaxchilán, it is demonstrably different from Piedras Negras.

That political frontiers in the Usumacinta were becoming more rigidly controlled during the Late Classic is therefore indicated by both epigraphic and archaeological data. When compared with earlier periods, the Late Classic includes increased evidence of both warfare events and of a powerful subroyal nobility. It is likely that threats to political authority drove this process, though the control of access to overland trade routes through the imposition of defensive settlements and the exercise of military power must not be ignored. I simply argue against the primacy of the economic or ritual in this case.

The implications for Maya polities in general are clear. By the eighth century A.D. in the Usumacinta River Basin, polities with definite boundaries and frontiers of political authority were in the process of developing or had in fact already developed. Beginning at least with the reign of Bird Jaguar IV, the k'uhul ajaw of Yaxchilán required the support of subordinates such as Tilo:m to achieve and maintain their throne. In return for their support in times of war aimed at the defense and extension of the boundaries of royal authority, sajal received their own political authority. Such authority was associated with material benefits, such as the privilege of text-bearing monuments carved by artists attached to the k'uhul ajaw. In the Yaxchilán polity, warfare played an important role in this process by providing an arena in which subordinate nobility such as sajal could be engaged in a process of exchange and negotiated authority.

Notes

The data for La Pasadita in this chapter were gathered in March 1998 by the Sub-Proyecto La Pasadita, one facet of the Piedras Negras Archaeological Project. Research was carried out by the author, Tomás Barrientos, Zachary Hruby, and René Muñoz. I wish to thank the Instituto de Antropología e Historia de Guatemala, Stephen Houston, and Hector Escobedo for the opportunity to work at La Pasadita. Funding for the La Pasadita Archaeological Sub-Project was provided by the Foundation for the Advancement of Mesoamerican Studies, Inc., Grant # 97042. I want to note my appreciation,

48 / Charles W. Golden

especially, to the men of Dolores, Guatemala, whose knowledge of the forest
and the archaeology of the Petén made this work possible. Finally, I would
like to thank George Cowgill, Amy Kovak, René Muñoz, Robert Sharer, David
Webster, and an anonymous reviewer for their constructive commentary on
earlier versions of this chapter.

1. In addition to the most exhalted title of *k'uhul ajaw* ("holy lord"), Late
Classic texts make reference to persons bearing titles such as *ajaw* ("lord"),
ch'ok ajaw ("young lord"), *sajal* (perhaps "he who fears"), *a-k'uh-hu:n* (a
scribal title), and *y-ajaw-k'ak* ("the fire's lord"), as well as others. For a more
thorough understanding of these and other Classic period Maya titles, see
Houston and Stuart (2000).

2. *Sajal* were members of the nonroyal nobility who sometimes served as
members of the royal courts or as governors of secondary centers within
Maya polities. This title appears only in the inscriptions of the Late Classic
period and is restricted largely to the western portions of the Maya lowlands.
Sajal could apparently become *ajaw,* but in no recorded instance was an individual of *sajal* status advanced to the highest position of *k'uhul ajaw* (Houston
1993; Houston and Stuart 2001; Villela 1993).

3. Such monuments tend to depict Bird Jaguar IV, though in a few
instances they do depict his successor, Shield Jaguar II, as well as his deceased
father, Shield Jaguar I.

Chapter Four

Imperialism in Pre-Aztec Mesoamerica: Monte Albán, Teotihuacan, and the Lower Río Verde Valley

Arthur A. Joyce

The term *warfare* subsumes a wide range of social interactions (Fried et al. 1968; Keeley 1996; Ross 1986). Warfare is a form of conflict that usually refers to organized violent encounters between members of different sociopolitical groups but can range from sporadic raiding for ritual purposes to large-scale warfare for territorial conquest with thousands of casualties. The motivations and outcomes of specific historical instances of conflict also vary greatly. To address warfare in the archaeological record, we need to define more precisely the variation in potential forms of interaction along with their archaeological correlates.

This chapter considers a specific category of interpolity conflict, that of imperial conquest and control where a state comes to dominate a multiethnic hinterland. The best-known example of imperial conquest in Mesoamerica is the Aztec Empire of the fifteenth and early sixteenth centuries. The record of Aztec imperialism is strengthened by both the archaeological data and the ethnohistoric record of the Late Postclassic period (Berdan et al. 1996; Davies 1987; Hassig 1988, 1992b; Smith 1987, 1996; Smith and Berdan 1992). Despite the seemingly rich database for Aztec imperialism, however, the nature and even the existence of the empire have been debated (Smith and Berdan 1992). Arguments for the presence of Mesoamerican empires prior to the Aztec Empire have had to rely primarily on archaeological evidence for imperial expansion, which, not surprisingly, has also triggered considerable debate (Cowgill 1997; R. Millon 1988; Smith and Montiel 2001; Zeitlin and Joyce 1999). Perhaps the two most controversial cases of Mesoamerican imperialism involve the highland Mexican polities of Monte Albán and Teotihuacan (figure 4.1).

In this chapter, I consider the impact of both Monte Albán and Teotihuacan on the lower Río Verde Valley on the Pacific Coast of Oaxaca. In particular, I examine the possibility that during the Terminal Formative (150 B.C.–A.D. 250), the lower Río Verde Valley was incorporated into an empire controlled by the rulers of Monte Albán in the Valley of Oaxaca. Marcus and Flannery (1996) have argued that the northern end of the lower Verde region was subjugated by Monte Albán. While Marcus and Flannery (1996) acknowledge various forms of imperial expansion, their model emphasizes direct territorial control either through military conquest or, in the case of weaker polities, through colonization under the threat of military action. As I will

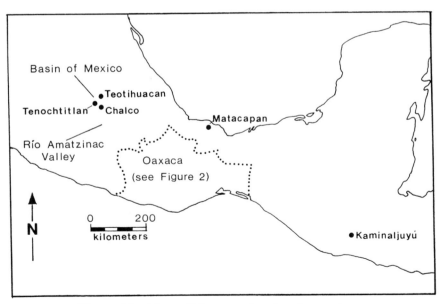

Figure 4.1   Map of Mesoamerica showing regions
and sites mentioned in the text

show in this chapter, however, the Terminal Formative data from the lower Verde suggest continuity in regional sociopolitical developments and do not meet the criteria for subjugation due to territorial imperialism. Instead, the evidence suggests a major sociopolitical disruption of the lower Verde during the Early Classic period (A.D. 250–500) that meets more of the criteria for subjugation than do the Terminal Formative data. Preliminary results suggest that the powerful center of Teotihuacan in the Basin of Mexico may have played a role in Early Classic sociopolitical change in the lower Verde. While the evidence for interaction between the lower Verde and Teotihuacan is intriguing, at present plausible models range from conquest to increased reciprocal exchange.

Archaeological Evidence
for Imperial Conquest

Comparative research on ancient empires such as the Wari, Inka, Roman, Assyrian, Vijayanagara, and Aztec indicates that imperial elites usually pursued a variety of strategies to control or influence hinterlands (Algaze 1993; Berdan et al. 1996; Fulford 1992; Hassig 1988; Postgate 1992; Schreiber 1987, 1992; Sinopoli 1994; Smith and Montiel 2001; Stark 1990; Stein 1999). These strategies vary from territorial conquest and direct administration, such as is emphasized by Marcus and Flannery (1996), to indirect hegemonic control achieved largely through the cooperation of local elites in peripheral regions, as was the case for much of the Aztec Empire (Berdan et al. 1996; D'Altroy 1992; Hassig 1988, 1992b). In cases of indirect control, the cooperation of local elites is often achieved through military threats backed up by occasional raids. Finally, imperial control can be exerted through asymmetrical alliances with local elites, often cemented via intermarriage and gift exchange (Stark 1990), and may involve the presence of outposts to facilitate trade (Algaze 1993; Stein 1999). Archaeological correlates of imperialism vary according to the nature of imperial conquest and control.

Archaeological correlates of territorial imperialism include evidence for military conquest or colonization and the direct administration of the province (Berdan et al. 1996; Fulford 1992; Postgate 1992; Schreiber 1987, 1992; Smith and Montiel 2001; Stark 1990; Stein 1999). Direct evidence for conquest warfare includes burials with traumatic war wounds, burned and/or intentionally destroyed buildings (see

Brown and Garber, chapter 6 in this volume), and the construction of defensive walls. Indirect evidence for war includes sites that have been suddenly abandoned, settlement shifts to defensible locations, and buffer zones between competing polities. Direct control over subjugated regions is often manifest in evidence of architectural remains, mortuary practices, or aspects of elite culture that reflect the presence of imperial administrators. The wholesale replacement of indigenous cultural patterns, such as ritual practices and styles of architecture and ceramics, would probably occur only with large-scale imperial colonization. The imperial reorganization of local political and economic systems would be suggested by changes in settlement hierarchy along with the presence of colonies, garrisons, and trading enclaves. Systems of craft or subsistence production would be expected to intensify as tribute was mobilized to the imperial core. Evidence for imperial storage facilities would be expected. Military conquest and imperial administration of a region may also be visible in iconographic and epigraphic data, especially at the capital of the empire.

Evidence for indirect hegemonic control is more difficult to identify archaeologically than territorial conquest and direct administration (Berdan et al. 1996; Schreiber 1992:32–34; Smith 1987; Smith and Montiel 2001; Stark 1990; Stein 1999). If conflict is sufficiently intense and protracted, defensive features and settlement shifts to defensible locations might occur in subject regions, although with politically weak polities even the threat of warfare can be sufficient for imperial elites to gain compliance (Hassig 1988:112–33). Imperial administrative facilities will not be as extensive under indirect control, and if local elites are left intact, there may not be any evidence of an imperial administrative presence. Even in the absence of imperial administrators, however, local elites often adopt imperial symbols of prestige and gain access to prestige goods from the core. Some degree of economic reorganization often occurs under indirect rule as tribute is mobilized for transport to the core (Stark 1990:257–58). Evidence of economic reorganization includes intensification in subsistence and craft production for tribute, a lowered living standard, and some counterflow of trade goods from the imperial core to the provinces (Smith 1987; Stark 1990).

Unfortunately, most of the potential indicators of imperial conquest and control, whether direct or indirect, can also result from other factors (see Schreiber 1992; Smith and Heath-Smith 1994; Stark 1990; Zeitlin 1993). For example, changes in settlement, economy, and sociopolitical organization can occur because of a multitude of factors, both internal and external. The diffusion of ideas and practices from core regions can result from emulation independent of conflict with that region (Renfrew 1986:8). The causes of the diffusion of elements of ceramic and architectural style from the imperial core are often extremely difficult to interpret (Cowgill 1997; Pasztory 1993; Stark 1990; Yarborough 1992). Burned structures can be the result of accidental fires or reverential termination rituals (see Pagliaro et al., chapter 5 in this volume). Finally, iconographic and epigraphic indications of imperialism must be viewed with caution since they reflect the viewpoint of core elites and can represent propaganda with little historical veracity (Marcus 1992b:401). These problems of equifinality require that researchers use multiple lines of evidence to support an imperialism argument. In addition, other factors that affect the probability of direct territorial control need to be considered, such as the relative size and complexity of core and peripheral polities, their distance from one another, the difficulty of travel, their relative military prowess, and the potential benefits to the core of subjugating the periphery (Stein 1999).

Monte Albán Imperialism

The interregional impact of Monte Albán during the Terminal Formative, from about 150 B.C. to A.D. 250, has become a topic of debate among Oaxaca archaeologists (Balkansky 1997; Feinman and Nicholas 1990, 1991; Finsten 1996; Flannery 1983b; Joyce 1991a, 1993a, 1994a; Joyce and Winter 1996; Joyce et al. 2000; Marcus 1983; Marcus and Flannery 1996; Redmond 1983; Spencer 1982; Workinger 2002; Zeitlin 1990, 1993; Zeitlin and Joyce 1999). Most researchers, including myself, agree that Monte Albán influenced many areas during the Terminal Formative. Evidence for contact with Monte Albán varies greatly, and this has led to a variety of perspectives as to the nature and effects of core–periphery relations in Terminal Formative Oaxaca. The most pervasive evidence of Monte Albán's interregional influence is the spread of certain gray-ware ceramic styles from the Valley of Oaxaca to the Mixteca Alta, Mixteca Baja, Ejutla Valley, Miahuatlán Valley, Sola Valley, Cuicatlán Cañada, lower Río Verde Valley, and southern Isthmus of Tehuantepec (figure 4.2). In addition, people in the Mixteca Alta and Mixteca Baja adopted a number of elements of Oaxaca Valley elite culture, including hieroglyphic writing and a distinctive style of anthropomorphic urn (Joyce and Winter 1996).

There is evidence for increased interpolity conflict during the

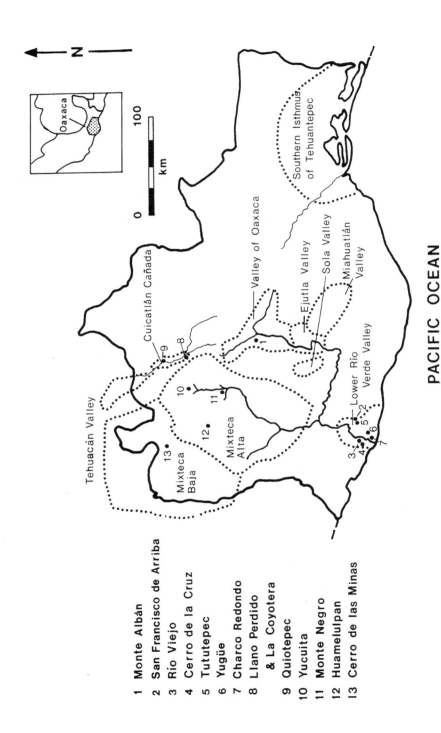

PACIFIC OCEAN

Southern Isthmus
of Tehuantepec

Valley of Oaxaca

Cuicatlán Cañada

Ejutla Valley

Sola Valley

Miahuatlán
Valley

Lower Río
Verde Valley

Tehuacán Valley

Mixteca
Alta

Mixteca
Baja

N

0   100

km

Oaxaca

1 Monte Albán
2 San Francisco de Arriba
3 Río Viejo
4 Cerro de la Cruz
5 Tututepec
6 Yugüe
7 Charco Redondo
8 Llano Perdido
   & La Coyotera
9 Quiotepec
10 Yucuita
11 Monte Negro
12 Huamelulpan
13 Cerro de las Minas

Figure 4.2 Map of Oaxaca showing regions and sites mentioned in the text

Terminal Formative (150 B.C.–A.D. 250) throughout the Oaxacan highlands and in the lowland Cuicatlán Cañada region (Feinman and Nicholas 1990; Joyce 1994a; Spencer 1982; Winter 1989). Evidence for conflict includes a shift in settlement locations to defensible hilltops. In many of the highland valleys of Oaxaca, early urban centers developed, all of which were located on hilltops or ridges. Urban centers often had defensive walls, such as at Monte Albán, Cerro de las Minas, and Yucuita. There are indications of warfare, such as the apparent burning and partial abandonment of Yucuita at approximately A.D. 200 and the abandonment of Monte Negro at about the same time. Probable trophy skulls have also been recovered at Huamelulpan, Yucuita, and Monte Negro (Winter 1989:37).

Marcus and Flannery (1996:206–7) argue that the Terminal Formative data from Oaxaca indicate that Monte Albán expanded beyond the Valley of Oaxaca through imperial conquest and colonization. According to their model, by the Terminal Formative, Monte Albán's empire covered an area of 20,000 square kilometers, stretching from the Cuicatlán Cañada in the north to the Pacific coast in the south (see Marcus and Flannery 1996:fig. 242). Imperial subjugation of these regions would have allowed Monte Albán's rulers to gain control over exotic goods and trade routes from the Pacific coast to Central Mexico.

Marcus (1983, 1992a:394–400) supports the imperialism argument through her study of the Terminal Formative "conquest slabs" from Building J in the Main Plaza at Monte Albán. The conquest slabs consist of over fifty carved stones that have been interpreted as representations of places conquered by and/or paying tribute to Monte Albán (Caso 1938, 1947; Marcus 1976, 1983, 1992a). Each slab contain two distinct elements: 1) a standardized "hill" glyph signifying a place and 2) a glyph or series of glyphs directly above the "hill" glyph, differing for each stone and signifying the name of a particular place (figure 4.3a). Many of the slabs contain an upside-down human head directly beneath the "hill" glyph, each with a distinctive headdress and interpreted as the dead ruler of a conquered locality. Marcus and Flannery (1996:197) suggest that the difference between the slabs that include effigy heads and those that do not is that the former refer to places incorporated into the Zapotec Empire by conquest with the latter subjugated by colonization. Some conquest slabs also exhibit a hieroglyphic text that in its most complete form includes a calendar date that may represent the date of conquest of the locality. By comparing the toponyms carved on the Building J slabs to those found in the Codex Mendoza, a sixteenth-century Aztec tribute list, Marcus

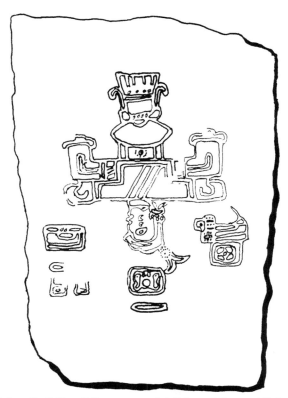

Figure 4.3a   Building J "conquest slab" from Monte Albán: slab 15

(1992a:395–96) argues that the specific location of seven of the localities can be identified.

One of the regions identified on the conquest slabs by Marcus
(1983:108) was the Cuicatlán Cañada, located about 100 kilometers
northwest of the Oaxaca Valley. Archaeological research in the Cuicatlán Cañada by Charles Spencer and Elsa Redmond (Redmond 1983;
Spencer 1982; Spencer and Redmond 1997) has provided the strongest
direct evidence for conquest by Monte Albán. Their data suggest military conquest followed by the imperial administration of the region by
Monte Albán. Evidence for the conquest and subjugation of the region
includes the following:

1. The surface survey showed a dramatic shift in settlement patterns from
   the high alluvium to defensible piedmont locations.

Figure 4.3b   Building J "conquest slab" from Monte Albán: slab 57

2. There was a decrease in the settlement hierarchy from three to two levels.
3. Terminal Formative ceramics showed a close stylistic affinity with those from the Valley of Oaxaca.
4. Evidence from excavations indicated that the Llano Perdido site was burned and suddenly abandoned.
5. Excavations at the site of La Coyotera exposed the remains of a *tzompantli*, or skull rack, possibly exhibiting victims of warfare or sacrifice.
6. The apparent establishment of a Zapotec administrative outpost and fortress at Quiotepec was inferred from a Oaxaca Valley–style tomb eroding from the surface.
7. An unoccupied buffer zone was indicated by survey data between the Cañada and the Tehuacán Valley to the north.
8. New forms of political organization were inferred from changes in public architecture.
9. A major economic reorganization was suggested, perhaps designed to produce surpluses in the form of tropical crops for tribute payments to Monte Albán. Economic changes included the development of irrigation systems as well as a decline in evidence for exchange and craft production.

While the data for Monte Albán's subjugation of the Cuicatlán Cañada are compelling, direct evidence for Zapotec conquest of other regions is thus far rare. Evidence for warfare is present in much of the Oaxacan highlands; however, the data are more consistent with a model involving conflict among multiple competing polities rather than defense solely against Zapotec imperialism (Joyce 1994a). Outside the Cuicatlán Cañada, Marcus and Flannery (1996) rely on indirect evidence of a Monte Albán presence to argue for imperial subjugation. In particular, they argue that the spread of Terminal Formative gray-ware ceramic styles from the Valley of Oaxaca is one of the best lines of circumstantial evidence for a Monte Albán takeover, either through conquest or colonization. They argue that subjugation is demonstrated in "those regions whose previously autonomous ceramics are literally swamped or replaced by Monte Albán gray wares" (Marcus and Flannery 1996:199). The lower Río Verde Valley is one of the regions with evidence for the diffusion of Monte Albán–style gray-ware ceramics.

Monte Albán and the Lower Río Verde Valley

The argument that the lower Verde was incorporated into a territorial empire ruled by Monte Albán is based on two lines of evidence: epigraphic interpretations and similarities in ceramic styles (Marcus and Flannery 1996:201–2). Among the places identified by Marcus (1983) on the conquest slabs was Tututepec in the northern part of the lower Verde region. Marcus and Flannery (1996:201) also cite ceramic evidence from a brief survey by DeCicco and Brockington (1956:59) at the site of San Francisco de Arriba, located 3 kilometers east of Tututepec. DeCicco and Brockington (1956:59) suggest that the ceramics from San Francisco de Arriba bear a strong resemblance to Late/Terminal Formative pottery from Monte Albán, although Brockington (1983:29) concluded that "Monte Albán never dominated the Coast at any time." According to Marcus and Flannery (1996:201–2), the conquest of the area around Tututepec and San Francisco de Arriba would have placed the northern part of the lower Verde region at the southern boundary of Monte Albán's empire (Workinger 2002).[1] They also suggest that the floodplain of the lower Verde "was so sparsely populated that the Zapotec would hardly have needed an army to subdue them" (Marcus and Flannery 1996:202). Balkansky (1997:222) is more specific in suggesting that San Francisco de Arriba may have been a Zapotec outpost from which local resources could have been exploited.[2] Imperial control over the Tututepec/San Francisco de Arriba area could have given Monte Albán's rulers access to exotic coastal items, such as ornamental shell, cacao, cotton, fish, *púrpura* dye, tropical fruit, and textiles. Archaeological research has shown that Pacific coast shell was reaching the Oaxacan highlands during the Terminal Formative (Feinman and Nicholas 1993; Winter 1984:204–7).

Archaeological research in the lower Río Verde Valley since 1986 has investigated the possibility of an imperial conquest by Monte Albán (Joyce 1991a, 1991b, 1993a; Joyce and Winter 1989; Joyce et al. 1995, 1998; Workinger 2002; Workinger and Colby 1997; Zeitlin and Joyce 1999). This research has included excavations at seventeen sites, a regional site reconnaissance, and a full-coverage survey over 152 square kilometers. The regional survey, reconnaissance, and excavation data do not indicate a shift to defensible piedmont locations or a disruption in sociopolitical organization suggestive of a Zapotec take-over during the Terminal Formative.[3] Population appears to have grown through this period based on occupational areas calculated from the surface survey. The area occupied in the 152-square-kilometer survey zone increases from 297 hectares in the Late Formative (400–150 B.C.) to 446 hectares in the early Terminal Formative (150 B.C.–A.D. 100) and to 699 hectares by the late Terminal Formative (A.D. 100–250). The settlement hierarchy, based on site size and volume of monumental architecture, increases from three tiers in the Late Formative to five by the Terminal Formative. The percentage of the occupational area in the piedmont fluctuates through this period, ranging from 43 percent in the Late Formative to 20 percent during the early Terminal Formative and 38 percent by the late Terminal Formative, so there is no evidence of a shift to defensible piedmont locations. In fact, the early Terminal Formative period, when piedmont settlement is at it lowest proportionally, is precisely when Marcus and Flannery (1996:202) claim that the lower Verde region was conquered. Defensive walls have not been identified. Survey and excavation data have yielded no evidence for burned sites or burials with traumatic wounds that would signal conflict. There are no indications of the presence of Zapotec administrators, such as elaborate pottery, tombs, or monumental architecture, in Oaxaca Valley style.

The primary center in the lower Verde by the early Terminal Formative was the site of Río Viejo, which reached 225 hectares. Since Monte Albán was only 416 hectares at this time, the lower Verde cannot be considered a sparsely settled and underdeveloped region but instead would have been a formidable opponent to Zapotec expansion.

In addition, the lower Verde lies 150 kilometers southwest and about a week's hard travel through the mountains by foot from Monte Albán, which would have created great logistical difficulties for imperial armies or administrators (Zeitlin and Joyce 1999).

Evidence for exchange between the Oaxaca Valley and the lower Verde declines during the Terminal Formative. Excavated Late Formative contexts at the sites of Río Viejo, Cerro de la Cruz, San Francisco de Arriba, and Yugüe have yielded several hundred examples of Oaxaca Valley pottery as well as exotic nonlocal ceramics from other areas (Joyce 1991a; Workinger 2002). By the Terminal Formative, however, few examples of imported pottery from the Oaxacan highlands have been recovered, and there also seems to be a decline in the importation of obsidian (Joyce et al. 1995; Workinger 2002). The decline in exchange may have resulted from the more competitive political landscape of the Terminal Formative, especially in the Oaxacan highlands (Joyce 1993a:73). There is no evidence, however, linking the decline in exchange to conquest by Monte Albán. Warfare in the highlands may have disrupted exchange routes to the coast even if coastal polities were not directly threatened.

The only evidence from the lower Verde that might suggest interaction with Monte Albán during the Terminal Formative is the diffusion of highland ceramic styles (Joyce 1991a, 1993b; Zeitlin and Joyce 1999).[4] Lower Verde gray-ware ceramics show stylistic cross ties with the highlands during the Terminal Formative, but the overall assemblage remains regionally distinct.[5] The only ceramics that bear a strong resemblance to Oaxaca Valley pottery are a category of conical bowls decorated with two incised lines on the interior rim and occasionally a combed base. This ceramic category is similar to type G.12 from the Oaxaca Valley (Caso et al. 1967). This vessel type, however, is found throughout much of Terminal Formative Oaxaca (Joyce 1993b), including regions with evidence for Monte Albán conquest, such as the Cuicatlán Cañada, as well as areas with no indications of Zapotec conquest, such as the Mixteca Baja (figure 4.4). The technology of manufacturing gray-ware pottery in a reducing firing environment appears to have originated in the Valley of Oaxaca (Winter 1984:203–4), but because the G.12 style bowl was being manufactured throughout Oaxaca by the Terminal Formative (Caso et al. 1967; Gaxiola 1984; Joyce 1991a; Spencer and Redmond 1982; Spores 1972; Zeitlin 1979), coastal potters could have adopted the technology to produce these ceramics from many regions. In addition, focusing solely on the Oaxaca Valley as the source area for the spread of gray-ware styles

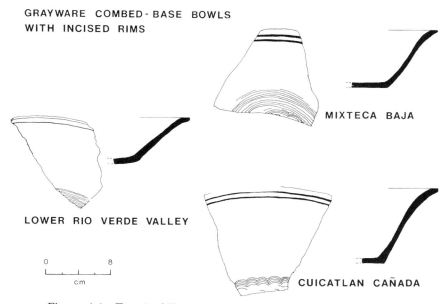

GRAYWARE COMBED-BASE BOWLS
WITH INCISED RIMS

MIXTECA BAJA

LOWER RIO VERDE VALLEY

0   8
cm

CUICATLAN CAÑADA

Figure 4.4   Terminal Formative gray-ware combed-base bowls

ignores other potential patterns of ceramic similarity that might be important for understanding Terminal Formative interaction (Joyce 1993b). For example, thin-walled composite silhouette bowls (figure 4.5) found at both Huamelulpan in the Mixteca Alta and Cerro de las Minas in the Mixteca Baja are almost identical to one another in technology, form, and style.

The overall distinctiveness of the lower Verde pottery is in sharp contrast to areas of the highlands such as the Ejutla, Miahuatlán, and Sola Valleys, whose pottery is so similar to the Valley of Oaxaca that an independent ceramic typology is not needed (Balkansky 1997; Feinman and Nicholas 1990; Markman 1981). The Oaxaca data are consistent with comparative studies of ancient empires indicating that general similarities in ceramic styles are a poor indicator of conquest (Bey, chapter 2 in this volume; Lind 1987:97–98; Schreiber 1992:263; Stark 1990).

A recent archaeological project at San Francisco de Arriba, the site supposedly conquered and administered by Monte Albán, has also failed to yield evidence of warfare or conquest (Workinger 2002; Workinger and Colby 1997). Survey, mapping, and excavation by Andrew

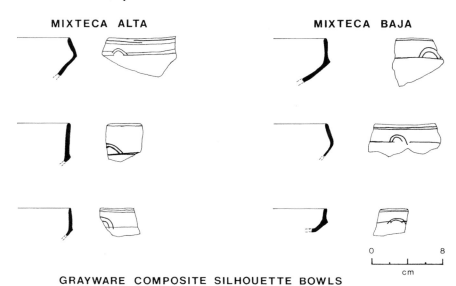

GRAYWARE COMPOSITE SILHOUETTE BOWLS

Figure 4.5   Terminal Formative gray-ware composite silhouette bowls

Workinger (2002) in and around San Francisco de Arriba has not recovered evidence of defensive works, Zapotec administrative facilities, site destruction, or economic reorganization during the Terminal Formative. A study of the ceramic assemblage at San Francisco de Arriba (Workinger 2002) indicates that the proportion of gray-ware ceramics at the site is lower than for sites studied in the lower Verde's floodplain (Joyce 1991a:694). These data argue against San Francisco de Arriba having been conquered by Monte Albán or having been the location of a Zapotec administrative outpost (Workinger 2002).

At this point, the only evidence for the conquest of the lower Verde by Monte Albán is the epigraphic data. Marcus (1976, 1992a) argues that Building J Slab 57, depicting the conquest of a "Hill of the Bird," refers to the coastal town of Tututepec, which was an important Postclassic polity (figure 4.3b). There are, however, many hills known by indigenous people in Oaxaca as "Hill of the Bird," and there is no reason to assume that the one on Building J should refer to coastal Tututepec. In addition, Whittaker (1980:92–106) questions Marcus's (1976) methodology for identifying the localities on the conquest slabs and especially critiques the reading of Slab 57 as the coastal town of Tututepec (also see Workinger 2002). As I have suggested elsewhere (Joyce 1993a), many of the "conquests" referred to on Building J may have involved nothing more than raiding. The nature, intensity, and goals of warfare in ancient Mesoamerica varied considerably across time and space (Hassig 1988, 1992a), so it is difficult to know what type of conquest is referred to on the Building J slabs. Given the potential importance of political propaganda (see Marcus 1992a, 1992b), regions that were occasionally raided might have been represented on the conquest slabs in an equivalent fashion to areas that were conquered.

The evidence from the lower Río Verde Valley does not support a model of military conquest and territorial control by Monte Albán. Except for the diffusion of some highland gray-ware pottery styles, there is little evidence that can be interpreted as resulting from interaction between the Oaxaca Valley and the lower Río Verde Valley during the Terminal Formative. If Monte Albán threatened the lower Verde militarily, it appears that those threats were not sufficient to motivate settlement shifts to defensible locations. The data at present leave open the possibility of a form of indirect control, perhaps via asymmetrical alliances with local elites, which left little evidence in the archaeological record, although even this form of interaction seems unlikely.

Even if Monte Albán did not conquer the lower Verde, the highland polity may still have had an effect on social developments on the Oaxaca coast (Joyce 1991a, 1991b, 1993a, 1994a; Joyce et al. 1995, 1998; Zeitlin 1990; Zeitlin and Joyce 1999). Exchange between the lower Verde and the Oaxaca Valley declined during the Terminal Formative, perhaps because of competition and conflict in the highlands. Monte Albán's rulers may have tried to coerce coastal elites into compliance by withholding crucial goods (Zeitlin and Joyce 1999). To replace the prestige items that had previously been obtained from the Oaxacan highlands, lower Verde elites probably forged new ties with elites from other regions and enlisted local artisans to manufacture exotic goods (Joyce 1991a, 1993a; Joyce et al. 1995). To the extent that the lower Verde was subject to raids by Monte Albán, the threat might have provided a rationale for elites to consolidate power, thereby contributing to political centralization, as appears to have happened in the Oaxacan highlands (Joyce 1991a:658–63, 1994a; Joyce and Winter 1996). Politicoreligious ideas and practices developed at Monte Albán appear to have been emulated by people in many parts of the Oaxacan highlands (Joyce 1991a, 1994a; Joyce and Winter 1996) and perhaps in more distant regions (Joyce 2000). It is possible that people in the lower Verde also adopted some of these ideas and practices, although present evidence is insufficient to assess this possibility.

Teotihuacan and the Lower Río Verde Valley

While the Terminal Formative data from the lower Verde do not suggest conquest, there is evidence from the Early Classic (A.D. 250–500) indicative of a disruption of settlement and social organization perhaps related to a foreign incursion (Joyce 1993a; Joyce 1999). The systematic survey data show an increase in regional settlement from 699 hectares in the late Terminal Formative to 807 hectares during the Early Classic. The percentage of the occupational area located in the piedmont increased from 38 percent in the late Terminal Formative to 63 percent in the Early Classic, suggesting a shift to defensible locations. There was a reduction in the settlement hierarchy from five to four levels. The full-coverage survey data indicate that during the Early Classic, the lower Verde region contained multiple first-order centers with perhaps as many as eight sites of roughly equivalent size. Río Viejo experienced a major decrease in size, going from 200 hectares in the late Terminal Formative to 75 hectares in the Early Classic. The construction of monumental buildings at Río Viejo appears to have declined.

Evidence from Río Viejo suggests the possible destruction of the main temple at the site. Large-scale excavations in the eastern end of the acropolis at Río Viejo show that a fourteen-meter-high adobe platform was constructed here during the late Terminal Formative (A.D. 100–250). The platform supported a probable public building made from adobe blocks covered in places by stucco. At about A.D. 250, this structure was abandoned and was not reoccupied until the Late Classic (A.D. 500–800). Burned adobes and floor areas suggest that the structure may have been destroyed by fire. The summit of the platform lay exposed to the elements for perhaps 250 years, resulting in erosion and disintegration of most of the building. Two AMS dates have been obtained from the remains of the adobe structure. A date of 1573 ± 40, or A.D. 377 (AA40036), was obtained from charcoal associated with adobe building materials. A second date of 1696 ± 43, or A.D. 254 (AA40037), was recovered from charcoal lying directly on a section of burned floor and sealed by overlying adobes. The latter sample appears to be more reliable in dating the abandonment and possible destruction of the building.

Several other large Terminal Formative floodplain sites with mounded architecture declined significantly in size or were abandoned. For example, during the Terminal Formative, Yugüe was a third-order site of 9.75 hectares. Most of the site was artificially elevated above the floodplain by a huge platform that supported at least one probable public building. During the Early Classic, Yugüe was virtually abandoned.

The decline of Río Viejo and other floodplain sites, the changes in the regional settlement hierarchy, and the dramatic settlement shift into the piedmont together suggest a major sociopolitical reorganization relative to the Terminal Formative. The sociopolitical disruption of the Early Classic is underscored by the Late Classic (A.D. 500–800) recovery of settlement patterns and sociopolitical organization to conditions similar to those of the Terminal Formative. The survey data show that, in the Late Classic, people left the defensible piedmont sites and returned to the floodplain. In the full-coverage survey zone, the percentage of settlement in the floodplain increases from its Early Classic level of 22 percent to 56 percent by the Late Classic. Settlement at Río Viejo grew to 250 hectares, and the regional settlement hierarchy increased from four to seven levels.

Excavation data indicate that the Early Classic disruption in settlement patterns and sociopolitical organization may have had something to do with the powerful central Mexican polity of Teotihuacan located about 400 kilometers northwest of the lower Verde (Joyce 1993a). Excavations at Río Viejo in 1988 exposed two high-status Early Classic burials with elaborate offerings, including green obsidian from the Pachuca source, controlled by Teotihuacan, and probable local imitations of thin-orange vessels, suggesting interaction with Central Mexico and probably Teotihuacan (Joyce 1991a:app. 1). Both burials were interred in simple graves in the eastern part of the site, which was probably the civic-ceremonial core during the Early Classic (Joyce 1999). Burial 7 was an adult male interred with twenty-two ceramic vessels, eleven greenstone beads, two shell ear flares, and a conch shell. Burial 15 was an adult female with twenty-nine ceramic vessels and two green obsidian blades.

A small proportion of Early Classic ceramics in the lower Verde exhibit formal and decorative attributes often linked to Teotihuacan, including thin-orange pottery, cylindrical tripod vessels with slab feet, coffee-bean appliqués, and *candeleros*. Pottery with Central Mexican attributes appears to be more common in high-status contexts, such as with Burials 7 and 15 from Río Viejo. Most of these ceramic cross ties seem to be with late Tlamimilolpa and Xolalpan pottery from Teotihuacan (Sejourné 1966a). The vast majority of lower Verde pottery, however, was purely local in style. Other ceramic types often linked to Classic period interaction with the Basin of Mexico, such as Teotihuacan-style *floreros* and *incensarios* (Berlo 1984; Santley 1983; Yarborough 1992), have not been recovered in the lower Verde.

While ceramic styles from the lower Verde provide ambiguous data on interaction with Central Mexico, the frequency of Pachuca obsidian suggests some type of intensive exchange (Joyce et al. 1995; Workinger 2002). Obsidian studies, including neutron activation analyses, have shown that Pachuca obsidian made up 61 percent of the seventy-one pieces of obsidian excavated from Early Classic contexts in sites on the lower Verde floodplain. This is the highest proportion known for a region outside the Central Mexican highlands. For example, in contemporaneous deposits at Matacapan in southern Veracruz, only 6 percent of the obsidian is from Pachuca, even though Santley (1989:140) views the site as an enclave permanently colonized by Teotihuacan merchants. The focus on Pachuca obsidian during the Early Classic continues a pattern of reliance on Basin of Mexican obsidian sources in the lower Verde that began in the Late Formative (Joyce et al. 1995; Workinger 2002). Several sherds from Early Classic contexts at Río Viejo are also likely imports from Teotihuacan, although sourcing studies have not been conducted.

Data from Workinger's (2002) recent project at San Francisco de Arriba, another first-order Early Classic site, reinforce the view that the lower Verde had a significant exchange relationship with Teotihuacan. Excavations at San Francisco de Arriba exposed a midden containing dense deposits of obsidian dating to the Early Classic. Of the 285 pieces of obsidian recovered from this deposit, 243, or 85 percent, were from Pachuca.

All the Early Classic Pachuca obsidian thus far excavated in the lower Verde region has been from the first-order sites of Río Viejo and San Francisco de Arriba. Test excavations at two lower-order Early Classic sites recovered eight obsidian artifacts, but none were green. These data suggest that elites may have controlled access to Pachuca obsidian.

The significance of the high percentage of Pachuca obsidian in the lower Verde is underscored by archaeological evidence from the eastern coast of Oaxaca that has yielded almost no Pachuca obsidian and few stylistic cross ties with Central Mexican pottery (Brockington 1987:231; Long and Brockington 1974:88; Zeitlin 1982). These patterns suggest that the nature of interaction with Central Mexico was different in the eastern versus the western coast of Oaxaca.

To better understand the possible role of Teotihuacan in the lower Río Verde, the coastal data can be placed in the context of evidence for Teotihuacan imperialism in other parts of Mesoamerica. As with other examples of pre-Columbian imperialism (Hassig 1992a; Smith and Montiel 2001; Zeitlin and Joyce 1999), the nature and extent of Teotihuacan's empire has been debated (Ball 1983; Clark 1986; Cowgill 1997; R. Millon 1988; Smith and Montiel 2001; Stark 1990). Research in many areas of Mesoamerica increasingly indicates that the rulers of Teotihuacan may have controlled a far-reaching though discontinuous empire. Regions in close proximity sometimes exhibit great variation in evidence of contact with Teotihuacan (Hassig 1992a; Joyce 1993a; Yarborough 1992). Teotihuacan's rulers appear to have targeted areas where they could control key resources, such as marine shell, cacao, cotton, and obsidian (Bové 1991; Hirth 1980; R. Millon 1988; Santley 1983, 1989). With the exception of portions of the Central Mexican highlands that may have been directly administered (Hirth 1980), Teotihuacan's imperial strategy was largely hegemonic (Cowgill 1997:134; Hassig 1992a:45–61; Smith and Montiel 2001; Stark 1990) via contacts with local elites and possibly the establishment of trading enclaves at sites such as Kaminaljuyú and Matacapan (Sanders and Michels 1977; Santley 1983; Santley et al. 1987; however, for a critical perspective, see Arnold et al. 1993:186–87; Clark 1986; Cowgill 1997:135). Most areas with evidence for contact with Central Mexico were not conquered but interacted with Teotihuacan both directly and indirectly via exchange, alliance, intermarriage, and diffusion (Cowgill 1997; Laporte and Fialko 1990; Pasztory 1978, 1993; Santley 1983; Stone 1989). The nature and extent of Teotihuacan imperialism, however, is still far from being clearly established, and in most cases alternative explanations are possible (Arnold et al. 1993; Clark 1986; Cowgill 1997:134–35; Pasztory 1993; Stark 1990).

The data from the lower Verde are as equivocal as in other areas of Mesoamerica in regard to possible conquest and incorporation into a Teotihuacan empire. The data could be used to argue for a Teotihuacan imperial presence, perhaps even involving military conquest and territorial control, although other explanations not involving conquest would also be consistent with the evidence (see Joyce 1993a:74–75). For example, it is possible that exchange relations with Teotihuacan altered the political economy of the region such that the power of the rulers of Río Viejo was undermined in a way that contributed to the decline of the polity. Further research is necessary to evaluate these alternatives.

Conclusions

To contribute to an understanding of warfare in ancient Mesoamerica, the data from the lower Verde must be viewed from a broader macro-regional perspective on the nature of Mesoamerican empires. The evidence from the lower Río Verde Valley is consistent with the developing view that Mesoamerican empires pursued the type of multifaceted strategy for dealing with their hinterlands that is found in other ancient empires, or what Schreiber (1992) has termed a mosaic of control. Imperial rulers had a variety of strategies for dealing with hinterland regions, ranging from territorial conquest to political alliance.

The Mesoamerican data suggest that in most cases the only areas to be conquered and directly administered were politically weak polities near the imperial core. Examples of territorial conquest in ancient Mesoamerica include the Aztec conquest of the Chalca city-states (Berdan et al. 1996; Hassig 1988:171) and perhaps Monte Albán's conquest of the Cuicatlán Cañada (Redmond 1983; Spencer 1982; however, see Workinger 2002). Given the scale of pre-Columbian polities and the rugged terrain that characterizes much of Mesoamerica, it is not surprising that territorial conquest was relatively rare and limited to areas near imperial centers.

Rather than territorial conquest, the dominant strategy of Mesoamerican empires was that of indirect hegemonic control (Berdan et al. 1996; Hassig 1988, 1992a; Smith and Montiel 2001; Stark 1990). Regions were brought under imperial control through the threat of warfare, which could be realized if local elites did not comply. Evidence for imperial administrative facilities is rare, and the data suggest that local rulers usually remained in place. Indirect control was also achieved through alliances with the more powerful imperial rulers having greater influence over economic and political relations.

The rich ethnohistoric record of the Aztec provides a detailed view of the dynamics of hegemonic control during the century before the Spanish conquest (Berdan et al. 1996). Yet the Aztec Empire provides an important control for the examination of imperialism during earlier periods in Mesoamerica, such as for Teotihuacan and Monte Albán, where textual data are limited. In the Aztec case, even when ethnohistoric records verify that a region was controlled by Tenochtitlan, it is often difficult to identify the archaeological evidence for hegemonic imperialism (Berdan et al. 1996; Smith 1987; Smith and Berdan 1992; Smith and Montiel 2001).

In regions that interacted with the earlier polities of Monte Albán and Teotihuacan changes in settlement, social organization, trade, and architectural styles that have been proposed as the result of conquest often have alternative explanations (Cowgill 1997:134–35; Stark 1990; Zeitlin and Joyce 1999). Powerful polities greatly influence their hinterlands through military threats, trade, and the spread of political, religious, and economic ideas even in the absence of conquest (Stein 1999). Given the difficulty of identifying imperial conquest and control in the archaeological record, it is important to be careful not to fit ambiguous data into preconceived models (Cowgill 1997:134). Multiple lines of evidence and improved analytical tools, such as refined chronologies, can help identify the dynamic and often short-lived periods of imperial control (O'Brien and Lewarch 1992; Smith 1987; Smith and Montiel 2001).

The data from the lower Río Verde Valley highlight these problems with the archaeology of empires. In the case of Monte Albán, evidence from the lower Verde and other hinterland regions indicates that a model of territorial imperialism alone is not appropriate (Zeitlin and Joyce 1999). Given the distance, difficulty in travel, and relative size and complexity of lower Verde society, it seems improbable that Monte Albán could have conquered and directly administered the lower Verde region. At present, arguments for Monte Albán conquest of the lower Verde hang on the iconographic interpretation of Building J Slab 57. While it is not yet possible to eliminate some form of indirect control of the lower Verde by Monte Albán, it is also quite possible that Slab 57 does not refer to the conquest of the lower Verde. The weight of evidence argues against an imperial presence by Monte Albán in the lower Río Verde Valley, including at San Francisco de Arriba and Tututepec (Workinger 2002).

It is also not yet possible to say whether Teotihuacan conquered the lower Verde region or even if the Early Classic disruption in settlement and sociopolitical organization resulted from foreign intervention of any sort. Yet given the archaeological criteria for imperialism, it appears more likely that the lower Verde was disrupted by foreign incursions during the Early Classic than during the Terminal Formative. Early Classic Teotihuacan was a much larger and more powerful polity than Terminal Formative Monte Albán. Militarism was a major theme in Teotihuacan art, although it is not clear how the iconography relates to the actual practice of warfare (Cowgill 1997:144–48; Headrick 1996 and chapter 9 in this volume; Taube 1992a). Archaeological research suggests that Teotihuacan may have achieved indirect hegemonic control over regions as distant as the Pacific coast and highlands of Guatemala (Berlo 1984; Bové 1991; Sanders and Michels 1977).

Further work is needed, however, to clarify the relationship between the lower Río Verde Valley and both Teotihuacan and Monte Albán. While this chapter has provided few definite answers regarding the impact of Monte Albán and Teotihuacan in the lower Río Verde Valley, it raises a number of questions that address the more general issue of ancient Mesoamerican imperialism. Long-term systematic research in core regions and especially in potential provinces will be necessary to tease apart and clarify the nature and extent of the putative empires of Teotihuacan and Monte Albán.

Notes

I would like to thank the Instituto Nacional de Antropología e Historia; especially the president of the Consejo de Arqueología, Joaquín García-Bárcena; and the directors of the Centro INAH Oaxaca, María de la Luz Topete, Ernesto González Licón, and Eduardo López Calzada, who have supported my research in Oaxaca. Funding for the field research in the lower Río Verde Valley has been provided by grants from the following organizations: National Science Foundation (grants SBR-9729763 and BNS-8716332), Foundation for the Advancement of Mesoamerican Studies (#99012), National Geographic Society (grant 3767–88), Wenner-Gren Foundation (GR. 4988), Vanderbilt University Research Council and Mellon Fund, Fulbright Foundation, H. John Heinz III Charitable Trust, Explorers Club, Sigma Xi, University of Colorado, and Rutgers University. Andrew Workinger kindly provided unpublished settlement data from his doctoral dissertation. The first draft of this chapter was completed while I was a Summer Fellow at Dumbarton Oaks, and I would like to thank that institution, especially Dr. Jeffrey Quilter, director of pre-Columbian studies. I would like to thank Cathy Cameron, Claudio Cioffi-Revilla, Steve Lekson, Jeffrey Quilter, Payson Sheets, Michael Smith, and Andrew Workinger for their comments on this chapter as well as Travis Stanton and Kat Brown for inviting me to participate in the volume.

1. Marcus and Flannery (1996:201) and Balkansky (1997:34) claim that the area of Tututepec and San Francisco de Arriba is too distant from the lower Río Verde Valley to "shed light" on each other's interactions with Monte Albán. The Tututepec and San Francisco de Arriba area, however, is located only 12 kilometers northeast of the lower Verde's floodplain and 16 kilometers east of the pre-Columbian regional center of Río Viejo. Since the mid-

1980s, archaeological projects in the lower Verde have included Tututepec and San Francisco de Arriba as part of the Lower Río Verde region, and there is no reason to justify modeling them as separate regions (see Grove 1988).

2. An article by Balkansky (1998:469–72) contains numerous factual errors and appears to misrepresent the work of several scholars who work on the archaeology of coastal Oaxaca. While many of the errors are addressed in a subsequent commentary (Joyce et al. 2000), his response to this commentary (Balkansky 2001) further misrepresents our research. A significant error by Balkansky (2001) that bears on the present chapter is his argument that burials from Late Formative Structure 1 at Cerro de la Cruz represent a massacre. Balkansky (2001:560) states that "the still-articulated bodies, moreover, are piled together in rooms without apparent disturbance." The burials in Structure 1 at Cerro de la Cruz have been discussed, often with illustrations, in several publications (Joyce 1991a, 1991b, 1994b; Joyce et al. 1998). As these publications show, "burial activities in both Structure 1 and Op. U (a nearby area with several interments) apparently occurred over a period of several generations, as shown by the frequent instances of later burials having disturbed earlier ones" (Joyce 1994b:158). The burials were underneath floors, and an analysis from the southern half of Structure 1, where stratigraphic relationships among burials could be clearly discerned, indicates that there were between six and twenty-one separate burial events (Joyce 1991a:732–39). Osteological analyses of the Cerro de la Cruz material have failed to yield evidence of traumatic wounds (Alexander Christensen, personal communication, 2001; Joyce 1991a:app. 1). It is also puzzling as to why Balkansky (2001:560) finds it exceptional that no grave goods were associated with the interments of Structure 1 since Late Formative burials found in the lower Río Verde Valley have rarely had grave offerings. Likewise, I do not know why burial patterns in the lower Río Verde Valley should conform to Formative period practices in other regions of Oaxaca, as Balkansky (2001:560) argues. Balkansky (2001:560) is incorrect when he argues that the age profile of the Structure 1 burials differs from formal cemeteries (see Joyce 1991a:255).

3. At present, an area of 152 square kilometers has been covered by full-coverage survey methods in the lower Verde, while the remainder of the region has been investigated through nonsystematic surface reconnaissance (Grove 1988; Joyce 1991a, 1991b, 1993a, 1999; Workinger 2002; Workinger and Colby 1997). The combination of survey and reconnaissance, along with excavation data, should be more than adequate to recognize the kind of dramatic settlement shifts noted for conquered regions like the Cuicatlán Cañada (Redmond 1983; Spencer 1982). For comparison, Spencer and Redmond (1997:25) covered 52.1 square kilometers in their survey of the Cuicatlán Cañada.

4. Balkansky (1998:470) argues that "epigraphic and iconographic data suggest that ties between the highlands and coastal Oaxaca began in Late Formative times, coincident with the Zapotec expansion." Joyce et al. (2000), however, stress that the epigraphic data from the coast is still equivocal in

terms of chronological placements and that the only nonportable carvings that might date to the Late Formative–Early Classic do not resemble Zapotec conventions. In his rebuttal, Balkansky (2001:560) contends that Urcid repetitively states that "highland-coastal epigraphic ties on stone monoliths also began in the Late Formative." Indeed, in the cited article, Urcid (1993:161) concluded that "the earliest [epigraphic] data [from the coast] can be dated to the late Formative" but qualifies this in the subsequent phrase where he states that such a conclusion is based only on a portable object of uncertain origin. The object, while technically a monolith, is merely 7 centimeters tall (Javier Urcid, personal communication, 2002). The object was not discussed by Joyce et al. (2000) because the statuette is in a private collection and has only a provenance attributed to Pochutla, which is outside the lower Verde region. To use such scanty epigraphic data in support of "an emerging regional pattern" is highly problematic.

5. Balkansky (2001:560) is in error when he argues that "by the Late/Terminal Formative, gray wares plus imitations made up almost 90% of the ceramics from coastal Río Viejo (Joyce 1993b)." The report he cites examines only ceramics from the early Terminal Formative Miniyua phase (150 B.C.–A.D. 100) rather than from the Late/Terminal Formative as a whole. During the Late Formative Minizundo phase (400–150 B.C.), there are virtually no locally made gray wares or Oaxaca Valley imitations, although 1.3 percent of rim sherds from unmixed deposits excavated in 1988 are from Oaxaca Valley imports (Joyce 1991a:129–47). Miniyua phase gray wares and fine brown wares include sherds with ceramic cross ties to styles from highland regions, including the Oaxaca Valley, Mixteca Alta, Mixteca Baja, Cuicatlán Cañada, Ejutla Valley, and the Miahuatlán Valley. Taken together, gray wares and fine brown wares make up 89.4 percent of the lower Verde rim sherds ($N = 273$) analyzed by Joyce (1993b) from a single feature at Río Viejo, although only about half of these exhibit cross ties with highland styles. Other ceramic types are regionally distinct. By the late Terminal Formative Chacahua phase (A.D. 100–250), gray wares are the dominant paste category, although they exhibit few cross ties with highland pottery. Questions about the diffusion of firing technologies used to make reduced gray-ware paste pottery and the spread of some ceramic styles throughout much of Oaxaca continue to be important subjects of study (Levine 2002). I agree with other researchers, however, that the diffusion of ceramic styles is a very poor indicator of conquest in the absence of other categories of evidence (Schreiber 1992:263; Stark 1990), evidence that has yet to be found in the lower Verde.

Part II

WARFARE AND RITUAL

Chapter Five

Evaluating the Archaeological Signatures of Maya Ritual and Conflict

Jonathan B. Pagliaro, James F. Garber, and Travis W. Stanton

Evidence for conflict and warfare among the pre-Columbian Maya has been gathered from epigraphic, iconographic, and archaeological contexts. Recently, some scholars have argued that particular ritual deposits constitute an important category of archaeological evidence pertaining to Maya warfare (Ambrosino 1997; Ambrosino et al., chapter 7 in this volume; Brown and Garber, chapter 6 in this volume; Freidel and Suhler 1998; Freidel et al., chapter 11 in this volume; Mock 1998b; Stanton 1999; Stanton and Pagliaro 1997; Suhler 1996; Suhler and Freidel 1995a, 1995b). Designated desecratory termination ritual deposits, they exhibit purposeful destruction of material culture and symbols of power, including elite architecture and burials. Similar acts of destruction have been observed within the archaeological records of cultures throughout the world (Tarlow 1997) and are related to an overarching ideological strategy used by individuals and/or groups of individuals attempting to establish dominance within prehistoric societies.

The identification and interpretation of these ritual deposits is becoming central to reconstructing the ideological and material goals behind ancient Maya conflict and warfare. Yet despite the increasing awareness that some ritual deposits can be related to warfare activities, a number of unresolved issues remain. First, criteria for distinguishing the remains of ritual behavior from other activities, such as refuse disposal, are not clearly defined (Stanton and Pagliaro 1997). Second, termination ritual deposits and destructive behavior manifesting similar material patterning appear to occur for a variety of reasons, including but not limited to conflict and warfare. Thus, separate subclasses of ritual deposits must be more clearly defined to reach an increased understanding of the behavior associated with Maya conflict and warfare as well as other ritual activity.

The Ritual Enigma

Maya ritual deposits represent a variety of ceremonial activities that are presently subsumed under a number of contextual subclasses, including reverential termination, desecratory termination, and dedication or consecration rituals. Although the material patterning for some of these classes of ritual activity is similar, the composition and contexts of these deposits, as well as artifact condition, vary among categories. While differences in material patterning between consecration and termination ritual deposits may be fairly simple to discern, identification of the subclasses of termination ritual deposits, namely, desecratory and reverential termination deposits, requires a more in-depth analysis of depositional context, artifact condition, and material patterning. Further, as within any classificatory system, categories of ritual deposits must also account for a degree of variability within each single type. Each category may vary across time and space as well as among communities of different sizes. Although such deposits may occur in a variety of contexts, architectural features will be the focus of this analysis.

Dedication or consecration ritual deposits have been identified by a number of Mesoamerican scholars (see Coe 1959; Mock 1998a; Monaghan 1998; Pendergast 1998). These deposits consist of materials that were cached in the attempt to charge a place or thing with supernatural power (see Freidel et al. 1993). The Maya, along with other Mesoamerican peoples, were very proficient in imbuing or ensouling places with supernatural power by placing material items within them, such as flint eccentrics, pottery filled with perishable goods, and even sacrificial victims. Archaeologically, these deposits are easily distinguishable from reverential and desecratory termination ritual deposits because the material items are not associated with destructive behavior, such as intensive burning, burial disturbance, destruction of material goods, and the destruction and desecration of architecture (Garber 1983).

In contrast, reverential termination ritual deposits often exhibit extensive destruction of material culture, including architecture and ceramics. These deposits often represent the ritual destruction or "termination" of one construction phase of a structure before an ensuing phase's construction may begin. Furthermore, ritual destruction of architecture and material goods linked to site or structure abandonment may also indicate reverential ritual activity by prehistoric inhabitants. These rituals are associated with the cyclical Maya belief system in which one cycle of life must be terminated before the next may begin.[1]

Similar in appearance to reverential termination deposits, desecratory termination ritual deposits have also been identified through the recognition of patterning in artifact consumption and depositional context (Ambrosino et al., chapter 7 in this volume; Brown and Garber, chapter 6 in this volume; Freidel et al. 1998; Garber 1981, 1989, 1993; Pagliaro et al. 1998; Stanton 1998, 1999; Stanton and Pagliaro 1997; Suhler 1996; Suhler and Freidel 1995a). In contrast to reverential termination ritual deposits, these deposits appear to be linked to destruction associated with warfare and, as with reverential deposits, can be followed by site abandonment. Simply stated, desecratory termination ritual deposits are the result of purposeful destruction and manipulation of material culture for the furtherment of goals aimed at destroying the supernatural power of a defeated community or faction. These rituals resulted in the formation of deposits that were used to "kill" the animate supernatural power of an object, person, place, or portal to the otherworld. Although the destruction and material patterning associated with these rituals linked to warfare and dominance may superficially resemble reverential termination ritual deposits, desecratory termination deposits present an archaeological signature that is contextually distinct from these acts of veneration.

Identifying and Categorizing
Termination Ritual Deposits

Analysis of depositional context and patterning in artifact consumption within ritual deposits has enabled researchers to establish a more concrete list of core signature features for the two general categories of termination ritual deposits noted previously. Generally, termination deposits have been and often are misinterpreted as squatter refuse or the product of natural processes of mound decay (Stanton and Pagliaro 1997). Suhler and Freidel (1995a) have noted that through the use of positive contextual patterning, a list of core signature features may be created that can be used to make a distinction between some of the more problematic deposits uncovered through excavation, such as those associated with warfare and those of reverential ritual behavior from squatter refuse and natural deterioration.

The confusion as to what constitutes ancient Maya refuse as opposed to the remains of termination rituals has been a result of their seemingly similar material patterning. On closer examination, these patterns diverge into identifiable categories separating the types of activities. Although materials such as pottery, faunal remains, *manos*, *metates*, and obsidian are found in both kinds of deposits, the condition and contexts in which they are found are different. Refuse is generally located beyond the outskirts of an architectural feature or group, while termination deposits are located on or within structures. Because refuse does not generally accumulate in sizable quantities within an inhabited and/or utilized structure, actual refuse found within architectural boundaries must be the result of dumping practices after an architectural feature or entire structure has been abandoned. The separation of these processes from termination rituals involves the examination of both the artifacts and the structure itself. Discussion of refuse disposal and midden accumulation has been considered in more detail elsewhere by the authors (Hutson and Stanton 2001; Stanton and Pagliaro 1997) and others (Deal 1985; Hayden 1979; Hayden and Cannon 1983) and will be only briefly summarized here.

Perhaps the best archaeological example illustrating patterns of refuse disposal comes from the site of Ceren, El Salvador (see Beaudry and Tucker 1989; Gerstle 1989, 1993; McKee 1989, 1993; Sheets 1992). Ceren is a small site consisting of a number of structures that were completely buried by a volcanic eruption in the sixth or seventh century A.D. This unique situation gives archaeologists a rare view of how refuse was distributed in a functioning pre-Columbian household (see also Deal and Hagstrum 1995).

The Ceren data support the model of Maya refuse disposal proposed here, namely, that refuse was disposed outside of architectural features. Although the floors of structures are littered with ceramics, a layer of tephra separates most of these artifacts from the floors, indicating that the vessels were suspended from the roof and broke only after the roof gave way to the volcanic activity. Other objects (obsidian blades and so on) that were stored in the rafters were also deposited on the floor in this fashion. What remained of the artifact assemblages that can be determined to have been in contact with the floors at the time of the eruption includes probable digging stick weights, jars, and a few scattered small sherds. Structure 1B, hypothesized to be a storage area, contained a large number of ceramic vessels (Beaudry and Tucker 1989). More than half these vessels were incomplete, suggesting that the vessels were reused and curated as long as they were not too severely broken. Based on this evidence, the Maya may not have left any pots or large sherds in structures on their abandonment. This may have depended on the distance between the original structure and the new locus of habitation. Objects that have a substantial capacity for curation are not often provisionally discarded (Tomka 1993). Digging-stick weights would also most likely be curated until they were too worn to be of practical use. On the other hand, the small sherds, never found in the centers of the floors, were most likely deposited and caught in artifact traps like those described by Deal (1985); thus, the functioning Ceren household was kept basically free of household refuse.

The refuse that has been identified at Ceren fits into two depositional categories. The first involves sweeping processes. An area adjacent to Structure 10 was identified where sherds seem to have been swept into a pile. Paths through household compounds were also kept free of refuse by sweeping activities. The second depositional category involves actual dumping activities resulting in the formation of middens. Several middens were located within household compounds. Some of these middens were excavated in close proximity to but never within the contexts of structures. Refuse was dumped in discrete areas within household compounds, most likely after being swept from structures, patios, and pathways. Apparently, the occupants of Ceren, like the Maya today (Deal 1985), threw their refuse outside in discrete midden areas. Similar results have been obtained in studies of Early Classic house lots at Chunchucmil, Yucatán, suggesting that this is a widely distributed pattern (Hutson and Stanton 2001).

Unlike ancient Maya refuse middens, termination ritual deposits are often located within architectural boundaries. Evidence for desecratory termination rituals located within architectural boundaries includes the following:

1. Intensive burning
2. Intentional structural damage, including floor damage, vault collapse, and the defacing of facades

3. Deposition of layers of white marl
4. Pot smashing and scattering resulting in ceramic sherd refits from wide areas and different levels
5. Rapid deposition of material
6. Dense concentrations of large sherds with sharp, angular breaks
7. Large quantities of "elite" artifacts

The most easily recognizable trait of desecratory termination ritual deposits is the condition of the ceramics recovered from these deposits. Ceramic sherd refits from different levels, often spaced quite far apart and from wide areas, are indicative of pot smashing and scattering associated with termination ritual deposits. Ceramics associated with archaeological trash are generally worn and cannot be refit. Thus, patterns of scattering are not discernible within these midden deposits.

In contrast to most domestic midden deposits, desecratory termination ritual deposits can also include primary- or secondary-context human remains. Deposit content and context suggest that desecratory termination deposits represent the literal termination of all cycles of life and death invested within all associated artifacts, structures, burials, and so on. Furthermore, desecratory termination deposits may include purposeful disturbance and/or desecration of elite burials as well as the remains of ritually sacrificed elite inhabitants of a Maya community (Ambrosino 1997; Ambrosino et al., chapter 7 in this volume; Mock 1998b; Suhler and Freidel 1998). For example, Mock (1994a, 1998b) reports a skull pit at Colha containing the decapitated heads of thirty individuals. Many of the skulls were found with articulated vertebrae and had indications that the skin had been flayed from their faces. She suggests that these individuals were sacrificed during a termination ritual ending the Terminal Classic occupation at Colha. In association with this skull pit, Mock reports additional building destruction and deposits of stacked polychrome sherds, teeth, scattered human remains, jade, and evidence of burning. Furthermore, Mock argues that the flaying of these individuals' faces is analogous to the defacement of monuments like those reported at Copán (Schele 1991b).

Although the ultimate target of desecratory termination ritual may have been the live members of a ruling elite and their buried ancestors, it appears as if the majority of desecratory rituals do not exhibit evidence of burial disturbance or the sacrifice of humans. Yet when this behavior can be identified, it may strongly suggest acts of conflict, including warfare. Associations between termination deposits and architectural defacement, human sacrifice, and intensive burning, such as that noted by Mock earlier, appear to be critical in determining the type of ritual deposit under investigation and any link these acts of prehistoric destruction may have had to conflict and warfare.

Distinguishing between ritual deposits associated with warfare and conflict (such as desecratory termination) and those indicative of reverential termination is a much more complicated affair because the core signature features used to identify these two types of ritual deposits are very similar. Furthermore, both desecratory and reverential termination deposits may often be found within similar depositional contexts. As will be discussed later in this chapter, a noted difference between reverential and desecratory termination deposits may be the intensity of both architectural destruction and burning. Deposits uncovered at a number of sites in the Belize River Valley, as well as in surrounding areas, will be used to illustrate patterns of building and artifact destruction associated with both types of termination deposits.

Archaeological Evidence of Ritual Deposits

The two most apparent features of desecratory ritual deposits are architectural destruction and evidence of burning. Excavations at the site of Blackman Eddy, Belize (Brown and Garber, chapter 6 in this volume), have uncovered episodes of burning and facade destruction. These deposits illustrate the archaeological signature of desecratory termination rituals, including, in many cases, extremely high temperature burning of plaster floors. Evidence for this type of burning, as seen on Structure B1–4th at Blackman Eddy, is clearly representative of much more intense episodes of burning and destruction than those represented within apparent reverential termination deposits located in other episodes of construction for this structure (Brown and Garber 1999). Although both desecratory and reverential deposits exhibit similar archaeological signatures, factors such as the intensity of structural damage and burning associated with these deposits may aid in determining observable patterning within the different categories of ritual deposits. Much of the archaeological database used in discovering patterns of artifact consumption and deposition within desecratory and reverential termination deposits has been gathered through excavations along architectural axes. Most, however, do not illustrate the spatial extent on which both reverential and desecratory termination rituals may have been carried out.

Archaeological studies have indicated that both desecratory and reverential termination deposits may often have had a site- or at least structurewide focus. For example, artifacts recovered from termination deposits located within the alleyway between Structures B1 and B2 at Blackman Eddy, such as ceramic vessels, obsidian blades, and stone *metates,* were only partially reconstructable. This may indicate that reverential deposits could conceivably constitute structure- or sitewide ceremonies that are only partially uncovered by a scattering of excavation units throughout an archaeological site. Suhler and Freidel (1995a) have noted that such rituals may leave behind involved and complex stratigraphic deposits, usually centered at the level of an entire building. Mock (1998b:115) has likewise noted that termination deposits may be scattered in "liminal interstices or places of transition, such as stairways, doorways, axial centers or lines, or the corners of structures." In other words, ritual deposits are not necessarily located solely on the axes of public architecture. Excavations at Blackman Eddy and other archaeological sites, such as Cerros and Yaxuná (Ambrosino 1997; Freidel et al. 1998; Suhler 1996), have demonstrated that ritual deposits can encompass an entire structure or extend across an entire site.

Excavations on Structure 4B-1st at Cerros, Belize, may be cited as evidence for the dispersed and, at least, structurewide nature of some ritual deposits. Walker (1998) notes,

> Analysis revealed that the matrix surrounding the cache held fragments of the same types of vessels as those found at the base of 4B-1st in Operation 25g. . . . Some sherds found in Operation 20 appeared to be fragments of pots deposited in Operation 25g, 13 m below at the base of the temple, although no fits were discovered. This surprising finding gave the first major analytical link between the two spatially distinct deposits, implying that a single ritual locus spanned the entire building. (89–92)

Likewise, a Late Formative/Protoclassic termination deposit uncovered on Structure B1–2nd at Blackman Eddy illustrates that ritual deposits may have been strewn over an entire structure. Garber et al. (1996:9) note that while the majority of this ritual deposit (containing 200 Late Formative/Protoclassic sherds, including three partial vessels, jute [*Pachyychillus claphyrus*] shells, riverine bivalves, several chert flakes, and a chopper) was located beneath the eastern corner of the eastern outset panel on Structure B1–2nd, the other half of a ceramic vessel from this ritual deposit was recovered from the lower portion of the mound.

On an apparently larger scale, excavations within Structure 6F-68 at the site of Yaxuná, Yucatán, are indicative of a larger termination event inclusive of at least several structures at the site (Ambrosino et al., chapter 7 in this volume). The desecratory termination of Structure 6F-68 included burial disturbance and desecration, intensive burning of plaster floors, deposition of large amounts of smashed ceramics and white marl, and intentional vault collapse (Ambrosino 1995, 1996; Ambrosino et al., chapter 7 in this volume). After excavations within other parts of Structure 6F-68 and nearby Structure 6F-3, also within the North Acropolis at Yaxuná, it was determined that this violent act of termination was carried out by people from Chichén Itzá and was performed on much of the North Acropolis (Ambrosino et al., chapter 7 in this volume; Suhler 1996). Therefore, in addition to the apparent similarities in both patterns of artifact consumption and deposition for Maya rituals of reverential and desecratory termination, both types of deposits seem to also share patterning in depositional context. This further complicates the differentiation between ritual deposits linked to reverence and those associated with violence and warfare.

Discussion

As illustrated earlier, it is apparent that continued observation of patterning in artifact consumption and deposition, as well as contextual patterning, is a necessity if we desire to establish a more refined archaeological signature for ritual deposits as a whole. A better understanding of the patterning within ritual deposits, as well as their association with other indications of violence, conflict, and warfare, is essential if we are to utilize these data as evidence for or as an indication of conflict and warfare. Previous research by the authors (Garber 1981, 1993; Pagliaro et al. 1998; Stanton and Pagliaro 1997) and others (Suhler and Freidel 1995a; Walker 1998) have attempted to identify patterning within the particular artifact types found in the context of Maya ritual deposits as well as refuse deposits. These contextual analyses of artifact remains have been successful in determining both patterns of ceremonial activity and artifact consumption.

For example, Garber (1993) illustrated a contextual covariance between jade artifact type, condition of preservation, and category of ritual deposit within contexts excavated at Cerros:

> Jades recovered from dedicatory caches are usually intact, and those recovered from termination rituals are usually broken. Thus, whole jades are associated with structure completion or dedication, and broken jades are associated with abandonment and destruction. Beads and flares are recovered from both contexts. The form and the event dictated whether or not the artifact was smashed. (171)

Continued analysis of artifact consumption within both trash and ritual middens is essential if a list of core signature features for both types of deposits is to be identified.

As stated earlier, further analysis of differences and similarities in contextual and spatial patterning for both reverential and desecratory termination deposits is a necessity if termination ritual deposits are to be used as evidence for conflict and warfare as well as other ritual activity. An association of ritual deposits to other factors indicative of warfare, violence, or acts of reverence, such as ethnographic accounts, archaeological evidence from multiple structures at a site, and evidence from surrounding sites, will aid in strengthening arguments identifying an act of reverence or warfare within a particular deposit or architectural feature. For example, Driver and McWilliams (1995) note that ritual middens excavated within structures at Ontario Village, Blackman Eddy, and Floral Park, Belize, all appear to indicate similar patterning that is suggestive of a type of "abandonment ritual":

> The deposits recovered at Ontario Village and Blackman Eddy consist of one or more whole vessels surrounded or buried by what appears to be primary midden-like deposits directly transported to the ritual location. Initial testing at the site of Floral Park has also identified a similar deposit of midden-like material, although of much greater volume. The deposition of these materials across the basal portion of the Structure A1 stair may have been intended to symbolically deny access to the summit, in effect, killing the structure. As no later construction was intended, such deposits may be seen as an "abandonment ritual," rather than a termination ritual enacted prior to the commencement of a new building episode. (34)

An additional example of this type of deposit may have been uncovered within the alleyway[2] between Structures B1 and B2 within the northern cluster of structures at Blackman Eddy, Belize (Hartman and Pagliaro 2000; Hartman et al. 1999). Excavations between Structures B1 and B2 at Blackman Eddy have thus far uncovered at least two ritual deposits covering the entire excavated portion of this alleyway. The first ritual deposit encountered in the alleyway, Problematic Deposit 1 (PD1), consisted of a high density of ceramic sherds, some of which were very weathered, while others may have been smashed immediately before deposition. Other cultural material found in the ritual deposit included chert flakes, granite ax fragments, partial vessels, obsidian blades, *metate* fragments, hammer stones, *mano* fragments, large chert bifaces, bone, and partial and whole ceramic figurines. This material was deposited directly on yellowish marl melt overlying the B1–1st alley floor. This Late Classic deposit may be linked to structure abandonment. PD1 exhibits the same pattern as other ritual middens deposited at the time of structure abandonment excavated within the Belize River Valley (see the previous discussion). Moreover, because there is no evidence of intense burning, architectural destruction, or other acts of violence, this deposit does not appear to be a desecratory termination event linked to warfare or conflict.[3] In other words, although indicative of the destruction of large amounts of material items, this problematic deposit does not appear to indicate evidence of conflict or warfare and may instead indicate yet another example of the abandonment ritual recorded by Driver and McWilliams (1995) at several sites located throughout the Belize River Valley. Although these deposits do not appear to indicate desecratory termination or acts of violence suggestive of warfare, similar deposits excavated throughout the Maya area do seem to illustrate that the abandonment or termination of structures or entire communities can correlate with warfare.

For example, two alleyways excavated at Cerros, Belize (between Structures 4A and 4B in the central zone and Structures 29C and 29D 300 meters to the south), may be indicative of a more violent end to the use of the surrounding architecture (Freidel 1986b). Although the termination ritual located between Structures 4A and 4B contained a number of artifacts similar to those found in the alleyway at Blackman Eddy, Freidel (1986b:9) noted that the deposit also contained a large number of fragments of modeled and painted stucco decoration "fallen or torn from the walls." The termination event located in the alleyway between Structures 29C and 29D was likewise inclusive of evidence of burning, including scorched plaster and charcoal. The investigators also indicated the presence of large quantities of smashed pottery vessels intermixed with plaster torn from the frieze and panels located higher on the structure (Freidel 1986b:11–12).

Garber (1986:118) indicated that these two termination events at Cerros, similar to those found on Structures 5C, 2A-sub-1st, and 3B, are indicative of termination rituals: a behavioral pattern associated with the abandonment of architecture. Garber (1981) noted that evidence of ritual structure termination and abandonment may include the destruction and removal of plaster facades, burning, broken artifacts including jade, white marl layers, and evidence of the preparation and consumption of a ceremonial beverage. While some of the features may be absent from a given ritual deposit, it appears that layering of white marl, destruction of material culture, and burning are consistent (Garber 1986:118).

Although these termination events at Cerros exhibit artifact patterning similar to those recovered from excavations at Blackman Eddy and those recorded by Driver and McWilliams (1995), the deposits at Cerros differ in some important aspects. The non-Cerros examples from the Late Classic Belize Valley offer many of the core signature features of a reverential termination deposit. For example, the surrounding architecture does not appear to have been disturbed, and there is no evidence of in situ, high-temperature burning as was the case at Cerros (for an example of warfare-related destruction at Blackman Eddy, see Brown and Garber, chapter 6 in this volume). Even though the previously mentioned termination events at Cerros and PD1 at Blackman Eddy were both located within alleyways, some differences in contextual patterning, artifact consumption, and association with other indications of violence and/or conflict may indicate two different types of ritual activity, namely, a ritual of desecratory termination within the alleyways at Cerros and an act of reverential termination and abandonment at Blackman Eddy.

Association of termination deposits with other evidence of warfare and conflict is therefore critical in the recognition of desecratory, war-related deposits as opposed to other, nonviolent forms of ritual deposits. For example, the association of midden-like material with other evidence of violence and warfare, such as architectural destruction and intensive burning, may indicate that deposits within two elite residential compounds at Copán were ritually terminated in a desecratory fashion. The 10L-33 complex at the south edge of the acropolis was covered with "domestic refuse" during the Terminal Classic "just prior" to the cessation of occupation. Not only do these deposits occur in the remains of collapsed elite structures at Copán, but they are also directly associated with intensive burning. In the words of Andrews and Fash (1992),

> It might be argued that our evidence for the destruction of buildings at the core of Copan is limited to four buildings and that fires in a few buildings could have come about in more natural and less meaningful ways. But it must be remembered that the four buildings mentioned are among the few vaulted structures of importance excavated in recent years. Such evidence was most likely overlooked in the past, and most of the great buildings in central Copan were cleared long ago, so that we will probably not find large numbers of structures with clear traces of destruction by burning. In considering the case for violent terminal events, we should recall the small round altars from Structures 10L-29 and 10L-43. Both commemorate 11 Ahau 18 Mac (790) and both were neatly and identically snapped in half. The one from 10L-29 was vandalized just before the building collapsed, and the one from 10L-43 may have been broken as part of the same event. The fragmentary rectangular altar excavated in 1990 from the building collapse behind 10L-32 (CPN 19222), probably a companion piece sitting next to Altar F on the bench of the center room, was badly shattered, and most of it was not found. Intentional vandalism preceding the destruction of 10L-32 seems indicated. (86)

Similarly, MacKie (1985:48–49, 65–71) identified several midden-like deposits located on plaster floors within the terminal construction phases of several structures at Xunantunich, Belize (as well as directly in front of these structures). While MacKie attributed these deposits (within Structures A-6, A-11, and A-15 at Xunantunich) and the "sudden" vault collapses located directly on top of them to a "natural disaster," such as an earthquake and/or natural decay, he does not rule out the possibility that "human agents" may have been involved. Of particular interest is MacKie's (1985) thorough description of deposits located within Structure A-15 and directly below the vault collapse:

> In room 2 the north half of the front wall had completely disappeared down to the plinth-top level. The plastered floor of the north half of the room was covered by a layer of black earth from 1–2 in (2–5 cm) thick and part of the floor was so blackened and warped as to suggest that fires had been lit directly on the plaster. (69)

As with the termination deposits from Copán noted earlier, the association of these midden-like deposits at Xunantunich with intensive burning of plaster floors, vault collapse, architectural defacement, and an "interruption" in both ceramic chronology (MacKie 1985:49) and structure use and occupation strengthen an argument that these deposits are not due to natural collapse or decay and instead may be attributed to acts of desecratory termination linked to conflict and warfare at the end of Classic period.

Houk (1996) has likewise made a potential link between the termination of the main acropolis at Dos Hombres (A.D. 840–850) and the "sacking" of nearby Río Azul in A.D. 840 (see Adams 1995). Associations of termination events (such as at Dos Hombres) to other war-related evidence within the same time period and region (such as that at Río Azul in this example) can only strengthen arguments intending to discern these ritual deposits as violent or war-like in nature (Brown and Garber, chapter 6 in this volume; Stanton 1999; Suhler and Freidel 1995a, 1995b). Association of these ritual middens with other evidence of conflict and violence, such as intentional destruction of surrounding architecture and material goods (as illustrated earlier at Copán and Xunantunich), is necessary if these deposits are to be used as evidence for warfare.

Again, the minimal amount of comparative data identifying Maya ritual deposits as a whole and their association with other evidence for warfare and conflict leaves us with a situation in which the recognition of these deposits as evidence of warfare, destruction, or reverence is often quite problematic. Further investigation of material patterning within all types of Maya middens (both domestic and ritual) is needed. Likewise, patterning for ritual deposits on a regional scale may also aid in determining the ideological and/or material goals behind these deposits. While some ritual middens or deposits may be more easily connected to warfare-related behavior, examples such as those noted earlier illustrate the need for caution when approaching the subject of Maya ritual deposits and their prehistoric implications.

Conclusions

Maya termination rituals exhibit an enormous amount of variability on a number of different regional and temporal scales. Variability in what are possibly the same types of ritual deposits within different archaeological settings must also be addressed and accounted for if a list of core signature features is to be defined for both desecratory and reverential termination deposits. Although desecratory termination deposits share some commonalities in patterns of both artifact consumption and deposition with reverential termination deposits, some variables thus far observed in the archaeological record may offer avenues of exploration that will further enhance our understanding and recognition of these two deposit types. While these ritual deposits may share some features in patterns of both artifact consumption and deposition, it must be remembered that desecratory and reverential termination deposits represent two very different sets of ideological and political goals. The similar patterning found in these ritual deposits also needs to be analyzed on a variety of different scales if their role as a useful indicator of warfare and conflict or other ritual activity and their underlying ideological and/or political goals are to be better understood. Furthermore, this evidence for conflict and warfare must be used in association with other contextual factors, such as epigraphic and iconographic evidence, and co-occurrences of similar patterns at neighboring sites and in other structures at the same site. The similarity between the archaeological signatures for reverential and desecratory termination deposits necessitates a better understanding of the patterning and context for both types of ritual deposits before their use as a mechanism for understanding the political and/or ideological objectives behind them can be refined.

Notes

1. Walker (1998) illustrated through her investigations at Cerros that reverential termination deposits may also represent attempts to rejuvenate power and life forces originally ensouled within structures through caching behavior.

2. The term "alleyway" is used in this case to define the plastered surface between Structures B1 and B2 at Blackman Eddy. The portion of this alleyway excavated thus far measures approximately 2.8 meters in width (east to west) and 7.0 meters long (north to south).

3. At approximately 166 to 176 centimeters below surface level, a similar ritual deposit was uncovered, again spanning the entire length and width of the excavated portion of the alley between Structures B1 and B2. This deposit (PD2) included a high density of ceramic sherds and refits (some again appearing to have been weathered, possibly before deposition), granite *metate* fragments, shell beads and fragments, *manos,* hammer stones, chert flakes, obsidian blades, chert cores, bone, and a minimal amount of burnt ceramics and daub.

Chapter Six

Evidence of Conflict during the Middle Formative in the Maya Lowlands: A View from Blackman Eddy, Belize

M. Kathryn Brown and James F. Garber

Examples of warfare and conflict are common during the Classic period in the Maya lowlands as indicated by iconographic, epigraphic, and archaeological data. Until recently, however, there was little evidence of warfare or conflict during the Middle Formative. Evidence from the site of Blackman Eddy, Belize, suggests that conflict was present as early as 650 B.C. in the Maya lowlands. In this chapter, we address the archaeological data from the site of Blackman Eddy and contextualize these data through the use of the Popol Vuh, a historic compilation of Maya mythology that appears to have deep roots in Maya culture. We suggest that warfare within ancient Maya society was a deeply rooted ritualized institution that was necessary for accomplishing both political and ideological objectives.

Webster (1976a) suggests that warfare began in the Maya lowlands in areas with the highest demographic potential, such as the Pasión drainage and the Belize River Valley. He also suggests that these productive environmental zones were the earliest to be colonized by agriculturalists. The recently discovered evidence from the site of Blackman Eddy in the Belize River Valley supports his model. Excavations at the site of Blackman Eddy have revealed early public architecture dating to the Middle Formative period. Investigations at the site indicate massive destruction and burning of this early public architecture. This evidence is important for several reasons. First, the desecration of the Middle Formative public architecture at Blackman Eddy suggests that some form of conflict or warfare was present at this time. Second, this evidence has important implications pertaining to the nature of sociopolitical complexity during the Middle Formative. Third, the evidence indicates that the pattern of burning and destruction of public architecture found in the Classic and Postclassic periods has antecedents in the Middle Formative. Finally, in order to fully understand the ritualized nature of Classic period warfare and conflict, it is necessary to examine earlier patterns of conflict in the archaeological record. Pattern recognition through time and space is essential to understanding the variability pertaining to rituals related to conflict and warfare.

Maya Warfare as a Ritualized Institution

Archaeological correlates of Maya warfare include severe burning and desecration of architecture, disturbance of burials, removal of valuable objects, and physical destruction of material culture. Material patterns of Maya warfare indicate continuity from the Formative through the Postclassic. Similar archaeological patterns are found throughout the lowlands, further supporting the ritualized nature of Maya warfare. We believe that the archaeological records left by prehistoric warfare events are indicative of specific rituals related to warfare and that Maya warfare was a ritualized institution with specified rules and goals that guided the participants. This ritualized institution was deeply embedded within ancient Maya ideology perpetuating the life, death, and rebirth cycle and is reflected in the Popol Vuh, an ethnohistoric document of the K'iche' Maya that describes the Maya creation myth. We suggest that this creation myth both legitimized and perpetuated the role of warfare within Maya society.

Suhler and Freidel (1998) have defined the deposits left by warfare rituals as desecratory termination deposits. These deposits are often difficult to distinguish from reverential termination remains (Pagliaro et al., chapter 5 in this volume). Reverential termination rituals were a form of dedicatory ritual and completed the cycle of life, death, and rebirth of a particular structure. These types of termination events rev-erentially caused the death of a structure and allowed its life force to be reborn within a new building episode.

On the other hand, desecratory termination deposits were the result of violent destruction of monumental architecture and material culture after a specific warfare event. The victors would ritually kill, burn, and deface monumental architecture; smash artifacts; loot and desecrate caches and burials of important ancestors; and take captives for sacrifice. This ritual destruction dismantled the losing communi-ty's ties to its ancestral power and deactivated the soul force, or *ch'ulel*, that animated its sacred space. It is not surprising that public architec-ture was the focus of desecratory termination events. Architecture was often the focus of public ritual functioning as a backdrop or perform-ance space (Miller 1998).

Freidel et al. (1993) were the first to suggest that Classic period warfare was intricately tied to the Maya creation story. Mythical beings from the underworld are often pictured as part of the sacrificial ritual portrayed on a number of Classic Maya polychrome vessels. Captive sacrifice and warfare themes are often associated with ball-game imagery as well. Classic period monuments also portray images of ritual associated with warfare that incorporate characters from the underworld and reflect passages within the Popol Vuh. A large stucco frieze from Tonina shows a skeletal dancer of the underworld holding a severed head of a noble captive. Behind the dancer is a large rat. In the Maya creation story, the rat plays an important role by delivering ball-game equipment to the hero twins (Freidel et al. 1993). In a sec-ond panel, one of the hero twins is portrayed as a dancing acrobat. Freidel et al. (1993:322) state, "This scene links war and the sacrifice of captives to the same mythology and cosmology that guided other Maya affairs of state."

Epigraphic and iconographic evidence suggests that captive sacri-fice is a ritualized institution associated with warfare and is deeply rooted within Maya mythology. Archaeological evidence suggests that desecratory termination is also a warfare-related ritual, and thus one should expect to find references of this type of ritual behavior embedded in the Maya creation story. Moreover, one should expect to encounter patterns in the archaeological record reflecting these rituals extending back in time. We believe that these desecratory termination events associated with warfare can be observed in the archaeological record of the Middle Formative.

Approaches to Identifying
Patterns of Warfare

Indications of prehistoric warfare or conflict can be direct or indirect. Compelling iconographic and epigraphic evidence of warfare has been documented at numerous sites in the Maya lowlands during the Classic period. Iconographic evidence of warfare and captive sacrifice is abundant, indicating both the frequency and the importance of warfare to the ancient Maya. For example, Lintel 8 from Yaxchilán clearly illustrates warriors dominating their captives (Schele and Freidel 1990). Stela 16 from Dos Pilas portrays a king standing over a war captive (Houston 1993), while the painted murals at Bonampak depict battle scenes and the ritual torture of captives (Miller 1986). Numerous other indications of warfare can be found within the corpus of Classic Maya carved monuments.

Classic Maya texts referring to warfare events are numerous and provide strong evidence for both the importance and the prevalence of warfare in Classic Maya society. The shell/star glyph has been deciphered as a verb representing warfare and has been linked to celestial events (Schele and Freidel 1990). Of special interest, the star glyph appears on a Late Formative text incised on a jadeite clamshell effigy pendant, which may indicate a reference to a warfare or destruction event at this early date (David Mora-Marín, personal communication, 2002). Chase and Chase (chapter 10 in this volume) examine the epigraphic record at Caracol, Belize, and identify four glyphs related to different forms of warfare. Epigraphic data can also provide clues to specific material targets of warfare, such as special architecture. Within the epigraphic record, there are references to burial houses of the Maya, or *muknal* (Stuart 1998b). These elite burial houses were places of importance that housed the ancestors. Because of the great importance of these places, they were often targeted in times of hostility. Stela 23 from Naranjo records such an event, namely, the desecration of a Lord of Yaxha (McAnany 1998). With the discovery of additional monuments and new advances in decipherment of the hieroglyphic texts, our knowledge of Maya warfare will no doubt increase substantially.

Ethnographic and ethnohistoric data provide useful information for interpreting the archaeological record because of the persistence and resilience of indigenous worldviews from the Formative to present-day Mesoamerica (Stross 1998). For example, Díaz del Castillo (1956) wrote of several Spanish expeditions within Mesoamerica that provide valuable information pertaining to indigenous warfare behavior in the Postclassic. This and other Spanish accounts are often used to contextualize Classic period warfare patterns as well. We believe that the Popol Vuh (Tedlock 1985, 1996), an indigenous document describing the Maya creation myth, can also aid us in better understanding ancient Maya warfare. The Popol Vuh contains references of conflict, burning, sacrifice, and material destruction. Interestingly, there are parallels between the accounts in the Popol Vuh and evidence for warfare in the archaeological record.

The archaeological evidence of conflict, unfortunately, is more obtuse than the iconographic, epigraphic, and ethnohistoric records. Consistent patterns across time and space do, however, indicate that rituals were associated with warfare. Although there is little consensus on the criteria used to identify evidence of conflict or type of warfare within the archaeological record, evidence of defensive works, material destruction, and population shifts is often interpreted as the result of some form of conflict. The evidence for conflict among the Maya, either internal or external, appears to be more widespread and variable than previously thought. This is perhaps a reflection of the variable nature of conflict itself. Conflict may take the form of large-scale conquest or perhaps, more commonly, small-scale raiding of site cores. Unfortunately, both types of warfare may in fact leave very similar archaeological remains. To understand the variability within the archaeological record, it is necessary to examine patterns in a diachronic fashion in conjunction with other lines of evidence.

Archaeological Examples of Warfare in the Maya Lowlands

Archaeological evidence of warfare in the form of material destruction and defensive works has been successfully documented during the Late and Terminal Classic at a number of sites. These include several sites within the Petexbatun region that were fortified by large defensive masonry walls and wooden palisades indicating extensive warfare during the Late Classic period (Demarest et al. 1997). Defensive walls constructed in a roughly concentric pattern with the palace group at the center (possibly the residence of the royal family) have been found at the site of Aguateca, Guatemala (Inomata 1997). The defensive walls date to the Late/Terminal Classic and appear to have been constructed in response to intensified warfare within the region.

Evidence from the epicenter of Aguateca suggests that the site was abandoned rapidly. The material culture that remained reflects complete assemblages, including prestige goods that were left behind. Excavations also detected evidence of extensive burning as indicated by the recovery of numerous charcoal pieces as well as a wide range of burned items, such as daub, wall stones, ceramics, lithics, and bone (Inomata 1997). It appears that the residents of the site were forced to flee rapidly while the attackers burned and desecrated the site core.

Strong archaeological evidence of a warfare event was also encountered at the site of Colha, Belize. At the end of the Late Classic period, Colha experienced a violent attack, indicated by widespread destruction within the site core. Evidence of burning, destruction, and smashed vessels was found on several elite structures at the site (Mock 1998b). A shallow pit placed next to an elite structure contained thirty human skulls: twenty adults and ten children (Massey 1989; Mock 1998b). A number of the skulls exhibited cut marks indicating the removal of soft tissue or flaying (Massey 1994). The destruction of the elite architecture and the mass sacrificial skull burial clearly reflects violent conflict and appears to be a desecratory termination event in which the elite family members at Colha were sacrificed and defaced (Mock 1998b).

Indirect evidence of warfare has also been documented for the Late Formative. Impressive fortifications were encountered at the site of Becán, Campeche, by Webster (1976a). He discovered that the site was encircled by an extensive dry ditch. Late Formative evidence of desecratory termination associated with warfare was also uncovered at the site of Cerros. This includes evidence of destruction on Structures 4B, 5C, and 21 as well as the destruction of a banner stone at the base of Structure 6A (Reese 1996). Given this evidence, it is apparent that Maya warfare was a significant aspect of the political process at a significantly early stage. However, warfare associated with prestate societies in the Middle Formative has not been systematically investigated.

Evidence for Complexity in the Middle Formative

Many scholars have noted that warfare is a general characteristic of prestate complex societies (Carneiro 1970, 1981, 1990; Earle 1987; Webster 1975). Competition over prime agricultural land, labor, and access to prestige goods may have motivated conflict in prestate societies. These societies, however, may not have had the political strength to conquer and control other polities. They may have opted to weaken their competitors by raiding and desecrating public buildings within the community and take prestigious captives for sacrifice (Marcus and Flannery 1996).

Evidence pertaining to the complexity of the Maya during the Middle Formative period has been uncovered at several sites in the Maya lowlands, including Nakbé, Cuello, Colha, Pacbitún, Barton Ramie, Cahal Pech, and Blackman Eddy. Intensive investigations of the Middle Formative have recently been undertaken in the Belize River Valley by several different researchers. Excavations at Blackman Eddy have revealed relatively large public architecture (Brown and Garber 1998; Brown et al. 1998, 1999; Garber et al. 1998). Elaborate ritual deposits were associated with the public architecture indicating continuity through later periods (Brown et al. 1999). Public architecture and associated ritual deposits have been documented at the nearby site of Cahal Pech as well (Awe 1992). Middle Formative ceramic material is widespread throughout the Belize River Valley, indicating significant population densities during this period. Domestic architecture has also been excavated at several sites, including Cahal Pech (Powis 1996), Barton Ramie (Willey et al. 1965), and Pacbitún. Further, possible evidence of craft specialization in the form of marine shell bead production is currently being investigated at the site of Pacbitún (Hohmann 2002).

Burial data elsewhere in Belize indicates ascribed status differences during the Middle Formative. The mortuary evidence from the site of Cuello, Belize, indicates the use of exotic items, such as jade and greenstone, as early as 650 B.C. Some form of social differentiation independent of age or sex may be inferred from the Cuello burial data, as multiple grave goods and exotic items crosscut sex and age boundaries (Hammond 1999; Robin 1989). Burial 1 from the Lopez Mamom phase at Cuello was missing the skull, possibly indicating sacrifice (Hammond 1999). Other earlier disarticulated burials may reflect sacrifice as well. With the new and increasing body of evidence pertaining to the complexity of the Middle Formative in the Maya lowlands, it is apparent that Maya society was stratified but had not achieved a state form of political organization.

Evidence from Blackman Eddy

The site of Blackman Eddy is located in the Belize River Valley. The site core consists of two main plazas and a ball court (figure 6.1). Structure B1 is strategically placed on an elevated ridge, allowing a commanding view of the Belize River and its alluvial plain. This structure has been severely damaged by bulldozing activity, and its western half has been completely removed. The resulting cut provided a complex profile of the central axis of the structure (figure 6.2). A construction history of seven major construction phases with various revisions and additions spanning over 1,900 years has been identified from both the profile cut and extensive excavation. Because of the severe damage to the structure, the Belize Department of Archaeology approved a detailed salvage excavation program consisting of total horizontal exposure and recording of the intact construction phases to bedrock.

Five of the construction phases encountered date to the Middle Formative. Of particular interest here is Structure B1–4th, which exhibits evidence of conflict during the Middle Formative. Structure B1–4th is a single-tiered rectangular platform that is oriented eight degrees west of true north, with an inset staircase and an extended basal platform (figure 6.3). The platform summit rises 1.58 meters above the associated plaza surface. A highly fragmented stucco mask armature flanked the staircase. The nose armature of the mask was still in place and rests directly on the associated basal platform (figure 6.4). This is the earliest documented mask found within the Maya lowlands to date (Brown and Garber 1998). Ceramic analysis, as well as one radiometric date, places this structure within the transition between the early Middle and late Middle Formative, approximately 650 B.C.

The summit of Structure B1–4th was constructed of thick plaster and was in excellent condition. This summit, however, was severely burned over much of its surface. In some places, the depth of the discoloration from extreme heat was approximately 8 centimeters. Postholes in the summit floor indicated the presence of a perishable superstructure. The summit of the platform did not have a large amount of debris on the surface and appears to have been swept clean prior to the construction of the overlying architectural phase. An unusual deposit was found abutting the back retaining wall of the structure consisting of a dense cluster of smashed ceramic material and carbon. The ceramic material was in secondary context, suggesting that it was smashed on the summit surface and deliberately swept

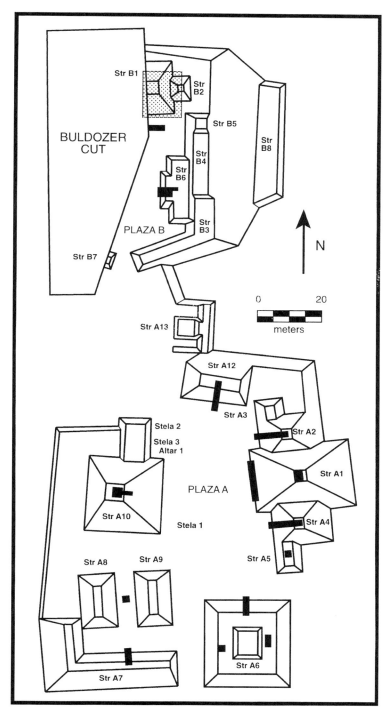

Figure 6.1   Blackman Eddy site map

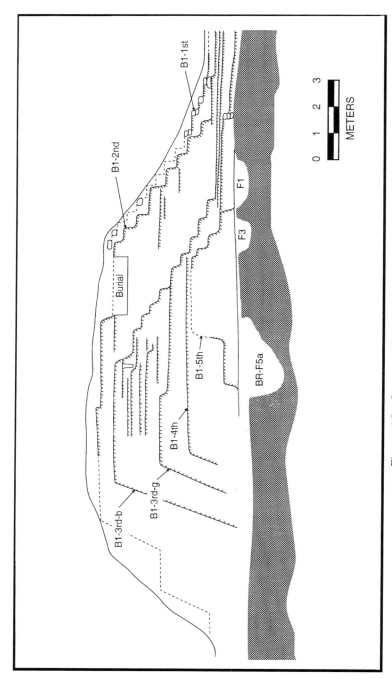

Figure 6.2   Structure B1 bulldozer-cut profile

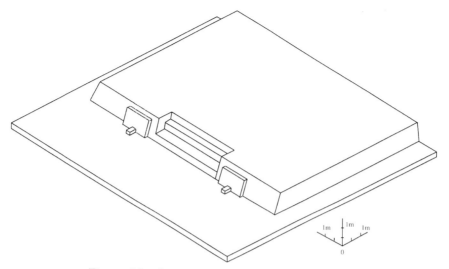

Figure 6.3   Structure B1–4th isometric drawing

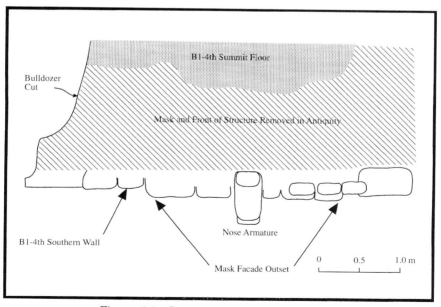

Figure 6.4   Structure B1–4th mask facade

off the back edge. The mask facade, summit, and basal platform were desecrated in antiquity, evidenced through extensive burning and physical damage to the building. The upper portion and backing to the mask facade were completely destroyed. The missing portions of the mask backing that were removed in antiquity were not recovered within the excavations, further supporting the notion that the building was cleaned prior to the construction of the subsequent building.

The desecration of the structure may indicate some form of conflict either external or internal at this early date (Brown and Garber 1998). It seems clear that the burning and destruction of public architecture at Blackman Eddy is consistent with the criteria used to identify patterns of desecratory termination events related to warfare as seen at Aguateca, Yaxuná, Colha, and Cerros. This indicates the longevity and consistent ritualized nature of Maya warfare.

Deposits that exhibit burning and destruction may also be interpreted as acts of reverential destruction (Pagliaro et al., chapter 5 in this volume). This does not appear to be the case on Structure B1–4th for several reasons. First, the structure was extensively and intensively burned to the point that burning occurred through the thick lime plaster. Second, the architectural decoration was deliberately pulled from the structure's frontal facade. Third, we did not encounter any reverential termination ritual deposits, such as smashed vessels, on any areas of the structure. The summit appeared to have been swept clean, and the debris from the destruction of the mask facade was removed before the construction of the later building phase. It appears that the inhabitants cleaned up after the burning and desecration of the structure, possibly to ritually purify the location. Also of interest, excavations of an earlier and several later construction phases of Structure B1 did reveal evidence of reverential termination rituals that were left in place on the structure immediately prior to the rebuilding of a new architectural phase.

The evidence for warfare at Blackman Eddy is consistent with the defensive location of the site, which was strategically placed on a hilltop. The nearby site of Cahal Pech was also strategically placed on a hilltop and has public architecture dating the early Middle Formative as well. Also of importance, the ceramics of the earliest phase at Blackman Eddy, Kanocha (1200–850 B.C.), show strong parallels to pre-Mamom, non-Maya ceramics of adjoining regions. This warfare event on Structure B1–4th comes at a time when unequivocal Maya ceramics are appearing in the Blackman Eddy sequence, and thus the conflict may be the result of ethnic tension (see also Ball and Taschek 2003).

Comparative Data from Cuello, Belize, and San José Mogote, Oaxaca

Evidence of a possible desecratory termination event dating to the late Middle Formative has been uncovered at the site of Cuello. Gerhardt and Hammond (1991) suggested that the construction of two large rectangular structures, 315d and 314, on the north and west sides of a Middle Formative patio, may reflect a change in status of the users or quite possibly a change in function from residential to ceremonial. Interestingly, Gerhardt and Hammond (1991:106) state that "the front-ages of all buildings around Patio Floor V—Structures 314, 315e, 316f and 318—were ripped away, the superstructures set on fire (witnessed by scorch marks on interior floors and on the patio floor in front of the buildings), and the patio filled in up to the tops of the building platforms." This event marks the initial construction of a large plat-form, Platform 34. Also of importance, a mass human sacrificial burial consisting of thirty-two individuals was placed within the construc-tion fill of this large platform (Gerhardt and Hammond 1991). White marl was dumped against the demolished north and west sides of Structure 315 (Gerhardt and Hammond 1991). The dumping of white marl appears to be a pattern associated with desecratory termination events (Ambrosino et al., chapter 7 in this volume; Pagliaro et al., chapter 5 in this volume). Above the fill and patio area, the excavators encountered a lens of what appeared to be midden material thought to have been redeposited from nearby. Two decapitated individuals (a male and a female) were placed in this upper fill prior to the comple-tion of Platform 34. Mass Burial 1 contained almost exclusively young adult male individuals, possibly suggesting captive sacrifice (Saul and Saul 1991).

From these data, an argument can be made for a desecratory ter-mination event related to warfare. The construction of larger rectangu-lar structures indicates some form of change within the patio group. This change of function or status may have caused the inhabitants to become a target for hostility. The massive destruction of frontal facades, combined with intentional burning, is suggestive of a hostile event. Further, the addition of a mass sacrificial burial of warrior-age males and dumping of white marl supports this argument. Above these deposits, two more sacrificial victims were encountered, and the building of Platform 34 was completed. The data from Cuello are con-sistent with archaeological evidence of desecratory termination events dating to the Classic period.

Evidence of conflict dating to the Middle Formative has been noted elsewhere in Mesoamerica. Interestingly, a similar pattern of material destruction has been documented during the Rosario phase at the site of San José Mogote in Oaxaca, Mexico. Marcus and Flannery (1996) argue that during this phase, the Oaxaca Valley was inhabited by several competing chiefdoms. Excavations at the site of San José Mogote revealed deliberate destruction of public architecture. Structure 28 was a large rectangular platform, covered in plaster, that supported a wattle-and-daub temple superstructure (Marcus and Flannery 1996). A severe burning event destroyed this upper building. Thousands of fragments of vitrified daub were encountered, indicating a massive and intense fire. Iconographic evidence of warfare was also discovered at San José Mogote for this phase. Monument 3 portrays a sacrificial victim laying on his back with the trilobed heart glyph on his chest and stylized blood drops flowing from his heart (figure 6.5). Marcus and Flannery (1996) argue that the evidence of the destruction of Building 28 combined with the iconographic evidence from Monument 3 indicates that the pattern of raiding, temple burning, and ritual sacrifice of captives evident in the later periods was present as early as 600 B.C.

Conflict Themes and Parallels from the Popol Vuh

The examination of prehistoric Maya ritual deposits in a diachronic fashion indicates strong continuity through time, retaining its basic structure and thematic content (Brown and Garber 1999; Hammond 1999; Marcus 1999). This trend has led some scholars to contextualize Middle Formative ritual behavior in Mesoamerica using ethnohistoric documents. For example, Marcus (1999) suggests that shallow plaster-lined basins may have been used in female household rituals of divination at San José Mogote. Ethnohistoric accounts document the use of similar basins in divination rituals. Can we use historic Maya documents focused on mythological events, however, to enlighten our understanding of Maya warfare from the Formative period?

The Popol Vuh has often been used to interpret Classic Maya ritual behavior. Clearly, the stories of the Popol Vuh are not a postconquest invention but rather are deeply rooted in ancient Maya mythology. Many of the references within the Popol Vuh text are evident within the corpus of ancient Maya iconography. For example, a relief panel

Figure 6.5   San José Mogote Monument 3 (after Marcus 1992:37)

from Late/Terminal Classic Chichén Itzá, Yucatán, portrays a ball-player with a severed head. This reflects the passage within the Popol Vuh when Hunahpu's head was severed within the house of bats and then tossed into the ball court by the Lords of Xibalba (Tedlock 1996). Other examples of Popol Vuh imagery are evident from Classic period vessels, as well as the Madrid codex, yet some have been traced back to Formative times. At the site of Nakbé, Guatemala, Hansen (1992) identified Formative images in the monumental mask program that reflect passages in the Popol Vuh. Late Formative Stela 25 from Izapa, Guatemala, clearly depicts one of the hero twins shooting Seven Macaw out of the Nance tree. This sculpture illustrates a scene from the previous creation, when the hero twins defeat Seven Macaw, who is portraying himself as the sun. The twins remove the shining jewels from his eyes and teeth to humble him. Without his jewels, Seven Macaw can no longer proclaim that he is the sun. These depictions, which are eventually incorporated into the Popol Vuh, are indicative of the longevity of this creation story.

There are parallels between the archaeological record reflecting warfare and the Popol Vuh text as well. Mock (1998b:119) suggests that the skull pit and the final warfare event at Colha may have been a reenactment of the original sacrifice from the third creation in the Popol Vuh text. The mutilation and flaying of the Colha victims mirror the destruction of the wooden people of the third creation, who had their faces smashed and pounded (Mock 1998b; Tedlock 1996). Other researchers have suggested that Maya warfare was often ritually based and may have been purposely timed with celestial events (Freidel et al. 1993; Schele and Freidel 1990). Evidence suggests that raiding for the purpose of capturing sacrificial victims was quite common and had strong ritual components. The ritual elements of warfare provided the necessary framework for economic and political competition. In Maya ideology, gods go to battle against and conquer other gods. Therefore, rulers, who were thought of as reincarnated gods, were supposed to go to war and defeat other rulers. This basic theme is evident within the Popol Vuh.

Some warfare events may have actually been a reenactment of the hero twins defeating the Lords of Xibalba. Just as the hero twins humbled Seven Macaw by taking his jewels, which made him powerful, and proclaiming that he was the "false sun," Maya rulers would seek to humble and humiliate enemy rulers by dismantling their power, destroying their temples, and taking their jewels, in essence, proclaiming that they were "false rulers." These actions were both legitimized and perpetuated through the creation myth. Other passages within the Popol Vuh reflect the struggle for power between the hero twins and the lords of Xibalba. One such passage describes how the hero twins were sacrificed by the Lords of Xibalba and their bones dumped into a river. The twins reemerged as fishmen with special powers. They could burn down structures and then rebuild them and sacrifice things and bring them back to life. The Lords of Xibalba heard about the strange twins and wanted to be part of this magic. The hero twins tricked the lords through the use of fire, sacrifice, and material destruction. The Lords of Xibalba asked to have their house burned down and themselves sacrificed:

> And then the hearts of the lords were filled with longing, with yearning for the dance of little Hunahpu and Xbalanque, so then came the words from One and Seven Death: "Do it to us! Sacrifice us!" they said. "Sacrifice both of us!" said One and Seven Death to little Hunahpu and Xbalanque. (Tedlock 1996:137)

This is how the hero twins defeated the denizens of the underworld within the creation story. Following their victory, the hero twins make a proclamation to the vassals of the Lords of Xibalba:

> The gifts you receive will no longer be great, but reduced to scabrous nodules of sap. There will be no cleanly blotted blood for you, just griddles, just gourds, just brittle things broken to pieces. Further, you will feed on creatures of the meadows and clearings. (Tedlock 1996:138)

This passage implies the dissolution of a tribute relationship, destruction of material objects, and quite possibly the removal of agricultural food supplies from the vassals of the underworld.

Archaeological correlates of warfare events seem to mirror the ethnohistoric texts through the use of fire, sacrifice, and material destruction. This archaeological pattern is seen from the Formative to the Postclassic and further indicates the ritual nature of warfare among the ancient Maya and its economic ramifications.

Summary and Conclusion

In this chapter, we suggest that the systematic examination of conflict within prestate Mesoamerican societies yields greater insights into the character of Classic period warfare and the origins of social complexity within ancient Mesoamerica. Unfortunately, investigation into early Mesoamerican warfare and conflict has been limited. It is known that prestate societies the world over practiced warfare and that conflict was an integral part of the development of complex society. In fact, Webster (1976a) suggested that warfare stimulates and intensifies political organization. The lack of attention given this topic reflects the difficulty in identifying patterns of warfare within the archaeological record. Several patterns have been recognized and proposed as criteria for identifying ritual warfare events (Pagliaro et al., chapter 5 in this volume). These include severe burning, desecration of important buildings, and extensive material destruction. Furthermore, the Cuello data provide complementary evidence of desecratory termination activity in the Maya lowlands during the Middle Formative. The burial data from Cuello also suggest that individual sacrifice was practiced during the Middle Formative and continued throughout the chronological sequence at that site (Hammond 1999). Ritual sacrifice and warfare appear to be intricately related as seen through archaeological, epigraphic, iconographic, and ethnohistoric evidence.

In Maya ideology, gods fought with and defeated other gods. Therefore, kings, who were thought of as reincarnated gods, were supposed to fight and defeat other kings. This basic theme is evident within the Popol Vuh creation story. The archaeological patterns for conflict are consistent through time and indicate the longevity and importance of ritualized warfare within Maya ideology. The burning and desecration of important buildings, as well as the taking of sacrificial victims, is a pattern that begins early in Maya prehistory and continues through Postclassic times.

The archaeological evidence for Middle Formative conflict at Blackman Eddy is consistent with previously documented evidence for warfare activities in ancient Mesoamerica. Although the use of other lines of evidence, such as iconographic and epigraphic data, will provide a better understanding of warfare, these data are not always available or are limited in nature, especially when dealing with the Middle Formative Maya. Ethnohistoric data, such as the Popol Vuh, can provide clues to the patterns found within the archaeological record. The reverse is also true. A careful examination of the archeological record yields important information relative to the origin and development of the ethnohistoric record. Clearly, the Popol Vuh was not an ethnohistoric invention but rather is an expression of myths and stories with deep roots in the past. Popol Vuh imagery is present within the corpus of Maya art as early as the Late Formative period. Warfare was both important and prevalent during the early stages of complexity in the Maya lowlands and therefore is emphasized within the Maya creation myth. In essence, the volatile nature of the prestate society helped shape the Maya creation myth, and in turn the Maya creation myth legitimized warfare within the society. With the ever increasing body of data on the Middle Formative in the Maya lowlands, it is apparent that the Maya were more complex than was previously thought. A critical factor in reaching an understanding of that complexity is a careful examination of the role of conflict and warfare.

Chapter Seven

The History of Warfare at Yaxuná

James N. Ambrosino, Traci Ardren, and Travis W. Stanton

In the early 1960s, political history gained a place in Maya archaeology when it was first established that Maya hieroglyphic inscriptions contained historical information (Berlin 1958; Proskouriakoff 1960, 1963, 1964). Much of the potential of this discovery was realized a decade later, when in 1973 the dynastic sequence for the site of Palenque was largely worked out (Mathews and Schele 1974). This in turn led to an explosion of research into the political history of the Classic Maya lowlands, culminating in the appearance of a number of recent syntheses (Culbert 1991b; Martin and Grube 1995, 2000; Schele and Freidel 1990; Schele and Mathews 1998). One of the significant results of this work was the identification of wars between various Maya polities throughout the lowlands during the Classic period. It has become clear, however, that although some inscriptions record warfare events, there rarely is any mention or even implication of the conduct or scale of that warfare (Stuart 1993:333). Moreover, the known warfare events derive from only a limited number of sites. The bulk of Maya sites do not have written records of warfare, as many contain limited, if any, hieroglyphic inscriptions. This is certainly the case for many of the smaller sites as well as for a number of the larger centers, especially in the northern Maya lowlands.

The lack of recorded warfare events at most Maya sites by no means implies that they did not participate in warfare or that they did not play important roles in the political struggles throughout the Maya lowlands. On the contrary, warfare-related iconography abounds throughout the lowlands (Freidel et al. 1993:293–336; Schele and Miller 1986:209–40). In order to address questions of the conduct and scale of Maya warfare as well as to obtain a more balanced picture of the history of warfare throughout the entire area, we must turn to archaeology. Unfortunately, archaeologists have had difficulty addressing specific historical problems. Because of the nature of the archaeological record, archaeology is much better suited to addressing anthropological questions, except where special circumstances exist (Binford 1962). It is our argument that just such special formation processes did occur in the Classic Maya lowlands. Thus, we are presented with an opportunity to at least partially address the history of warfare and its impact on settlement, even at sites that lack specific epigraphic records of warfare. We will demonstrate our point by tracing the history of warfare at the site of Yaxuná, Yucatán.

Evidence for Maya Warfare

In the literature, archaeological evidence of warfare is commonly restricted to aspects of defense. Usually, this has to do with the presence of constructed fortifications or natural barriers but may also be inferred from more general settlement pattern data (Rowlands 1972). Traditionally, Maya archaeologists have argued that the essentially open nature of Classic period lowland settlements would run counter to purposes of defense (Bullard 1960; Thompson 1966). The discovery of fortification systems at sites including Tikal (Puleston and Callender 1967), Aguacatal (Matheny 1970), Becán (Webster 1976a), Muralla de Leon (Rice and Rice 1981), and various centers in the northern lowlands (Kurjack and Andrews 1976; Ruz L. 1951; Webster 1979) was the first archaeological evidence for the prevalence of warfare. Although difficult to date, many of the currently known fortifications appear to be Late Classic constructions, possibly built in response to the economic and social upheaval associated with the southern lowland Classic collapse. Following these discoveries, researchers in the Petexbatun found a series of sites that were sequentially fortified during the final years of the Classic period, when the area witnessed a pattern of increasing balkanization and political devolution (Demarest et al. 1997). Thus, much of the defense-related evidence seemed to suggest that warfare was a significant factor in the shaping and transformation of Maya society at the end of the Classic period.

Other fortification systems, however, have been dated to the Late Formative and Postclassic. Late Formative fortifications are most well known at Becán (Webster 1976a) and El Mirador (Dahlin 1984). In Yucatán, Postclassic defensive walls not only are known from archaeological remains, such as the wall at Mayapán (Shook 1952) and Dznote Aké (Webster 1979), but were described by various conquistadores who had interests in native military practices (Díaz del Castillo 1963). Such features suggest that warfare was a significant force within Maya society throughout a much greater span of time (see Brown and Garber, chapter 6 in this volume).

Yet it was not until the presentation of epigraphic evidence for an Early Classic war of conquest in Petén between Tikal and Uaxactún (Schele and Freidel 1990:130–64) that scholars realized the importance of correlating warfare and politics prior to the Late Classic. In this particular case, Freidel and Schele argued that Tikal was able to wage a victorious war over its political equal to the north, Uaxactún, and place one of its *ajaws* on the throne of the conquered center (see also Laporte and Fialko 1990; Stuart 1993). Thus, the idea was raised that warfare was sometimes the means by which the political landscape could be altered prior to the "Classic collapse."

A question that follows is whether the Early Classic Tikal-Uaxactún war represents a unique occurrence. The presence of Late Formative fortifications at some sites and the abundance of warfare-related iconography throughout the lowlands suggest that it is not unique. The absence of warfare-related texts during a time such as the Early Classic does not necessarily indicate the absence of warfare. Given recent arguments such as those proposed by Martin and Grube (1995, 2000) concerning far-reaching "superpower" conflicts centered on the polities of Tikal and Calakmul, the investigation of archaeological correlates of Early Classic warfare may provide a much better understanding of the lowland political arena. We suggest that the absence or, for that matter, the presence of hieroglyphic inscriptions concerning conflict should not be equated automatically with the absence or presence of war. Instead, the content and role of any historical moment should be a question investigated through the archaeological record.

Besides these historical questions, anthropological questions also remain. Foremost among these are the societal impact of Maya warfare and how it changed over time. Recent work in the Petexbatun has emphasized how Terminal Classic wars drastically affected the settlement of the region, with whole populations being displaced and the entire economy disrupted (Demarest 1997a; Demarest et al. 1997). Christopher Jones (1991) suggested that the proposed defeat of Tikal by Caracol explains not only the hiatus at Tikal but also the massive monument destruction and the change in ceramic complexes from Manik to Ik. The evidence for earlier wars throughout the Maya lowlands, such as the Tikal-Uaxactún war, likewise bespeaks of drastic effects on the elite stratum of society with particular dynasties expanding while others were displaced or exterminated. Yet it is unclear how the lower strata of Maya society were affected by warfare prior to the Classic collapse. In order to investigate the effects of warfare on the lower strata of Maya society, we need to be able to identify war in the archaeological record. That is, we need to develop culture histories of warfare at particular sites. At the site level, we could then attempt to correlate the history of war with changing settlement patterns and concomitant population shifts and economic change. Granted there is a difference between correlation and causation, but if we have the ability to identify individual warfare episodes, we would have a much better basis from which to argue for the effects of warfare on Maya society as a whole.

Clearly, defensive features do not always offer the resolution we require to develop detailed culture histories. As mentioned previously, these features can be difficult to date. In addition, when they can be dated, their functions can sometimes be equivocal. Moreover, these functions, being culturally attributed aspects of the features, can change over time. For example, the Late Formative defensive ditch and parapet feature at Becán attests to the need for defense at this time, but it is unclear whether it continued to function in this same capacity during all or part of the following Classic period. Thus, more reliable archaeological indicators of Maya warfare are needed.

In addition to evidence concerning preparations for warfare at Yaxuná, we have been able to isolate a program of ritual destruction as the outcome of warfare among the Maya. This has been referred to in the literature as ritual termination (Brown and Garber, chapter 6 in this volume; Freidel 1986b; Freidel and Schele 1989; Garber 1983, 1989; Mock 1994a; Pagliaro et al., chapter 5 in this volume; Robertson 1983). We agree that a further distinction should be made between desecratory termination, which the pattern discussed here represents, and reverential termination (see Pagliaro et al., chapter 5 in this volume).

The latter is performed out of deference and, despite its formal similarities to desecratory termination, may be understood to be more akin to or at least closely related to dedication rites. Just as dedication rites were methods by which buildings and objects were invested with *ch'ulel*, or soul, termination rituals were employed to release this *ch'ulel* (Freidel and Schele 1989; Freidel et al. 1993:234). Whereas reverential termination was intended to release the *ch'ulel* of an object in a venerating manner, the purpose of desecratory termination was to defeat and destroy the living object. Thus, the desecratory termination of monumental architecture, the sacred mountains of the Maya (Freidel et al. 1993; Stuart 1987:16–24, 1997), was a powerful statement of victory and quite possibly subjugation. Both portable and nonportable objects could be terminated, as both were invested with *ch'ulel*. In this chapter, we will restrict ourselves to the termination of architecture, which will specifically be referred to as structure termination.

The material signature of structure termination typically involves the destruction of architecture in prescribed manners, the laying down of white marl, the smashing of ceramics, and the ritual sacrifice of items of power. The full pattern of architectural destruction is still being cataloged, but it is clear that it can include a number of aspects. The defacement of veneers appears to be a common practice associated with termination. For example, at Cerros the facade of Structure 5C-2nd was systematically defaced with specific portions of the stucco masks being torn away, some of which were actually placed within a ritual deposit associated with a different structure (Freidel and Schele 1989:239). At Yaxuná, several large veneer columns from the terminated *popol nah* (council house), Structure 6F-68, were removed and dragged to various positions around the plaza of the North Acropolis. Likewise, portions of the basal molding within doorways were chopped out and deposited at great distances from the structure. Another common feature of architectural defacement concerns large V-shaped cuts that are typically placed in stairways and facades above doorways. Other architectural damage resulting from termination involves the pulling out of lintels, systematic dismantling of vaults, and chopping and removal of floor sections (Ambrosino 1996, 2003; Suhler and Freidel 1995a, 1995b).

One of the telltale signs of structure termination is the presence of large amounts of white marl banked against walls. These white marl deposits, which can measure between several centimeters to several meters thick, tend to be placed in specific locations inside rooms and outside around buildings. They tend to be heaped in doorways, cover benches, and bury important facade elements, such as the masks of Cerros Structure 5C-2nd (Freidel 1986b; Freidel and Schele 1989). Placed within, under, and/or above these layers of white marl are varying amounts of smashed ceramic vessels. Some of these vessels appear to have been smashed in place, while others were broken prior to deposition. In many cases, sherds from individual vessels are found scattered around buildings, and refits are encountered within spatially separated but presumably contemporaneous termination deposits. In cases where the layer of smashed ceramics is unusually thick, ceramic refits often occur between sherds separated by great vertical distances, thus underlying the singularity of particular deposits. Also commonly occurring within these deposits are items such as jades, obsidian implements, and human and animal bones that are often ritually broken and scattered in a similar manner to the ceramics.

Typically, desecratory termination deposits can be dated to transitions between chronological phases. This has to do with the nature of the ceramics incorporated as well as stratigraphic placement. Stratigraphically, such deposits tend to mark final episodes in structure phases, after which they are immediately capped by further construction or followed by site or area abandonment. The ceramics within these deposits tend to be representative of the chronological assemblage that is ending with the addition of various new types. We refer to these new types that first appear at the site in these special deposits as "signature vessels" because they can be used in the identification of the perpetrators of the termination rituals (Dave Johnstone, personal communication, 1994).

History of Warfare at Yaxuná

A series of desecratory termination deposits have been identified at Yaxuná dating from the Early Classic through the Terminal Classic. We propose that these be taken as evidence for warfare and for the periodic shifting of power and political allegiances over time. We also maintain that this interpretation holds significant implications for the meaning behind abrupt ceramic change in the archaeological record as well as for the cultural significance of ceramic typology in general (see also Bey, chapter 2 in this volume).

At the present time, we believe we are able to identify four distinct episodes of defeat in the archaeological record of Yaxuná. All four warfare episodes appear to mark shifts in political power at the site facilitated and/or perpetrated by outside help. Before we start to think of the ancient Yaxuneros as perennial losers, we should keep in mind that the evidence is based on the presence of desecratory termination deposits representing victory statements by their vanquishers. It logically would follow that after warfare episodes in which Yaxuná was victorious, such deposits would not be present at the site. Therefore, victorious wars would be archaeologically invisible or at least could be detected only by other means, such as the erection of stelae or other monuments. Unfortunately, the known glyphic texts from Yaxuná are too fragmentary or eroded to provide much information.

The first archaeological evidence for defeat has been dated to the Early Classic, which in the local chronology corresponds to the transition between Yaxuná IIa and IIb, around A.D. 400, and appears to be a violent conflict between rival families for control of the city after the death of a powerful king (Freidel et al., chapter 11 in this volume; Suhler et al. 1998). The pivotal evidence is Burial 24, a mass grave of twelve individuals entombed in a vaulted chamber within Structure 6F-4 on the North Acropolis (Suhler and Freidel 1998; Suhler et al. 1998:173–76). The central figure of the tomb was a decapitated male over fifty-five years of age with a charred white shell crown and royal jades at his feet. He was placed on top of a desecrated ancestor bundle and surrounded by the other ten individuals, representing men, women, and children of a whole range of ages, including one infant, some decapitated, many in contorted positions having been irreverently thrown down the stairs into the chamber. The grave furniture included a mix of local and foreign ceramics, jade jewels, carved bones, and small mosaic pieces in addition to other white crowns worn by two of the females. Burial 24 has the look of a royal family that had been murdered in a violent takeover of Yaxuná, presumably to exterminate an entire line of descent (Ardren 2002).

This action may have been perpetrated by a rival local lineage with ties to the large center of Oxkintok located in the northern Puuc Hills region. Oxkintok is one of the largest known Early Classic centers with a Maxcanú ceramic assemblage (Varela T. 1998). It also has ambiguous ties to Teotihuacan, as evinced by the ceramics and architecture (see Varela T. 1999). Many of the vessels found within the Burial 24 tomb have been identified as typical Oxkintok wares, which do not appear at Yaxuná prior to this interment. These include an Oxkintok Thin Monochrome bowl with three incised faces, a nearly identical example of which was recovered from a royal interment at Oxkintok (Rivera D. 1987; Suhler et al. 1998:175). Also associated stratigraphically with Burial 24 but in another part of the structure was a cache including a Maxcanú Buff vessel that held royal jades and had a stone ax jammed into it. This is reminiscent of the "ax" verb used in warfare statements in hieroglyphic texts that has the general meaning "to destroy" (see Chase and Chase, chapter 10 in this volume; Matthews 1994). Finally, as a victory statement, the new ruler of Yaxuná dedicated Stela 1 at the site on which he is portrayed in Teotihuacan warrior garb (Freidel 1987). A similar portrait, quite possibly of the same individual, appears on a Tituc Polychrome bowl found within Burial 24.

Also indicative of new rule at Yaxuná at this time is the introduction of new syncretic architectural concepts, such as the patio-quad compounds at the outlying Xkanha group (Ardren 1997). This palace group, located on the northern frontier of the Yaxuná polity, uses local construction techniques but attempts to convey the plan of a Teotihuacan apartment compound. Thus, we believe that one ruling family of Yaxuná was defeated, sacrificed, and placed within a tomb marked by foreign elite ceramics from Oxkintok. A deposit of jades in a bowl was ritually terminated and placed in a cache at the summit of the structure containing the tomb. After this event, a new ruler adopting Teotihuacan regalia ascended to the throne, and Teotihuacan-style architecture was constructed. We suggest that these data indicate a violent shift in political power at Yaxuná, possibly supported by economic or regal ties to Oxkintok.

The second set of evidence for warfare appears to have occurred at the Early Classic to Late Classic transition, Yaxuná IIb–III between A.D. 550 and 600, which has been identified through a drastic shift in material culture. The most dramatic evidence denotes increased ties to sites in the north, specifically with those in the eastern half of the northern lowlands. The arrival of people from Cobá, Quintana Roo, is indicated by the construction of Sacbe 1, the longest known Maya causeway, connecting Yaxuná with Cobá 100 kilometers to the east. Yaxuná was in a relatively weakened state, having let economic ties to the southern lowlands wither away or be seized by ascending polities. Cobá, on the other hand, experienced continuous growth during the Classic period and aggressively moved to control the central portion of the peninsula.

Sacbe 1 has been argued to represent the western expansion of the Cobá polity at its height, physically integrating Yaxuná as a frontier settlement (Andrews and Robles C. 1985; Freidel 1992; Suhler et al. 1998). Construction details indicate that it was built in haste, incorporated earlier sites such as Ekal along its length, and utilized ramparts to facilitate the movement of troops or personnel from the countryside (Villa Rojas 1934:198). Iconographic data from panels located along the causeway and at its terminus in Cobá convey a decisive message of subordination (Brasderfer 1981:53; Thompson et al. 1932).

Peoples from Cobá also built a residential structure on the Xkanha Acropolis, in a distinctive east coast style, after terminating the Teotihuacanoid patio-quads built during the Early Classic period. The main patio-quad had partial ceramic vessels smashed on the interior floor and sterile soil brought in to cover the ritual debris (Ardren 1997). These structures were then abandoned while the Cobá-style residence was occupied. The burials and ceramic inventory from Late Classic Yaxuná are completely distinct from earlier and later patterns (Shaw 1998; Suhler et al. 1998). Late Classic burials are placed without a crypt, and all contain Arena Red vessels, a ceramic type most common at Cobá and its east coast ports (Robles C. 1990:149). The overall ceramic inventory is very restricted, and there are no trade wares or imports from the southern lowlands.

Associated with these termination events, Stela 1 on the North Acropolis appears to have been reset from a prominent location to a less visible location on the northern side of Structure 6F-4. It is significant that this stela was left intact and not destroyed. A possible reason for this is that the new ruler may have still legitimized his claim to the throne through the ruler depicted on Stela 1. By this, we mean to suggest that even when victors introduce foreign ceramics at a site, the new rulers most likely still represent local individuals with distinctly local claims of legitimacy who are backed by foreign allies. Similar dynamics have been proposed in the southern lowlands based on hieroglyphic data (Schele and Freidel 1990). Although the evidence points to the arrival of a significant occupying force from Cobá, it is likely that this was legitimized at Yaxuná through the manipulation of locally established claims to the throne.

The next suggestion of warfare or sustained conflict is seen at the transition between the Late and Terminal Classic. This is locally designated as the transition from Yaxuná III to IVa and dates to around A.D. 700–750 (Suhler et al. 1998). At this time, there was a series of architectural terminations accompanied by distinctive ceramics. Local patterns of burial, house-mound construction, and ceramic use return, and we postulate that the Cobá-affiliated Late Classic ended with a large-scale reorientation to local rule. The crude Late Classic modification of the temple at the terminus of Sacbe 1 was terminated with a deep deposit of burned wood and stucco (Ardren 1994). There is also evidence for the termination of Structure 6F-8, a small vaulted building constructed during the Yaxuná III phase on the North Acropolis. The vault of this building was deliberately collapsed and the structure razed after ceramic vessels were smashed on its floors. The vault of the central gallery on the west side of Structure 6F-4 was also brought down on a deposit of smashed ceramics. Additionally, a large V-shaped cut was placed along the centerline of the megalithic staircase in front of the gallery to further desecrate this building. A stone of the proper size and shape containing large hieroglyphs was located in the ball-court plaza off the North Acropolis to the south, possibly representing one pulled from the staircase. At a possible elite residential group located just to the south of the E-Group, a similar pattern of destruction was recorded. Large quantities of broken ceramics exhibiting patterns typically associated with termination deposits were located along the basal platform and on the floor of the three-room superstructure. The ceramic types were a mixture of Cobá and western Cehpech types. Also at this time, it appears that Structure 6F-68, a *popol nah,* or council house, constructed in the Western Puuc tradition as defined by Pollock (1980:586), was added to the south side of Structure 6F-4, violating the triadic arrangement on the North Acropolis by reorienting the focus of this structure away from the central plaza. Significantly, an iconographic analysis of the *popol nah* indicates that the leading members of Yaxuná now legitimized their claims to council through extensive warfare imagery (Suhler and Freidel 1993).

As in previous cases, these terminations associated with the third identified warfare event are accompanied by sitewide ceramic shifts, in this case toward the arrival of a complete Cehpech ceramic sphere assemblage indicative of the western Puuc region (Suhler et al. 1998:177–78). Although the Cehpech ceramic sphere is now understood to have had at least five regional centers of production (Fernando Robles C., personal communication, 1999), the Terminal Classic termination deposits at Yaxuná appear to have Cehpech ceramics associated with the Puuc Hills region. Along with the introduction of Puuc-style architecture and crypt burial patterns, this mix of ceramics associated with the destruction event suggests that the Puuc forcefully took control of Yaxuná around A.D. 700. After this event, settlement data suggest drastic population growth associated with very simple foundation brace structures. These may suggest an influx of peoples from the western portion of the peninsula.

The fourth and most clearly demonstrated warfare event identified at Yaxuná occurred during the Terminal Classic at the Yaxuná

IVa–IVb transition, around A.D. 850–900 (Suhler et al. 1998:178–79). This time period saw the construction of fortification walls encircling the North Acropolis (figure 7.1) and protecting the entrance to Xkanha (Ambrosino et al. 2001). The outcome of this war saw the termination of Structure 6F-68 as well as buildings elsewhere on the North Acropolis and in the ball-court plaza south of the North Acropolis. The terrace of Structure 6F-68 was destroyed and had vast amounts of ceramics smashed on it. A burial within one of the rooms was desecrated, the skull and parts of the upper torso were removed with the rest of the upper torso left in a jumble around the entry hole, grave

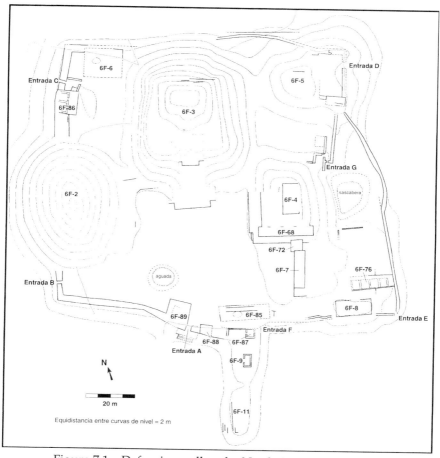

Figure 7.1   Defensive wall at the North Acropolis, Yaxuná

offerings were removed and smashed, and a fire was lit in the entry hole. The rooms were burned, white marl and smashed ceramics were heaped in doorways, and finally the roof was weakened and the front of the building pulled down on top of the front terrace (Ambrosino 1995, 2003). In addition, the construction of the large staircase on the central pyramid of the North Acropolis (Structure 6F-3, the *kun*, or royal stone seat, of the Yaxuná kings since the Early Classic [David Freidel, personal communication, 1997]) was violated with key architectural blocks dislodged and sent to the bottom (Suhler 1996). Smashed ceramics indicative of termination deposits were also noted on the exposed staircase core of Structure 6F-3.

Much of Yaxuná was left in ruins, and very little construction followed this large-scale termination (see also Stanton and Gallareta N. 2001). In fact, among the few known new constructions is Structure 6F-9, a small one-room vaulted building placed on a tiny extension on the south side of the North Acropolis outside the previous defensive fortifications. This new construction is associated with a newly imposed ceramic complex, the Sotuta complex, most likely centered at Chichén Itzá (Robles C. and Andrews 1986; Smith 1971). Likewise, many of the smashed ceramics in the termination of Structure 6F-68 were Sotuta varieties. In addition, green obsidian, previously unknown at Yaxuná but prevalent at Chichén Itzá, was recovered from this termination deposit. Thus, we believe that Yaxuná was conquered by forces from nearby Chichén Itzá at this time. Moreover, given the extremely limited nature of the Sotuta occupation at Yaxuná, it appears that the site was more or less decimated after this war. Local rule appears to have been annihilated, and settlement data suggest a massive depopulation of the site.

Impact of War Events on Population

Through careful analysis of the archaeological record, we have been able to identify evidence for four distinct warfare events at Yaxuná. As noted previously, we believe that these were events in which the rulers at the site were defeated and ousted. The victors commemorated and otherwise finalized their victories in rituals and other actions that left unique archaeological signatures identifying both the actions and the actors. The transfer of power at these various times had far-reaching effects for the entire community.

The first war ushered in the Yaxuná IIb phase at the site, a time that saw new ceramic intrusions indicative of contact with the large

Early Classic site of Oxkintok to the west and possibly important sites of the Petén in the south. The prior Yaxuná IIa phase saw extensive construction within the monumental core and the residential zones of Yaxuná. The limited evidence we have to date suggests that the Yaxuná IIb occupation was equally robust. The transfer of power does not appear to have greatly affected the character of the settlement in a positive or negative way. We have little evidence to date for a strong ceramic disjunction in the settlement zone between Yaxuná IIa and Yaxuná IIb. Thus, the local economy does not appear to have been greatly impacted despite the introduction of new elite wares indicative of Oxkintok, although continued research may alter this view.

The second war event seems to have occurred at or just prior to the arrival of forces from Cobá, at the transition from Yaxuná IIb to III. The period in question roughly corresponds to the so-called hiatus in the Petén (Willey 1974). Thus, the conflict we envision may have risen out of the temporary political demise of many Petén centers and may represent a local struggle over the political pieces left at Yaxuná. Depending on the timing of the second warfare event at Yaxuná, an impoverished community may have been left in its wake, only to pick up years later with the arrival of Cobá. Alternatively, if a later date for the warfare event is correct, Cobá or a local group with close ties to Cobá may have exploited the weakened economic and political backing of the local rule at Yaxuná and invaded. On victory and the termination of the old rule and its cosmological sources of power, a much more prosperous time for the community would have been ushered in, judging from renewed building activity and the presence of relatively rich graves (Johnstone 1994; Suhler et al. 1998:177).

Following on the heels of the third identified warfare event at Yaxuná is what appears to be the greatest population boom in the history of the site. Yaxuná IVa ceramics are the most prevalent types found throughout the residential zone, indicating extensive occupation (Suhler et al.1998:177–78). This is especially true of the densely packed southern portion of the site. Along with this residential expansion, significant monumental construction and modification were undertaken in the site core. These included two Puuc-style palaces appended to and reorienting earlier pyramids (Ambrosino 2003) as well as smaller structures employing the Puuc construction technique of stone veneer over concrete and rubble core. The ceramics introduced in the wake of the third warfare event comprise a mixture of Cehpech forms (see Robles C. and Andrews 1986). The pattern evident throughout this time period is the initial predominance of western

Cehpech followed by the gradual transition toward eastern Cehpech varieties by the end of Yaxuná IVa (Suhler et al. 1998:178). The ceramic and architectural evidence points toward a strong Puuc influence at the start of Yaxuná IVa and thus implicates a Puuc-allied force as the victors of the third warfare event and the subsequent governors of the site. The immediate outcome of this violent takeover of Yaxuná was an economic and demographic resurgence after a much more modest Late Classic occupation. Not to be overlooked in the search to explain this resurgence is the old idea that it may have a great deal to do with an influx of refugee populations from the war-ravaged southern lowlands.

Puuc expansion across the peninsula may have been quickly curtailed as Chichén Itzá grew to prominence. It is clear that Yaxuná did not sustain relations with Chichén Itzá, its close neighbor to the north, since Sotuta ceramics, indicative of the latter, are completely absent from Yaxuná at this time. Also belying this situation of hostility (Andrews and Robles C. 1985) is the fortification of the North Acropolis at Yaxuná and its northern outlying group of Xkanha before the end of Yaxuná IVa (Ambrosino et al. 2001; Ardren 1997). Colonial native documents also mention a less-than-cordial relationship between the two communities (Andrews and Robles C. 1985; Roys 1933).

The final outcome of this apparent tension was the fourth war, in which forces from Chichén Itzá were the ultimate victors. The following Yaxuná IVb phase was characterized by little monumental construction or residential occupation (see also Stanton and Gallareta N. 2001). One of the only structures known to have been built at this time was Structure 6F-9, a small one-room vaulted building situated on a narrow extension to the North Acropolis immediately outside the destroyed fortification walls. Possibly a victory monument, this structure may have also served as a station from which the site could be policed in order to prevent the return of occupants. It is significant that most Sotuta ceramics so far identified at Yaxuná derive from ritual as opposed to occupational contexts (Suhler et al. 1998:178–79). This indicates that the purpose of warfare changed drastically at this time from conquest to virtual annihilation. This development appears symptomatic of a much larger region and is clearly visible in the archaeology of the Petexbatun region (Demarest et al. 1997). At Yaxuná, we can suggest a reason for the change on the basis of the specific historical context. Yaxuná appears to have been located in a hotly contested strategic area in the center of the peninsula. All the previously described conflicts may have erupted over control of this location. Chichén Itzá, also existing within the center of the peninsula a mere 22 kilometers away, would have had no reason to control the nearby site of Yaxuná. From a simple standpoint of cost efficiency, annihilation rather than occupation may have been the preferable option. Additionally, we have suggested that previous wars at Yaxuná represented conflicts between local groups who were backed by foreign patrons or allies. We suggest that the victor of the fourth war was an entirely foreign group from Chichén Itzá who had no vested interest in the government of Yaxuná. Essentially, the Terminal Classic showdown at Yaxuná was not a dynastic struggle at all; it was a war for economic and political control of the entire Yucatán peninsula.

At Yaxuná, warfare played a decisive role in the evolution of the site. There is rarely a period of more than 200 years without evidence of conflict at a sufficient scale to interrupt daily life for most members of the community. As the population in the northern lowlands grew through the Late Classic and Terminal Classic periods, the practice of war also matured in scale and cost to the community. The eventual abandonment of Yaxuná as a residential center is now tied directly to the wars of conquest practiced by Chichén Itzá. It is tempting to focus on this evidence as the primary factor in the history of Yaxuná, but this would oversimplify a complex system of environmental, economic, and social processes at work prior to the appearance of war.

Part III

EPIGRAPHIC AND ICONOGRAPHIC
APPROACHES TO WARFARE

Chapter Eight

The Symbolic Representation of Warfare in Formative Period Mesoamerica

F. Kent Reilly III and James F. Garber

Recent archaeological and historical investigations clearly establish that warfare figures as prominently in the artistic, social, and political histories of Mesoamerica as it does in the cultures of the primal civilizations of South America and the Old World. However, the depictions of Mesoamerican warfare have not always been easily recognized and, when recognized, not always completely understood.

Certainly, images of war and conquest are explicit in Postclassic Aztec art. Not only is the meaning of these Aztec warfare depictions explicit, but their interpretations are supported by a plethora of Spanish colonial ethnographic and historical sources as well (Townsend 1992). However, to the modern observer, warfare themes are not as readily recognizable in the earlier art of Classic period Teotihuacan. At this Valley of Mexico metropolis, warfare themes do not appear to be presented explicitly. Warfare imagery is rather implicitly depicted or symbolized within an iconographic complex whose major motifs are the atlatl, owls, and feathered serpents who carry a goggled-eyed war helmet on their tails (Sugiyama 1989; Taube 1992a). War banners also figure prominently within this "Teotihuacan War Complex." As physical objects and ideological symbols, these war banners function as battle standards and as portals through which the war gods enter natural space, bringing with them the gift of victory (Freidel et al. 1993:296–317; Reese 1996).

On the other hand, the warfare imagery of the contemporaneous Classic period Maya is often dramatically explicit. Maya elites are shown in the act of both capturing and sacrificing their enemies. Such explicit warfare representations are augmented with hieroglyphic inscriptions describing the capture of kings and nobles and thus the defeat of one Maya polity by another.

Iconographic investigations suggest that, rather than the explicit warfare representations of the Classic Maya, Olmec-style (Coe 1965b) images of conquest are expressed within an overarching iconographic complex. This complex is more closely akin to those seen at Teotihuacan. In other words, Olmec-style warfare depictions are implicit and contained within a larger motif set. Within this motif set, a close evaluation of elements, symbols, motifs, and themes strongly suggests that the ideology of warfare, as expressed in Olmec-style art (1200–400 B.C.), was couched in a supernatural framework based on images depicting feline domination over humans as well as the ideological concept of jaguarian transformation itself. This recognition lends support to our hypothesis, which interprets Olmec and other Formative period warfare representations as an expression of paradigmatic ideology strongly grounded in the larger artistic corpus of the Mesoamerican supernatural.

The Iconography of Classic Maya Warfare

In order to support the previously mentioned hypothesis, it is first necessary to summarize our knowledge of Classic period Maya warfare iconography as a basis for the more implicit Formative period iconographic interpretations. This comparison between these two cultures can be made with some assurance, as it is now known that a highly developed Maya Formative period culture is contemporaneous with the culture of the heartland Olmec. Intensive and ongoing research illustrates that important linguistic and iconographic loans occurred between these two cultures between 900 and 300 B.C. (Campbell and Kaufman 1976; Coe 1976, 1977; Freidel et al. 1993; Hansen 1993; Kappelman 1997; Reilly 1991, 1994, 1995; Taube 1995, 1996).

Archaeological excavations reveal that the Maya engaged in warfare as early as the Middle Formative period (Brown and Garber 1999, chapter 6 in this volume; Schele and Freidel 1990). However, the iconography of war does not become prominent in Maya art until the Early Classic period. Undoubtedly, like their South American and Old World counterparts, the Maya of the Mesoamerican Classic period (A.D. 300–900) engaged in war for political, territorial, and material gain (Martin and Grube 1995; Schele and Miller 1986; Suhler and Freidel 1998).

Conversely, as is the case with other primal civilizations, the iconography of Classic period Maya warfare was closely linked to the symbolism of rulership. However, explicit artistic compositions through which the Maya expressed victory in war most often concentrated on depictions of those rituals associated with the degradation and sacrifice of aristocratic war captives after success on the battlefield. Though actual depictions of battles are rare, they do occur. To date, the most explicit rendering of an actual Maya battle is the wall paintings from Bonampak, Structure 1, Room 2 (Miller 1986).

In Maya warfare iconography, captives are often identified as elite personages through hieroglyphic "tags" or inscriptions. Most often they are shown stripped of the elaborate costumes in which they are usually depicted. However, when a captive was of a sufficient rank, he is sometimes shown wearing an article of clothing that illustrated that rank. This is certainly the case of the image of the captured Palenque King K'an-Hok'-Chitam, who, on Tonina Monument 122, is depicted supine and bound but still wears the royal *Sak Hunal* (jester god) headband. Within the overall context of Maya works of art, captives are usually presented as bound beneath the feet of their captors or in a posture of supplication in front of them. It should be noted that often the images of captives show the results of the horrible tortures to which they have been subjected before death (Schele and Miller 1986; Taube 1988).

Unlike the degraded depictions of captives, the costumes and accompanying imagery of the captors are replete with elaborate feather headdresses and other costume details. Though certain aspects of these costumes vary from site to site, they often incorporate jaguar pelts and jaguar symbolism or the iconography of the Tlaloc/Venus war complex, which, as has been stated, originated at Teotihuacan and was adopted by the elites of the Maya lowlands sometime in the fourth century.

Pre-dating the symbolism of the Tlaloc/Venus War complex is an earlier war complex whose visible form consisted of elite costumes derived from zoomorphic supernaturals. Prominent among these zoo-morphic costumes is the imagery that has come to be identified as the "War Jaguar" (Freidel 1989). Another feature of elite war costuming is avian symbolism. However, within the broader motif set of war imagery, warriors wearing avian images are, more often than not, defeated by warriors wearing jaguar costumes (Schele and Miller 1986:214).

The Maya Ideological View of War

The needs of Maya ritual life were, in the minds of both elites and commoners, the ultimate ideological justification of warfare (Freidel et al. 1993:334). The Maya indicate, throughout their art and hiero-glyphic writing, that they associated war and the sacrifice of prisoners with specific episodes in their creation chronicle. The beheading of captives in ceremonies of human sacrifice was, in effect, the reenact-ment of the defeat and death of "First Father," the maize god. Through the death and resurrection of this deity, the world was made and humankind brought into existence.

Inscriptions from the Temple of the Sun at Palenque clearly state that, for the Maya, success in war was through supernatural interven-tion and that the "power of war comes from the Otherworld" (Freidel et al. 1993:307). Furthermore, there is another aspect of Classic period Maya warfare ideology that has only recently come to be recognized (Freidel et al. 1993:293–336). When the Maya elite dressed for battle in the costume of zoomorphic feline supernaturals, they were making a statement about their perception of the ideology of war and not just putting on battle armor. Putting on such costumes was taking on the identity of a spirit companion who was an important supernatural source of victory in war (Freidel et al. 1993:190–93).

The discovery that the Maya believed that their elites possessed supernatural spirit companions, or *way*, has been one of the great insights into ancient Maya worldview (Freidel et al. 1993; Houston and Stuart 1989; Stuart 1988). The *way* glyph is a depiction of an *ajaw*. This glyph designates the first day in the Maya Tzolkin calendar but also functions as a title for rulers, with half its face covered by a jaguar pelt. As currently understood, a *way* is an animal spirit companion, a trance state, and the ability to transform into that spirit companion and overcome enemies through bewitchment (Freidel et al. 1993:190). In the Maya belief system, even the gods have *wayob* (plural of *way*). In Classic period iconography, the *wayob* could take the forms of humans, animals, and zoomorphic supernaturals. Before the adoption of Teotihuacan's Tlaloc/Venus war complex, jaguarian imagery was associated with the most powerful of the *wayob*. Even after the adoption of this Central Mexican war complex, jaguarian imagery continued to feature prominently among the Maya *way* imagery.

Victory or defeat in battle was even described in terms of the *wayob*. When the Spanish conquistador Pedro de Alvarado (called Tunadiú by the Maya) entered the Guatemalan highlands in 1523, he was opposed by Tekum Uman, a great lord of the K'iche' Maya, the most powerful of several Maya kingdoms. The Spanish account of their defeat of the K'iche' is not extraordinary and is described in purely Eurocentric, logistical, and tactical terms. Alvarado merely mentions in his dispatches that a K'iche' lord is killed, but he does not bother to identify him (Bricker 1981:29–42).

However, the K'iche' version of their defeat is an extraordinary tale couched in terms of a cosmic battle of opposing *wayob*. The K'iche' viewed the battle as the defeat of their spirit companions by the spirit companions of the Spanish (Bricker 1981:29–42). In their eyes, the Spanish were defended by a maiden who was aided by footless birds. This description of the Spanish *wayob* is the K'iche' perception of the Spanish battle banner with its image of the Virgin Mary. As described in the K'iche' chronicle,

> At midnight the Indians went and the captain of the Indians who became an eagle became anxious to kill the Adelantado Tunadiú, and he could not kill him because a very fair maiden defended him; they were anxious to enter, but as soon as they saw this maiden they fell to the earth and they could not get up from the ground, and then came many footless birds, and those birds had surrounded this maiden, and the Indians wanted to kill the maiden and those footless birds defended her and blinded them. (Bricker 1981:39–40)

The footless birds described in this chronicle may very well have been how the K'iche' understood the angelic images that surrounded this Marian depiction.

The K'iche' description of their defeat of their great captain, at the hands of Alvarado, was described in the following terms:

> And then Captain Tecum flew up, he came like an eagle full of real feathers, which were not artificial; he wore wings which also sprang from his body and he wore three crowns. . . . And when he saw that it was not the Adelantado but the horse that had died, he returned

to fly overhead, in order to come from there to kill the Adelantado. Then the Adelantado awaited him with his lance and he impaled this Captain Tecum with it. (Bricker 1981:40)

This K'iche' account helps us considerably in our understanding of the Maya ideological concept of war. Like all cultures, wars conducted by K'iche' and their ancestors against the Maya of the Classic period were fought for many of the same reasons that they have always been fought: control of labor and resources and the amassing of territory and power. However, the ideological explanation for victory or loss in warfare was a uniquely Mesoamerican supernatural expression.

Thus, for the Maya as well as other Mesoamerican cultures, warfare occurred on two planes: the supernatural and the natural. Victory in the supernatural realm ensured victory in the natural world. Defeat in the supernatural realm could be the explanation for the reality of defeat in the natural order. The visualization of this distinct warfare ideology was often expressed through hieroglyphic inscriptions and artistic representations that mentioned or depicted the spirit companions of those elites who made up the command structure. Defeat, as previously mentioned, could be explained as the defeat of one *way* by the more powerful *way* or *wayob* of the victor. "Victory not only secured wealth and power for the winners, it demonstrated to all that the gods were on their side" (Freidel et al. 1993:323).

The question now arises as to whether the heartland Olmec and the other cultures of the Mesoamerican Formative period also possessed a warfare complex in which defeat and victory were visualized through depictions of *wayob*. That question is best answered with a discussion of the transformation imagery in Olmec-style art, followed by a survey of certain categories of Olmec sculpture from the heartland site of San Lorenzo and bas-reliefs from the highland site of Chalcatzingo, Morelos.

Transformation Imagery in Olmec-Style Art

In Olmec studies, the transformation theme has been discussed by numerous authors (Coe 1972; Furst 1968, 1995; Kappelman 1997; Reilly 1989, 1994). Coe (1972), in his groundbreaking analysis of Olmec religion, elucidated the role that shaman-jaguar transformation played in the visualization and validation of heartland Olmec rulership. Working from Coe's model, more recent research has emphasized the concurrent validation of Olmec and Izapan rulership through the public performance of transformation rituals that stressed both jaguarian and avian imagery (Freidel et al. 1993; Kappelman 1997; Kappelman and Reilly 1999; Reilly 1989, 1994).

In Olmec-style art, monumental sculptures such as San Lorenzo Monument 10 depict Olmec elites either as were-jaguars or wearing masks and other costume elements that identify them as beings who have the ability to transform into supernatural jaguars (figure 8.1a). The "Transformation or Were-Jaguar Motif Set" has been identified through the analysis of both monumental sculpture and a series of portable objects. The small-scale objects consist of figurines embodying depictions of the several ritual episodes in the transformation sequence from human to jaguar or vice versa (Reilly 1989). This interpretation is further supported by numerous other examples, but none is more striking than a clay figurine head from the Early Formative period Valley of Mexico site of Tlatilco. This figurine depicts a face that is half human and half jaguar (figure 8.1b), clearly another Formative period source for what will eventually become a component of Classic Maya hieroglyphic writing (Reilly 1996).

For this discussion, one of the most important transformation depictions is the Olmec-style Juxlahuaca Cave Painting 1 (Griffin 1967; Guy 1967; Tate 1995). Juxlahuaca Cave Painting 1 depicts two individuals dressed in elaborate costumes in a dominant and subordinate relationship (figure 8.2). The ritual costume worn by the taller figure

Figure 8.1a   San Lorenzo
Monument 10

Figure 8.1b   Head of clay
transformation figure, Tlatilco

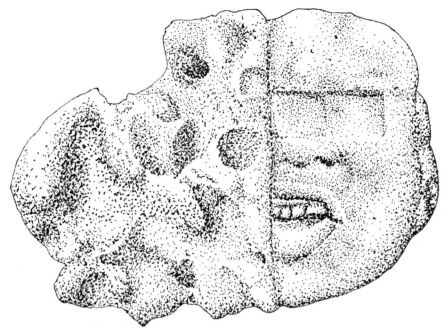

Figure 8.1c   San Lorenzo Monument (unnumbered),
perhaps depicting Olmec-style *way*

(5 feet, 5 inches) consists of an elaborate headdress and a striped tunic. However, the arms and legs of this standing figure are covered in jaguar skin, and a jaguar tail can be seen swinging below the hemline of the multicolored tunic. This specific costume, with its jaguarian elements, is almost certainly another prototype template for the *wayob* costumes worn by the Classic Maya elite.

The Juxlahuaca Cave Painting 1 jaguar-costumed figure holds a rope in his left hand that leads to the second figure, who, though also elaborately costumed, is seated in a subordinate cross-legged posture. Both figures appear to be linked by the rope held in the hand of the standing figure. Considering the overall context of this painting, with its transformational content, the jaguar-costumed individual is best interpreted as an ancestor linked by a cosmic cord to his petitioning descendent who has entered the cave in search of a ritualized ancestral vision (Kappelman and Reilly 1999). The jaguarian costume elements identify the *way* or spirit companion that this founding ancestor has passed down to his descendents. Juxlahuaca Cave Painting 1, through

Figure 8.2   Juxlahuaca Cave Painting One

its underworld location and thematic organization, depicts both a supernatural Otherworld and the actual costuming worn by Formative period elite participants in rituals of transformation.

Iconographic interpretations of this pervasive transformation theme suggests, in the belief system of the Olmec creators, that the journey into the supernatural Otherworld was an undertaking fraught with danger. The transformation figurines, in combination with the jaguar-costumed individual in Juxlahuaca Cave, demonstrate that overcoming such dangers depended on a ruler's ability to transform into a spirit companion who possessed the strength and cunning to overcome Otherworld dangers. Jaguars appear to have been the real-life source of many of the spirit companion depictions in Olmec-style art. Depictions of jaguars dominating humans should reveal whether specific Olmec-style transformational imagery can also function in the ideology of Formative period warfare similarly to the *wayob* of the Classic period.

Images of Human/Jaguar Interaction from the Olmec Heartland

Excavations at San Lorenzo in the Olmec heartland have revealed a monument that is almost certainly a prototype of the Classic Maya *way* glyph. Currently unnumbered, this boulderlike San Lorenzo Monument (figure 8.1c) is highly reminiscent of the Classic period *way* glyph. Like the *way* glyph, it is carved in a form that presents a face half hidden by an object that may be an animal pelt (Cyphers 1996:58–59). The "half-hidden" theme of this monument is not unique but certainly rare within the corpus of heartland monumental sculpture and strongly suggests that the *way* template was first expressed in Olmec-style art. Other examples of jaguarian imagery (as opposed to were-jaguar representations), in the form of sculptural monuments, are plentiful at Olmec heartland sites. The majority of these representations portray individual felines that in some instances hold ropes or cords in their mouths (Gonzalez L. 1988; Kappelman and Reilly 1999). Such monuments include La Venta Monument 80 (Gonzalez L. 1988), and Los Soldados Monument 1 (Stirling 1955).

In particular, the Olmec site of San Lorenzo possessed a plethora of monuments that depict jaguars dating to the San Lorenzo phase (1150–900 B.C.). Among these sculptures are Monument 7 (Coe and Diehl 1980:312), Monument 37 (Coe and Diehl 1980:344), Monument

90 (Cyphers 1997:207), Monument 108 (Cyphers 1997:212–14), and, from the subsidiary site of Tenoctitlán, Monument 2 (Cyphers 1997:220). San Lorenzo Monument 7 has strong water and fertility associations because of the Lazy-S or cloud symbol carved on its flank (Reilly 1994). Another San Lorenzo jaguar image that connotes such water and fertility imagery is the recently discovered Monument 77 (Cyphers 1997:205–7), which is unique within this jaguar-image sculptural corpus. This monument depicts a crouching jaguar that has a drain stone in place of a head (figure 8.3a). San Lorenzo Monument 77

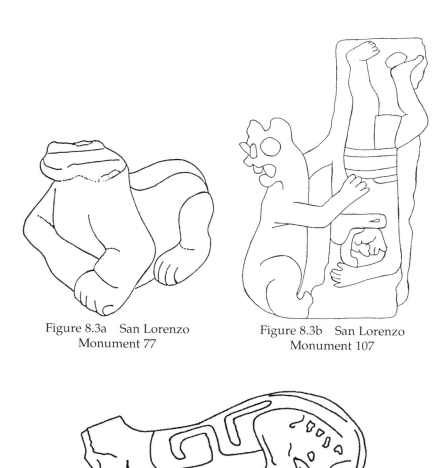

Figure 8.3a   San Lorenzo
Monument 77

Figure 8.3b   San Lorenzo
Monument 107

Figure 8.3c   San Lorenzo Monument 7

is convincing evidence that within the Olmec heartland—and, as we will see, within other Formative period ideological systems—there was a strong connection between jaguars, water, and fertility.

Within the Olmec heartland, sculptural portrayals of jaguars interacting with or dominating humans are not as plentiful as monuments that depict jaguars standing alone. The appearance of this "jaguar dominating humans" motif subset was first reported by Stirling in 1955. Initially, this motif subset consisted of only two monuments in the Olmec heartland, each found in the vicinity of San Lorenzo Tenoctitlán. These two monuments, Portero Nuevo Monument 3 and Río Chiquito Monument 1, are so badly battered that their subject matter is difficult to ascertain (Stirling 1955:8, 19–20, pls. 2, 25, 26a).

Trying to make sense of these monuments, even in their broken and battered state, Stirling (1955) hypothesized that they had been intended as representations of the act of sexual intercourse between a human female and a jaguar. Stirling further proposed that these two monuments were an attempt by their carvers to visualize the underlying myth through which the Olmec people explained their ideological conception of their cosmogenic origins. Stirling felt that the many half-human, half-jaguar (were-jaguar) portrayals in Olmec-style art were undoubtedly meant to be understood as the offspring of just such a sexual union.

However, a close analysis of these two sculptures reported by Stirling reveals that, in their battered state, the most that can be said is that they depict what appear to be supine human figures pinned down by upright figures (figure 8.4a). As Davis (1978) describes them, neither of the two supine figures is equipped with any physical fea-

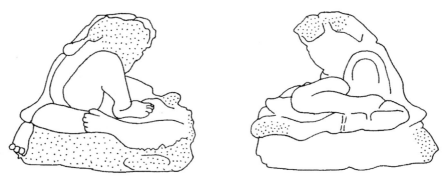

Figure 8.4a   Río Chiquito Monument 1

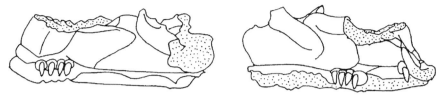

Figure 8.4b   Portero Nuevo Monument 3

ture that is identifiably female. Certainly no sexual organs are evident in either composition. What can be ascertained from these two badly broken monuments is that each portrays a domination scene in which one figure is pinned to the ground by another. Only in the case of Portero Nuevo Monument 3 (figure 8.4b) are any jaguarian features clearly evident. On this monument, the jaguarian aspect is unclouded because the dominating figure possesses clawed paws (the feline dewclaw is strikingly evident) and a curved tail.

Recent and ongoing excavations conducted by Cyphers on the San Lorenzo Tenoctitlán Acropolis and at nearby subsidiary sites have uncovered dramatic monumental sculptural depictions of jaguar/human interaction. In particular, San Lorenzo Monument 107 (95 centimeters high) depicts a pop-eyed jaguar standing on its haunches that drags down (perhaps from the sky) an avian-costumed human figure (figure 8.3b). The fact that this jaguar displays a triangular-shaped "shark's tooth" between its upper eyeteeth supports a supernatural identification for this jaguar as well as another instance of jaguar/water associations.

One of the most important San Lorenzo subsidiary sites where Cyphers has conducted excavations is Loma del Zapote (Cyphers 1996). There, on the slopes of an earthen platform/pyramid construction (acrópolis de El Azuzul), she discovered dramatic proof that Olmec depictions of jaguar/human interaction could be positioned in sculptural "scenes" or tableau (Cyphers 1993). In this case, two identical elaborately costumed human figures are positioned facing a jaguar sculpture who in turn faces them (Cyphers 1997:184–94). An identical jaguar was uncovered farther up the slope and may also have been originally incorporated into this tableau (figure 8.5a).

The two human figures of this scene are not only elaborately garbed but also depicted grasping a ceremonial bar in the same posture as that of Monument 1 from San Martín Pahapan (figure 8.5b). This "lacrosse posture" has been shown to be linked to the raising of

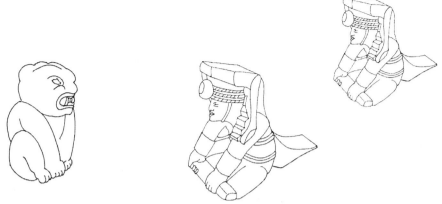

Figure 8.5a   El Azuzul Monument grouping

Figure 8.5b   San Martín Pahapan Monument 1

the cosmogenic world tree, an important episode of Maya creation whose origin is to be found in the Formative period (Freidel et al. 1993:132–38; Reilly 1994; Schele 1995b:108). The entire context of this El Azuzul sculpture scene suggests that Olmec-style human/jaguar interaction scenes and figures, like their Classic Maya counterparts, had a strong cosmogenic as well as a warfare association for their creators.

Images of Human/Jaguar Interaction at the Highland Site of Chalcatzingo, Morelos

Chalcatzingo, Morelos, Mexico, is a Formative site possessing an extensive corpus of bas-reliefs and carved monuments (Grove 1968, 1984, 1987). Much of the iconography of Chalcatzingo is devoted to themes of water and fertility (Angulo V. 1987; Grove 1984; Reilly 1996). However, one monument in particular, Chalcatzingo Monument 31, takes major symbolic elements of jaguars, bloodletting, and warfare and incorporates them with such images of water and fertility as the Lazy-S and the phallic-shaped raindrop symbols.

Chalcatzingo Monument 31 (1.3 meters high) depicts a supernatural feline who is much larger than the human figure lying below him in a prone position (figure 8.6a). The jaguar is identified as supernatural through its flame eyebrow and a striking ear configuration. This ear element has been compared by some scholars to the Venus/Star or Lamat hieroglyph of the Classic period Maya (Angulo V. 1987:121; Grove 1972:157). For the Maya, the Venus/Star or Lamat hieroglyph had strong warfare associations. However, it can be argued that this ear configuration also resembles a water lily and that the water-lily jaguar is an important spirit companion for Classic period Maya rulers.

The Monument 31 jaguar has struck his human victim from behind and while holding him down has reached under to his soft abdomen and disemboweled him with its razor-sharp claws. Intestines can be seen spreading out from under this victim. Above this gruesome scene, three phallic-shaped raindrops fall from a Lazy-S cloud symbol. The implication is that the scene below is the causative agent for the rain falling from above (Reilly 1996).

The overall context and theme of Chalcatzingo Monument 31 relates it to Monuments 3 an 4 from the same site. Chalcatzingo Monuments 3 and 4 are bas-reliefs carved on boulders in close proximity. Monument 3 is difficult to read because of damage sustained when a fiberglass mold was made of the bas-relief in the 1950s (figure 8.6b). This monument depicts a long-necked feline (perhaps a puma) crouching atop a supine human figure (Angulo V. 1987; Grove 1987). The human figure wears a necklace and an elaborate headdress. His left arm is raised as if to protect his face. A branching motif, perhaps a cactus (Grove 1984:116), appears to emanate up from behind this supine figure. The feline supernatural's tongue licks this upraised arm, and the overall impression is that he is devouring the human (Angulo V. 1987:144). Though the features of the feline are obscured,

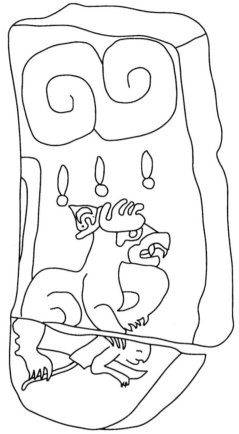

Figure 8.6a   Chalcatzingo Monument 31

its ear appears to contain the same star or water-lily symbol as the jaguar supernatural depicted on Chalcatzingo Monument 31.

This same symbolic element also appears in the ear of the upper jaguar carved on Chalcatzingo Monument 4 (figure 8.6c). This jaguar is one of a pair. Both jaguars have flame eyebrows and are depicted in the act of ripping apart supine human victims (Angulo V. 1987; Grove and Angulo V. 1987). The splayed posture, arms askew, of the victims portrayed on Monument 4 is highly reminiscent of the images of slain sacrificial victims (*danzantes*) from Formative period San José Mogote and Monte Albán (Marcus and Flannery 1996:129–30, figs. 137, 151–154).

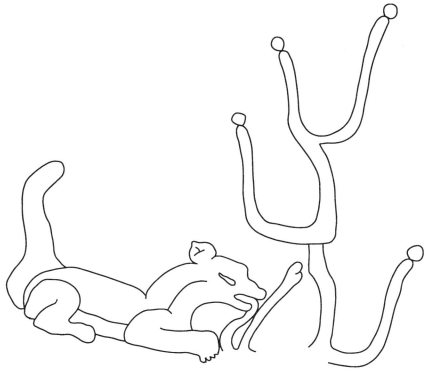

Figure 8.6b   Chalcatzingo Monument 3

The felines depicted on Chalcatzingo Monument 4 are not identical. Among the observable distinctions is the fact that only the upper of the two carries the same ear element as the feline depicted on Monument 31 (Grove 1984:114). The headdress or headband worn by the two animals is also comprised of distinctive elements. The upper jaguar possesses a cartouche containing a crossed-bands symbol that is positioned over its eye. From this cartouche, vegetative elements emerge. In fact, a vegetative element emanates from the forehead of the upper jaguar's supine victim.

The lower jaguar also posses a cartouche above its L-shaped eye, but if that cartouche ever contained symbolic elements, they are no longer discernible. The ear of the lower jaguar is cleft, perhaps invoking the image of a vegetative element, and vegetative elements in the form of a trefoil motif are positioned on its forehead. The tail of the lower jaguar ends in a trefoil arrangement of three cleft jade celts

Figure 8.6c   Chalcatzingo Monument 4

(Grove 1984:114). This repeated arrangement of Olmec-style vegetative elements in a trefoil configuration is highly reminiscent of the Classic Maya jester god or trefoil headband, a costume detail that we now know originated with the Olmec in the Formative period.

The Trefoil Headband

For the Classic period Maya elites, the single most important object of royal costuming was the *Sak Hunal,* or jester god headband. Functioning as a "royal crown," the *Sak Hunal* identified the wearer as both ruler and god. As a physical object, the jester god headband or headdress consisted of a cloth headband with a central jade mask topped by vegetative elements arranged as a trefoil. Sometimes the trefoil elements appeared to stem from an underlying anthropomorphic face.

This central trefoil-shaped jewel was usually flanked by four jade seed or flower motifs, two to a side. Not only are Maya rulers depicted wearing the jester god headband, but the headband has been recovered archaeologically as well (Freidel 1990).

The work of Fields (1989, 1991) conclusively established that the central jewel of the Maya jester god headband was a sprouting maize plant. Iconographic studies illustrate that, when worn, the headband identified the Maya ruler as "First Father," the maize god (Freidel 1990; Freidel et al. 1993). Fields also successfully illustrated that the trefoil element worn in the Olmec-style headdresses of Formative period rulers is the prototype of the Maya jester god headband (figure 8.7). She also demonstrated that the origins of the Classic period Maya trefoil symbol are to be found in the Olmec-style symbol system and that within that system its real-life source is a maize ear.

Recent iconographic analysis clearly illustrates that when worn by a Formative period ruler, in several instances emerging from a crossed-bands symbol, the Olmec-style version of the jester god headband had an identical ideological function as its Classic Maya descendant (Reilly 1994; Taube 1996). It should be noted that physical examples of the Formative period jester god headdress have also been

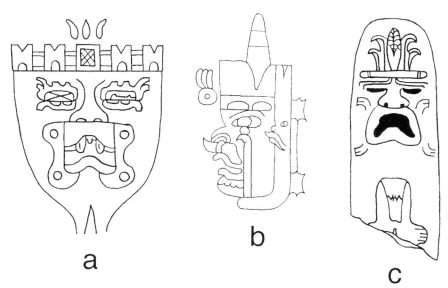

Figure 8.7a–c   Formative Olmec-style examples of the trefoil headdress

d   e

Figure 8.7d–e   Examples of Maya jester god headdress

archaeologically recovered at the Olmec heartland site of La Venta (Reilly 1999).

Comparisons of Jaguars Overpowering Human Imagery: Implications for an Understanding of Warfare Imagery within the Corpus of Formative Olmec-Style Art

The fact that felines on Chalcatzingo Monuments 31 and 3 and the upper feline on Monument 4 carry the same symbolic element in the ear and that all four are shown in the same sanguinary act of destroying supine victims certainly suggests that these jaguars are, if not identical, closely related supernaturals. One can say with some certainty that they also fall within the same jaguar dominating a human category as the previously discussed San Lorenzo Monument 107 (figure 8.3b). The most obvious symbolic clue as to what these scenes of supernatural jaguars overpowering humans depict is given by the trefoil vegetative elements incorporated into the headgear of several of these jaguarian supernaturals (figures 8.6b and 8.7a–c).

As stated earlier, the trefoil headband is one of the most distinctive elements of rulership costuming throughout the Mesoamerican Classic and Formative periods. The fact that it is incorporated as costume elements into two of the jaguarian images and that it may very well be worn by one of the victims is a clear sign that these figures should be understood at one level as supernaturals and at another level as human rulers who have transformed into their jaguarian spirit companions. In other words, these depictions of jaguars overcoming humans are also depictions of human rulers overcoming their enemies in warfare, the same situation that was described in the K'iche' account of their defeat by the Spanish. The fact that one of the victims at Chalcatzingo wears the vegetative motif on his forehead suggests that he was a ruler of some rank. Certainly, as has been discussed, the Classic Maya also depicted high-ranking captives wearing symbols of their rank.

Keeping in mind that Mesoamerican art is thematically conservative but stylistically and iconographically vigorous, it can be argued that warfare representations are almost certainly present somewhere within Olmec-style art. But where? The monuments and figures discussed in this chapter illustrate that, contrary to previous thinking, the theme of warfare is not lacking in Olmec-style art; it is simply not an overt or explicit representation.

As we have illustrated, it can be argued through ethnohistoric evidence that the Maya specifically and Mesoamericans in general conceived of war as supernatural battles waged between the spirit companions of opposing elites. We argue that the answer to the question of depiction or visualization resides within the belief of the spirit companion as a necessary feature for success in war.

Images of jaguarian transformation are recognized within Olmec-style art. Monumental depictions of elites in the Olmec heartland conflate their human identity with supernatural zoomorphs. Obviously, sculptures of jaguar supernaturals, in some instances wearing the accoutrements of rulers, are depicted overcoming and dominating human beings. This can be considered the representation of human rulers who, on the battlefield, have taken the form of their jaguarian spirit companions and with this supernatural identification overcome their enemies. In other words, one can say that while warfare imagery is explicit in the art of the Classic period Maya and other, later Mesoamerican cultures, the same subject is implicit and couched in supernatural were-jaguar imagery within the Formative period Olmec style.

War is waged for practical considerations; however, the reasons for war are universally expressed in ideological terms. In Olmec-style art, the jaguar-dominating-humans motif set is linked to the inclusive themes of water and fertility. Taube (1995:83) has called the Olmec Mesoamerica's first rainmakers and has demonstrated the iconographic debt owed by later Mesoamerican rain god images to the Olmec style. The fact that several of the jaguarian images discussed earlier (San Lorenzo Monument 77 and Chalcatzingo Monument 31) are also associated with Olmec-style cloud and rain symbols supports a linkage between the theme of jaguars overcoming humans, warfare, bloodletting or sacrifice, and water/fertility (figures 8.3a and 8.6a).

When all this imagery is viewed as a series of interlocking iconographic themes, it can be argued that there exists a "grammar" through which the seeming oppositions of warfare and fertility become linked or ideologically reconciled within the Olmec style. As Knight (1986) expressed it in his analysis of the organization of the religion of the Mississippian period southeastern United States, fertility and warfare are cult manifestations that are balanced by the institution of rulership. Within such a model, fertility (thesis) is a cult open to the many, while the ideology of warfare (antithesis) is a cult restricted to the few (figure 8.8). Functioning as a synthesis between these two oppositions, the ruler, with his ability to ritually transform, travels to the Otherworld and obtains the knowledge necessary to sustain life and also becomes the spirit companion who ensures victory in war.

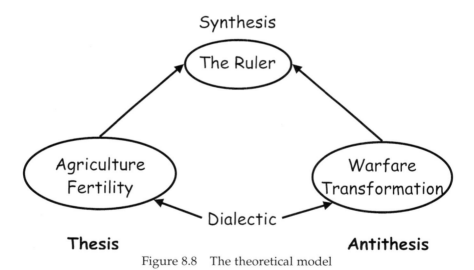

Figure 8.8   The theoretical model

Chapter Nine

Butterfly War at Teotihuacan

Annabeth Headrick

Though a seemingly unlikely candidate in a discussion of warfare, the fragile insect that is the butterfly became one of the premier instruments of war at Teotihuacan. In our own culture, this winged insect symbolizes such qualities as delicacy, spring, and brevity of life. Although the Teotihuacanos may have associated similar qualities with the butterfly, for them the creature was unmistakably martial. What many see as a gentle creature, one of the few insects that we encourage to alight on our arm and gently tickle us with its step, for the Teotihuacanos became an immutable reminder of the duty of war.

That this duty was an ever present aspect of life is clear, for the butterfly is a common feature in Teotihuacan art. It appears in the art directly produced in the city and also at Teotihuacan-influenced places such as Esquintla. The frequency of its appearance in the visual record has led to several studies of butterfly iconography. Early scholars like Seler (1990–1998) and Beyer (1965) discussed the butterfly, and more recently von Winning (1987) and Berlo (1983, 1984) have conducted in-depth analyses. The purpose of this chapter is not so much to refute previous ideas about the butterfly, for I believe that these earlier attempts are quite accurate. Instead, this investigation will add an additional twist to our understanding of the butterfly. I hope to demonstrate that the butterfly was an important propagandistic tool used by the Teotihuacan state. That is, the butterfly permeated the everyday life of the Teotihuacanos and thereby shaped their understanding of their role in society, their relationship to the state, and their duty to the state.

Iconographic Characteristics of Butterflies

Some butterflies are easy to recognize in Teotihuacan art. On one frescoed bowl (figure 9.1a), the artist carefully delineated the fore and aft wings as well as the long tubular body. Circular rings mark the eyes on this and many other butterflies, and above the eyes there is a prominent curl that represents the proboscis of the butterfly. Finally, to either side of the proboscis are the antennae. There is an anatomical specificity to this image that reveals the artist's interest in copying from nature. This particular butterfly appears to frolic among the multicolored raindrops. Yet this scene may not be as bucolic as it seems because there are attributes that are disturbingly suggestive of war.

For instance, the circular eyes are visually identical to the goggles worn by Tlaloc. Imagery from Teotihuacan often shows Tlaloc as a deity associated with rain, depicted with both a lightning bolt and a water vessel streaming with liquid (Miller 1973:fig. 360). This might explain the coupling of the raindrops with the Tlaloc goggled butterfly. However, Schele and Freidel (1990) have definitively shown that Tlaloc is equally connected with war, the Tlaloc image appearing on square war shields and seeming to be associated with Venus-regulated warfare at Tikal. The authors argue that the Tlaloc deity

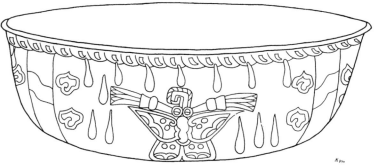

Figure 9.1a   Frescoed bowl with butterfly

may have spawned a new form of warfare among the Maya, who borrowed motifs and concepts from Teotihuacan. More recently, Stuart (1998c; see also Freidel et al., chapter 11 in this volume) has built on the earlier ideas of Coggins (1979) and Proskouriakoff (1993) to argue that the appearance of Tlaloc and other Teotihuacan imagery at Tikal probably arose through direct contact, possibly including Teotihuacanos actually going to Tikal. Stuart's convincing argument, coupled with Schele and Freidel's observations on the Tlaloc cult, suggests that the militaristic aspects of this deity were strong enough to be exported over vast distances in Mesoamerica.

In addition to the Tlaloc goggles, the antennae on this painted butterfly (figure 9.1a) have an eerie resemblance to the fletched ends of atlatl darts. In Teotihuacan images, the fletching generally consists of a round ball capped by a swath of feathers, and the butterfly's antennae surprisingly take the same form (figure 9.1b). A mural in the Palace of the Sun (Zone 5-A) indicates that this visual double entendre was an intentional one (figure 9.1c). As von Winning (1987:I:116) pointed out, the mural depicts a butterfly with the points of atlatl darts below the aft wings. Though badly damaged, the curled proboscis and round eye goggles are still quite visible, securely identifying the image as a butterfly. The feathered ends of the antennae frame both sides of the

Figure 9.1b Warrior with atlatl darts, white patio, Atetelco, Teotihuacan
(adapted from von Winning 1987:I:fig. 3a)

Figure 9.1c   Mural depicting butterfly with atlatl darts, Zone 5-A,
Teotihuacan (adapted from Miller 1973:86)

goggles, but the lower portion of the body reveals that the antennae
are not as much the parts of an insect as they are the fletched ends of
a pair of crossed atlatl darts. In this case, the artist provided a direct
substitution in which the atlatl darts create a visual pun on the component shapes of a butterfly's body (Mayhall 1991). Undoubtedly, the
success of this pun relied on the fact that the military association of
butterflies was a strong one at Teotihuacan.

Indeed, there is an abundance of images depicting warriors with
butterfly attributes. On another frescoed vase (figure 9.1d), a human
dresses in a butterfly costume, indicated by a small proboscis on top
of his head that curls to the left. Behind this is a feathered eye that,
like the Tlaloc goggles, frequently appears in butterfly imagery at Teo-

Figure 9.1d   Butterfly warrior with shield on frescoed vase
(adapted from Sejourné 1966a:fig. 94)

tihuacan. Tucked next to the eye is one of the butterfly's antennae with its feathered or fletched end. On this vessel, the artist has eliminated the human body, but there are two prominent wings where the individual's shoulders might be, and these wings emerge from the circular shape of a warrior's shield. Though no other weapons appear in this image, the shield indicates the martial associations if the butterfly itself were not enough to cue the viewer.

The warrior's shield is more fully visible in another frescoed tripod vessel (figure 9.2a). In this version, the shield is fully round, but the warrior's body is similarly hidden behind the shield. The figure also has the distinctive curling proboscis and feathered eye on the top of his head that position this warrior inside the butterfly complex. However, the butterfly is not the only animal attribute worn by this warrior. Below the proboscis, the beak of a bird clearly frames the warrior's face, and this time the tail feathers of a bird project from the shield instead of the butterfly wings seen earlier. The composite nature of this figure indicates that butterfly costumes did not exclude the imagery of other animals.

In truth, the butterfly–bird conflation is extremely common in Teotihuacan art (Mayhall 1991; Parsons 1988). A fine example appears on a tripod vessel that is divided into two opposing yet complementary sections (figure 9.2b). On one side, the artist portrayed a frontal individual with outstretched arms waving two rattles or staffs. The figure

Figure 9.2a Warrior with shield on frescoed vase

Figure 9.2b   Vase with frontal figure (adapted from Sejourné 1966b:fig. 130)

wears a broad headdress crowned by the butterfly proboscis, yet once again the bird attributes are equally apparent. He wears a hook-beaked bird on his chest, and the costume hanging from his arms seemingly transforms into the extended wings of the raptor. The opposite side further reinforces the butterfly associations, for here an oddly compiled butterfly with proboscis, antennae, feathered and goggled eyes, and fully splayed wings confronts the viewer.

The most integrated example of the butterfly–bird conflation appears on a relief-decorated vessel (figure 9.2c). Initially, the creature seems mostly butterfly because it has the clearly delineated fore and aft wings of a butterfly that, in this case, emerge from a four-petaled flower resting over the area of the butterfly's body. In addition, the creature has the feathered eye and the expected proboscis and

Figure 9.2c   Avian butterfly from relief vessel
(adapted from von Winning 1987:I:fig. 7a)

antenna. Further examination of the head, however, reveals that the butterfly proboscis sprouts from the hooked beak of a bird that fully merges with the butterfly features. The butterfly–bird conflation on this vessel seems extraordinarily complete because the features of the two animals merge with perfect fluidity.

In the extant examples of Teotihuacan art containing this butter-fly–bird conflation, the bird has a distinctive short, hooked beak (figure 9.2c). This same bird is one that von Winning (1948:131–32; 1987:I:85–90, 121) identified as an owl. He went even further to give a label to the combination of an owl, shield, and atlatl darts, calling it the "*lechuza y armas.*" He suggested that it was a Teotihuacan emblem for war and possibly a heraldic sign of the warrior class (von Winning 1987:I:85–90). Recently, Stuart (1998c) has revisited the *lechuza y armas* motif, building an intriguing argument that it may instead represent the name of a powerful warrior-king of Teotihuacan who was influential in moving his descendant onto the throne of Tikal. This exciting interpretation may lead to new revelations in Teotihuacan hiero-glyphic readings and force the field to reassess the relationship between iconography and epigraphy at Teotihuacan; nevertheless, whether name or heraldic symbol, the owl at Teotihuacan is decidedly militaristic in keeping with the martial themes of the associated but-terfly imagery. Butterflies, it would seem, were an integral part of the iconography of war at Teotihuacan.

Of further note is the fact that on this and other vessels with but-terfly–bird conflation, the feathered eye seems fully integrated into the hooked beak of the bird. Likewise, in images of the owl, indepen-dent of butterfly references, the feathered eye invariably appears. I would suggest that the feathered eye is actually an avian feature and that when it appears on the butterfly, it is a direct reference to the owl. Thus, a butterfly with a feathered eye may carry owl associations even when there is no other reference to bird features.

Returning to an earlier image (figure 9.2a) introduces another important iconographic element of this butterfly assemblage. The warrior carries a war shield that obscures his body, and his costuming fits within the iconographic cluster developed previously of an indi-vidual or group who wears militaristic butterfly–bird paraphernalia. Yet there is one more part of the costume that frequently appears in the art. This butterfly warrior has a distinctively shaped nose plaque that apparently hangs from his pierced septum; likewise, this same nose plaque adorns the shield held in his hand.

This nose plaque makes an even more prominent appearance in

the many incensarios found at Teotihuacan and the Teotihuacan-influenced site of Esquintla (Berlo 1984; von Winning 1987:I:118–24). In what von Winning calls an altar-type incensario (figure 9.3a), a masklike face peers out from between plaques representing decorated standards that the figure holds in his hands. Just as in the frescoed vase, the face wears the same nose plaque, as do many masks in both the Teotihuacan and the Esquintla incensario. In an incensario from Tetitla (Berrin and Pasztory 1993:217), there is a row of naturalistic butterflies above the mask wearing the nose plaque, suggesting a close association between the two.

Von Winning (1987:II:59) securely identified this nose plaque as butterfly related, though he argued that it was an accoutrement of his "Butterfly God." In essence, the nose plaque is an abstracted version of the shape of a butterfly's body that is best demonstrated on a plano-relief vessel (figure 9.3b). On the vase, the relationship between the nose plaque and the butterfly is explicit because the artist carefully delineated the shape of the nose plaque and surrounded it with the wings of a butterfly. The artist clearly tells the viewer that the upper portion of the nose plaque represents the forewings of a butterfly and

Figure 9.3a   Teotihuacan incensario with figure wearing a butterfly nose plaque (adapted from von Winning 1987:I:fig. 18b)

Figure 9.3b   Vase decorated with nose plaque surrounded by butterfly wings (adapted from von Winning 1987:II:fig. 3b)

that the lower portion of the plaque represents the aft wings, while the lower portion of the butterfly's tubular body extends from the bottom of the nose plaque to tighten the visual association. To be sure, the nose plaque is a butterfly. In a wonderfully animated example of a nose plaque serving as a butterfly body (figure 9.3c), the naturalistic proboscis appears on the top. Below this, the atlatl dartlike antennae flare to each side of the feathered and goggled eyes, but the butterfly's body is gone. In its place is a stylized version of the animal with the crisp outlines of a nose plaque. In this case, the nose plaque unambiguously replaces the butterfly's body.

Figure 9.3c   Frescoed vase with butterfly head above a nose plaque, Tetitla, Teotihuacan (adapted from Sejourné 1966b:fig. 100)

Butterfly Symbolism

Seler (1990–1998) began the discourse on Mesoamerican butterfly symbolism in his many papers concerning the art and thought of the Aztec. In a discussion of Aztec creation beliefs, he cites the ethnohistoric work of Sahagún, who wrote on the different afterlife locations in Aztec thought (Seler 1990–1998:V:39). In particular, Sahagún explained that warriors killed in battle or sacrificed after capture resided in the heavens, a privileged place of death:

> The brave warriors, the eagle-ocelot warriors, those who died in war, went there to the house of the sun. And they lived there in the east, where the sun arose. And when the sun was about to emerge, when it was still dark, they arrayed themselves, they armed themselves as for war, met the sun as it emerged, brought it forth, came giving cries for it, came gladdening it, came skirmishing. Before it they came rejoicing; they came to leave it there at the zenith, called the midday sun. (Sahagún 1950–1982:6:162)

Thus, initially on the warrior's death, he and other warriors would spend each day greeting the sun, celebrating the arrival of the sun by beating their shields, and following the sun to its zenith. Sahagún continues by stating,

> And when they had passed four years there [in the home of the sun], then they changed into precious birds, hummingbirds, orioles, yellow birds, yellow birds blackened about the eyes, chalky butterflies, feather down butterflies, gourd bowl butterflies; they sucked honey [from the flowers] there where they dwelt. And here upon the earth they came to suck [honey] from all the various flowers. (Sahagún 1950–1982:6:49)

In this passage, we see that after four years of service to the sun, the warriors' souls then transformed into butterflies and birds to live a joyous life sucking the nectar of the earth's flowers. Thus, Seler (1990–1998:III:102, IV:9, V:39) settled on the concept that the butterfly represents the souls of dead warriors.

While in Seler's day there was much confusion about the time spread between Teotihuacan and the Aztec, subsequent scholars (Berlo 1983, 1984; Beyer 1965; Kubler 1985; Pasztory 1976:157–59; Toscano 1954:33; von Winning 1987:I:111–24) have accepted Seler's basic premise and applied it, in varying degrees, to Teotihuacan. Beyer (1965:465–68) added that butterflies represented the qualities of fertility and flames as well as those deities associated with these properties, but he still followed that butterflies were the souls of dead warriors. He carefully recognized that the documentation came from a Postclassic source, but he reasoned that the Aztec concept developed from beliefs that were already present at Classic Teotihuacan. Von Winning (1987:I:116–17) endeavored to add some chronology to the question, offering that butterflies were connected with fertility since the earliest of Teotihuacan times but that in later phases the animal took on associations with war and the souls of the dead. As always, Kubler (1985:270) was particularly suspicious of using Aztec ethnohistory to elucidate Teotihuacan, yet he did nevertheless arrive at a funerary association for butterflies through his methodology of iconographic clusters. Noting that butterfly iconography appeared on incensarios, he supposed a funerary use and reasoned that the butterfly could be an image of a soul. Throughout the literature on the subject, scholars may report additional symbolism for the butterfly, but all are in agreement that one viable meaning for the butterfly is the souls of dead warriors.

As suggested by Berlo (1983, 1984:30–31, 63–65), Kubler (1985:270), Taube (1998), and von Winning (1987:I:121–22), the frequent appearance of butterfly imagery on incensarios works well within this context, for incensarios seem to have been important features of funerary rites. Throughout Mesoamerica, burning incense and the subsequent cloud of smoke were an important means for contact with the dead. As the smoke rose from the tube of the incensario, it seemingly bridged the distance between earthly and celestial realms, providing visual evidence of a link to the ancestors. Von Winning (1987:I:122) argued that the masked face in the center of an incensario was the face of the deceased individual. These clay masks are stylistically similar to Teotihuacan's famous stone masks, and I (Headrick 1996, 1999) have argued that these stone masks were originally attached to mortuary bundles. Taube (1998) has even suggested that the conical shape of many incensarios purposefully mimics the bundles of the dead. That is, it may be that the incensarios actually are effigy mortuary bundles. Such reasoning, coupled with the fact that incensarios frequently come from burials, indicates that incensarios are funerary related (Berlo 1984:30–33; Linné 1942:125–32; Manzanilla 1993; Manzanilla and Carreón 1989; Sejourné 1959:667).

Although Kubler (1985:270) and von Winning (1987:115–24) broadened the funerary association to suggest that butterflies could be the souls of the dead in general, Berlo (1983, 1984) returned to the earlier ideas of Seler (1990–1998:IV:9) and Beyer (1965:465–68) to emphasize the ethnohistoric accounts that identify butterflies not only with any dead souls but also with the souls of dead warriors. Another incensario mask seems to validate this stance (figure 9.3d). As on many incensario masks, this example depicts a face with a butterfly nose piece; however, less typical are the three human skulls that decorate the upper portion of the nose plaque. The skulls convey the concept of death in a chillingly graphic manner and strengthen an argument for incensarios having strong ties to the worship of the dead. In addition, this butterfly nose plaque also doubles as the trapeze-and-ray year sign (Seler 1990–1998:VI:pl. LXIV). Looking to the tripod feet of many Teotihuacan cylindrical vessels (figure 9.3e), it is evident that this visual overlay of the year sign on the butterfly shape is a fairly common visual trope in the Teotihuacan ceramist's repertoire. The year sign, like other elements in the butterfly complex, often shows up in warfare-related contexts. As Teotihuacan warriors frequently wear the year sign in their headdresses (figure 9.1b) and the Teotihuacanos exported the year sign along with its military symbolism when they contacted the Maya (Berlo 1984:111–12; Coggins 1979; Proskouriakoff 1993; Schele and Freidel 1990; Stuart 1998c), the death imagery of the skulls on the incensario mask quite likely represents a warrior's death.

Holy War

If the Teotihuacanos shared the Postclassic belief that butterflies were the souls of dead warriors, then it seems that we should explore the

Figure 9.3d   Incensario mask with butterfly nose plaque and three skulls, Tlamimilolpa, Teotihuacan (adapted from Linné 1934)

Figure 9.3e   Feet from tripod vases decorated with the year sign (adapted from Sejourné 1966a:88, 100)

nature of such a belief in greater depth. For the Aztec, the afterlife of dead warriors was to exist in a privileged realm. It was an honor to be in the close proximity of the sun, and the life of sucking nectar that followed was a pleasurable one. In his text, Sahagún (1950–1982) makes it clear that this heaven was reserved for dead warriors; that is, this afterlife was the reward for bravery on the battlefield. Thus, Sahagún describes a system of incentive. To do battle for the state or to sacrifice one's life for the state was amply rewarded. The incentive of a glorious afterlife enticed people to risk their very lives.

In order to gain insight into such a belief system, it may prove helpful to explore a similar incentive system found in Islamic fundamentalism. While the following is but a brief overview with little space for inevitable variations, this general sketch of the concept allows for rudimentary comparisons. In its simplest translation, the word *Islam* means "submission," as in the submission to God (Johnson 1997:161). In essence, an individual submits to the will of God and, in turn, to the state that represents that god, as there is no distinction between religious and political aims. To this end, Muslims have certain devotional duties, or obligations. These are ranked from mandatory to recommended to forbidden, and one of the mandatory duties is jihad (Peters 1979:3–12, 1996:3).

In the West, *jihad* often appears in translation as "holy war"; however, a more accurate translation might be "to strive" or "to struggle." Clarification of this concept comes from books on Islamic law and the Koran that indicate that the term means "to struggle against unbelievers"; thus, it is a Muslim's duty to fight unbelievers whenever the Muslim caliph, or leader, announces a holy war (Martin 1991:92; Peters 1979:9, 1996:1–3). Interestingly, not all members of the community must fight in the holy war because it is part of a category called universal duties. In universal duties, the obligation is for the community as a whole; therefore, everyone in the community need not participate as long as the participating members of the community, in this case able-bodied men, can accomplish the obligation (Peters 1977:9–10, 1979:12).

Most pertinent for the discussion at hand are the motivational tools incorporated into the religion to ensure adequate participation throughout the community. For one, to be Muslim is to believe in one's duty to bring all of humanity into the submission of Allah. The driving force is the belief that one's actions will restore the world to its proper condition by eliminating the forces of deception and unbelief (Martin 1991). Tangential to this is a more individual reward system that appeals not as much to what is right but to personal gain. As an added incentive to participate in a jihad, those who die in such a war are declared martyrs, and verses in the Koran indicate that these martyrs are guaranteed entrance into Paradise without any preconditions (Peters 1977:4, 1996:5). This latter motivational stratagem is most profitable when compared to Central Mexican notions of warfare.

The parallels between the Aztec account of their warriors' afterlives and Islamic jihad are intriguing. Both cultural traditions promise a better afterlife in return for fighting the state's war. To the Aztec, the afterlife bestowed the honor of accompanying the sun, the greatest celestial force then known, followed by a leisurely life sustained by the sweet nectar of flowers. For a Muslim, the reward is immediate acceptance into his own concept of paradise. In turn, using the afterlife as a motivational tool encourages the individuals in both societies to endanger their own immediate living existence to follow the will of the state. The incentive of enhanced afterlife incorporates the will of the individual into the collective goals, thereby enticing the individual to abandon his instinct for survival.

As argued earlier, so much of Teotihuacan butterfly iconography is in accord with Aztec traditions, especially in its military and funerary senses, that it is likely that the Teotihuacanos may have also believed in a Mesoamerican form of holy war. Perhaps they too believed that an enhanced and noble afterlife awaited those who died in battle or suffered the fate of sacrifice after capture. If so, the butterfly iconography seen in Teotihuacan art could have had a very distinct social message about the obligations of the individual to the state and the rewards for proper behavior. It is plausible, I would suggest, that butterfly imagery at Teotihuacan functioned as a propagandistic tool to motivate the people into war by holding out the carrot of a pleasurable afterlife.

The search for evidence of a Teotihuacan form of holy war leads directly to the so-called Tlalocan murals of the apartment compound of Tepantitla. In the upper register of the east wall, a frontal view of the Great Goddess dominates the mural (figure 9.4). Approaching from either side are priests who sprinkle offerings on the ground before the goddess. In return, the goddess sprouts verdant vegetation from her head while life-sustaining water drips from her open hands and gushes out of the womblike opening at her base. Both butterflies and birds flit around the flowering branches of the tree, while below,

Figure 9.4   Mural of the Great Goddess, Tepantitla, Teotihuacan
(drawing by Linda Schele © David Schele)

in the lower register, people frolic about. The themes of reciprocity and fertility are explicit, yet, I would argue, so is the theme of the duty of war.

This Tepantitla mural has been the subject of much discussion, but for the purposes at hand, I will limit discussion to the seminal work on the deity at the center of the image.[1] Until recently, most scholars accepted Caso's (1942) identification of the image as Tlaloc, but this began to change with Furst's (1974) identification of the figure as a goddess and Pasztory's (1976) thorough investigation of the Tepantitla murals. In that work, Pasztory left the identification of the deity open, although in other publications she refined her definitions of Tlaloc and the Great Goddess, landing firmly on the side of the Tepantitla mural depicting the latter (Pasztory 1974, 1988, 1997). The imagery of the Great Goddess was further elaborated on by Berlo (1992), and most scholars now accept this identification.

In an interesting study of the particulars of the tree sprouting from the head of the goddess, Taube (1983) highlighted the fact that spiders decorate a branch of the tree and a spider drops down on a thread to dangle just above the goddess's head. Building his argument from a pan-American perspective, he compares the image to the spider woman myths found in Mesoamerica and the Southwest. His work represents an important step in fully understanding the multifaceted nature of this image, and I would build on his work by focusing on the other branch of the tree.

On careful observation, it is clear that the Tepantitla goddess has two distinct branches rising from the top of her head. One, as Taube (1983) recognized, has spiders decorating it, but the other has butter-flies marking it.[2] The iconographic command that each insect has over half the tree indicates not that the spider is the dominating icono-graphic element of this deity but that the two forces are somehow bal-anced. I would argue that this balance is the equilibrium of gender. In short, these two halves of the tree show a male/female opposition.

As previously argued, butterflies at Teotihuacan represented the souls of dead warriors. With some exceptions, the iconography and archaeology of Teotihuacan indicate that war was largely a male enter-prise; thus, the butterfly half of the tree would represent the male side. By symbolizing the male as a butterfly, the image characterizes just what it means to be male in Teotihuacan society. Rather than empha-sizing a masculine craft or male roles in food acquisition, the artist chose to highlight warfare and, in particular, the reward offered to those who never returned from the battlefield. The mural would have reminded male members of this society that their role in life was to do battle for the state.

Pasztory (1976:160–61) recognized the feminine associations of spiders when she linked the spiders on the other branch of the Tepantitla tree with the female activities of spinning, weaving, and childbirth. For the Maya, the spider is a symbol of the goddess of spinning and weaving, a natural connection drawn from the spinning activities a spider makes when it weaves its web (Taube 1992b:99–105; Thompson 1970:247). For the Aztec, Mixtec, and Maya, the female goddess of weaving also was the goddess of childbirth; therefore, the female side of the tree nicely emphasizes the female duties of weaving and childbirth (McCafferty and McCafferty 1994).

This connection to childbirth is especially important and further tightens the argument when we consider a certain Aztec belief recorded by Sahagún. For the Aztec, childbirth was connected to battle, and a woman experiencing labor pains was compared to a warrior. As Sahagún (1950–1982:6:167) describes the moment of birth, "When the baby arrived on earth, then the midwife shouted; she gave war cries, which meant that the little woman had fought a good battle, had become a brave warrior, had taken captive, had captured a baby." In this passage, the comparison to the male role of warrior is clear, for childbirth was a woman's struggle and battle, and her child was her captive (Berlo 1983:92–93; Klein 1988). Even more interesting is the belief that women who died in childbirth went to the same celestial paradise as men who died in war (Sahagún 1950–1982:6:161–65). Like men, they accompanied the sun along its path across the sky, and they too sucked the nectar of flowers. If we apply this to the Tepantitla Great Goddess, we see a new message. The tree explicitly states the roles of males and females, and it does so in terms connected to warfare. Females were to be metaphorical warriors in childbirth and to risk their very lives in this endeavor. Males were warriors in the traditional sense, imperiling their lives on the battlefield. For females and males alike, the reward was the same if they died in the process; they gained entrance to the celestial paradise of the sun.

To emphasize how deeply engrained this duality was in Mesoamerican thought and, in turn, expressed in art, other iconographic traditions demonstrate that this male/female dichotomy was not limited to Teotihuacan. In the Codex Vindobonensis, the Mixtec show a tree similar to the Great Goddess called the Tree of Apoala (figure 9.5a). In this case, the artist inverted the female head to the ground and drew the lineage founders emerging from her vaginal area up

Figure 9.5a   The Tree of Apoala, Vindobonesis Codex 37
(drawing by Linda Schele © David Schele)

above. Just as with the Tepantitla tree, the Mixtec tree has two branches with opposing iconography, and the paired themes are decidedly similar to Teotihuacan. On the left side of the tree, circular motifs with holes in their center appear. Aside from the fundamental association of circularity with female concepts, the round shapes can be identified as spindle whorls, a primary symbol of the female craft of spinning and weaving and, in turn, the battle of childbirth. In opposition, the long atlatl darts on the right side of the tree are both phallic and representative of the male endeavor of warfare. Here, as in the

Teotihuacan tree, the male symbol has a strong military association, and the female symbolism is almost identical with its reference to spinning, childbirth, and a female brand of war.

Thus, we can see gendered roles clearly emerging in Mesoamerican art, with a constant that warfare was an important male duty. In the case of Teotihuacan, as suggested by the Tepantitla mural, the butterfly became the gender-laden symbol of males; thus, its appearance in Teotihuacan art served as an ever present reminder of the male duty to risk his life on the battlefield. However, at Teotihuacan, butterfly imagery is not limited to a few vases, incensarios, and isolated murals. I believe that the propaganda of butterfly war was even more insidious in nature and that the Teotihuacan state made such iconography impossible to escape.

Architectural Butterflies

While the shape of the butterfly nose plaque does seem to derive from the stylized shape of a butterfly, I believe that it also bears a resemblance to the distinctive *talud-tablero* architecture that envelopes the city. As von Winning (1947, 1979:321, 1987:II:60) pointed out and Mayhall (1991) further asserted, when the Teotihuacanos themselves drew pictures of their architecture, it takes the same shape as the butterfly nose plaque. The horizontal bar on top and the triangular base not only resemble the shape of a butterfly's body but also reproduce the silhouette of *talud-tablero* architecture. On an architectural scene from a tripod vessel (figure 9.5b), the stairs, superstructure, and decorative *almenas* clearly identify the image as a temple; however, the shape is also strongly reminiscent of the nose plaque. Likewise, in a figurine headdress, three *talud-tablero* temples appear (figure 9.5c), each with a superstructure and decorative *almenas* on top of the *talud-tablero* form. Assuredly, these are temples, but anyone versed in Teotihuacan iconography would see the resemblance to the nose plaque. Von Winning (1987:II:60) found the proverbial "smoking gun" on a molded plaque that depicts a temple, complete with crowning *almenas*, but this time the temple superstructure rises from a carefully delineated butterfly nose plaque (figure 9.5d). On this example, instead of stairs, the depression meant for the wearer's nose substitutes for the temple stairs. It is well known that Teotihuacan artists enjoyed such visual puns, and because the forms of the architecture and the nose plaque are so similar, Teotihuacan *talud-tablero* structures surely carried some degree of butterfly symbolism.

Figure 9.5b   Temple with stairs (adapted from von Winning 1947:fig. 1)

Along these lines, I would contend that when the Teotihuacanos saw the *talud-tablero* style of architecture, they also saw butterflies, yet it was not just the creature that the architecture brought to mind but also the symbolism attached to the butterfly in Teotihuacan belief. As such, the *talud-tablero* architecture would have constantly reminded Teotihuacanos, especially the male members of society, of their duty to the state as associated with concepts of butterfly warfare. Their very gender may have determined the supreme directive in their lives, for their duty, their goal in life, was to do battle for the state. They were

Figure 9.5c   Three temples in figurine headdress
(adapted from Sejourné 1966b:fig. 44)

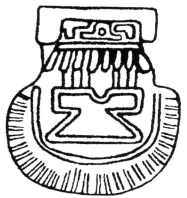

Figure 9.5d   Molded plaque with butterfly nose plaque serving as temple substructure (adapted from von Winning 1987:II:fig. 6a)

to go to war and fight valiantly. The dividend that enticingly pulled them into action was a belief, for if they died in war or as sacrificial victims, they were rewarded in the afterlife. They would go to the paradise of the sun and eventually reemerge on earth as the carefree birds and butterflies.

In short, the architecture seemingly was propaganda. It lined the Avenue of the Dead for at least the 1.5 miles that archaeologists have presently exposed. If the architecture was perceived as symbolic butterflies, then the street could be viewed as a long line of stylized butterflies that completely filled the peripheral vision. The propaganda would have also entered domestic spaces in the form of additional temples. Inside the apartment compounds, the temples around the ritual patios had *talud-tablero* architecture as well. For the Teotihuacan eye and, therefore, the mind, the butterflies were literally everywhere. Visually, the Teotihuacanos could not escape them; thus, the propaganda of warfare would have permeated their lives, subsuming the desires of the individual into the goals of the state.

If we return to our initial image (figure 9.1a), the temptation to view this only as a charming scene of a butterfly dancing through nature seems less tenable. Because our goal should be to view the art as the Teotihuacanos may have seen it, we must entertain the idea that such butterflies likely carried a deeply engrained association with social concepts of duty and gender. If the Teotihuacanos saw this butterfly as an image of a heroic warrior enjoying the fruits of the exalted afterlife he earned through service to the state, then the image becomes propaganda, designed to manipulate the actions of the population into the act of war. That this intent bled into the ubiquitous architectural style that was identifiable with the city throughout Mesoamerica was a brilliant, if hauntingly exploitative, maneuver by the state that was Teotihuacan.

Notes

This chapter would not have been possible without the profound insight of Marguerite Mayhall both in her 1991 paper and in subsequent conversations. Indeed, her work should be viewed as the foundation from which this chapter sprang.

1. For the most thorough analysis on the history of the research, see Pasztory (1976).

2. In a paper produced for a seminar with Linda Schele at the University of Texas, Mayhall (1991) first emphasized the complementary balanced nature of this opposition. She cogently emphasized that the equal treatment argued for equal symbolism for the butterflies.

Chapter Ten

Texts and Contexts in Maya Warfare: A Brief Consideration of Epigraphy and Archaeology at Caracol, Belize

Diane Z. Chase and Arlen F. Chase

> Epigraphy and archaeology need each other. If a truly *objective* history is ever to emerge from prehispanic Mesoamerica, much of it will have to emerge at the point of a trowel. (Marcus 1992a:445)

A primary focus of research at Caracol has been the examination of the archaeological responses to and manifestations of successful warfare. Thus, we have attempted to correlate the warfare events epigraphically recorded on the stone monuments and stucco facades in Caracol's epicenter with the archaeological record found in the outlying settlement. Caracol's texts include the earliest known example of a Maya "shell-star" event, taken to be the most consequential kind of Maya warfare (Houston 1991:40). Dated to A.D. 562, it marks the defeat of Tikal, Guatemala, a site 76 kilometers distant. Other defeats, decapitations, destructions, and captures are also present in Caracol's extensive hieroglyphic record. These events generally cluster in two time horizons, between A.D. 550 and 700 and again after A.D. 790. Because the material remains at Caracol can be tightly dated, it is possible to correlate the two epigraphically recorded periods of successful aggression with other social contexts. Settlement in the post–A.D. 550 time frame indicates significant population growth, increased construction activity, as well as widespread cohesion and prosperity among Caracol's populace. In contrast to the earlier warfare episode, the post–A.D. 790 episode is marked by epicentral but not core settlement growth conjoined with selective rather than widespread cohesion and prosperity. Our investigations have revealed that both the textual references and the archaeologically recoverable responses vary between the two definable warfare episodes in Caracol's history. Maya warfare was not a monolithic activity. The Caracol data demonstrate that the archaeological record can be effectively used to monitor the effects that different kinds of epigraphically noted warfare had on a given population.

Epigraphic Interpretation of Maya Warfare

Epigraphically recorded war events between known Maya sites span the entire Late Classic era (table 10.1). While warfare was certainly practiced by the Maya from a very early date (cf. Webster 1977; see also Brown and Garber, chapter 6 in this volume), epigraphic indications of warfare prior to the Late Classic are somewhat problematic. The hypothesized Early Classic warfare between Tikal and Uaxactún (Freidel et al., chapter 11 in this volume), for example, originally derived from the monumental texts at these two sites (Mathews 1985; Schele and Freidel 1990), has been disputed on both epigraphic (Stuart 1993) and archaeological (Laporte and Fialko 1995) grounds. Starting at the very end of the Early Classic period, epigraphic references to Maya warfare increased throughout the Late Classic period (cf. Schele and Miller 1986:209). Stuart (1993:334) argues that the explosion in Late Classic narrative exposition related to Maya warfare represents a profound shift between the Early and Late Classic periods. Whether this was a shift in written emphasis and/or a shift in the scale of warfare, however, can be addressed only with a conjunctive approach. Nowhere within the epigraphic and archaeological records of the Maya can warfare's long-term impact be better studied than at Caracol, Belize. It was here that the earliest known shell-star event was recorded (Houston 1991), and it is here that some of the latest known warfare events of the Classic period are also in evidence (Mathews 2000).

Hieroglyphic Representations of Warfare: General Considerations

A number of hieroglyphs are associated with Maya warfare. While there is some variation in emphasis and use of these glyphs among

Table 10.1   Epigraphically known war events in the Maya area[1]

Date	Distance (km)	Victor	Defeated	Nature of Warfare
9.6.2.1.11	76	Tikal	Caracol	Axe event
9.6.8.4.2	76	Caracol	Tikal	Star-war
9.6.10.14.15	25	Yaxchilan	Lacanha	Capture
9.9.13.4.4	42	Caracol	Naranjo	*Hubi*
9.9.14.3.5	42	Caracol	Naranjo	*Hubi*
9.9.18.16.3	42	Caracol	Naranjo	Star-war
9.10.3.2.12	42	Caracol	Naranjo	Star-war
9.11.1.16.3	153	Palenque	Site Q	Axe event
9.11.6.16.11	128	Palenque	Yaxchilan	?
9.11.11.9.17	51	Dos Pilas	Machaquila	Capture
9.11.17.18.19	111	Dos Pilas	Tikal	Star-war
9.12.0.8.3	111	Tikal	Dos Pilas	Star-war
9.12.5.10.1	105	Site Q	Tikal	Star-war
9.12.7.14.1	42	Naranjo	Caracol	Star-war
9.13.1.4.19	30	Naranjo	Ucanal	*Hubi*
9.13.2.16.0	40	Naranjo	Tikal	*Hubi*
9.13.3.7.18	105	Tikal	Site Q	*Hubi*
9.13.13.7.2	111	Dos Pilas	Tikal	Star-war
9.13.19.13.3	65	Tonina	Palenque	Star-war
9.14.17.15.11	25	Yaxchilan	Lacanha	Capture
9.15.4.6.4	24	Dos Pilas	Seibal	Star-war
9.15.6.14.6	47	Quirigua	Copan	Axe event
Pre-9.15.9.17.17	54	Aguateca	Cancuen	?
Pre-9.15.10.0.0	78	Machaquila	Motul de San Jose	?
9.15.12.2.2	30	Tikal	Yaxha	Star-war
9.15.12.11.13	36	Tikal	Motul de San Jose	Star-war
Ca. 9.16.0.0.0	87	Dos Pilas	Yaxchilan	?
Ca. 9.17.0.0.0	45	Aguateca	El Chorro	?
9.17.3.5.19	54	La Mar	Pomona	?
9.17.16.14.19	47	Piedras Negras	Pomona	Capture
9.18.3.9.12	47	Piedras Negras	Pomona	?
Pre-9.18.10.0.0	32	Caracol	Ucanal	Capture ?
Post-9.19.9.9.15	76	Caracol	Tikal	Axe event

[1] After A. Chase and D. Chase 1998a:19. Data derived from Grube (1994), Houston (1993), Houston and Mathews (1985), Jones and Satterthwaite (1982), Nahm (1994), Schele (1982, 1991a), Schele and Freidel (1990), and Schele and Mathews (1991).

sites in the southern lowlands, four major warfare-related hieroglyphs enjoyed widespread and fairly consistent usage over time and space (figure 10.1). Other glyphs have also been suggested as having war-related meanings, such as "shell kin" and "flint and shield" (Schele and Freidel 1990), but the interactions implied in texts that use such hieroglyphs do not appear to be of the same order as the four major event glyphs described here. For example, the flint-and-shield glyph

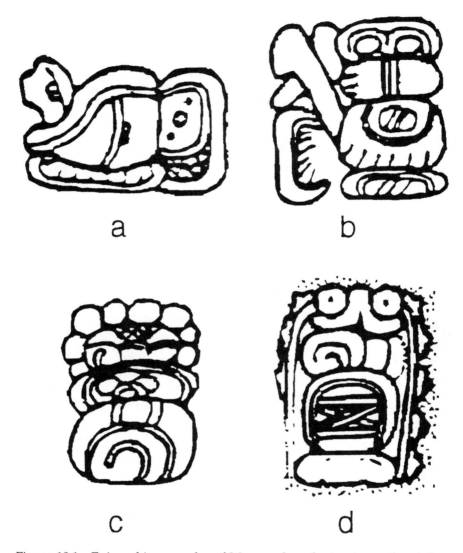

Figure 10.1   Epigraphic examples of Maya verbs referring to warfare (after A. Chase and D. Chase 1998a:20): (a) *chuc'ah*, ''capture'' (Proskouriakoff 1960:470); (b) *ch'ak*, ''decapitation'' (Schele and Freidel 1990:456, n. 17), or *batcaba* or *batelba*, ''to wield an axe'' or ''to do battle'' (Marcus 1992a:420); (c) *hubi* ''destruction'' (Grube 1994:103); (d) star-war (Schele 1982:99)

is often combined within texts with one of the war-related verbs, most likely indicating that the flint-and-shield glyph represents a particular object. The shell-kin glyphs that are particularly found at Naranjo (Schele and Freidel 1990:186–95) may not be involved as much in war events as in ritual burning events (Stuart 1998b). While other hieroglyphs and phrases may be related to aggression, the four most secure and consistent warfare-related hieroglyphs are *chuc'ah* (capture), *hubi* (destruction), *ch'ak* (axe), and shell-star (star-war) events. These distinct glyphic expressions surely represented different kinds of warfare events; however, their meanings also may have been contextually variable.

Chuc'ah, or "capture," is probably the least constant and most controversial kind of aggression mentioned in the hieroglyphic record. The act of capture is perhaps best represented on certain Yaxchilán lintels that combine both imagery and text to ensure meaning (cf. Marcus 1992a:419). Whether "capture" relates only to specific individuals or symbolically refers to towns, communities, and regions is a matter of current debate. The differences in opinion over this issue, however, have major ramifications on the interpretation of Maya warfare. If only specific individuals are named, then an argument can be made for elite ritual warfare with little impact on the overall population (cf. Freidel 1986a). However, if the portrayed individuals symbolically represent larger entities, then Maya warfare could be seen as involving territorial gain and tribute. For instance, it has been suggested that the Palenque ruler Kan-Xul (also now known as K'an-Hok'-Chitam) was captured and executed by Tonina (Schele and Freidel 1990:487). Kan-Xul is both named and portrayed on a Tonina carved monument. But did his capture have an impact on the general populace at Palenque? While Palenque's succession may have been altered, it is not known whether tribute was given by Palenque to Tonina as a result of this event or if there were any other local changes that would have affected the population at large. In another case, the hieroglyphs associated with a captive have been interpreted in two very different ways. On Naranjo Stela 24, Schele and Freidel (1990:188–89) suggest that the captive in the lower register, on whom the ruler stands, was an individual named "Kinichil-Cab" from the site of Ucanal. Marcus (1992a:414) alternatively reads the hieroglyphs associated with this captive as a nonpersonal name meaning "western land" and views the captive as an artistic symbol for captured territory. The implied difference between these two viewpoints, as it relates to the scale of the associated warfare, is striking. We suspect that both readings of *chuc'ah* may sometimes be appropriate and that the meaning is context dependent.

Hubi and *ch'ak* events clearly represent military endeavors. *Hubi* has been translated as "destruction" (Grube 1994) and appears to refer to the attainment of specific goals and objectives in warfare. For instance, an A.D. 695 event records Tikal's "destruction" of the "flint and shield" of Jaguar-Paw of Site Q. The use of this verb to indicate warfare between Caracol and Naranjo seems fairly well established (A. Chase and D. Chase 1998a; Schele and Freidel 1990), especially given the multiple records that exist at Caracol and Naranjo for specific *hubi* events. Yet *hubi* has also been taken to read "to come down" in accession contexts (Harris and Stearns 1997:48), and it is conceivable that the translation of this glyph may be modified in the future.

Ch'ak, or "axe," events have been interpreted both as "decapitation" (Schele and Freidel 1990:456, 487) and as important "battles" (Marcus 1992a:420). Recovered archaeological records that are relevant to the verification and assessment of *ch'ak* events are available from several sites. In all cases, an argument can be made that while *ch'ak* events were undoubtedly significant to the victors, they may not have greatly impacted the losers. Perhaps the best-known *ch'ak* event is the one carried out by Quirigua against Copán in the Late Classic (9.15.6.14.6; A.D. 738) with the resultant loss of the current Copán ruler 18-Rabbit and the installation of a new Copán king thirty-nine days later (9.15.6.16.5). As noted by Sharer (1978), this event appears to have had a major effect on Quirigua. The actual impact on Copán, however, is still a matter of debate (Fash 1991; Marcus 1992a; Webster 1989). A *ch'ak* event by Tikal against Caracol in A.D. 556 (recorded on Caracol Altar 21 and, to some extent, set up textually as a propaganda counterbalance for later antagonisms by Caracol against Tikal) was obviously offset six years later by a more conclusive shell-star event against Tikal (also recorded on Caracol Altar 21).

Of all epigraphically known warfare events, shell-star, or star-war, events are interpreted to be of the greatest consequence. They are thought by most epigraphers to represent the defeat of one site by another (Schele and Mathews 1991:246). Thus, epigraphic data suggest that one polity may interrupt the succession at another site, exert dominion over another polity, and/or, alternatively, break free in a war of independence (A. Chase and D. Chase 1998a; Marcus 1992a). We have argued elsewhere for the territorial impact of this kind of warfare (A. Chase and D. Chase 1998a; D. Chase and A. Chase 2000). Indeed, the substitution of the *caban,* or "earth," glyph in lieu of a specific emblem glyph as the center sign in the shell-star hieroglyph has been taken to indicate that this kind of warfare had a territorial dimension (Hammond 1991:277; Mathews 1985:321). Despite arguments to the contrary (Haviland 1994), it would seem that the star-war event against Tikal recorded on Caracol Altar 21 had devastating consequences at Tikal while positively impacting on Caracol (A. Chase 1991; A. Chase and D. Chase 1996a, 1996c; Jones 1991).

Hieroglyphic Representations of Warfare: Caracol

Two episodic periods of warfare may be found in Caracol's hieroglyphic record. The first covers a period of nearly 150 years and defines the site's early Late Classic history from roughly A.D. 550 to A.D. 700. The second period of warfare at Caracol may be inferred from the texts, iconography, and extant archaeological record that define the site's Terminal Classic era after A.D. 790.

Caracol Warfare A.D. 550–700

Initiating the first episode of widespread war at Caracol is a *ch'ak* event, most likely a battle (in our estimation) carried out by Tikal against Caracol in A.D. 556. This is followed in A.D. 562 by a full-blown star-war against Tikal. Even though recorded seventy years after the actual event, thus permitting some historical modification or correction (cf. Haviland 1994; Marcus 1992a:429–30; Webster 1993), this event left clear marks in the archaeological and iconographic records of both sites. That the war was consequential is indicated by the marked absence of hieroglyphic history from Tikal for over 120 years (A. Chase 1991) and by the fact that the Tikal settlement pattern underwent a major constriction after this date (Puleston 1974). In contrast, Caracol underwent a period of incredible growth (A. Chase and D. Chase 1989) and prosperity (A. Chase and D. Chase 1994a, 1996a, 1996b) while undertaking further warfare to maintain its hold on the eastern edge of the southern lowlands. Bound prisoners occur on four Caracol stelae (4, 5, 6, and 21) dating from A.D. 603 (9.8.10.0.0) to A.D. 702 (9.13.10.0.0). *Hubi,* or destruction, events are recorded by Caracol against Naranjo, Guatemala, twice, in A.D. 626 and once in A.D. 628. A star-war against Naranjo is recorded in A.D. 631 and again five years later. That the star-war event had a major impact on Naranjo is shown by the presence of hieroglyphic texts celebrating Caracol kings at

Naranjo itself. Naranjo is located exactly halfway between Tikal and Caracol (42 kilometers from each site). An application of military theory and the concept of marching distance (Hassig 1992b:85) have led to the suggestion that direct (as opposed to hegemonic) territorial control was possible for Maya sites within a 60-kilometer marching radius (A. Chase and D. Chase 1998a:17). Thus, we believe that Caracol, through its conquest of and incorporation of Naranjo, was able to capitalize on the A.D. 562 defeat of Tikal to at least temporarily control a larger territory. The flow of tribute from the central Petén to Caracol continued until at least A.D. 680, at which time texts suggest that Naranjo regained its independence from Caracol through a shell-star event. Reference to this event is found not at Naranjo but rather on a partial building facade at Caracol. That the text continues to extol Caracol successes after this event suggests that the A.D. 680 star-war was not the real end of the saga but rather the prelude to some other as-yet-unknown Caracol success after this date.

Caracol Warfare Post–A.D. 790

The second episode of warfare at Caracol was initiated sometime around A.D. 790 and is credited to Caracol ruler Hok Kauil by his descendants. Caracol Stela 11 indicates that Hok Kauil took a series of eight captives from neighboring sites. Like rulers from other sites (Stuart 1985:100), Hok Kauil may have claimed prisoners taken by others as his own. Two of these eight prisoners are shown on Caracol Altar 23, where both are credited to Tu-mu-ol (Chase et al. 1991; Grube 1994); another is shown on Caracol Stela 17, a posthumous monument to Hok Kauil in which a vision serpent is situated above the prisoner. It would appear to us that Hok Kauil (and his prowess in taking captives) was further lionized by his descendants to serve their political ends. Yet another set of paired and bound prisoners are portrayed on Caracol Altar 22 in a social context that is meant to demonstrate the importance of someone other than the Caracol ruler (Chase et al. 1991). Within an A.D. 820 text on Caracol Altar 12, a ch'ak event against k'ul mutul, most probably Tikal, is recorded (Grube 1994:97). An A.D. 835 text from Mountain Cow (Altar 1) contains a "he of 20 captives" expression (Stuart 1985:101). As Grube (1999) has noted, these constitute some of the latest textual (as opposed to iconographic) expressions of warfare known from the Maya epigraphic record.

From the epigraphy alone, it would appear that Caracol's two episodes of warfare are different. Most notable are distinctions in the hieroglyphs used, particularly the mention (and/or depiction) of captives. The first episode is concerned textually mainly with *hubi* (destruction), *ch'ak* (axe), and star-war events, while the second is marked predominantly by *ch'ak* (axe) and *chuc'ah* (capture) events. The first episode is comprised generally of specific activities that are contextually and internally consistent at Caracol as well as Naranjo. The second episode contains elements that are as yet not entirely clear-cut; captives are taken and alliances are made, but the full extent of relationships among individuals and sites is not immediately apparent. Thus, contextualizing the warfare statements within the archaeological record is important to any interpretation of these events, as such analyses can provide additional information on the similarities, differences, and realities of stated aggression.

Archaeological Interpretation of Maya Warfare

Most scholars would generally agree that the nature of Maya warfare changed over time. Innovations in both weapons and techniques of war are evident throughout Maya prehistory (Hassig 1992b:172). And the kind of warfare that was practiced may also have shifted (A. Chase and D. Chase 1992). Once thought to be primarily an elite-dominated raiding activity with little impact on day-to-day life or territorial control (Freidel 1986a; Schele and Mathews 1991:245–48), it is now apparent that Late Classic Maya warfare could be waged for territory (A. Chase and D. Chase 1996a, 1996b) and tribute (Stuart 1998c). Late Classic Maya warfare not only impacted many members and levels of Maya society (A. Chase 1992; A. Chase and D. Chase 1989, 1996c) but also involved ever larger warfare arenas (A. Chase and D. Chase 1992, 1998a) and political alliances (Martin and Grube 1995). Rather than being directly related to the agricultural cycle (Marcus 1992a:430–33) or to celestial events (Lounsbury 1982), it is also evident that Late Classic Maya warfare was a year-round occurrence (Nahm 1994) and a part of daily life.

Warfare also has become an increasingly popular topic for archaeological research. While many Maya research projects have encountered data relative to ancient Maya warfare, two recent projects have made warfare a major focus of research. These projects are the Petexbatun Regional Archaeological Project, focusing on the Guatemalan site of Dos Pilas (Demarest 1993, 1997b; Demarest et al. 1997; Houston

1993), and the Caracol Archaeological Project, focusing on its Belizean namesake (A. Chase and D. Chase 1987; D. Chase and A. Chase 1994). Both projects openly attempted to integrate hieroglyphic texts with archaeological data. The Petexbatun Project examined Maya warfare from the standpoint of a site that was both largely produced and destroyed by warfare. Dos Pilas appears to have rapidly expanded its polity in the Late Classic period (at least according to the epigraphy) and then suffered a relatively early and catastrophic decline through a siege and sacking shortly after A.D. 760 (at least according to the archaeology). Continued Classic period warfare resulted in a subsequent destabilization of this region despite the presence of Seibal, a Terminal Classic capital (A. Chase 1985; Willey 1990). The archaeological record demonstrates the influx of new populations to Seibal in both the ceramic and the burial data (Tourtellot 1990); the epigraphic interpretations associate this influx with Ucanal (Schele and Mathews 1998:179; Thompson 1970). Almost two decades of research at Caracol, Belize has also revealed a site whose Late Classic rise and decline was directly related to warfare. Epigraphic evidence of warfare events has been recorded at Caracol on stone monuments, stucco facades of buildings, and monuments at Naranjo. Archaeologically, Caracol appears to have sustained benefits from successful aggression throughout the Late Classic era, at least until its own epicenter was burned and presumably destroyed at the very end of the tenth century by unknown individuals. Caracol's elite utilized the spoils of war to integrate its huge population and to build and maintain a large primate city and polity (A. Chase and D. Chase 1989, 1996a, 1996b, 1998a; D. Chase and A. Chase 2000).

Despite the flurry of interest in Classic period war by Mayanists, warfare is extremely difficult to see in the archaeological record. There are any number of reasons for this. Warfare activities often leave little tangible archaeological residues (but see Ambrosino et al., chapter 7 in this volume; Brown and Garber, chapter 6 in this volume; Pagliaro et al., chapter 5 in this volume). Warfare may take place in vacant terrain. Other cultural activities may result in material manifestations that are very similar to those that would be expected to result from aggression, leading to problematic or nonconclusive interpretations of the archaeological record. Weapons and hunting items may not always be distinctive. Buildings may be burned, but the burning may be accidental or purposeful; Maya burning may as easily result from a purposeful reverential termination ritual (Pagliaro et al., chapter 5 in this volume) as from hostile aggression (Brown and Garber, chapter

6 in this volume). Artifacts found smashed on building floors likewise may be the result either of termination rituals or of rapid abandonments. Archaeological data are more often than not open to multiple interpretations with careful analysis of context providing the only potential resolution of meaning.

Notwithstanding the previously mentioned caveats, material remains of weapons and defensive systems have been recovered and reported throughout the Maya lowlands (A. Chase and D. Chase 1992; Repetto Tio 1985). While Caracol evinces no permanent fortifications, such as those noted for Dos Pilas (Demarest et al. 1997), Becán (Webster 1976a), and possibly Tikal (Puleston and Callender 1967), its archaeological record has yielded a multitude of artifactual materials that are suggestive of aggression, especially at the end of Caracol's epicentral occupation (ca. A.D. 900). Various kinds of remains are found on the floors of Caracol's buildings. Some of the artifacts, such as mace heads (found both on palace floors and in outlying residential areas at Caracol), are likely weapons based on their form. Other artifacts, such as bifacially worked points, are viewed as weapons primarily because of their archaeological context. Broken vessels on Caracol's floors (mostly epicentral palace but also in some outlying residential groups) are interpreted as the evidence of latest occupation rather than as the remains of termination rituals for a variety of reasons. They are generally found in residential as opposed to ritual areas, the recovered ceramics are predominantly residential rather than ritual debris, and the vessels are generally found unburned and broken in situ (or in localized areas) as opposed to being burnt and smashed over a large area. Importantly, the articulated bones of an unburied child on a palace floor also imply rapid abandonment and, presumably, aggressive activity. Where burning does occur, it appears as a layer over these remains, suggesting (at least to us) sacking as opposed to reverential termination. Carbon-14 dating of this burning indicates the possibility of a single event throughout most of Caracol's epicenter at about A.D. 895. Only Caracol Structure A6, the primary eastern temple in the A Group, appears to have been the locus of long-term use-related activity that included the deposition of cooking vessels and burning into the eleventh century.

Apart from the artifacts themselves, other archaeological data permit extrapolation about the potential impact of aggression. Among the data that can be considered are changing population numbers and/or the spatial location of a given population. Still other kinds of data permit the archaeological determination of changes in the degree of a population's relative prosperity and cohesion (for a general discussion of the potential effects of successful warfare, see Otterbein 1973). While population increases or large building efforts do not directly reflect warfare and aggression, if tightly dated, these data may be correlated with historically known warfare events to reveal the potential scope and/or the effects of warfare on a local population.

Archaeology and Warfare: Caracol

Because of Caracol's rich hieroglyphic history, warfare has been the focus of two distinctive programs of the Caracol Archaeological Project. During 1988 and 1989, under the sponsorship of the Harry Frank Guggenheim Foundation, Caracol Archaeological Project research focused on testing the settlement in the southeast sector of the site during and following the Tikal-Naranjo wars (A. Chase and D. Chase 1989). This sector of Caracol is located between and to the sides of the Conchita and Pajaro-Ramonal Causeways (see figure 10.2). Following initial survey of this approximately 2.5-square-kilometer area, investigations focused on ascertaining the time of occupation, construction activities, and the indications of prosperity and cohesion within the sample. Excavations were undertaken directly in residential groups, causeways, and fields. This program of work, in combination with Jaeger's (1987, 1991, 1994) dissertation research, resulted in the testing of thirty-seven groups. Overall, recovered remains were found to date from approximately 300 B.C. to post–A.D. 900.

From 1994 through 1996, with support from the National Science Foundation, investigations focused on comparing growth, cohesion, and prosperity for the two defined epigraphic episodes of Caracol aggression (A.D. 550–700 and post–A.D. 798) in a different part of the site. Investigations focused on the systematic survey and excavation of settlement in the northeast sector of the site, mostly located east of the Puchituk terminus (see figure 10.2). Four square kilometers of settlement were transit mapped as part of this program, with 2 square kilometers being intensively surveyed to include all agricultural terraces (A. Chase and D. Chase 1998b). Excavations were undertaken in thirty-three groups with additional tests being undertaken in causeways, fields, and "vacant terrain." A chronological sequence extending from approximately 600 B.C. to post–A.D. 900 was recovered.

Significant additional information has also been derived from other investigations undertaken at Caracol that were not specifically focused on war and aggression. The current Caracol settlement map

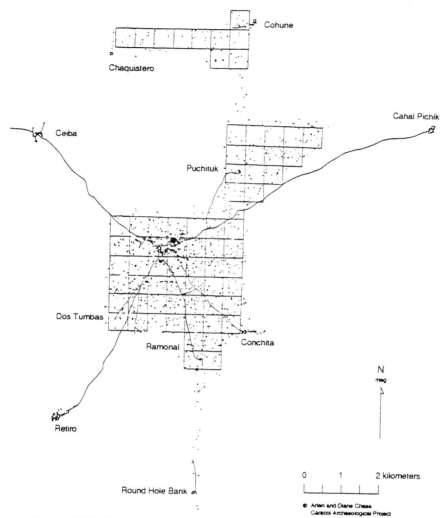

Figure 10.2   The mapped settlement of Caracol, Belize (as of 1998)

covers some 17 square kilometers out of an estimated 177 square kilometers and portrays approximately 1,000 residential groups representing almost 5,000 structures (figure 10.2). Within this area, other
excavations have focused intensively on epicentral remains, exposing
several palace complexes (A. Chase and D. Chase 2001), and have also
tested thirty-eight additional residential groups that were not

included in the warfare program samples (A. Chase and D. Chase 1987; D. Chase and A. Chase 1994). In combination with the warfare samples, this work has resulted in the recovery of approximately two dozen in situ floor deposits as well as over 250 burials (D. Chase 1998) and over 200 caches (D. Chase and A. Chase 1998). By combining hieroglyphic statements of warfare with such archaeological information, it becomes possible to assess the impact and manifestations of Maya warfare at Caracol.

Caracol Warfare A.D. 550–700

Investigations indicate substantial growth, prosperity, and cohesion at Caracol following the conclusion of the Tikal-Naranjo wars in A.D. 636. There was a building boom at Caracol that included all parts of the site. Population growth is indicated by a substantial increase in residential units following A.D. 550. Elsewhere, we (A. Chase and D. Chase 1989:15) have suggested that Caracol underwent 325 percent population growth in a span of 130 years. Monumental architecture was constructed in the site epicenter at the same time that major public works projects, such as the construction of causeways and agricultural terraces, were undertaken in the surrounding Caracol core. Information suggests that much of the special function architecture found in the Conchita, Ramonal, and Puchituk causeway termini also were constructed and utilized shortly following Caracol's wars with Tikal and Naranjo (A. Chase 1998; A. Chase and D. Chase 1989, 1994a). Thus, the causeways and termini themselves may have formed important mechanisms for site integration and boundary maintenance (cf. Kurjack and Andrews 1976:323) as well as have directly resulted from successful war.

Other recovered data additionally indicate increased prosperity and cohesion throughout all parts of the site during the beginning of the Late Classic period. This is especially seen in ritual activity as expressed in caching practices and the widespread interment of the dead in tombs (A. Chase 1992; A. Chase and D. Chase 1994b, 1996a; D. Chase and A. Chase 1998). Caracol's Late Classic burial pattern, with the site's notable emphasis on interments in specially prepared chambers containing multiple individuals (D. Chase and A. Chase 1996), is distinctive from the pattern found at excavated northern Petén sites (cf. W. Coe 1990:917; Smith 1950:88–91:table 6; Haviland et al. 1985:142) and at sites in northern Belize (Pendergast 1969, 1979, 1981:38–40, 1982, 1990). Mortuary patterns similar to those at Caracol have been noted for the settlement in the southeast Petén (Laporte 1994; Laporte et al. 1989), and it is probable that this area was under direct Caracol dominion during most of the Late Classic. The specially prepared domestic cache containers found throughout the core of Caracol (A. Chase 1994; A. Chase and D. Chase 1989, 1994b, 1996a, 1996c; D. Chase and A. Chase 1998; Jaeger 1991) are not, however, noted from this southeast Petén region, thus potentially suggesting the existence of hierarchical relationships within the broader Caracol polity (perhaps similar to those that existed in the ritual realm during the Postclassic period in the province of Chetumal [D. Chase 1986]). We have argued (A. Chase and D. Chase 1996a, 1996b) elsewhere that these distinctive burials and caches were part of an intentionally fostered Caracol identity and may well have been a key part of Caracol's successful internal organization during the Late Classic period.

Caracol Warfare Post–A.D. 798

From A.D. 702 to 798, there are no known hieroglyphic texts carved on stone monuments at Caracol. Archaeologically, however, this era is correlated with substantial continued prosperity (D. Chase and A. Chase 2000). After A.D. 798, while aggressive activity is again indicated in the monument texts, the archaeological manifestations of such warfare are different from those of the earlier episode. Specifically, there is uneven prosperity, no clear population growth, and decreased cohesion between central and outlying settlement. Substantial prosperity and monumental construction activity are evident only in the site epicenter. This is perhaps best seen in the massive rebuilding effort undertaken on the largest palace compound, Caana (A. Chase and D. Chase 1994a); its final phase dates to well after A.D. 800, and this massive complex is not abandoned until shortly before A.D. 900. Use-related debris left on the floors of epicentral palaces indicates substantial prosperity for at least the elite segment of Caracol's population (A. Chase and D. Chase 2001). Palace debris includes consistent groupings of artifactual items, including specific ceramic trade wares (including Pabellon Modeled-Carved, Trapiche Incised, Sahcaba Modeled-Carved, and Silho Orange but no slateware), jadeite, and carved bone. The palace diet continued to be good, as indicated by the extremely varied faunal remains that have been recovered (Giddens 1997) as well as through stable isotopic analysis of bone (D. Chase et al. 1998; A. Chase and D. Chase 2001). Indications that warfare may have been widespread during this era also are found both in the on-floor remains of weapons and in the presence of an unburied child on the floor of one of the palaces (A. Chase and D. Chase 1994a). In contrast to the successful epicenter, the population in the outlying settlement only infrequently buried their dead in elaborate tombs or participated in vestiges of the earlier pan-Caracol caching practices. Unless more formal palace-type buildings are present, the outlying inhabitants also do not appear to have been included in distributions of trade wares and specific types of ceramic vessels. These data suggest a Terminal Classic breakdown in Caracol's unique and carefully crafted Late Classic social and ritual identity, a breakdown that may well have played a key role in the site's ultimate demise.

Conclusions

The research at Caracol affirms the legitimacy of hieroglyphic texts relating to the site's successful warfare but also indicates the need to use archaeological information as part of a critical methodology to test the validity and significance of historic statements. The combined archaeological and historic information indicate both the reality and the variability in Maya warfare. Maya warfare cannot be considered as a single monolithic activity. It was not merely comprised of insignificant raiding activity, as it has sometimes been portrayed (Freidel 1986a; Webster 1993). Different levels of aggression are indicated within Maya hieroglyphic texts, and it is logical to assume that more than one kind of warfare activity was practiced during the Classic period. At least in the case of Caracol, shell-star warfare resulted in the physical incorporation of Naranjo into the Caracol polity. This is amply attested to in the hieroglyphic records and in the physical presence of stone monuments celebrating Caracol's ruling dynasty at the site of Naranjo itself. Thus, Caracol's warfare during the early part of the Late Classic had a manifest territorial aspect. This successful warfare also materially benefited a large segment of Caracol's residents; it may be credited with the extension of what is normally an elite ritual realm into most residential groups at the site. These combined factors indicate that Maya warfare could be both large scale and regional in nature. This finding, in turn, has implications for how the Maya world was organized, especially as it brings the Maya into line with general military theory involving such considerations as marching distance and the maintenance of territory (A. Chase and D. Chase 1998a; D. Chase and A. Chase 2000).

We have previously used archaeological data, ethnohistorical inference, hieroglyphic statements of aggression, warfare distance, and military theory to argue that Maya warfare could be broken into wars between primary centers and wars for border control (A. Chase and D. Chase 1998a). Border wars between primary and secondary centers that are recorded as formal star-wars had an average distance of 36 kilometers between the two antagonistic centers. In contrast, the distance between primary centers who warred with each other averaged 96.5 kilometers. Both of these distances are in accord with military theory concerning marching distance (Hassig 1992a) and suggest that Maya polities could reasonably maintain physical and territorial borders to a radius of 60 kilometers, which translates into the distance that could be effectively marched by an army in three days. The direct territorial control implied by effective marching distance, in turn, has implications for the average size of Classic Maya polities. Following the logic of this military theory, polities that were dominated by primate centers (such as Caracol) could approach a spatial size of approximately 11,300 square kilometers. Larger-size polities could have been accommodated but likely would have been correlated with hegemonic control, more like that undertaken by the later Aztecs.

Marcus (1992a:360) has stressed that Maya epigraphic texts contain selective propaganda and self-serving history and that such records should not be accepted on face value alone. Archaeological data from Caracol indicate that the site's epigraphic record of aggression in the early part of the Late Classic period is strongly correlated with stunning growth, site cohesion, and great prosperity throughout all social levels. These are all expected outcomes of successful warfare. However, relatively similar hieroglyphic and iconographic expressions may have dissimilar outcomes. Although the epigraphy and imagery would lead one to conclude that Caracol enjoyed a similar success in war at the close of the Classic period, the archaeological record indicates a far different situation. And a closer examination of the Terminal Classic hieroglyphic records finds only *chuc'ah* and *ch'ak* events with a complete lack of *hubi* and shell-star events. Thus, while the results of some forms of successful warfare are amply reflected in Terminal Classic imagery at Caracol (not only on monuments but also on molded-carved ceramics), the general Caracol populace does not appear to have benefited from warfare in the same way that it did earlier. Prosperity is evident only among the site's latest epicentral elite and not at all materially evident among the site's general populace. Thus, Caracol's cultural contexts help interpret and amplify differences that are apparent in the epigraphic statements. *Hubi* and shell-star warfare impacted the site as a whole, while *ch'ak* and *chuc'ah* events appear to have impacted mainly the elite sector of Caracol.

In summary, warfare played a significant role in the waxing and waning of individual sites and in regional Maya political history. As indicated in the Caracol data, increased aggression appears to be a factor in transitional eras of Maya history, especially those that have been labeled the "hiatus" and the "collapse." While epigraphy permitted initial insight into Maya warfare and political relations, the diverse and variable nature of the recorded events (their impacts and their broader relationships) can be fully understood and explored only through the archaeological contextualization of the epigraphic history.

Note

An earlier version of this chapter, titled "Settlement Patterns, Warfare, and Hieroglyphic History at Caracol, Belize," was presented at the ninety-seventh annual meeting of the American Anthropological Association in Philadelphia in December 1998. The authors wish to thank George Cowgill, an anonymous reviewer, and the two editors for comments on an interim version of the chapter. The research on which this chapter is based is indebted to the University of Central Florida and the Belize Department of Archaeology. Besides the government of Belize, the United States National Science Foundation (Grants BNS-8619996, SBR-9311773, and SBR-9708637), the United States Agency for International Development, and private donations to the UCF Foundation, Inc., the Caracol Archaeological Project has been supported by the Harry Frank Guggenheim Foundation, the Miami Institute of Maya Studies, the Dart Foundation, the Foundation for the Advancement of Mesoamerican Studies, Inc., the J. I. Kislak Foundation, the Ahau Foundation, and the Stans Foundation.

Chapter Eleven

Early Classic Maya Conquest in Words and Deeds

David A. Freidel, Barbara MacLeod, and Charles K. Suhler

The Fog of War:
Epistemology and Context

The fog of war has descended on ancient Maya civilization. Having moved successfully into the arena of warfare through the urging of articulate exponents like Webster (1977, 2000) and prophetic fieldworkers like Rands (1973), we now encounter patterns in evidence—archaeological, epigraphic, and iconographic—subject to a bewildering array of contested interpretations. This is not a bad thing, for eventually when the fog lifts, the field will be a more certain place than our intellectual forebears could have ever imagined. But it makes virtually every report from the front at this time subject to dramatic reinterpretation. In light of the presently ephemeral nature of conclusions about Maya warfare and its consequences, we can still provide some discussion of how those conclusions are being derived from evidence that might prove helpful in anticipating where such conclusions may lead.

The most volatile material is, in our view, the epigraphic. Ironically, the process of decipherment is generating new readings because of the exceptional insight of the epigraphers and the power of the methods they collectively employ. It is hard for us to gauge such fundamental matters as the reliability of the texts as chronicle as opposed to disinformative propaganda (Marcus 1992a) when the first-order substance of the texts continues to change. Nevertheless, we are confident that the direction of decipherment of texts is toward more clarity and that the texts that declare history will be proven to contain important and independently verifiable discussions of actual events (Houston 2000). That independent testing of textual statements will have to come from archaeological contexts. Concomitantly, archaeological interpretations will necessarily benefit from information and insight derived from the texts. The conjunctive approach (Fash and Sharer 1991) in Maya studies is no doubt perplexing and frustrating as the epistemological uncertainties of two perspectives are compounded, but it is the productive way to proceed.

The primary issue at hand is conquest warfare in Classic lowland Maya civilization and, in particular, conquest initiated by foreign invaders. How can episodes of conquest be identified in the archaeological, epigraphic, and iconographic records? Once identified, how can they be analyzed both for historical information and for purposes of anthropological comparison? These are not new issues. Sabloff and Willey (1967) addressed them squarely in the context of the archaeology at Seibal on the Pasión River in Petén, Guatemala. They argued that non-Classic Maya peoples invaded the lowlands and precipitated the ninth-century collapse (see also Graham 1990:6). In this chapter, we compare two cases of Early Classic conquest warfare in the Maya lowlands: Tikal, Guatemala, where both epigraphy and archaeology inform us of political struggle and usurpation, and Yaxuná, Yucatán, where textual evidence is absent.

Conquest in Texts and Contexts

At the 1998 Maya Glyph Workshop meetings in Austin, Texas, the teams of Grube and Martin (1998) and Stuart (1999) offered epigraphic arguments that Teotihuacan had sponsored a conquest of Tikal under the auspices of a lord named Siyah K'ak', or Smoking Frog, in A.D. 378. Grube and Martin also made allusions to the mutilation of Early Classic period carved stone monuments at Tikal, actions that may have accompanied such a conquest. These new inferences from ancient Maya texts provide fresh incentives to reconsider Coggins's (1976) original proposal, following the thought of Proskouriakoff, to the effect that Mexican foreigners placed an interloper named Yax Nuun Ain, or Curl-Snout, on the throne of Tikal following the death of the Tikal king Toh Chak Ich'ak, or Great-Jaguar-Paw, on this date. Mathews (1985) subsequently proposed that as Siyah K'ak' occurred on Stela 5 at Uaxactún with the Tikal emblem glyph, he must have been an *ajaw* of Tikal, then dominant at Uaxactún. He suggested that either marriage between Tikal and Uaxactún or conquest of the latter by the former generated such a circumstance. Schele and Freidel (1990) pursued the conquest hypothesis and elaborated it, agreeing with Mathews's general premise that the royal line of Tikal remained intact through the period in question. Laporte and Fialko (1990) proposed internal factional dispute between rival Tikal lineages, one represented by Siyah-K'ak' and the other by Toh-Chak-Ich'ak, as a way of looking at the relevant archaeological evidence generated by the Proyecto Nacionale Tikal during the 1980s. More generally, these latest arguments concerning Maya words by Grube, Martin, and Stuart spur us to continue to refine our views about Maya deeds as seen in the archaeological patterns of conquest and political usurpation. Whether outsiders or leaders of internal factions, what might such usurpers leave in the stratigraphic record of Maya urban centers? Is it possible to distinguish internal from external takeovers in Classic Maya contexts?

Before proceeding to analyze some problematic evidence that illustrates both the potential and the challenges of determining such military and political dynamics, it is worth suggesting some points on which consensus seems to be emerging. The bold and productive core of Coggins's thesis on Tikal was the idea that outsiders could be interjected into the royal succession without destroying the principle of legitimacy in rule. That idea, generally supported by archaeologists working on the Tikal data, has been reinforced in several specific instances, including the succession through women at Palenque and the restarting of the dynasty of Naranjo by a woman of Dos Pilas and the establishment by Siyah K'ak' of a conquerors line at Uaxactún (for reviews of these cases, see Schele and Freidel 1990). In the case of Tikal in particular, then, the numbered succession reckoned from the founder of the dynasty, Yax Eb Xok, continues unabated through several proposed breaks in the line. In our view, the implication of such reckoning of succession is that while the norm seems to have been that a male would succeed from a male of the ascending generation, usually his father, the critical criterion was actually enactment of the required rituals of accession (Schele and Freidel 1990). Once a would-be king had carried out such rituals, he or she was in the dynastic succession as an irreversible fact of subsequent history. Such a conclusion is a source of both doubt and opportunity. It is a source of doubt because it means that a numbered succession is no ready guide to blood relations between the dynasts, any of which might turn out to be an interloper. It is a source of opportunity because it implies that all succession events were, in principle, elaborate and materially substantial to declare the legitimacy of the new dynast. Close examination of the archaeological data surrounding dynastic succession events might provide valuable clues as to the peaceful or hostile nature of a given succession. As we note in this chapter, this kind of examination can raise as many questions as it answers. However, the general consensus that dynastic "Holy Lordship" was permeable is a major advance. Schele and Freidel (1990) postulated that conquest warfare in southern lowland civilization could not lead to lasting imperial consolidation because local nobilities would regard the imposition of usurpers on their thrones as an ideological and religious heresy and affront to the prior royal ancestors. Evidently, local nobilities were quite capable of acknowledging usurpers if circumstances warranted or demanded it.

Such political intricacies have bearing on the organization and scale of Maya polities. Martin and Grube (1995) have outlined an impressive and persuasive case of long-term struggle to forge "superstates" in the Classic southern lowlands. We prefer the term "empire." For all the difficulties of employing that term, it is the proper comparative category when looking at the Maya relative to other ancient civilizations. The Maya evidently failed to forge empire for reasons other than local nobility's stubborn adherence to local kings. Identifying and documenting the actual takeover events in the archaeological record are key tasks if we are ever to figure out what actually blocked the evolution of Maya empire in the southern lowlands.

The Decapitated King

Part of Grube and Martin's argument for a Teotihuacan takeover, as presented in oral arguments at the 1998 workshop in Austin, refers to a patterned and deliberate destruction of carved stone monuments from the reign of Great-Jaguar-Paw. This includes a decapitated sculpture in the round of a seated man (Hombre de Tikal) found by the Proyecto Nacional Tikal (PNT) in Structure 3D-43 of Group H (Fahsen

1988) and halved Stela 39 discovered by the PNT in excavations in Structure 5D-86–7, the central temple of the eastern range of the Lost World pyramid group.

We will deal first with the Hombre de Tikal sculpture (figure 11.1). This is a seated and realistic sculpture-in-the-round of a middle-aged and rather rotund man. The sculpture has Great-Jaguar-Paw's name, Toh Chak Ich'ak, inscribed on his left shoulder. It has an inscription written on the back in a different style and with slight differences in spelling conventions (Marc Zender, personal communication, 2000). There are two possible explanations for the two writing styles. They were either carved by two artists at different times, or they were carved by two artists working on the sculpture at the same time, a practice attested in later Classic Maya sculpture (Coe and Stone 2001). In light of known examples of Tikal kings wearing their names as insignia, for example Sian-Kan-K'awil's crown on Stela 31 (figure 11.2), this sculpture might well have been a portrait of King Toh Chak Ich'ak commissioned by that king or his family. Subsequently, the sculpture would have been inscribed on its back during the reign of the king who succeeded Toh Chak Ich'ak, King Nuun Yax Ain. Alternatively, the sculpture may have been commissioned as a portrait of his predecessor by King Nuun Yax Ain, with two artists inscribing the back and the name of his predecessor on the shoulder.

The sculpture was headless when found. Grube and Martin have suggested, in oral discussions at the Maya meetings in Austin, that this portrait was ritually killed at the time of a Teotihuacan conquest

Figure 11.1   Hombre de Tikal

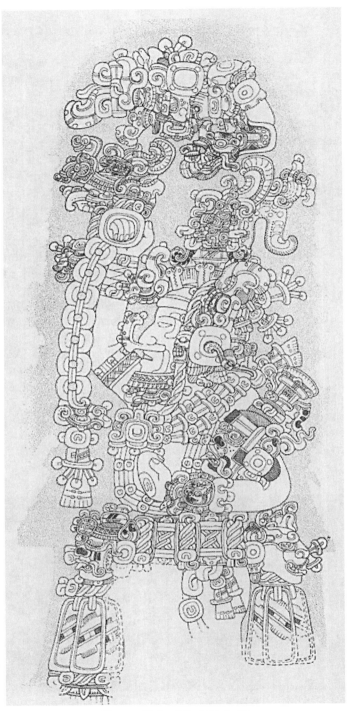

Figure 11.2 Tikal Stela 31

of Tikal. While we quite agree that the sculpture was ritually killed, we see evidence for a complicated and magical manipulation of the portrait that might have been part of the hostile dynastic succession by Nuun Yax Ain over Toh Chak Ich'ak. The text inscribed on the back of the image remains incompletely deciphered. It does, however, refer to Nuun Yax Ain, Curl-Snout, as king of Tikal and as a major protagonist in the events transpiring late in his reign (indeed just before his untimely death) dedicating the sculpture and perhaps bringing the image to life (Stanley Guenter, personal communication, 1999, 2000). Intriguingly, the back text is, like the sculpture itself, desecrated. Someone drilled a large jagged hole through it, ending in a deep, round socket in the back of the figure. If the desecrated Hombre de Tikal sculpture were laid prone (the typical pose for a Maya elite captive), the drilled hole would be suitable for insertion of the wooden shaft of a battle standard. The stone effigy of such a wooden standard with a feathered shield on the top was discovered in Early Classic context at Tikal in Group 6C-XVI (Laporte and Fialko 1990, 1995). We would suggest that even after Nuun Yax Ain and his allies took the Tikal throne from Toh Chak Ich'ak, he carried out a series of magical acts designed to legitimize his insertion in the dynastic succession. Whether or not Nuun Yax Ain was present at the time of his predecessor's death and was able to manipulate the actual body of the defeated king is an open matter, although this is implied in the text of Stela 31. We will return to this issue in regard to Stela 39. Houston and Stuart (1998) point out the intimate spiritual relationship between kings and their portraits. The key to understanding the Hombre de Tikal as an artifact is the sequence of events: carving the portrait, inscribing the name of the portrayed, inscribing the back with the name of the enemy and successor of the portrayed, the drilling of the back, and the decapitating of the portrait.

The Hombre de Tikal was discovered in the course of axial tunneling excavation in the primary pyramid of Group H, north of the main center at Tikal, under the direction of archaeologist Jorge Mario de Leon of the PNT. This pyramid faces south toward the Maler Causeway, and that causeway, along with the Maudslay Causeway, was constructed in the Late Classic, probably in the reign of King Yik'in Chan K'awil, to make Group H the apex of a grand sacred triangle encompassing the center of Tikal. Evidently, the Hombre de Tikal sculpture was interred in the passageway of an elaborate tomb. Should this prove to be the case, the sacrificed portrait of Toh Chak Ich'ak may have been used once again as a sacrifice in conjunction with the burial of a member of the Late Classic royal family. Yik'in Chan K'awil, like his father Hasaw Chan K'awil, was interested in making allusions to his connections with the family of Nuun Yax Ain and his son Siyan Chan K'awil. If the tomb was Late Classic, manipulation of this image in particular might have reminded Yik'in Chan K'awil's contemporaries of the legitimacy of his descent from those Early Classic kings who had magically usurped power from Toh Chak Ich'ak and entered into the succession of Yax Eb Xok. If the tomb was Early Classic, then manipulation of the image would have been part of the assertion of legitimacy of Nuun Yax Ain's descendants.

While the precise events on the Hombre de Tikal remain to be elucidated, there is the prospect that the dedication rituals were designed to bring the sculpture to life at the behest of Nuun Yax Ain and other protagonists. That act would certainly be appropriate if the "sacrifice" of the image were designed as a reiteration of an original sacrifice of Toh Chak Ich'ak that was ritually required to place Nuun Yax Ain in the successor line of the dynastic found of Tikal, Yax Eb Xok. The necessity of such a reiteration, we suggest, was the problematic nature of the succession between Nuun Yax Ain and his son Siyan Chan K'awil. Just what happened between the death of Nuun Yax Ain and the accession of Siyan Chan K'awil is not clear, although there is the prospect that an adult regent, Siyah Chan Kinich, ruled for Siyan Chan K'awil as a minor child until the accession of this son some years after the death of his father (Stanley Guenter, personal communication, 2000). Coming at the beginning of this interregnum and in the context of a father–son transfer following a usurpation of the throne, the magical second sacrifice of Toh Chak Ich'ak may have served to remind the Tikal nobility of the legitimate authority of Nuun Yax Ain resulting from his appropriate rituals of accession and also to reinforce the legitimacy of his heir, Siyan Chan K'awil.

The Murdered Scion

Stela 39 is an equally interesting and complicated case of monument desecration relevant to the proposed conquest of Tikal by Teotihuacanos and their Tikal allies (figure 11.3). The stela fragment portrays a king stepping on a bound sacrificial victim. The king is carrying a decapitator blade in the shape of a claw, which is the name insignia of King Toh Chak Ich'ak. The stela was broken in half, and the top half is missing, so that like the Hombre de Tikal the image was decapitated. Excavated by the Proyecto Nacionale de Tikal and described and ana-

Figure 11.3   Tikal Stela 39

lyzed by Laporte and Fialko (1990, 1995) as burnt and broken, the stela fragment is illustrated by them as being found inside a masonry temple, Structure 5D-86. Apparently, it was found located on the east–west axis, inside of room 3 of the last construction phase of the temple, which was built in the Early Classic period, at the end of Manik II or beginning of Manik III. This, incidentally, is the period when King Toh Chak Ich'ak reigned.

Stela 39 was found placed on end, off the main axis, on or above the access step between rooms 2 and 3 (Ayala Falcón 1987). The stela's stratigraphic relation to the earlier building, Structure 5D-86–6, which contained desecrated stucco images of captives along the battered lower portion of the back wall of the front room, is only after the fact. Structure 5D-86–6 was raised in conjunction with the construction of a masonry tomb chamber on the stairway centerline to the west. The PNT found that this vaulted tomb contained the remains of a middle-aged man with fragments of a mosaic greenstone mask pectoral, a chest bead carved as a mat symbol, and very elaborate pottery vessels. Laporte and Fialko regard this interment as royal, and a murdered royal at that (the center section of the otherwise articulated body was missing or disturbed). They propose that the individual in question is portrayed on Stela 39. While the stratigraphic associations are indirect, it is clear that the stela, dated textually to A.D. 376, is roughly coeval with the ceramics in the tomb below, which are Manik II in style (Laporte and Fialko [1990, 1995] date the advent of Manik IIIa to A.D. 378). In the flanking buildings of this complex, coeval tombs contained the remains of men, women, and children, a pattern that bears comparison to that found in Early Classic Yaxuná as discussed later in this chapter. The stela fragment had smashed Etznab period (Terminal Classic) ceramics up against it. It seems most unlikely, however, that the fragment was reset in that period. The temple witnessed no further modification on the main western side in Late Classic times. We infer that the fragment was reset in later Early or Middle Classic times.

As did Laporte and Fialko (1990, 1995) and Schele and Freidel (1990), Grube and Martin identified the protagonist portrayed on Stela 39 as Great-Jaguar-Paw, Toh-Chak-Ich'ak. For this reason, Grube and Martin reasoned at the 1998 Maya meetings in Austin that the destruction of the stela and the interment of the murdered individual, perhaps the king himself, again registered the conquest of Tikal in the time of that king. The reasoning here, iconographically, is that the individual is carrying his name glyph as a sacrificial axe. Epigraphically, the argument for Toh-Chak-Ich'ak as the protagonist is not as neat, and we suggest an alternative in which a man named Skull-Feathers is the patron of the stela. In the last analysis, our alternative reading does not substantially affect the general trend of events proposed by Grube and Martin, but it does point to the kinds of complex sequencing that magical manipulation of royal portraits likely entailed.

A reading that includes an informed speculation of the upper, broken part will provide a sense of the whole. Opening the text, we would propose a date or Initial Series if the missing portion occupied as much space as the preserved remainder. Then we would expect a lost lengthy first clause including a major event, such as heir designation with, we postulate, Skull-Feathers as subject. Then we would see a second clause, a father's parentage statement, "his person/self was the man's-son of Father (*bah-ih y-une*, Toh-Chak-Ich'ak)." Here we presume the lost verb to have been the rare *bah-ih*, "became the self or image," as opposed to *u-bah*, "was the self/image." The preserved text begins in the middle of this second clause of the text. The third clause is complete, and it is the mother's statement, which shows *bah-ih* unequivocally. The Maya liked to create parallel couplets, which is why we reconstruct *bah-ih* in the father's clause.[1] This third clause then reads "his person/self was the cherished one of mother" (*bah-ih u-huntan*, Na'Balam Yaxun). The fourth clause is dedicatory: "rose his creation-darkness Skull-Feathers the son" (*t'abay u-ch'ab y'ak'abil* "Skull-Feathers" *p'enal*).[2] The fifth clause is "he closed (*u-tsutsuw*) the seventeenth *k'atun*." The sixth clause is "it happened at the Tikal sky-seat" (*uhti mut ka'an-kun*). The seventh and final clause is "it was his seat" (*u-kun*). There is deliberate restatement here, first in saying "Skull-Feathers the son" (*p'enal*), then in saying "it was his seat."

The unusual use of *t'abay* with *ch'ab-ak'ab* makes sense in light of this identification of Skull-Feathers as the patron of the stela. This verb has no agent grammatically; it is mediopassive (as in "the door closes"), in which we presume some unstated agency. Similarly, *t'abay* cannot take an object; it is not transitive, and "*u-ch'ab y-ak'abil*," "his creation his darkness," is hence the grammatical subject of the verb. These possessive pronouns *u-* and *y-* refer to Skull-Feathers, and the whole can be parsed as "this is the creation-darkness of Skull-Feathers, the son, which rose." What is such a "creation-darkness"? On lintels at Yaxchilán, we see such active and subjective representations in the vision serpents that arise from the bowls of smoldering bloody rope. But we understand why colleagues might discern some parental relationship in this complicated clause, for *ch'ab-ak'ab* is not just any sacrifice but also one that recalls the ancestors and underscores lineage charter. Thus, it is intimately linked with the parentage statement, and, in some way we do not yet understand, they must ultimately have converging meanings. In sum, we identify Stela 39 not as the monument of Toh-Chak-Ich'ak, the son of a man dubbed Skull-Feathers, but rather as a monument dedicated by Skull-Feathers, a son of Toh-Chak-Ich'ak. Again, Laporte and Fialko point out the correlation of the associated ceramics in PNT-019, which are exclusively Manik II, and this Katun 17 period–ending monument.

Martin and Grube (2000) have persuasively argued that Toh Chak Ich'ak was the fourteenth successor of Yax Eb Xok and that his father was King Skull-Feathers, the thirteenth successor. On the face of it, this would seem to contradict the reading we offer for Stela 39. However, another clear feature of the Tikal dynasty outlined by Martin and Grube (2000) is the repeated use of personal names in the succession. We would suggest that the individual portrayed on Stela 39 is not Toh Chak Ich'ak or his father Skull-Feathers but rather another Skull-Feathers, his son and heir, namesake of his grandfather. In order to discourage the return to power of the nobility who supported Toh Chak Ich'ak, the faction supporting Nuun Yax Ain would have needed to kill and magically destroy his heir as well.

The next question is, Who is in the tomb, PNT-019, below the broken stela reset over it? First, PNT 019 was placed on the centerline in a room of Structure 5D-86–7, the final phase of construction on this building. The adjacent structures on the shared platform, Structures 5D-84 and 5D-88, had slab-topped cyst tombs built into their centerlines in the final Early Classic phases of construction, contemporaneous with the tomb built into 5D-86–6. Each tomb housed the remains of one person. They contained the remains of a middle-aged male, a middle-aged female, two young male adults, a female adolescent, and an infant (Salas and Pijoan 1982, cited in Laporte and Fialko 1990). All these tombs contained rich offerings of ornate ceramics dating to Manik II times and exotic materials including, in the case of PNT 019, the previously described fragmentary greenstone mosaic face mask incised with *kin* and *akbal* glyphs such as appear on the legs of the protagonist of Stela 39.

Laporte and Fialko (1990:45) proposed that the other people were relatives of the deceased individual in PNT 019, possibly sacrificed, and that the central man was Great-Jaguar-Paw. We have given epigraphic reasons for thinking that the protagonist of Stela 39 is Skull-Feathers II. Iconographically, the fact that the man portrayed carries an axe in the form of Great-Jaguar-Paw's name is no more a clue to his own name than is the crown marked "Spear-Thrower-Owl" lofted by Sian-Ka'an-K'awil on Stela 31 at Tikal. Tikal kings had a penchant for identifying with ancestors through such insignias. We do think that it is possible to postulate that the man in PNT-019 is a murdered royal individual accompanied by close kin, quite possibly Skull-Feathers II, and that the pattern here represents an important change in government at Tikal. We think that Skull-Feathers II was the heir of Great-Jaguar-Paw and that Nuun Yax Ain wrested the throne from him before he could enter the line and after the death of his father. Was this the act of conquerors from outside the community, as proposed by Stuart, Grube, and Martin? Or was it an "inside" job? In our view, it was probably accomplished by a coordinated effort of local Tikal nobility in league with Teotihuacanos and their allies at Kaminaljuyú. Moreover, we think that the factional struggles involving Teotihuacanos and their allies at Tikal have considerable time depth before the takeover by Nuun Yax Ain. There are several archaeological contexts relevant to this history at Tikal. We will attempt to briefly review one of them, an elite residential compound, Group 6D-V, that apparently housed members of the Teotihuacan-Tikal noble faction during the critical period of the Early Classic.

The Early Fall and Rise of the Teotihuacan Faction at Tikal: Group 6D-V

Group 6D-V is an elite residence complex located south of the main ceremonial center of Tikal, 300 meters northeast of the more famous Group 6C-XVI. Laporte and his colleagues discovered two highland-style seated burials, each covered by a small platform resembling an altar. These burials, akin to seated burials at Kaminaljuyú in Teotihuacan-affiliated contexts, were clearly early in the group's history. The tombs were placed in what would traditionally be considered Manik II chronological times on the basis of most ceramics in them. However, they also contained Manik III materials, which is to say, Teotihuacan-style diagnostics. These burials look early in the Early Classic period. Burial PNT-168 was set within a void, 1.2 meters deep by 1 meter in diameter, placed into the fill of the group's plaza. As mentioned, the tomb was covered by a small rectangular platform that was made of packed earth. It was covered by stucco, and the resulting platform had round corners. This would be appropriate for a revered ancestor to the household. The individual was seated and facing east. The entrance to the tomb was covered by four tabular limestone blocks. Burial goods consisted of two vessels (an Aguila pedestal bowl and a Balanza bowl), a shell pectoral, and three jade beads (Laporte et al. 1992:41). The second tomb, Burial PNT-177, also had Manik IIIa ceramics in it. It was placed within a large compound-silhouette vessel that was within a *chultun* (underground storage chamber) 1.3 meters deep by 1.1 meters in diameter. The burial was covered by a small platform located under Structure 6D-04 on the south side of the plaza. Again, like Burial 168, this was a primary burial of a seated individual, again facing east. One tooth was filed of the Type 5B (Romero 1986), and another tooth had a circular inlay (possibly pyrite). There were seven ceramic vessels (two Aguila tripod cylinders, an Aguila tripod bowl, an Aguila anular-base bowl, a Lucha Incised basin [bowl], a Caldero Buff basal flange bowl, and a Caldero Buff basal flange tripod with hollow, almost mammiform supports). Laporte et al. (1992:30–68) remarked on the presence of the Teotihuacan-affiliated cylinder tripods in a burial otherwise dateable to Manik II times (before the time of Nuun Yax Ain). All together, these tombs suggest that the group was founded in Manik II times, well before the takeover by Nuun Yax Ain, and was founded by nobles who were affiliated with Teotihuacan, if not from that city.

While this household apparently was founded by individuals affiliated with Teotihuacan, it was eventually destroyed by enemies. The destruction debris from the group's violent termination was discovered as a massive problematic deposit behind the principal structure of the group, 6D-20, a C-shaped structure. The sequence of events we infer is that the group was first sacked and littered with debris, then the debris was cleaned up, dumped behind the main building, and sealed in by people refurbishing the group. Designated DP-21, this deposit encompassed an area of thirty-four meters north/south by seventeen meters east/west and in places reached bedrock. The deposit was sealed by a stucco floor preserved in areas, indicating that construction continued after its creation; we would identify this construction as a healing event that followed the cleanup of the desecration debris. The reoccupation suggests that the deposit was created and covered during Manik III late Early Classic times, for this group shows little, if any, Ik ceramic material indicative of Middle Classic period occupation.

Problematic Deposit 21 contained 186,547 sherds (including 812 incensario fragments and 220 miniature vessel fragments), 7,154 lithics, almost 300 pieces of worked shell, and 600 bone artifacts. It also contained two primary human interments and the scattered remains of seventeen other individuals as well as numerous animal bones and unworked shell pieces. While the two primary interments might suggest that this was a burial place, the scattered remains of the other individuals suggests that victims of human sacrifice or desecrated primary burials were in the debris. Among the scattered human remains were some instruments manufactured from human bone, polishers or burnishers, which employed cranial parts, such as foreheads and parietals. Also included were punches made from human long bones. The use of human bone in this fashion supports the argument for sacrifice and dismemberment. The deposit was also rich with painted sherd material and precious items, such as clay figurines, coral, pearls, and spondylus, as well as shell pendants, beads, plaques, and buttons. Animal remains included deer, peccary, turtle, rodents, and birds. Also found were objects of pyrite, mica, and quartz crystal. Within the fragmented objects were ceramic sherds with complex decorations, such as panels with deities, zoomorphic figures, and glyphic elements. Historically, this is a vital context, for it contained an incised sherd with the name Lady Une Balam, Tikal *Ajaw*. Martin and Grube (2000) identify this Lady Une Balam as either the thirteenth successor of the Tikal dynasty or the wife and consort of a thirteenth successor who was not named in later times.

Logically, the people who smashed the vessel naming Lady Une Balam were her enemies. Lady Une Balam was succeeded in the dynastic line by Skull-Feathers I, the fourteenth successor and the father of Toh Chak Ich'ak. Toh Chak Ich'ak, the fifteenth successor, was mortally wounded, as recounted on Stela 31, and replaced in turn by Nuun Yax Ain, the sixteenth successor. This sketch of the epigraphic history has, we suggest, a parallel in the archaeology of this elite residence complex. We would hypothesize that Lady Une Balam was associated with an existing faction of Tikal nobility allied with elite from Teotihuacan and Kaminaljuyú who were maintaining residences at Tikal such as Group D-6V. The founders of this group were buried as Teotihuacanos like those buried at Kaminaljuyú. When Lady Une Balam and her consort were overthrown, this group was sacked and littered with the rich debris of sacrificial rituals and shrine desecrations, including the breaking of the vessel naming Lady Une Balam. Skull-Feathers I and his son held power at Tikal in the ensuing period, and Group 6D-V was abandoned. Subsequently, however, the

Tikal faction, supporting an alliance with Teotihuacan and Kaminaljuyú, returned to power. As Stuart and others would have it, this was a conquest of Tikal led by Siyah K'ak', a Teotihuacan lord, that resulted in the installation of Nuun Yax Ain on the throne. Group 6D-V was sufficiently important that it was cleared of the desecration debris, which was carefully deposited and sealed with a plaster floor adjacent to the main building, and the group was reoccupied during this period.

The desecration of the homes, shrines, and burials of an enemy faction holding the Tikal succession was, in our view, not simply an act of violence designed to destroy the partisans and warn off supporters in the community. These homes were seats of power for the ancestors of those successors and shrine places for their household gods. Destroying those places broke the sustaining sources of supernatural power seated in buried ancestors and in spiritually charged buildings containing dedicatory offerings and altars. At the present time, we have not yet identified material evidence of the usurpation and magical insertion of Skull-Feathers I into the dynastic succession of Tikal to parallel the magical destruction and manipulation of stelae and sculpture marking the return to power of the Tikal-Teotihuacan faction. The archaeological record of the North Acropolis, however, is a rich and detailed resource for investigating this category of events and may yet yield clues to the original imposition of the fourteenth successor over Lady Une Balam and her probable Teotihuacano consort. The "healing" of such desecrated places as Group 6D-V was as complicated and ritually circumscribed a matter as the original violence. In our conclusion, we will return to this issue in reference to the North Acropolis at Tikal, where the later desecration, burial, and eventual "healing" of Structure 5D-33–2nd through superimposition of Structure 5D-33–1st remains one of the most important examples of this kind of stratigraphically registered political event.

Usurpers into Dynastic Lines: The Yaxuná Case

The Tikal pattern just described is not unique and may represent a more general way of signaling usurpation of royal power through sacrifice and the magical manipulation of sacred objects and localities. The pattern seen at Tikal, which includes multiple Early Classic rich interments in a centerline tomb and evidence of sacrificed elite, probably royal individuals, is also reflected in deposits of Structure 6F-4 at Yaxuná. So our perspective on this pattern is informed by our field experience at that site, where we began looking for evidence of warfare in 1986 (Freidel 1992; Schele and Freidel 1990). The Selz Foundation Yaxuná project detected evidence for a conquest and usurpation in the early fifth century A.D. (Ambrosino et al., chapter 7 in this volume; Freidel and Suhler 1998; Suhler 1996; Suhler and Freidel 1998). The Early Classic Yaxuná event, as seen in Structure 6F-4, has implications for studying hypothesized takeover at Tikal in the same period. The problems of identifying war and conquest events in the middle of stratigraphic and historical sequences can be different from those associated with final conquest and sacking leading to abandonment. To this end, we need to review the patterns we discovered at Yaxuná before turning again to the Tikal case.

We discovered the evidence for an Early Classic attack at Structure 6F-4 at the North Acropolis. Structure 6F-4 is the easternmost structure of a triad of pyramids on the 100- by100-square-meter basal platform of the acropolis. Excavations on the summit of Structure 6F-4 revealed a buried masonry superstructure facing west toward the main plaza. This construction, Structure 6F-4/4th, was ceramically dated to the late fourth or early fifth century A.D. The plaster had been stripped off its walls and floors and the roof removed. A trench had been excavated in antiquity along the central corridor, and a layer of gray marl had been deposited along the main east–west centerline. In this gray marl, two flaring-necked jars were placed, one red to the east and one black to the west. Red is the color associated by the Maya with the east, the direction of the rising sun and cosmic rebirth (Freidel et al. 1993), while black is the color associated with the west. The two vessels have been identified as Maxcanú Buff: Tacopate (the black pot) and Hunabchen Red. These are extremely rare types at Yaxuná prior to this event but common at the coeval city of Oxkintok in far western Yucatán (Johnstone 2001; Suhler 1996; Suhler et al. 1998). The builders encased this desecrated superstructure in a new retaining wall, built outset panels on the western (front) side of it suitable for stucco decorations, and transformed it into an open-summit platform. Further to the west on the centerline of the pyramid, the people who laid down these offerings in the upper platform built a tomb into the hearting of another platform area fronting it. This was clearly performance space, for a narrow stairway on the northern side of this platform containing the tomb gave access to it from the broad plaza to the west of Structure

6F-4. The two vessels and the tomb established the east–west axis of performances to be carried out on these upper platform surfaces.

The black pot contained sixty-one pieces of worked greenstone and four of spondylus (figure 11.4). Common forms of the greenstone were collar beads, ear-flare elements, and crown jewels. The arrangement of the collar beads showed that they were deposited strung in a circle around the interior of the pot. Data further suggest that the

Figure 11.4   Maxcanú Buff vessel cache

seven diadem jewels clustered in the middle of the deposit were likely attached to cloth bands. The largest of these jewels had the trefoil headdress of the jester god *Sak Hunal,* diagnostic of Maya kingship. This jewel was of the bib-and-helmet style characteristic of the Late Formative period. It had been so worn by rubbing against soft material like cloth that the eyes had been re-etched to define them as open. Two other pendants in the set are also clearly bib-and-helmet style. These royal insignia, then, were likely heirlooms. The contents of this pot resemble the contents of the Late Classic royal god bundles of Palenque, Chiapas, described by Hanab Pakal in the Temple of the Inscriptions: "Each patron god had a bundle with his specific ear flares (*tup*), necklace (*uh*), head cover (*pixom*), headband (*sak hunal*), and headdress (*kohaw*). Presumably, *itz'at* opened these bundles to show their contents to the gathered lords, and perhaps dancers wore these accouterments in ritual that materialized the gods from the Otherworld for the k'atun-ending rituals" (Schele and Mathews 1998:106).

The other pendants in the black pot included several that are characteristic of Late Formative royal offerings, including the goggle-eyed or butterfly-eyed type and the "charlie chaplin" form. Additionally, there was a small owl pendant. This is a unique artifact, but the owl was very important as an emblem of conquest warfare in the Classic period. As Schele and her colleagues demonstrated (Freidel et al. 1993; Schele 1986; Schele and Grube 1994), Classic Maya kings fought conquest warfare employing several divinities and symbols imported from highland Mexico, and the owl was one of these insignia. To our knowledge, this is the earliest archaeological occurrence of the owl diadem in a lowland Maya context. Its earliest iconographic depiction as a Maya royal diadem jewel was on the crown lofted by King Sian-Ka'an-K'awil of Tikal on Stela 31. Stuart (1998c) identified the epithet "Spear-Thrower-Owl" on that stela with the foreign lord under whose auspices Smoking-Frog, Siyah-K'ak', conquered Tikal in the Early Classic. He has even speculated that Spear-Thrower-Owl might be the king of Teotihuacan. We will return to this scenario later in this chapter.

Another prospect is that the owl diadem, following the epigraphic analyses of MacLeod, might signify the word *kun,* meaning "throne" or "seat," although if the owl occurs glyphically without the *V-n* suffix, it simply reads *kuh,* "owl." *Cha'k-ah kun,* "ax the throne," is a textual expression for military attack (Martin and Grube 2000). The axe, *cha'k-bah,* verb actually occurs on a later Classic text at Yaxuná on a fragmentary monument exposed by recent INAH work in the ball-court group adjacent to the North Acropolis (Freidel 1999). When Suhler (1996) discovered the black pot containing the owl head, it had a black stone axe (carved as a god effigy) jammed down into its mouth. In sum, the offering on the western side of the open summit platform is the material expression of a war event against a royal bundle or seat and suggests the participation by the protagonist in "owl" war as fought and commemorated by coeval Early Classic kings at Tikal. Owl iconography and epigraphic statements register at Tikal during the initial expression of significant ties with Teotihuacan. The same holds for Yaxuná in this case.

Other events documented in Structure 6F-4 confirm the conclusion that the destruction of Structure 6F-4/4th and the construction of 6F-4/3rd were related to conquest warfare and usurpation of power. Further excavations on the western side of Structure 6F-4/3rd that buried the temple containing the royal jewels exposed the vaulted tomb chamber on the centerline where the main stairway of the previous building had been partially dismantled. This chamber contained a royal mass burial. Bennett (1993) and Suhler (1996; see also Freidel and Suhler 1998; Suhler and Freidel 1998) identified twelve individuals buried in the mass deposit. There were five women, one in an advanced stage of pregnancy or with a newborn child on her lap, two men as articulated skeletons, a third as burned fragments of a desecrated bundle burial, and three children. There was no evidence of bone disturbance of the kind that might accompany periodic reopening of the chamber to place new bodies into it. They were all placed into it at one time and as part of one event. Two of the women, those flanking the decapitated body of the central adult male (the king in our interpretation), were adorned with *Sak Hunal* jewels. The young woman to the west was wearing a white crown of worked strombus shell segments with a single *Sak Hunal* greenstone jewel in the middle. The adolescent girl on the east was wearing a pectoral of three greenstone jewels, one *Sak Hunal,* one dancing "charlie chaplin," and a profile of the old god who wears a *kin* symbol in his headdress.

The decapitated man in the middle was buried in a semiflexed position with an obsidian blade where his head should have been and with some jade and shell adornments. Near his feet, excavators found a crown of white shell segments like the white crown worn by the young woman to his west. However, this white crown had been burnt, evidently in situ. The central individual was decapitated, as was the maize god in the creation story of the Maya (Tedlock 1996). He is also flanked by young women bearing the royal jewels, as was the maize god in the depictions of his resurrection (Freidel et al. 1993). The reference to birth is underscored in the real infant held by one woman and the ceramic doll (discussed later in this chapter) cradled in the arm of the other woman. One of the other victims, an old man placed seated in the southeast corner of the tomb, had been evidently defleshed before burial, turning him into an image of a death god, performers in sacrifices from the creation myths. There is some evidence, then, that the principal people in this tomb were carefully arranged in a macabre tableau symbolizing mythical sacrifice and resurrection.

The nine vessels found in the deposit confirm an Early Classic date for the tomb and sacrificial event. Among those vessels are a Teotihuacan-style slab-footed tripod vase and unique goddess effigy with attributes of the Teotihuacan Great Goddess (the doll alluded to previously). The hypothesis that the tomb contains signature ceramics of the victor is consistent with the previously mentioned arguments concerning the offering pots in the desecrated shrine structure on the summit of this building and with the clearly sacrificial nature of the interments. One vessel in particular is relevant here: A plate placed next to the burnt crown was decorated with a depiction of a warrior wearing a fire macaw effigy costume and carrying a turtle shell. The fire macaw occurs as an insignia on the headdress of the personage depicted on Uaxactún Stela 5, identified by Mathews (1985:44; see also Schele and Freidel 1990) as Siyah-K'ak' in his status as conqueror of that city on behalf of Tikal. Whether or not Siyah-K'ak' also conquered Tikal, as proposed by Grube, Martin, and Stuart, virtually all investigators studying this matter agree that he is an emissary of Teotihuacan and lived during the introduction of Teotihuacan-style ceramics and "owl" warfare iconography at Tikal. We would identify this Macaw man in the tomb in Structure 6F-4 as the conqueror and usurper at Yaxuná, placing his image in the tomb of his victim. That portrait is adjacent to and above the burnt crown of his predecessor. It is also "above" the two young women who flank his predecessor, for they are oriented with their heads to the south, while the body of the decapitated predecessor is oriented to the north.

The east–west centerline of Structure 6F-4–3rd registers two ritual performances associated with conquest: the "axed" black pot containing a bundle of royal jewels suitable for gods and kings and the sacrifice and interment of twelve individuals with royal insignia jewels and extralocal signature ceramics. We think that these two performance deposits were flanked by two others to the east and west that marked the accession of the conqueror and usurper. To the east is the second offering vessel under the open summit of the upper platform. This red pot contained a single carved greenstone head pendant of a distinctive style that evidently was an attempt at portraiture (one that resembles the individual painted on the Macaw pot found in Burial 24). That pot also had a large spondylus bead and a square plaque of the same material. The red pot offering was not symbolically "axed" like the black pot offering. Thus, this offering was not "killed." The spondylus bead accompanying the diadem head is very large. There is reason to believe this bead held particular significance in the deposit, for in addition to being large, a second spondylus bead of similar size was discovered as an isolated offering above the red pot. The word for red shell bead, *k'an*, is the same word used to name the birth place of the maize god in the Classic Maya story of creation (Freidel et al. 1993). The story of the creation and the maize god's resurrection is strongly linked to Classic Maya accession rituals (such as at Palenque; see Freidel et al. 1993). The location of the red pot offering would be appropriate for a scaffold accession throne used by the conqueror of Yaxuná. As depicted on accession stelae at Piedras Negras, Guatemala, for example, the king seated in the scaffold throne has a sacrificial victim in an offering vessel placed before him at the foot of the scaffold (Taube 1988). In the case at hand, the sacrificial vessel (black pot) and the victim (in the tomb) are in front of this eastern location on the summit.

The second performance place that might register the rule of the conqueror is on the grand stairway of Structure 6F-4–3rd (see also Ambrosino et al., chapter 7 in this volume). This stairway had a great hole dug into it on the centerline and the steps removed, evidence of yet another destruction event, this time on the building marking the conquest of Yaxuná. There was nothing much in the hole, and it evidently was made primarily to remove something rather than to place something. There is something that would have appropriately stood on the stairway at this place, and that is the portrait stela of an Early Classic Teotihuacan-style warrior, Yaxuná Monument 1 (figure 11.5), reset by later Classic people on the north side of Structure 6F-4 (Brainerd 1958). That stela had been desecrated in antiquity. The head had been sheared off the upper surface of the stone. The portrayed individual was carrying in his left hand a bunch of atlatl spears horizontally. In his right hand, he held a spear-thrower upright.

Our hypothesis is that the Yaxuná tomb is a family of royalty exterminated to prevent succession in the line, analogous to the argument made by Schele and Freidel (1990), following Maricela Ayala

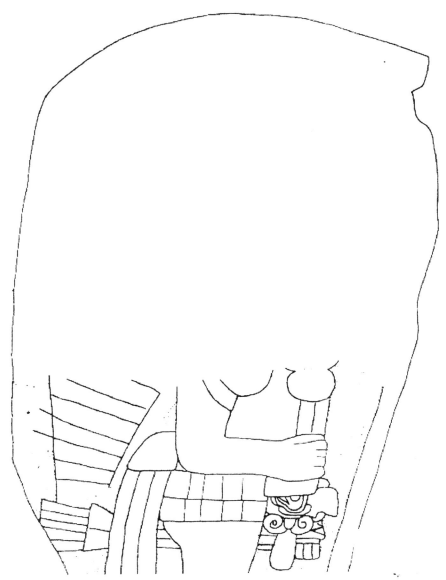

Figure 11.5   Yaxuná Monument 1 (adapted from Brainerd 1958)

Falcón, to explain the unique Early Classic multi-individual tomb in Temple B-VIII at Uaxactún as the family of the defeated king of that city killed after Tikal's conquest in A.D. 378. There, as in the postulated arrangement at Yaxuná, the victory stela (Stela 5) of the conqueror is placed in front of the building containing the sacrificed remains of the vanquished. And as at Uaxactún (Mathews 1985; Schele and Freidel 1990), we think that the conquerors at Yaxuná installed a usurper and his line there after the victory.

The magical manipulation of people and powerful objects at the North Acropolis may not have ended with the events on Structure 6F-4. The conqueror may have entered the tomb of another king (Burial 23), one buried in Structure 6F-3, the northern building of the triadic North Acropolis. Burial 23 was reentered after the original interment (Suhler 1996). The king, laid out as a single individual in majesty perhaps a generation earlier than the conquest of Yaxuná evinced in Structure 6F-4, showed clear evidence of careful manipulation. Rough stone of the kind that composed the hearting of the subsequent construction was placed around the king in two neat piles of rubble to either side of the body. The piles of stone reflect a clefted mountain, a symbol of resurrection. Three *Sak Hunal* jewels were found in association with Burial 23. One was located in the southwest corner of the tomb near three carved tibiae, and a second was found in the fill of the antechamber next to the tomb. A third jewel was encountered higher up in the construction of the pyramid above the tomb. Nearly identical stylistically, these *Sak Hunal* jewels likely formed a single crown worn by the interred king in Burial 23. They were probably arranged by the person entering the tomb to form a connection to the new pyramid covering it and, in particular, a connection with a new subterranean corridor inside that pyramid. There are several clues suggesting that the person who entered Burial 23 was none other than the conqueror who had deposited the sacrificed king in Burial 24. The most compelling is an enigmatic flat incised bone artifact found up against the far western wall of Burial 23. The incised symbols on this bone include a profile owl. The owl, as mentioned previously, is a symbol in this period of Teotihuacan warriors and their Tikal royal allies. A clue to the function of this artifact comes from two artifacts in Mesoamerican collections on display in Berlin. These are two ornately incised flat bone artifacts that were panels inset into the backs of atlatls. The Burial 23 bone artifact appears to be an example of such an atlatl panel. The person who entered the Burial 23 tomb apparently placed an atlatl inside it, a clear signature of his Teotihuacan affiliation as depicted on Monument 1. Indeed, with a spear-thrower decorated with an owl, one must wonder whether this is not a signature artifact of Spear-Thrower Owl, the father of Nuun Yax Ain and the great warrior of Teotihuacan. But why would the conqueror and usurper enter the tomb of a king who was clearly not his ancestor but rather the ancestor of the man he was replacing through magical sacrifice and resurrection? We would propose that he did so precisely to behave as if that ancestor were his own, indeed, to make him his own through magical manipulation of the artifacts inside that tomb. We predict that this conqueror later had himself interred in the construction phase enveloping Burial 23 at the end of a subterranean corridor that we discovered but did not have opportunity to explore. Only future work at the North Acropolis of Yaxuná can settle this question.

Tikal Revisited: How Do the Tikal and Yaxuná Cases Compare?

Investigators should begin to look at related coeval patterns at Tikal as we have touched on in this chapter and as we have attempted to do at Yaxuná. At Tikal, for another example, Burial 22 in the North Acropolis contains a vase with a glyphic inscription proclaiming its ownership by a "nine successions" lord. Not only is Burial 22 in a focal position in the North Acropolis, but it also contained Manik III ceramics, including Teotihuacan materials. He also wore broad mosaic ear flares of a kind found on portrayed Teotihuacanos at Tikal and found in elite tombs at Kaminaljuyú associated with the Teotihuacan occupation there. It is impossible to tell how this man died, as his bones were disturbed in later times. However, Burial 10, identified by Coggins (1976) and others as the tomb of Yax-Ain on the basis of a specific greenstone name jewel, also contained glyphically inscribed vases, at least one of which says, "his drinking cup, son of the 'nine successions' lord." In light of such proclaimed ties, we propose that the person interred inside Burial 22 is Spear-Thrower Owl himself, the father of Nuun Yax Ain. While Stuart (1999) has speculated that Spear-Thrower Owl was the king of Teotihuacan, we are of the view that the ubiquitous representation of owls at that city had to do with a more generic royal symbolism personalized by an exceptional individual who was a representative of Teotihuacan in Maya country, the kind of remarkable merchant warrior who later helped to establish the hegemony of the Aztecs in far-flung parts of Mesoamerica.

There is a formidable set of new glyphic interpretations building on the side of the hypothesized takeover of Tikal by Teotihuacan, and Stuart, Grube, and Martin have already begun to discern patterns in the archaeological record supporting their interpretations. First, the "ball-court marker" proclaims the accession in A.D. 374 of a "Spear-Thrower Owl" as the fourth lord of some unstated realm. The prospect of this being the same "Spear-Thrower Owl" as declared the father of Nuun Yax Ain on Stela 31 is a reasonable one, although it would make Nuun Yax Ain probably a child on accession less than five years later. Second, the last date on Stela 31 registers the death of a "Spear-Thrower Owl" person. This date was terribly important to the Late Classic king Hasaw-Kan-K'awil, who keyed the rededication of the center of Tikal to one sacred cycle of nearly 260 years after that death date. Schele and Freidel (1990) presumed that Hasaw-Kan-K'awil saw Stela 31, reinterred it, and hence knew the death date on it. However, scrutiny of the stratigraphy of the Stela 31 deposit shows that this stela was desecrated and dumped as part of a spectacular repudiation of the Teotihuacan affiliation (which Coe [1990] observed but thought Hasaw-Kan-K'awil undertook). Not only did that deposit bury Structure 5D-33–2nd and Stela 31 sealed by structures built before Hasaw-Kan-K'awil's time (indicated by the ceramic data), but it makes no sense for this king, who revered the Mexican affiliation, to have presided over the desecration. In short, he did not see the stela, and he knew the death date of the "Spear-Thrower Owl" person as a matter of history and sacred lore. If it was the same "Spear-Thrower Owl" who sired Yax-Ain according to Sian-Kan-K'awil, he outlived that son by nearly two decades and well into the reign of his grandson. A careful and systematic consideration of evidence from both central public places and elite residences in the city of Tikal will be needed to really understand the way that factional politics coordinated with outside strangers in "takeovers" by kings not directly descended from the prior kings in the succession. The notion of conquest of Tikal by armies marching halfway across Mesoamerica seems implausible to us. However, the notion of local factions attaching their ambitions to the military and commercial representatives of lucrative long-distance trade agreements not only makes reasonable sense but also echoes in the political machinations of the rulers of Mayapán, Yucatán, the last great lowland capital.

Houston (2000) reviewed the arguments favoring disruption of dynastic lines and came out in favor of such a prospect in Maya history as viewed through the texts. He noted that we had made arguments for such usurpation of royal power at Yaxuná on the basis of archaeological evidence, but he judged those more speculative. To be sure, archaeological evidence cannot provide the precise declarations that the texts occasionally can. But the kinds of magical manipulation of succession we propose are not so clearly seen in the texts. Without such material evidence of how Maya hostile takeovers actually unfolded as we have begun to explore here, we doubt that we would ever really understand the rationales that allowed holy lords from foreign places, be they far away in highland Mexico or closer to hand in Maya country, to effectively graft themselves into dynastic successions stretching into the distant past and incorporating ancestors who must have been also enemies and victims transformed into allies and progenitors. Dennis Tedlock once remarked to Freidel on seeing a photograph of the human remains in Burial 24 that it looked like black magic and sorcery to him. Indeed, we think he was quite correct. Understanding such magical behavior is not merely an aesthetic enterprise in Maya studies. Without insight into it, we could not really make sense of the more practical dimensions of political interaction that shaped Maya history and the archaeological record of the Maya public places in which that history unfolded. Understanding both the words and the deeds and the potential of generating independent tests of hypotheses across these domains is a more promising enterprise than ever in Maya studies.

Notes

1. There was some question in MacLeod's mind as to whether the suffix was a *hi* or *li*. The matter was settled by Freidel's identification of relevant comparative texts on the belt plaques from Tomb I, a royal interment in Structure III, at Calakmul (Folan et al. 1995:Figure 14). The example occurs on plaque II, and following discussion of the general category by Grube and Martin (1998:34–41), it appears to be a variant of the *hu-li-ha*, "to arrive," verb. To quote from MacLeod's correspondence with Freidel (September 30, 1998), "I received the celt and given the context (short text, initial glyph) I really think it's a *li* after all—and by extension, so is the putative *hi* on the Tikal monument. There's a real *hi* on the same celt; the characteristic 'toes' of the crocodile are very evident. *y'ak'ab-il* would just be the full possessed form with pronoun and possessive suffix (often optional)."

2. Attributions: *t'ab*: David Stuart; the *Vy* suffix as in *t'abay* as self-agentive: Barbara MacLeod; the syllable *p'e*: Werner Nahm; the reading *p'enal* "the son," Barbara MacLeod; *u-huntan* "her cherished one," David Stuart; *Ich'ak*: David Stuart; *Yaxun*: Nikolai Grube; *ch'ab-ak'ab*: Barbara MacLeod and David Stuart independently; Tikal Emblem Glyph as *mut* or *mutul*, David Stuart.

Part IV

ETHNOHISTORIC AND ETHNOGRAPHIC APPROACHES TO WARFARE

Chapter Twelve

Ethnic Conflict in Postclassic Cholula, Mexico

Geoffrey G. McCafferty

Making Military Histories

Ethnohistoric sources describe a sequence of ethnic changes in the Puebla/Tlaxcala Valley of Central Mexico beginning at the end of the Classic period and continuing up to the Spanish conquest (figure 12.1). In this chapter, I contrast the documentary accounts with archaeological evidence derived primarily from Cholula, the major urban center of the Puebla/Tlaxcala region with continuous occupation since at least the Middle Formative (McCafferty 1996a). Cholula is notable for not experiencing a collapse at the end of the Classic period as did other prominent urban centers, such as Teotihuacan and Monte Albán. It was the focus of panregional religious ceremonies for much of its history, with ethnohistoric accounts identifying it as an important pilgrimage site, especially during the Postclassic, when visitors came from diverse parts of Mesoamerica to worship at the temple of Quetzalcoatl (McCafferty 2001; Olivera 1970; Ringle et al. 1998). Thus, the socioreligious influence of Cholula spread far and wide, as can be measured by the dispersal of its characteristic artifact style known alternatively as the Mixteca-Puebla style (McCafferty 1994; Nicholson 1960, 1982) or as the Postclassic International style (Robertson 1970; see also Smith and Heath-Smith 1980).

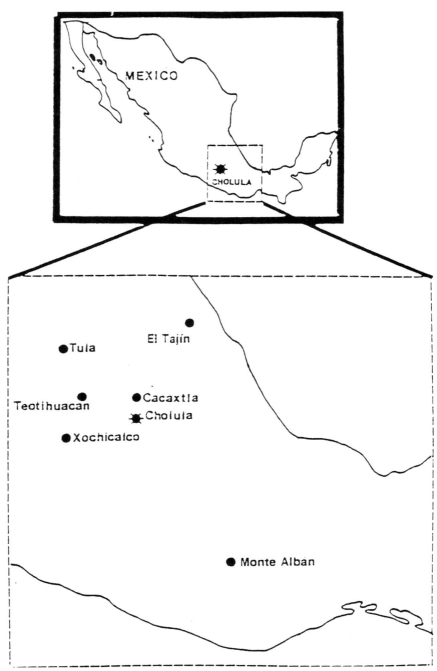

Figure 12.1   Map of the central highlands showing the
locations of Cholula and Cacaxtla

If Cholula enjoyed a wide sphere of influence over Postclassic Mesoamerica, however, it was through this combined practice of religion and trade; militarism does not seem to have been a significant characteristic of its hegemonic strategy. No evidence of "conquest" monuments are found in Cholula's artistic program, and while colonial period accounts mention Cholula as part of a rival "Triple Alliance" with Tlaxcala and Huejotzingo in the "Flowery Wars" against the Aztecs and their allies (Durán 1994), it is not renowned for having done particularly well. In fact, in the case studies to be examined in this chapter, Cholula is consistently known for its military defeats, as foreign groups conquered and occupied the city in successive waves. What is notable about this sequence of military failure is the resilience with which the city continued to flourish and remain a constant force in the religion, economy, and culture of Central Mexico throughout the turbulent Postclassic period. Thus, Cholula provides an alternative to the militaristic model of political organization, and this alternative may have value for explaining the longevity of the Cholula polity.

The first episode occurs around A.D. 700, at the end of the Classic period. It is described by colonial chroniclers such as Ixtlilxochitl (1975–1977) and Torquemada (1975–1983) and may be represented in the Cacaxtla Battle Murals (McCafferty and McCafferty 1994; McVicker 1985; Quirarte 1983). In contrast to the accounts of violent interaction between the Olmeca-Xicallanca and existing populations identified as Quinametinime, excavations on the northeast platform of Cholula's Great Pyramid suggest a gradual integration of the two groups (McCafferty 1996a).

The second example is documented in the *Historia Tolteca-Chichimeca* (1976), with the arrival to Cholula of immigrant Toltecs and Chichimecs around A.D. 1200 (various interpretations of the historical accounts have produced several specific dates, but all cluster around this more generic date). Architectural features at the Great Pyramid indicate a violent end to the ceremonial center, followed by a major reorganization of the site's ceremonial landscape as a new Pyramid of Quetzalcoatl was built in what is still the town's civic-ceremonial center (McCafferty 1996b). Additional evidence for this change is found at the residential site of UA-1, about 2 kilometers east of the Great Pyramid, where evidence of burning and a high incidence of projectile points are among the evidence of warfare-related destruction (McCafferty 1992).

Finally, the Spanish conquest of Mexico is among the most violent episodes of world history and resulted in radical changes in cultural organization. At Cholula, Cortés and his soldiers perpetrated the famous "Cholula Massacre," in which nobles from the city were gathered in the plaza associated with the Temple of Quetzalcoatl and attacked at the same time that indigenous allies swarmed into the city to attack and sack the residential areas (McCafferty 2000a). The massacre is one of the best-documented events of the conquest, with more than a dozen colonial period accounts from conquistadores, Spanish priests, and indigenous chroniclers (including codex-style pictorial versions). This provides the opportunity for critical evaluation of the different sources. Archaeological evidence for the massacre was recovered in the form of 671 burials found in the central square, many showing diagnostic sword cut marks (Castro Morales and García Moll 1972). The archaeological evidence therefore provides an independent perspective for further evaluation of the chronicles regarding this crucial event of the conquest.

The documentary and archaeological evidence for pre-Columbian warfare at Cholula provides an opportunity not only to infer how and why militarism occurred but also to evaluate how the colonial historians chose to accentuate or minimize the role of violence in the past. The theoretical framework that I employ here is based on practices derived from historical archaeology where documentary and archaeological data are not simply combined to construct a more complete story of the past but rather are treated as somewhat independent representations of the past that can reveal aspects of the "formation processes" of the distinct lines of evidence (Leone et al. 1987). For example, by contrasting the various ethnohistorical accounts of the Cholula Massacre against the archaeological evidence, a variety of perspectives is revealed relating to specific agendas of the chroniclers. Furthermore, the archaeological evidence derives from limited excavated contexts. Thus, the documentary accounts can be used to suggest additional arenas of action that have not been adequately sampled and thus identify topics for future investigation while pointing out gaps in the archaeological record that may lead to skewed interpretations.

The methodology, therefore, is explicitly dialectical, as it seeks not for an ultimate truth in the past but rather for the overlaps and ambiguities of the various lines of evidence. Both provide useful information. In the present study, ethnohistoric and archaeological evidence shed light on pre-Columbian warfare. But on a higher level, the contrast between the two data sets reveal distinctions in the Mesoamerican "history-making" process; what was worthy of being recorded and especially how propagandistic histories, often written by the victors, portrayed a biased vision of the past.

The "Invasion" of the Olmeca-Xicallanca

Mythicohistorical accounts describe the arrival of the Olmeca-Xicallanca during the Epiclassic period (ca. A.D. 700; McCafferty 1997). According to Ixtlilxochitl (1975–1977:I:529), the Cholula region was inhabited by "giants" (Nahuatl = *quinametitzúcuil*) following the Second Age, or Tlalchitonátiuc. These were the beings who built the pyramids of Teotihuacan and Cholula (Sahagún 1950–1982:X:192; see also Davies 1977:46). In archaeological terminology, they correspond to the Classic period. When the Olmeca-Xicallanca arrived in the Cholula area, the giants who had survived the cataclysmic end of the Second Age enslaved them. Yet the Quinametinime giants were eventually defeated and "consumed," at which point the Olmeca-Xicallanca became the rulers of Cholula. The same historical tradition was also shared by the Tlaxcaltecas (Armillas 1946; Torquemada 1975–1983:I:51–55), who kept a "femur the height of an ordinary man" (probably from a prehistoric mammoth) as evidence of giants, at least according to the testimony of Díaz del Castillo (1963:181).

Shrouded in the mists of time and fantasy as these accounts are, archaeological evidence provides some evidence to substantiate at least the outline of an ethnic invasion of the Puebla-Tlaxcala area following the Classic period. The Olmeca-Xicallanca originated in the Gulf coast region of Veracruz, as implied by their names as well as by later ethnohistoric sources (McCafferty 1997; Sahagún 1950–1982:X:187–88). Olman ("place of rubber") is located in the southern Gulf coast, where Formative period remains were designated as relating to the "Olmec" culture (since no original name was recorded for this culture, the term "Olmec" was adopted from the colonial period Nahua name for the region). The historic Olmeca-Xicallanca also came from the same area, perhaps more specifically from the area surrounding the Laguna de Terminos, where the Postclassic city of Xicalango was an important port and trading city (Berdan 1978; Chapman 1957).

Sahagún (1950–1982:X:187–88) wrote that the Olmeca came from the east, where their homeland was a land of abundance where flowers, cacao, and liquid rubber grew and where exotic birds with beautiful feathers lived. The wealthy were known as "sons of Quetzalcoatl," a name that was also used to describe successful merchants.

One of the greatest problems faced when trying to identify the Olmeca-Xicallanca is the chronology of when they were active in Central Mexico. While this has been discussed in several historical interpretations (Davies 1977; Jiménez M. 1966; McCafferty 1997), the actual evidence is extremely tenuous, based on Torquemada's (1975–1983:I:452–54; see also Fowler 1989) account of a migration out of Central Mexico (initiated by Olmec "tyranny") by Nahua groups who would eventually settle in Central America. Since this allegedly took place "7 or 8 lifetimes of an ancient person" prior to Torquemada's time (ca. A.D. 1600), and a "lifetime of an ancient" is generally interpreted as twice the fifty-two-year calendar round (Davies 1977:117–20), this would push the migration back to around A.D. 750–850. Thus, the ethnohistorical record indicates the arrival of ethnic Olmeca-Xicallanca sometime after the fall of the Classic empires but before the expulsion of the Nahua Nicarao (ca. A.D. 800). Furthermore, Ixtlilxochitl's (1975–1977) account implies an initial period in which the Olmeca-Xicallanca were dominated by the resident population, followed by their overthrow and violent destruction.

Archaeological evidence to evaluate this scenario is available from two sources: the Cacaxtla Battle Murals and an excavated elite residential area on the northeast platform of the Great Pyramid of Cholula. Although each provides relevant information relating to the ethnohistorical account, they are not consistent in supporting that account.

Cacaxtla, including the adjoining hilltop site of Xochitecatl, was occupied during the Epiclassic period, A.D. 650–850 (López de Molina 1981). Colonial period chroniclers still recalled its affiliation with the Olmeca-Xicallanca (Torquemada 1975–1983:I:353–54). It features extensive monumental architecture in the construction of the acropolis area. The acropolis probably combined elite residential as well as administrative functions, while religious/ceremonial functions were centered at the pyramids of adjacent Xochitecatl (Serra Puche and Lazcano Arce 1997). In addition to the Battle Mural, other polychrome murals have also been discovered that reveal historical as well as religious concepts (Stuart 1992). Of particular significance to the question of Cacaxtla's ethnic identity is a mural located in an early construction level that depicts a merchant, identified by a carrying pack (Nahuatl = *cacaxtli*) containing quetzal feathers and rubber, both deriving from the Olmeca-Xicallanca heartland. The merchant is further identified by the calendar name "4 Dog" and by costume elements, including a distinctive hat, all of which serve to identify him as the Maya God L, patron deity of merchants (Carlson 1991).

The Cacaxtla Battle Mural consists of a long panel painted on a building facade facing out onto the main patio of the acropolis (Foncerrada de Molina 1976). It represents two warring armies dressed in jaguar and bird insignia (figure 12.2a), respectively, with the jaguar army consistently depicted as victorious (McCafferty and McCafferty 1994; McVicker 1985; Quirarte 1983). The right side of the panel shows the battle still in progress, while the left side (divided by a central staircase) depicts the immediate aftermath of the battle. In addition to the contrasting costume elements, the two armies are distinguishable on the basis of facial features, the defeated bird warriors represented with Maya-like cranial deformation and the jaguar warriors lacking this characteristic (Quirarte 1983). This facial feature, combined with the artistic style and identifiable costume, jewelry, and other objects, has been interpreted as evidence that the mural was painted by artists with Maya background, with the closest stylistic parallel being the murals of Bonampak.

The Battle Mural does relate to the ethnohistoric account of ethnic conflict, but whereas Ixtlilxochitl describes the defeat of the Central Mexican "giants" by the Olmeca-Xicallanca, the mural depicts the defeat of a Maya-like group by non-Maya warriors, presumably residents of the central highlands. Yet this defeat is depicted in a style characteristic of the Maya, and earlier-phase murals clearly depict the Maya merchant god at Cacaxtla. This apparent contradiction has bewildered archaeologists and art historians alike.

An interpretation that provides a possible way out of this conundrum relates to an engendered reading of the Battle Murals (McCafferty and McCafferty 1994). Two standing members of the bird warriors are represented in female costume, including triangular *quechquemitl* capes, knee-length skirts, elaborately decorated textile patterns, and the absence of a loincloth (figures 12.2b and 12.2c). Both are shown confronted by a leader of the jaguar army, identified by the calendar name 3 Deer Antler "Tlaloc-mask." Since the Mesoamerican convention for representing captives is to show them nude, as are most other members of the Cacaxtla bird army, it can be suggested that the fate of the female-costumed individuals (or more likely a single individual depicted twice) was not to be sacrificed. Instead, McCafferty and McCafferty (1994) suggest that this noblewoman of the bird clan was captured for the purpose of marriage, thus forging an alliance with the jaguar clan that resulted in a combined bird/jaguar dynasty. This is precisely what is then represented on the portico murals of Building B at Cacaxtla, where two complementary individuals, in bird

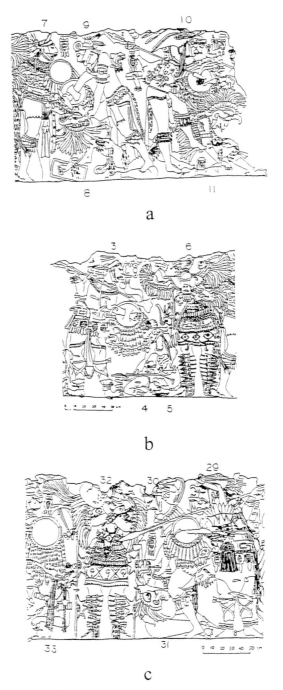

Figure 12.2 Cacaxtla Battle Murals: (a) warring armies;
(b–c) bird warriors in female costume

and jaguar insignia, respectively, are shown on either side of the doorway as descendants of the union implied in the Battle Mural. Thus, while the overall theme of the Cacaxtla Battle Mural was one of ethnic conflict and explicit violence, the conclusion was one of marriage alliance to unite the two groups into a multiethnic lineage. This same process may also be present in the archaeological record of Epiclassic Cholula.

Cholula was a major ceremonial center during the Classic period, peripheral to the political sphere of the great Basin of Mexico center of Teotihuacan, even though it probably shared ethnic traits with the Teotihuacan population (McCafferty 2000b). Recent investigations at Cholula have fundamentally challenged traditional interpretations of the Classic to Postclassic transition at the site (McCafferty 1996b, 1998, 2000b), as it is now believed that Cholula did not suffer a collapse as did its mighty neighbor to the northwest but instead went through a prolonged period of monumental construction. The Great Pyramid of Cholula was expanded from 180 meters on a side to 400 meters (Marquina 1970; McCafferty 1996a, 2001), more than three times the volume of Teotihuacan's Pyramid of the Sun. It is precisely at this time that the ethnohistoric chronicles indicate "invasion" by the Olmeca-Xicallanca.

Architectural evidence from the Great Pyramid and its surrounding ceremonial precinct supports the idea of ethnic change, with iconographic elements that create an eclectic mix of Maya, Gulf coast, and Central Mexican traits. The pyramid itself was built as a four-sided, radial pyramid, with access to the top from any direction (for Maya parallels, see Schele and Mathews 1998). The facades represent a change from the previous construction phase (Stage 2), in that Stage 3 used the *talud-tablero* format usually associated with Teotihuacan; *talud-tablero* facades were introduced only after the fall of Teotihuacan's ceremonial center and may have been a symbolic expression by Cholula's elite that they were appropriating Teotihuacan's role as Central Mexico's premier religious center (McCafferty 2000b, 2001). Sculpted and painted across the *tableros* of the Great Pyramid were Gulf coast– and Maya-inspired symbolic elements, including mat motifs, greca friezes, and scrollwork volutes. Two massive stela/altar groups were located in the Patio of the Altars on the south side of the Great Pyramid (figure 12.3); these are also Maya characteristics without precedent in the central highlands (McCafferty 1996a, 2001). The eclectic blending of highland and lowland traits is a characteristic of the Olmeca-Xicallanca, as they introduced an international theme that

Figure 12.3   Stela/Altar Group 1, Patio of the Altars, Cholula

developed into the Mixteca-Puebla stylistic tradition (McCafferty 1994; Nagao 1989; Robertson 1985). A skeleton of an adult male was found associated with Epiclassic architecture adjacent to the Patio of the Altars with distinctive cranial deformation that Suárez Cruz argues may even represent a Maya merchant or priest (Suárez C. 1985).

Archaeological evidence for the process of ethnic change comes from a small-scale excavation at the Patio of the Carved Skulls, located on the northeast platform of the Great Pyramid (McCafferty 1996a; McCafferty and Suárez C. 1995). This area was originally explored in the 1930s by Noguera (1937), who identified a small patio relating to an elite residence with a miniature pyramid-altar in the patio. This location corresponds to the palace of the Olmeca-Xicallanca high priest (figure 12.4), the Aquiach Amapane, as recorded in the colonial period *Historia Tolteca-Chichimeca* (1976; see also McCafferty 1996a).

As part of a project to consolidate the architectural remains uncovered by Noguera and to map the exposed features, several units were excavated that recovered artifactual material relating to the construction sequence of the patio and its associated architecture. Six phases of construction were encountered, including an earlier pyramid-altar that had been partially dismantled and covered over when a new staircase was built (figure 12.5). Since the original altar discovered by Noguera (1937) contained the skeletal remains of an adult male and female, associated with grave offerings and dental mutilation to indicate elite status, it is inferred that the altars may have served as shrines

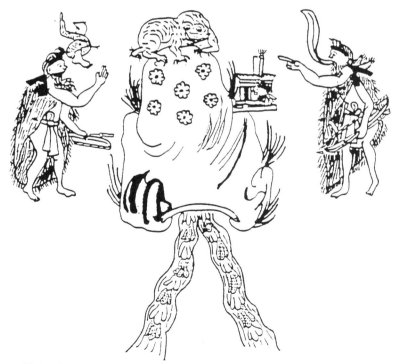

Figure 12.4   Great Pyramid of Cholula with the palace of Aquiach Amapane
(adapted from *Historia Tolteca-Chichimeca* 1976)

Figure 12.5   Remains of partially dismantled pyramid-altar

for revered lineage founders (McCafferty 1996a, 2000b). Thus, the intentional destruction of the earlier pyramid-altar may indicate a break in the dynastic history.

The material culture recovered from the patio features a blend of Classic period diagnostics together with ceramic types that later became prominent in the Early Postclassic period. Although no arch-aeometric dates could be established, the pottery suggests a relative date between A.D. 700 and 900 (McCafferty 1996a). That the ceramics represent a cultural blending of Classic and Postclassic types suggests that the transition was not abrupt but rather gradual, as would be the case with ethnic in-migration and intermarriage. Notably, both serving and utilitarian wares were introduced, including *comales*, which make their first appearance in Cholula in this assemblage. As cooking and particularly tortilla production were characteristic female tasks (Brumfiel 1991), the implication is that females were important agents of the ethnic change, perhaps as the result of marriage alliances with lineages from the Gulf coast.

In summary, ethnohistoric accounts indicated a fairly dramatic and violent ethnic change as the existing population of Classic "giants" was exterminated. In contrast, however, both the Cacaxtla

Battle Murals and the archaeological evidence from the Patio of the Carved Skulls suggest that intermarriage and especially lineage alliances through marriage may have been the process through which the Classic was transformed into the Postclassic. At Cacaxtla, the union of the bird and jaguar clans may have initially been brought about through military conquest in which the highland army was victorious, resulting in the capture of a dynastic founding queen. At Cholula, too, Gulf coast and Maya design elements on the ceremonial architecture support the arrival of ethnic immigrants, while the introduction of "foreign"-style cooking wares and forms such as the *comal* imply the presence of foreign women. The destruction of the earlier pyramid-altar also suggests a break in the lineage sequence, and the later shrine featured innovative pottery with Gulf coast origins (including imitation Fine Orange), while the two skeletons featured Maya-style dental mutilation. In this case, the archaeological evidence does not support the ethnohistoric record, but through a dialectical analysis, a broader and anthropologically richer interpretation is presented.

The Arrival of the Tolteca-Chichimeca

The Olmeca-Xicallanca domination of Cholula lasted for approximately 500 years, at least according to the mythicohistoric accounts of Ixtlilxochitl (1975–1977) and Torquemada (1975–1983). During this time, the Great Pyramid was built to truly monumental proportions; it was compared to the Tower of Babel, as it provided a means of ascending to the heavens (Durán 1971). Cholula was ruled by the priesthood of Ehecatl-Quetzalcoatl, to whom the pyramid was dedicated (Rojas 1927; Torquemada 1975–1983).

Around A.D. 1200, however, a new group, the Tolteca-Chichimeca, arrived on the scene and conquered the city. Again based on ethnohistoric accounts, especially from the *Historia Tolteca-Chichimeca* (a "history" clearly written by the victors), the Tolteca-Chichimeca left Tula after its fall and migrated east, following their priest-king Topiltzin Quetzalcoatl. Arriving in Cholula, the first group of immigrants was given land to the northwest of the ceremonial center and was subservient to the dominant ethnic group. But when the Toltecas called on ethnic allies for support, they were able to overthrow the Olmeca-Xicallanca and establish a new civic administration. The Great Pyramid was abandoned, and a new ceremonial center was established in the Tolteca-Chichimeca community around a "new" Pyramid of Quetzalcoatl. According to the colonial period *Descripción de Cholula*, the

Olmeca-Xicallanca were "vanquished" (Carrasco 1971; Rojas 1927; but see Olivera and Reyes 1969).

Archaeological evidence for the arrival of the Tolteca-Chichimeca and their subsequent conquest of the Olmeca-Xicallanca is available from the ceremonial precinct of the Great Pyramid and also from a residential site on the campus of the University of the Americas. Unfortunately, because the modern urban center of San Pedro Cholula is built on top of the Late Postclassic center, relatively little information is available to interpret the Tolteca-Chichimeca ceremonial complex.

Stage 3 of the Great Pyramid covered an area of 350 meters on a side and reached 65 meters in height (Marquina 1970; McCafferty 1996b). Several modifications were made to the west side of the pyramid, including Stage 3B, which featured a *tablero* decoration of a mat motif, followed by a steep-sided, rounded structure (Stage 3C) that caused the destruction of the front stairs of Stage 3B (figure 12.6). These represent the outermost facades of the Great Pyramid. But over the top of these construction levels was another layer of adobe brick that extended the Great Pyramid to its greatest dimension of 400 meters to a side. No finished stonework is preserved from this final construction level, raising the question of whether Stage 4 was ever

Figure 12.6   Stages 3B, 3C, and 4 of the Great Pyramid, Cholula

completed or whether instead the building stone had been stripped away for other construction projects (McCafferty 2001).

An incomplete pyramid would imply a radical shift in political organization as resources were channeled in a different direction. Alternatively, building materials were a rare commodity in Cholula since it is situated in the center of an alluvial plain with the closest source of building stone over 50 kilometers to the southeast (Sergio Suárez Cruz, personal communication). Quarrying stone from an existing building would be a cost-efficient means of procuring construction materials. Furthermore, stripping away the outer face of the Great Pyramid could be perceived as a form of humiliation. Pyramids were known as *cue* in the central highlands (Díaz del Castillo 1963), derived from the Nahuatl word *cueitl* for "skirt"; in support of this concept, Mixtec codices depict temples decorated with the same textile patterns as female costume (McCafferty and McCafferty 2003). Stripping away the outer layer of the skirt may have been perceived in the same way as stripping the clothing from a captive, as a sign of humiliation and defeat.

Further evidence of conquest is found in the Patio of the Altars on the south side of the Great Pyramid, where the large stone stelae of the stela/altar groups were thrown down and intentionally smashed. Stela/Altar 1 measured 3.85 meters in height and 35 centimeters in thickness (figure 12.7a) yet was shattered into at least seventeen fragments (Acosta 1970). Stela 2 (also known as Altar 3; Contreras 1970) was of comparable size and was broken near the base with the upper section dragged 40 meters to the base of the pyramid's south staircase (figure 12.7b), where it has been reconstructed (probably incorrectly since it was likely the complementary stela to Altar 2; McCafferty 1996a, 2001). The thickness of the slabs, as well as the small size of some of the fragments of Stela 1, suggests the intentionality of the breakage, as it would have required considerable force and labor to break this stone into so many small fragments. Furthermore, the act of dragging the multiton top portion of Stela 2 to the base of the pyramid suggests some ritual act. This may have been part of a termination ritual for the monument (cf. Mock 1998b), perhaps related to the destruction and desecration of the Patio of the Altars as a ceremonial space.

After the architectural facades had been stripped of their stone facing and the south ceremonial plaza had been destroyed, the major ceremonial functions were moved to the "new" Pyramid of Quetzalcoatl in what is now San Pedro Cholula. The Great Pyramid maintained some of its importance as a shrine dedicated to a rain deity,

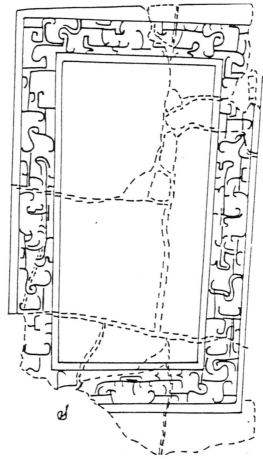

Figure 12.7a   Cholula Stela/Altar 1

Chiconauquiahuitl (Rojas 1927), and as a mortuary site for ceremonial interments (López et al. 1976). The Great Pyramid was allowed to become overgrown with trees and grasses, perhaps as another form of humiliation to the religious practices of the Olmeca-Xicallanca (for a similar case relating to the Tenochca treatment of its rival Tlatelolco's own pyramid, see López Luján 1998).

Evidence of violent destruction is also available from the outskirts of the urban center at the UA-1 locus of the University of the Americas. UA-1 was excavated in 1968 as a field school under the direction of

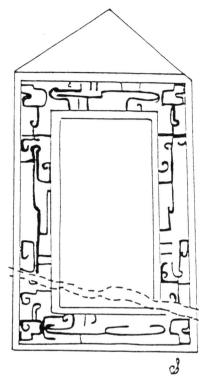

Figure 12.7b   Cholula Stela 2

Daniel Wolfman (1968; McCafferty 1992). Three structures were encountered (figure 12.8); the most extensively tested was Structure 1, a residential area that dated to the Middle and Late Tlachihualtepetl phases (A.D. 900–1200). Structure 1 consisted of four rooms plus associated porch areas and a deep trash midden. A thick layer of ash and charcoal on the surface of a charred plaster floor led excavators to suggest that the house had been destroyed by fire. Objects including vessels, spindle whorls, grinding stones, and projectile points were found as de facto refuse on the floor, suggesting rapid abandonment with objects left in their systemic context (Schiffer 1972). A cache box, lined with adobe bricks, was set into the plaster floor of Room 3 but was empty except for a fragment of a charred, carved bone; since the box was covered by collapsed adobe walls, it is possible that it was looted at the time that the house was burned. Room 4 featured a multiple burial of an adult female, three children, and two infants. These

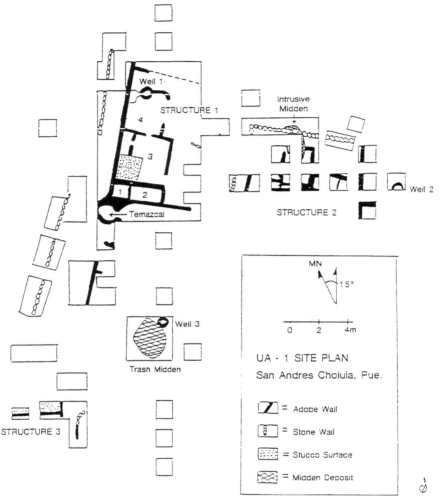

Figure 12.8   UA-1 site plan

skeletons were buried in flexed, seated positions in a shallow pit dug through the plaster floor, with their heads above the floor level. The base of the burial pit featured a 3-centimeter layer of carbon and ash. The collapsed adobe walls covered the burial pit, again implying that the interment probably took place shortly after the house was destroyed.

Although the evidence is not conclusive, Structure 1 apparently was destroyed in a cataclysmic fire during the Late Tlachihualtepetl phase (A.D. 1050–1200), about the time of the invasion of Cholula by the Tolteca-Chichimeca. Was the destruction of Structure 1 related to the invasion? Mixed in with the artifacts of UA-1 were remains of 102 projectile points, a remarkable number considering that the excavation only covered 200 square meters (McCafferty 1992:570–74). Many of these points (37 percent) were found in association with the occupation level of Structure 1, including direct floor contact (figure 12.9). The majority of the measurable projectile points were long (6–8 centimeters) side-notched points of the type usually associated with atlatl darts. Many other points were found in the extramural portions of the excavated site, suggesting that darts were not simply curated but were discharged and subsequently abandoned.

In summary, the arrival of the Tolteca-Chichimeca (ca. A.D. 1200) was noted in the ethnohistoric accounts as a period of violent upheaval, with the resident population of Olmeca-Xicallanca uprooted and "vanquished." This is substantiated by archaeological evidence from the Great Pyramid and from the UA-1 residential area.

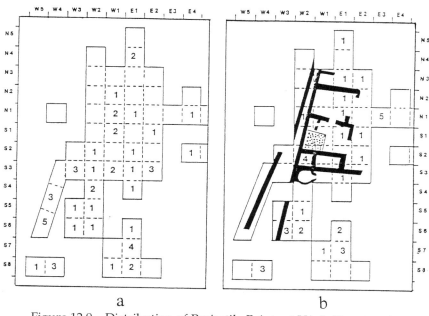

a   b

Figure 12.9   Distribution of Projectile Points at UA-1, Structure 1;
(a) levels 1 and 2; (b) level 3 and below

The Great Pyramid was not only abandoned as the principal ceremonial center of the city but also intentionally desecrated through the destruction of stone stelae in the Patio of the Altars and the (possible) stripping of finished masonry from the exterior of the Stage 4 pyramid facade. Structure 1 of the UA-l locus exhibits evidence of violent abandonment associated with the burning of the structure, looting of its cache box, and possibly the death of a mother and her children. A high concentration of projectile points within the occupation context and in the surrounding area indicates that this destruction was related to military attack.

While the archaeological evidence agrees with the outline of the ethnohistoric account, it remains unclear the extent to which the resident Olmeca-Xicallanca were, in fact, "vanquished." Colonial period accounts indicate a political division between the original Olmeca-Xicallanca part of town and the area occupied by the Tolteca-Chichimeca (McCafferty 1997; Olivera and Reyes 1969). This boundary exists up to the present in the distinct municipalities of San Andrés Cholula and San Pedro Cholula, which make up part of the same metropolitan area but maintain very different political, religious, economic, and cultural practices (Bonfil Batalla 1973). As will be seen in the next section, the multiethnic division of Late Postclassic Cholula had an important impact on the strategies behind the Cholula Massacre during the Spanish conquest.

The Spanish Conquest of Cholula

One of the most violent yet best-recorded events of the Spanish conquest of Mexico occurred in Cholula in October of A.D. 1519, when Cholulteca nobles were gathered in the plaza of the Pyramid of Quetzalcoatl and attacked at the same time that indigenous allies of the Spanish swarmed in to sack outlying parts of the city. This event, known as the Cholula Massacre, was recorded by virtually all chroniclers of the colonial period, including Spanish conquistadores (Cortés 1986; Díaz del Castillo 1963), Spanish priests and historians (Las Casas 1992; López de Gómara 1964; Sahagún 1950–1982; Torquemada 1975–1983), and indigenous scholars (Ixtlilxochitl 1975–1977; Muñoz Camargo 1966) as well as several pictorial representations in indigenous style (Bittman Simons 1968a, 1968b; Lienzo de Tlaxcala 1979; Muñoz Camargo 1966).

Each of these accounts represents what would be considered a primary source, and in isolation each would be relied on for historically accurate evidence. By critically analyzing all of these sources, however, clear differences become apparent that imply the agendas of the particular "historians." Such critical analysis of the Cholula Massacre has been presented by Dudek (1993) and Peterson and Green (1987), and recently I compiled the documentary and pictographic evidence into a study of factional competition relating to the massacre (McCafferty 2000a). Clear distinctions appear among the different accounts, with the most significant being events and/or strategies that may have provoked the massacre. Was it a justified defensive maneuver to forestall an imminent ambush, or was it a strategic offensive move predicated on Cortés's desire to instill fear among the Aztecs of Tenochtitlán, or was there some other political reason?

Cortés (1986) and other members of his army (Díaz del Castillo 1963; López de Gómara 1964) relate evidence that there was an impending ambush, perpetrated by deceitful Cholultecas and supported by their Aztec allies. Claims were made that battlements could be observed in the city and that the women and children had been sent away so that the city was filled only with warriors. There was even the rumor of 50,000 Aztec warriors hiding outside the city, waiting to ambush the Spaniards.

In contrast, however, one of Cortés's officers, Vazquez de Tapia, stated before the Inquisition that he had no warning when Cortés gave the order to attack the assembled Cholultecas (Wagner 1944:173, cited in Peterson and Green 1987:209–10). A similar account was recorded by Sahagún (1950–1982:XII:29–30), based on Aztec informants, that the Cholultecas were gathered unsuspectingly and slaughtered "treacherously." And it is curious that the alleged Aztec army did not join in the battle, especially once the Tlaxcalteca and Cempoalan allies entered the city in support of the Spanish.

Even if an actual ambush was not planned, the fear of one may have loomed large in the minds of the Spanish. Numerous accounts refer to warnings given by the Spaniards' Tlaxcalteca allies, who cautioned that the Cholultecas were allied to the Aztecs. A key element in the "conspiracy theory" was a warning that was allegedly given to Cortés's indigenous translator and adviser, Malintzin, who learned from a Cholulteca noblewoman that an ambush had been plotted (Díaz del Castillo 1963; Torquemada 1975–1983). When Malintzin informed Cortés of the plot, he set the wheels in motion to punish the city.

Was there ever such a plot? Virtually all information passed through Malintzin, including the warnings from the Tlaxcalteca. Was she a passive conduit, as has so often been inferred (Messinger Cypress 1991), or did she have political motivations of her own? Malintzin joined the Spanish in the southern Gulf coast, the Olmeca-Xicallanca heartland, and although she was presented to the Spaniards as a servant, she had been raised as a noble trained to inherit rulership (Kartunnen 1994; McCafferty 2000a). Malintzin's participation throughout the conquest demonstrates her skill as a political adviser and strategist. Arriving in Cholula to find a complex system of political factionalism based on ethnic differences between Nahua Tolteca-Chichimeca and Olmeca-Xicallanca, perhaps including lineages familiar to her, did Malintzin take a role in maneuvering the Spanish into siding with her own clan?

Several lines of evidence suggest that Malintzin did influence events of the Cholula Massacre. First, the indigenous depiction of the massacre presented in the *Lienzo de Tlaxcala* (1979) clearly shows her in the center of the action, pointing her hand to direct the assault on the Tolteca-Chichimeca Temple of Quetzalcoatl (figure 12.10). Second, in the account of Muñoz Camargo (1966; see also León Portilla 1992:48), the Tlaxcaltecan allies of Cortés wore plaited grass in their hair in place of their traditional war headdresses. While this may have been a practical means of distinguishing themselves from the similarly dressed (at least to European eyes) Cholultecas, it could also have been a sign of affiliation with Malintzin since *malintzin* means "precious grass" in the Nahuatl language. Finally, both Díaz del Castillo (1963) and Torquemada (1975–1983) recorded the aftermath of the massacre when a separate group of nobles from Cholula appeared, claiming to be leaders of different factions who were sympathetic to the indigenous allies of Cortés. Peace was immediately restored, and Cholulteca warriors joined in the final assault on Tenochtitlán.

The Cholula Massacre presents a complex scenario of ethnic conflict that was not simply a case of the Spanish versus the Native Americans but also included diverse groups, including the dominant Tolteca-Chichimeca and the subordinate but rival Olmeca-Xicallanca, both of Cholula, as well as Tlaxcalteca and Cempoalan allies of the Spanish. Although still preliminary in scope, archaeological evidence for the massacre illuminates some of the ethnohistorical confusion over this event.

Castro Morales and García Moll (1972) published a brief summary of their excavations in the courtyard of the Cathedral of San Gabriel in downtown San Pedro Cholula, where they had excavated 671 skele-

Figure 12.10   Malintzin directing the attack during the Cholula Massacre
(adapted from Lienzo de Tlaxcala 1979)

tons that they interpreted as victims of the Cholula Massacre (see also
McCafferty 2000a; Peterson and Green 1987). The Cathedral of San
Gabriel represents the most likely location for the Late Postclassic Pyramid of Quetzalcoatl (Marquina 1970), though attempts to locate the
foundations of the pyramid have failed. The skeletons combined pre-
and postcontact characteristics, leading to the interpretation that they
dated from the moment of European contact. Many featured cranial
deformation, a practice that was discouraged under the Spanish, yet
they were buried in the traditional Christian position, extended with
the head to the east, as opposed to the more typical pre-Columbian

burial position of a flexed, seated position facing north. Few grave goods were found, again a divergence from the pre-Columbian tradition, and those that were found were principally items of personal adornment, such as a lip plug, jadeite beads, and copper "buttons." Two Spanish coins were also found, including one dated to A.D. 1512 (Peterson and Green 1987:211).

Evidence to indicate that these were victims of the Cholula Massacre derives from the pathology of numerous individuals, forty-three of whom had been decapitated or dismembered (Castro Morales and García Moll 1972:383). Others showed deep cut marks in the bones consistent with trauma from a sharp blade.

The demographic profile of the skeletal population provides some hints that can be used to evaluate the ethnohistoric accounts of the massacre. Approximately 51 percent ($n = 342$) of the skeletons were adults, while juveniles ($n = 47$) and infants ($n = 256$) were also present. The analysis of the population by sex has not yet been reported, but some were pregnant women (Peterson and Green 1987:211). This information conflicts with the statements by Cortés and others that the women and children had all left the city prior to the planned ambush. Further osteological analysis of the skeletons would provide additional information relating to the ethnic factionalism of the battle, particularly if facial anatomy and DNA testing could isolate specific biological populations among the victims.

The variety of perspectives in the ethnohistorical accounts of the Cholula Massacre incorporate enough contradictions to call into question the events and particularly the motivation behind the attack. Specifically, most interpretations have been strongly Eurocentric, focusing on the Spanish as actors, with little attention paid to the multiethnic factionalism of the indigenous actors. Could Malintzin have manipulated Cortés and his companions into attacking the pro-Aztec faction at Cholula, thus promoting the subordinate pro-Tlaxcala, Olmeca-Xicallanca group, who were themselves her own kin? The accounts present only faint clues, but the archaeological record does contain information on the demographics of the massacre that challenge the accounts of Cortés and his supporters. Future problem-oriented archaeology to address the early colonial period of Cholula may produce additional information for evaluation of ethnic change, including intrasite organization of the Tolteca-Chichimeca versus Olmeca-Xicallanca rivalry.

Conclusion: A Dialectical Approach to Postclassic Warfare

Cholula experienced several violent conflicts during the Postclassic period, some of which can be further evaluated using archaeological evidence. In none of the cases examined was there a perfect fit between the ethnohistoric accounts and the archaeological record. There can be several explanations for this, the most direct being simply the fragmentary state of the archaeological material. Further problem-oriented archaeology to investigate specific periods of ethnic conflict would undoubtedly recover additional information that could be used to modify the interpretations presented here. On the other hand, the archaeological evidence, fragmentary as it is, consistently contradicts facets of the ethnohistoric accounts, challenging the veracity of the written records. This is particularly true for the case of the Cholula Massacre, where the accounts themselves are internally inconsistent. This lack of fit should be viewed not as a problem, however, but rather as varying perspectives on a complex mosaic of human experience. Certain lines of evidence, especially the ethnohistoric accounts, were constructed purposely to project specific ideas about the past, and it should never be forgotten that these projections were created strategically to accomplish certain agendas. The archaeological record, on the other hand, may be less "constructed" but is nevertheless a creation of the various interpreters of the patterned material culture who choose to emphasize or ignore attributes as they "reconstruct the past." An example of this practice is found in the many interpretations of the Cacaxtla Battle Murals that fail to consider the significance of the two bird figures wearing female costume. By engendering this scene, a radically different interpretation of the action can be realized, though again it is an act of manipulating the evidence into a particular pattern. The task at hand is to most completely and consistently incorporate all the information without leaving out any nonconformist pieces.

But what to do with the pieces of information that still do not fit? That is the interesting part of the analysis, for it provides the means to widen the net beyond events of the distant past to question the history-making process itself. Using a dialectical approach, we can critically evaluate the agency of the colonial historians as they embellished to suit their own purposes. Furthermore, we can examine our own prejudices as contemporary archaeologists manipulate their sherds

244 / Geoffrey G. McCafferty

and skeletons in support of the theoretical agenda du jour. By considering the multiple "voices" of the ethnohistoric and archaeological records, the past becomes more complex and much more interesting.

Acknowledgments

Thanks to Arqlgo. Sergio Suárez Cruz for collaborating on the investigations at the Patio of the Carved Skulls and for many hours of lively debate. Also thanks to the late Dan Wolfman, whose field school excavations at UA-1 produced such a wonderful database. And, as always, thanks to Sharisse McCafferty for her artwork, insight, and support.

Chapter Thirteen

A Macabre Sense of Humor: Dramas of Conflict and War in Mesoamerica

Shirley Boteler Mock

As archaeologists, our mission is to interpret spatial patterning in the material remains we recover, seeking to discover certain features of form and redundancy as a mode of understanding, in order to sort out the "structures of signification" (Geertz 1973:9). In the realm of middle-range theory, through the embracing of epigraphy, ethnography, ethnohistory, linguistics, and other academic fields, archaeologists have made important intellectual advancements in understanding the social reality of the past. For instance, the iconography provides daunting evidence that war was a persistent social drama in Mesoamerica, of varying degrees and intensities, carried out within a distinctive pattern of structuring principles merged with ideology and power (see Brown and Garber, chapter 6 in this volume). In this chapter, I seek to enliven the archaeological record by contextualizing these skeletonized life and death events into social dramas of conflict. From this middle-range perspective and guided by the nexus of belief and action, I merge humor with the macabre and sacrifice with war in an examination of the trickster complex. Thus, the archaeological record becomes not the static remains of postdepositional processes or someone's leftover sacrifice but rather a tantalizing piece in the patterns of inception, execution, and termination of changing dramas of conflict in ancient Mesoamerica.

Humor and the Macabre

It is ironic that while writing this chapter, I happened to read an article in the journal *Ethnohistory* (Brandes 1998) focused on the origins of the Day of the Dead iconography in Mexico. The author describes the iconography of the dead at Tenochtitlan as "rigid and serious," attributing the Day of the Dead humor and satire to modern contexts. "These archaeological remains display nothing of the playfulness and humor so essential to contemporary Mexican skull and skeletal representations" (Brandes 1998:193). He adds that "it appears unlikely that these lifelike skeletons, today an isolated archaeological find, would have themselves survived into the colonial and postcolonial eras in Mexico in the form of figurines associated with All Saints and All Souls Days" (Brandes 1998:191; see also Garciagodoy 1998).

From a Western perch, we may view the skulls on the *tzompantli* (skull rack) of ancient Tenochtitlan as grim and grisly reminders of death and war. However, even death and war had their sardonic and ironic twists within the Mesoamerican worldview. As Taube (1989:351) observes, the prominence of death, mutilation, and sacrifice in the iconography of ancient Mesoamerica seems to make humor incongruent. The Nahuatl and Maya worldviews (Burkhart 1989; Carlsen and Prechtel 1997; Freidel et al. 1993) incorporated punning and paradoxical conjoining, of "always becoming" rather than "being." Humor and conflict, then, although two seemingly discordant contexts, are conceptualized together in a broad and timeless pan-Mesoamerican cosmology. It is a matrix composed of overlapping yet complementary oppositions, such as order and chaos, purity and filth or pollution, and ethereal and grotesque. I contend that these conjoined "always becoming" ideas tenaciously continue as a substratum in present-day conflict dramas among the Nahuatl and Maya as personified by the ritual trickster (Bricker 1973). The accommodation of present to past is illuminated by Bricker's (1981) seminal work, *The Indian Christ, the Indian King* (Carlsen and Prechtel 1997:8; Freidel and Schele 1989; Gossen 1986).

In this chapter, I examine this macabre trickster and his presence in war events chronicled on the stone monuments and ceramics. I argue for his presence as a mediator or transformative agent in social dramas of war or conflict. These analogues, although gleaned from varying contexts and derived from different paradigms, inform us of the tenacity of this association of trickster with war, transformation, and sacrifice.

The Cosmic Trickster

The trickster is a character who presumably served (and continues to serve) a number of functions within a society, playing an active role in ordering, interpreting, resolving social contradictions, and acting as a catalyst for change. In many ways, the trickster is analogous to a clown. We must, however, be careful not to confuse our own understanding of humor and sensitivities with that of the Mesoamerican. The trickster, whether manifested as a clown or a misshapen fool, is a liminal character. He is often incomplete, not in control of his actions or bodily functions, or malformed in some manner, reflecting the liminality invoked by Turner (1969) in his study of such figures. Dwarves, because of their liminal characteristics, were often cast in the role of ritual tricksters and, as I discuss later, associated with transformation and war (Houston 1992). The trickster also incorporates features that juxtapose humor and joking to chaos or terror. Barbara Tedlock (Tedlock and Tedlock 1975:107), in their cross-cultural study of the trickster complex, observe that the (Navajo) Assinibone clowns of the Southwest provoke laughter but at the same time frighten their audience. The trickster dancers of the Kwakiutl, of northeastern America, when possessed by supernatural power, not only play practical jokes but also terrorize, stab, and even occasionally kill people. A clown's medicine may be nothing but "common filth." He may wear shabby clothing or display an "aggressive shamelessness . . . that goes with a sudden opening or dislocation in the universe" (Tedlock and Tedlock 1975:115). Barbara Tedlock observes also that the clown or trickster as a liminal character can symbolically be equated with decomposition, or the ambiguous, equivocal, or inchoate state of being. Incomplete as opposed to complete is a characteristic of liminality. Illness, deformities, and physical handicaps had a special meaning among the people of ancient Mesoamerica. Durán (1971:280) observes that one of the dances of conflict in Mexico featured old hunchbacks, simpletons, and jugglers. Despite our Western sensitivities to such ideas, these liminal actors were often associated with immorality, chaos, and filth (Burkhart 1989:177; Sahagún 1982:42, 44; see also Mock 1999), states of being that were incorporated into and controlled by this ritually potent figure.

248 / Shirley Boteler Mock

How does the trickster operate within the ancient humor of Meso-america, and what does he have to do with conflict? Within the Meso-american cosmology centered on the paradigm of war or dueling opposites, we might assume that the trickster was a symbol contra-dicting or overturning the moral order or the normative. In highland Chiapas today, any kind of physical difference or deformity is the sub-ject of jokes or ridicule (Bricker 1973:148). As a means of reinforcing norms, there is a direct relationship to the proper wearing of one's clothes, posture, or demeanor, to conducting one's life and duties in a proper manner (*costumbre*). Whether his aberration was natural or artificially contrived through costume or dress, the trickster purpose-fully overturned social convention and thus was a potential conveyor of power and ideology.

The fiesta of Carnaval held in Chamula, Chiapas, commemorates war and conquest and provides a multilayered context for the release of inhibitions and social critique through drinking ceremonies, humor, ridicule, distortion, parody, and punning. Music, mock pray-ers, and imitation also play crucial roles in the contrast of "normative features with deviant ones" (Bricker 1973:154) in these events, as do the Dance of the Warriors and displays of banners, flags, and spear-tipped poles (Bricker 1973:88, 103, 150). Monkey impersonators (often playing more than one role) with sooted faces and Blackmen (con-nected to caves and having the ability to fly) compose the abnormal or deviant components of the ritual as opposed to the norm.[1]

The trickster "hoots and whistles; he flicks his tail back and forth; he imitates the quick nervous gestures of monkeys"(Bricker 1973:152). During this social drama symbolizing chaos and disorder, Blackmen also are associated with presentation of stolen tribute, ridicule, and sacrifice centered on the display and decapitation of a turkey and the pursuance of fugitives. Bricker emphasizes that these "terrifying per-formances" are enough to "dislodge the soul of even the most stout-hearted Pedrano" (Bricker 1973:143). The period of fiesta ends with the Blackmen beating the other participants for their inappropriate behavior. As the reader will observe in a following section of this chapter, these ritual dramas offer striking parallels to the iconography of human sacrifice, soul loss, capture, tribute presentation, and war events depicted on the ceramics, wall paintings, and stone monu-ments of ancient Mesoamerica.

Bricker (1973:178–79), citing Barrera Vasquez (1965:71) on the Twelfth Song of Dzitbalche (see also Taube 1989), notes the promi-nence of ritual humor among the Maya of Yucatán during the five

Wayeb day dramas at the end of the Old World. These days, which also welcomed the arrival of the New Year, were synchronized with war. Ritual players included musicians, singers, comedians, contortionists, and hunchbacks. Pendants representing hunchbacks have been found in the Cenote of Sacrifice at Chichén Itzá and in earlier contexts at Quirigua, Guatemala, and Copán, Honduras (Ashmore 1980:figs. 10 and 11).

The Dirty Side of Ritual Tricksters

As mentioned previously, humor and conflict are conceptualized together in a broad and timeless pan-Mesoamerican cosmology composed of overlapping binary oppositions such as order and chaos, purity and filth, and ethereal and grotesque. Examination of these concepts helps us understand the complex interworkings of the trickster in conflict dramas depicted in the iconography. The Nahuatl language makes subtle references to dirt, linking it with the trickster. *Tlazolli,* derived from *izolihui,* means "rubbish" or "old, worn-out things." The transitive form *izoloa* means "to abase oneself." *Tlazolli* also can mean something used up, out of place, or swept up with a broom, such as muck, dirt, broken sherds, dust, excrement, or sweat (Burkhart 1989:199). Klein (1991) discusses the moral connotations of excrement, which is connected to the Land of the Dead. She also describes *tlazollalli* as earth filth that becomes "fertilizing humus." Clearly, as noted, dirt and filth were connected to the trickster complex.

For example, the Yucatec word for "comedy" or "farce" was *tah* or *taa, ta* also being the word for "dirt." Soot and dirt as transformatory agents is suggested by Landa's observations of ritual fasting (Tozzer 1941:161, 165; see also Stone 1995) in Yucatán. A central theme was "fasting and abstinence" during which the participants often covered themselves with soot or blackening. Tozzer (1941:165, n. 872) notes that the Guatemalan priests blackened themselves when they sacrificed, considered to be a kind of penance. During rituals of passage young, potential Aztec priests called *tlazoyotl* would grow long braids and smear themselves from head to foot with black soot from the smoke of pine trees. Often this blackened, thick headdress would attract all sorts of plant growth; in reality, they became a walking and flowering World Tree, certainly humorous figures in their religious soberness.

In some respects, *tlazolli* is analogous to the term *itz,* translated as "witch" by the highland Maya (Freidel et al. 1993:211), also meaning "sap," "wax," "sacred liquids," or "to make magic" among the Yucatec Maya (Schele and Mathews 1998:265). The hole in the middle of the ball court was called *Itzompan,* or "Skull Place," where plants were cultivated in the beginning of creation. The ball court and skull rack are found together in many archaeological contexts. *Itz* also has moral connotations as personified in *Itzama* and *Itzam-Yeh,* the great cosmic bird also known in the Popol Vuh as the Seven-Macaw, who was teased and deceived by the Hero Twins because of his arrogance (Freidel et al. 1993:211, 215).

This transformative aspect of the trickster complex also is reflected in the Maya *Ah Itz,* or wicked clown sacrificer, whose humor and punning play a crucial role in the present-day Dance of the Conquest during the New Year's Festival or Wayeb among the K'iche' (Freidel et al. 1993). The Nahuatl had a similar five-day period of bad luck they called *Nemontemi* (Weaver 1972:64).

Other Ritual Tricksters

The *itz,* or sage, also appears in dwarf form (Schele and Miller 1986:pls. 41 and 43), such as the Jaina-style figurine with a flayed face. Flayed faces were typically connected to war and Xipe Totec, "Our Lord the Flayed One" of the Nahuatl, and were an integral part of the Maya Tlaloc-Venus war complex (Freidel et al. 1993:24, 409; Schele and Freidel 1990). A flayed face is depicted on an unusual, applique-incised-resist decorated late Terminal Classic censer from the Northern River Lagoon site in Belize. A typical figurine whistle from the same site and time period represents the chubby, childlike dwarf, in this case wearing ballplayer attire. Kerr (1989:88 [1456], 116 [1837]) shows two rollouts of an angry-looking dwarf, in the latter case dancing with elegantly attired rulers. This distinctive attire and its relationship to war is discussed in more detail later in this chapter. During the Maya Terminal Classic to Early Postclassic, this dwarf type is modified to serve as part of a tripod vessel support.

Miller (1985) tabulated the various dwarf figures in Maya iconography, concluding that they are historical figures who once lived in Maya kingdoms (cf. Houston 1992:526). This manifestation of the trickster seems to appear in many contexts and take on many different attributes: a marked brow ridge, prominent nose, protruding belly, and buttocks as seen in Schele and Miller (1986:pl. 42). In this case, the old-man trickster wears an unusual hat and holds symbols of war such as a shield. He may represent god N, in the Pauahtun complex a prominent participant in New Year ceremonies among the Yucatec, or the old Mam effigy (Taube 1989:354–55), an object of ridicule as he ended the Old Year, his belly distended with sin. Subsequent to the ritual, he was discarded or destroyed, having absorbed the sins, evil, or corruption of the community.

Dwarves were considered to have special transformational powers among the pre-Columbian people of Mesoamerica (Laughlin 1988:273). Schele and Mathews (1998:77; see also Houston 1992:531) state that the Maya called dwarfs *mas*, or hobgoblins, with power to tap into the supernatural. It is interesting that the Maya word *max*, meaning "monkey" (Brian Stross, personal communication, 1999), forges yet another connection in this vast cast of character manifestations, becoming the focus of decorative ceramic treatment during the Late Classic, as typified in this Palmar Orange polychrome plate (figure 13.1a) (Mock 1997, 1999; see also Guderjan and Garber 1995:98–99). The reader may recall the monkey scribe depicted in a Late Classic sculpture at Copán. Like other monkey scribes, the figure is depicted with an ugly face, a flat, pug nose, almost as an incomplete figure with human and monkey characteristics, an echo of the previously described monkey impersonators of contemporary conflict dramas. The dwarf parallelism is carried through in highland Guatemalan ethnographic accounts of the earth lord who appears in openings in the earth (Vogt 1993). Similarly, Klein (1990–1991) notes the dwarfish Tlalocs associated with the orifices of the Underworld. Among the Nahuatl, dwarves were also of symbolic significance, serving as special "courtiers" to entertain the court and retainers (Schele and Miller 1986:150).

Figure 13.1a   A late Classic Palmar Orange polychrome plate with monkey design (drawing by Richard McReynolds, taken from Mock 1994b, 1997)

The Trickster as Mediator

The permutations of these figures in highly charged social dramas are clearly paralleled in examples of Late Classic Maya iconography. The trickster as mediator appears in contexts interacting with supernatural beings. Houston (1992:526–27)[2] singles out the dwarf for detailed analysis, concluding that a distinctive complex of kilted dwarfs and royals appears together in association with major period-ending rituals. This role is a significant association. In terms of the other ideas presented in this chapter, it is also of note that *caban* markings, "carnality, filth, or earth," are associated with one depiction of a dwarf. This is clearly in line with the Nahuatl concept of *tlazolli* discussed previously.

We find similar macabre tricksters in the murals and lintels at the Late Classic site of Bonampak in Chiapas. The murals depict a series of captive events, music, and dances, coordinated with the presentation of the ruler's son as heir. According to Miller (1986), the next event, dedicating the structure, occurred 236 days later on the first appearance of Evening Star, a Tlaloc war event. This occasion included bloodletting by the ruler, sacrifice and humiliation of captives, and war (Freidel et al. 1993:284; Schele and Miller 1986:217). The macabre tricksters on the west wall of Room 3 (figure 13.1b) bear a drum-playing (*huehuetl*) dwarf on a litter (Miller 1986:pl. 54). Miller describes the musical group as "deformed, perhaps an entire troop of cripples, hunchbacks, and dwarves, normally seen one at a time"(Miller 1986).

Wren (n.d.) observes a similar accession rite and decapitation sacrifice in the iconography of the Terminal Classic site of Chichén Itzá, Yucatán. She interprets the rite as the Warrior Dance, similar to that described previously in highland Guatemala and Yucatán. The aged Mam or Pauahtun discussed previously also played a central role in this procession of dancing warriors. Clearly, the Bonampak murals mirror a similar meaning. The macabre band on the western wall are holding up the Underworld while they make a din rather than melodious music in preparation for war and conquest. Coincidentally, the slit drum, or *teponaztli*, was associated with both rainmaking and war among the Maya and Nahuatl (Bricker 1981:148–49). This coincides with the Tale of the Red Dwarf also connected to war (see Stone 1995:153). "The whirlwind and the thunderbolt, which accompany rain, are also magical weapons of war, and the slit drum, which is played during a feast in honor to the rain god, is also a rain drum" (Bricker 1981:18).

Figure 13.1b   Macabare tricksters on the west wall of Room 3 at Bonampak bear a drum-playing (*huehuetl*) dwarf (adapted from Miller 1986)

An analogous palace scene takes place on another Late Classic vase from Motul de San José (Schele and Miller 1986:pl. 71) in the court of the "Fat Cacique" (figure 13.2), where he is being entertained by three twirling, painted figures performing a bloodletting dance on a lower level. In the midst of this commotion, the "Fat Cacique" sits on his jaguar-covered bench attended by a kneeling lord and a small, dark, deformed dwarf (Schele and Miller 1986:pl. 71, 193, 204–5). The Motul de San José site has been mentioned frequently in the context of wars with Petexbatun lords (Demarest 1997b:215); however, the site has never been identified archaeologically (see Reents-Budet and Bishop 1989; see also Houston 1992:fig. 3).

In Schele and Mathews (1998:82, fig. 2.23), there is a similar scene displayed on Pot 2D in the Dance of the Jaguar. It is a masked transformation dance centered again on the "Fat Cacique" from Motul de San José. He is attended in a palace scene by a small, chubby dwarf, attired as a ballplayer, echoing similar characteristics of the previously described figurines and vessel effigy supports.

At Yaxchilán, Bird Jaguar plays ball at the Three-Conquest-Ballcourt Stair accompanied by two dwarflike creatures. Freidel et al.

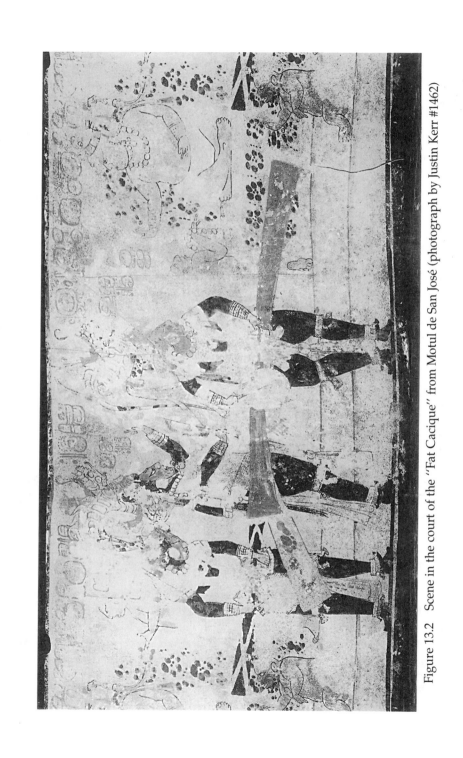

Figure 13.2 Scene in the court of the "Fat Cacique" from Motul de San José (photograph by Justin Kerr #1462)

(1993:360–61) note that one dwarf wears the shell ear flare of Chak, and both wear the Venus or star signs connoting war. Taladoire and Colsenet (1991:172) observe that dwarves are among the spectators at other ball-game activities. However, these liminal characters are not silent or passive; as tricksters, they are transformative and thus crucial to closing or initiating a social drama or sacred place. Just as they accompanied the victim to the Underworld, these tricksters probably accompanied the ruler to war and its counterpart, the ball game, frightening the enemy with their cacophonous din and appearance. Reents-Budet (cited in Cohadas 1991) noted the presence of a dwarf and a hunchback as attendants to dancing lords on a certain type of ceramic painting popular in the Naranjo-Holmul region. She interprets the individuals as shaman who would guide the deceased noble into the Underworld, just as the Evening Star guides the sun into the Underworld. As Freidel et al. (1993:361) note, "These conquest sacrifices are linked to battle and the unfolding of fate in warfare. These mythic decapitations and conquests have their parallel in the decapitation of real-world victims." As agents of change, these macabre joksters had simultaneous roles as shaman sacrificers, as suggested in the ceramics recovered from the site of San Motul de San José.

Mirrors of Sacrifice

In the iconography, the ritual trickster as sacrificer is often associated with both mirrors and ruler/captor in graphic court scenes. I find this interesting in that Houston (citing Schele and Miller 1986:20), in attempts to decipher the name of the kilted dwarf, notes the connection of the initial sign of the name with a mirror.

As another example, consider the cast of characters in this palace scene (figure 13.3) from a rollout vessel; the bleeding captive sits across from the ruler prior to or subsequent to a war event. An attendant holds up a mirror to the ruler while the captive looks on unhappily; perhaps it is his mirror, captured on the field of battle, representing a reversal of reality and capture of his soul, or *tonali*. The captive, presumably a noble, must now pay for his transgressions by being sacrificed and beheaded. He has created disorder and chaos through war or rebellion against this particular ruler or his ancestors. The typically tangled, snarled, or twisted hair of the captive (Mock 1998b; see also Stone 1995) symbolizes this impure and profane state prior to sacrifice.

Similarly, the captive may be forced to view his own captured

Figure 13.3   Palace scene depicting ruler with captive (photograph by Justin Kerr #5416)

mirror and his captured battle standard in a public display; his icons of power held by a attendant before he is sacrificed. In another scene (figure 13.4), the ruler may be preparing for war (Schele and Mathews 1998:76–77). Certainly as potential sacrifices and, thereby, mediators of order and chaos, certain captives may have been "banked," so to speak, with these rituals in mind. Painted with soot or paint suggesting a trance state, the ruler faces an unusual group of attendants: two dwarflike figures, the smaller of whom holds up a mirror; the other drinks a potion. Schele and Mathews (1998:77), noting both the bowl and the gourd container under the bench, interpret the glyph text above the drinking figure as *tos utz*, or "powdered good." The mirror may belong to the captive, in this case possibly represented by the figure of an old man demonstrating a submissive gesture. Taube (1989:351) has discussed captured figures being represented as wrinkled and old, with lumpy noses or sagging bellies (like the figurine discussed previously). He also notes their connection to war events. Two other attendants (*itz'at*, or "sage") seem to enjoy this form of ultimate captive humiliation. The violence of the occasion is enhanced by music and noise from another macabre band whose instruments include simulated long bones and large conch shells signifying war. This recalls the contemporary Blackmen of Zinacantan and Chenalho, who, as buffoons and clowns, chastise and insult, teasing the crowd and asking, "Are you suffering from magical fright?" Then they pretend to restore missing parts of their soul (Bricker 1981:136).

Perhaps these graphic dramas incorporate captives into the onset of new wars, as a result of revenge motives, or accompanying accession or Tlaloc-Venus events as seen in the murals of Bonampak. I am led to this interpretation by the previously mentioned Pot G2:A (Schele and Mathews 1998:89), in which the presence of the mirror and ruler with the *itz'at* suggests the presentation of captured mirror along with other conquest tribute. Another pot (Pot G2:A in Schele and Mathews 1998:89, fig. 2.32) shows the central figure, the ruler, sitting on his bench with a mirror before him.

In a scene displayed on a vessel from the Ik site (Motul de San José), clown musicians, dressed in Xipe masks and hats, perhaps wearing flayed skins (see Durán 1971:lamina 4), mock the intended victim, who is forced to gaze at his own captured mirror, his access to the spirit world denied in a reversal of reality (figure 13.5). He is losing his *way* or *tonalli* to the captor, bound by bloodied ropes symbolizing his wrongdoing and immorality (Klein 1991). Analogous to the sinner described in Sahagún (1950–1982:4, 11), he is depicted as wallowing

Figure 13.4   Black-painted ruler looks at mirror held by a dwarf (photograph by Justin Kerr #1453)

Figure 13.5   Rollout of vessel from the Ik Site (Motul de San José) showing clown musicians dressed in Xipe masks and hats (photograph by Justin Kerr #2025)

in disorder, "with blanched or reddened face debauched, with hair tangled, uncombed, twisted, and matted."

Grotesque realism emphasizes the brute, physical, and scatological properties of the clowns. They wear skins dripping with blood. Their tumbling, rapid movements, and mocking contribute a new dimension to the trickster complex, opposed to the pure and proper presentation of the masked captor. The clowns have Xipe-like mouths, swollen under the skins (Karl Taube, personal communication, 1999) that make noises. One holds a knife to the captive's ear while another mocks his throne, simultaneously tormenting him with the heart extraction pose. As symbolic inversions, these clowns cavort and dance like monkeys (see Bricker 1973:183), in ludic actions counter to the social order, loosening the disorder of chaos to incorporate order.

Like others, the captive's body has been tortured, now an incomplete body, invaded, dismembered, and degraded. As discussed previously in conflict dramas of today, his presence echoes the Sun-Christ, banished by monkeys to the Underworld in the five-day Wayeb ritual of San Juan Chamula of highland Chiapas. Freidel et al. (1993:265) have noted the "dichotomy of the monstrous and the bizarre in one phase and the stately and exemplary in another" among the Maya. Discourses of the grotesque and the ethereal are often opposed in such rituals, loosened in a pre- or postconflict ritual that condenses a cosmology in iconography (see also Taube 1989). The social drama encompasses Tezcatlipoca, the Nahuatl cosmic trickster, with attributes of pollution and chaos. Like a mirror, he could look into people's hearts and determine hidden deeds (Burkhart 1989). His manifestation is the flayed god, Xipe Totec, his attributes previously noted on an anthropomorphic vessel and figurine from the Northern River Lagoon site in Belize.

And Time Goes On

The epigraphy, iconography, ethnography, and ethnohistory of Mesoamerica have provided patterns and redundancies to assist us in contextualizing the social reality of past events. Contemporary social dramas also continue to assist us in crossing the bridge of time and space. The Dance of the Devil and the Dance of the Underworld (Bricker 1973:187), historically focused on war and conquest, continue to take place during the Wayeb days in Yucatán, in which the world is destroyed and recreated (Freidel et al. 1993). The ritual trickster, reflecting the winds of change, continues to transform time and bridge sardonic humor in the Dance of the Warriors, or *Holcan okot,* of the ancient Maya. The war-like steps reenacted in the festival of Carnival in Chamula today (Bricker 1989:143) fuse the historical and mythological, structure, and practice.

These "structures of signification" (Geertz 1973:9) make it clear that dramas of warfare, conflict, and sacrifice were also part of the stage from which the Late Classic Maya viewed their world (Demarest 1997b). In this chapter, I sought to enliven this stage with human actors. The popularity of the frightening but yet humorous trickster, dwarf, monkey, and other misshapen or grotesque characters makes sense within the context of endemic war and conflict in Mesoamerica. Their prominence in graphic depictions and the "wealth of dwarf glyphs" during the Maya Late Classic, in particular, can be explained by the turbulence of this time period. As discontent increased, so did the cast of characters appropriated by the ruling class to maintain order through increased ritual activity. As a social critic, the trickster also mediated relationships between elites and nonelites, rulers and nobles, on both intra- and interpolity levels. Presumably on the fringes of the elite, at the village level, the trickster complex (like the ball game) was replicated in different ways, to resolve gender, age, and kinship issues carried on today in myths and legends (Laughlin 1988). This frenzy to keep up with the forces of chaos created by war is reflected also in the regionality and heterogeneity of the ceramic assemblages of this time period (Mock 1994b).

Perhaps the cast of liminal, "always becoming" tricksters examined in this chapter will ultimately reveal their macabre secrets. Now that Pandora's box has been opened, so to speak, perhaps they can assist scholars in adding to the attenuated bits and pieces from which we adduce the culture of Mesoamerica. Within an interdisciplinary, contextual approach, an understanding of this complex cosmology may also allow us to fathom gleanings of the political agencies and practices of human players on this changing battlefield of time and space.

Notes

1. These are overlain with Turkish, French, and Latino costume elements reflecting the bricolage of historical conflicts (Bricker 1973:143).

2. The name glyphs of these figures depicted have yet to be revealed (Houston 1992:526).

Part V

COMPARATIVE STUDY AND SUMMARY VIEW

Chapter Fourteen

Warfare in the American Southwest and Mesoamerica: Parallels and Contrasts

Steven A. LeBlanc

There has been a long tradition of looking for links between the American Southwest and Mesoamerica but less interest in simply comparing the two regions. To some, the southwestern United States is recognized as the northern periphery of Mesoamerica, and archaeologically it is usually defined to include a good portion of the states of Chihuahua and Sonora in northern Mexico (Cobb et al. 1999; Cordell 1997). In fact, Phillips (1989) proposes the term "Northern Mexico" to imply a fundamentally Mexican aspect of what is known as the Southwest. Others see the two areas as much more distinct. Despite the nature of the relationship, it can be argued that the American Southwest is an area relevant to greater Mesoamerica, for which we have a considerable degree of information. Even though the Southwest is peripheral, we should make use of this knowledge in dealing with Mesoamerica proper (hereafter simply referred to as Mesoamerica).

The amount of research done in the U.S. portion of the Southwest greatly exceeds that of Mesoamerica in proportion to the extant size of the archaeological whole in each area. This intensity of research in the Southwest, combined with the wealth of tree-ring dates, typically makes more fine-grained analysis possible than in Mesoamerica.

Conversely, Mesoamerica had a literate tradition that provides a class of information unavailable in the Southwest. Moreover, although both areas have important oral traditions, much of the Mesoamerican oral history was recorded in the 1500s, while most of the Southwestern oral history was not recorded until the late 1800s or even more recently.

These various differences are reflected in the study of warfare in the two areas. In the Southwest, arguments on the subject focus on site locations, site configurations, regional settlement patterns, and so on, with only minor mention of iconography or oral histories. Conversely, much of the discussion of Mesoamerican warfare involves iconography, textual information, and appeals to models based on warfare at Spanish contact. Perhaps the most dramatic difference is in the contrasting use of iconographic evidence for warfare in the two regions. Iconography, such as murals and rock art, has been given short shrift in the Southwest (with notable exceptions, such as Cole 1993; Crotty 1995; Jacobs 1998; Schaafsma 1992). Is this omission a result of the unwillingness of Southwestern archaeologists to recognize warfare in the past? Or is Southwestern iconography truly so vague and uninterpretable that it cannot usefully be considered for this purpose?

Even though the two geographic regions are culturally closely linked, the nature of the information about their warfare is rather different and complementary. Thus, comparisons between the two should be useful for improving our understanding of warfare and related social processes in both areas. Of particular interest is how common warfare was in both areas, its importance in culture change, and why it took place. Also of interest are several aspects of southwestern warfare that might be usefully considered by Mesoamericanists. These include methods for recognizing warfare, the evolution of weapons technology, and the apparent linkage between the intensity of warfare and climate change. Conversely, knowledge about the social mechanisms of Mesoamerican warfare might be far more relevant to southwestern cultural developments than has been previously recognized.

Two particular topics seem worthy of consideration. The first is the extent of prestate warfare in Mesoamerica. The social organization of the Southwest even in late prehistory was no more complex than for the Early and Middle Formative in Mesoamerica. There is ample evidence for very significant warfare in the prehistoric Southwest, yet very little warfare has been recognized for the Early and Middle Formative in Mesoamerica. That is, when we compare the two areas at the same level of complexity, we seem to find much greater evidence for warfare in the Southwest than Mesoamerica. Is this because we have better data from the Southwest, or were the trajectories different?

The second issue is that it appears that warfare was significantly affecting the social organization of various southwestern societies (LeBlanc 1999, 2000), yet few such similar arguments seem to be made for Mesoamerica. For example, in the Maya area during the Classic and Postclassic periods, warfare seems to be every bit as prevalent as in the Southwest, yet there seems to be little belief among scholars that this warfare was causing significant changes in social organization. Is this a real difference or an interpretive problem?

The History of the Approach to Warfare in the Southwest and Mesoamerica

Over the years, attitudes toward warfare in the Southwest have changed. This topic has been reviewed by Haas and Creamer (1993, 1997), LeBlanc (1999), and Wilcox and Haas (1994) and is only briefly summarized here. The early explorers and archaeologists saw evidence for warfare in the locations and configurations of sites as well as the presence of unburied or obviously killed individuals, but little effort was made to include warfare in interpreting these societies. This early period was followed with ever decreasing concern for warfare. More and more, explanations both for site layouts and locations and for culture change avoided the role that warfare might have played. This culminated in the 1980s with claims that warfare was almost non-existent in the prehistoric Southwest and was irrelevant to understanding the cultural processes that took place. Then the trend began to reverse, and by the early 1990s increasing appeal to warfare to explain the locations of sites, the burning of sites, and so on was being made. Only recently has it been recognized that we can go beyond recognizing the existence of warfare and begin to include it in our model building of cultural change. Thus, while it may appear that we have only come full circle and are now recognizing evidence for warfare that was first recognized more than a century ago, this is not the case. We have moved beyond simply the recognition of warfare and now are beginning to see it as an important component of social behavior that must be integrated into models of social change.

It appears that a similar trajectory has taken place in Mesoamerica. The early historical documents demonstrated ample evidence for the importance of warfare in Mesoamerica at the time of European contact, and precontact histories did the same for the late prehistoric period. Thus, the early archaeologists knew full well that warfare had been an important component of late prehistoric Mesoamerican society. However, over time one can see an ever decreasing recognition for warfare during the past century of research. As the earlier periods were recognized and synthesized, they were increasingly seen as peaceful, culminating in a rather peaceful Formative period and even a peaceful Maya Classic period. Of course, as Freidel et al. (chapter 11 in this volume) point out, there was always the recognition that some warfare had taken place in the past, just as there was the recognition that some warfare had taken place prehistorically in the Southwest. Nevertheless, model building of how the Mesoamerican societies developed, evolved, and collapsed paid precious little importance to the role of warfare before the events of the Postclassic. Again, beginning in the 1970s and 1980s, recognition of warfare in earlier periods began to increase with broader acceptance of its presence and importance continuing into the 1990s. To what extent, however, have Mesoamerican archaeologists begun to build the existence of warfare into their models of cultural change? It is my view from a distance that this process has barely begun, with Flannery and his colleagues being the most notable example of actually integrating the role of warfare in their interpretations (Flannery and Marcus 1983b; Marcus and Flannery 1996; Redmond 1983).

Southwestern Warfare: A Summary

While far from worked out, an overall pattern of the nature of warfare in the Southwest is beginning to emerge (Haas and Creamer 1993; LeBlanc 1998, 1999, 2000). Virtually all classes of evidence for warfare can be found in the Southwest. This evidence includes sites built defensively and defensively located, communities clustering with large no-man's-lands between them, and communities located to effect line-of-sight communication between them. Cases of massively burned sites with in situ deposits and unburied bodies, including extensive massacres, are also known. Further indicators of warfare include weapons, iconography, human body-part trophies, as well as possible evidence of sacrificed captives. Many of these lines of evidence are complex in their interpretation and are not necessarily convincing in isolation, but the sum of the evidence is substantial in many times and places. For summary purposes, it is useful to divide the temporal sequence into three broad time intervals: an Early period prior to A.D. 900, a Middle period from A.D. 900 to 1150/1200, and a Late period from the 1200s to Spanish contact.

The Early Period

There is insufficient evidence to discuss southwestern warfare prior to the introduction of agriculture into the Southwest. Although an early farming period can be defined beginning around 1000 B.C. (Huckell 1995; Mabry 1997; Matson 1991; Wills 1988), overall archaeological evidence is rather sketchy until in the last few centuries B.C. and the first few centuries A.D. Thus, the interval for which one can say anything useful is about 1,000 years, from the last few centuries B.C. to A.D. 900. Evidence for warfare is surprisingly common in this interval.

Although there is not enough information to formulate a model for just how common warfare was during the Early period, how much it changed over time, or how much it was impacting these peoples' lives, given the paucity of information for this time in general, the evidence for warfare is surprising. Some sites are located in defensible locations, and some make use of hillside terraces, or *trincheras* (Roney 1996a, 1996b; Wilcox 1979). There is evidence for massacres (of up to one hundred people) as well as conflict-related iconography depicting trophy heads (Cole 1993; Hurst and Turner 1993). Perhaps more surprising is the presence of standardized basketry frames for stretching scalps and very standardized atlatl fending sticks (Heizer 1942; Howard and Janetski 1992). Both these items are found in contexts prior to the introduction of the bow and arrow around A.D. 200 in the northern Southwest. In the first few centuries A.D., it is generally assumed that no community had as many as one hundred residents, so a massacre of one hundred people is shocking. Where was the polity that could have executed such a massacre? In addition, the scalp stretchers were for displaying scalps; thus, people were being killed and scalped often enough to have a specialized artifact to use with them. All these lines of evidence imply rather widespread and formalized warfare.

From A.D. 200 to 600, the settlement pattern in the Mogollon area (the southern portion of the region) consists of almost all villages being located on hilltops. Such defensive locations were less common earlier. While site burning is not common, it does occur. Only rarely are these sites additionally fortified. Most interestingly, these hilltop locations are used for about 400 years, then never again used. In the

Anasazi area to the north, small hamlets with palisades occur, and some larger sites are located on mesa tops but are not additionally fortified. By A.D. 800, there are very large communities in the northern Southwest, and their destruction by burning is ubiquitous. In many of these instances, and in situations mentioned later in this chapter, it is assumed that the simultaneous burning of large suites of rooms or structures, the presence of in situ materials, and the abandonment of the community at the time of burning are a result of warfare. This pattern is referred to as "massive burning" to distinguish it from random and occasional burning of structures that may not be the result of warfare.

Early pit-house settlement patterns were also being influenced by warfare. The clearest example of this comes from the early Mogollon sites. During the period A.D. 200–600, as noted, virtually all villages were on hilltops. This was also a time before the introduction of the bow. Trying to throw an atlatl uphill is quite difficult, and these hilltops appear to have offered good defense even when unfortified. However, around A.D. 500–600, the bow was rapidly adopted in this area (it was adopted earlier in the Anasazi area to the north), and the hilltops were soon abandoned. Did hilltops not afford sufficient protection from the bow and arrows, so that the high cost of their use could no longer be justified and they were no longer inhabited? The important point is that not only was Early period settlement location being dictated by defensive concerns, but it was susceptible to technological change in warfare, a point quite relevant to the Mesoamerican situation.

Several points are of particular interest during this Early period. First, this rather chronic and pervasive Early period warfare takes place as agriculture is introduced and becomes increasingly reliable. Because one would assume an increasing carrying capacity during this interval due to the increased productivity of the new cultigens, one might posit a decrease in warfare because of lack of stress on resources. But this does not seem to be the case. Rapid population growth, competition for favorable farmable areas, lack of established usufruct rights, or other factors seem to dominate. Warfare may or may not have accompanied the initial adoption of agriculture in the Southwest, but it certainly accompanied the process of its becoming well established.

The final point is that this Early period warfare was not "ritual warfare," as is proposed for some ethnographically known warfare, such as in the New Guinea highlands or desert Australia or as has been argued for the Aztec "Flowery Wars" (Hassig 1988; Isaac 1983a). The idea of ritual warfare is that it is pretend war. The goal is not to really kill the enemy, capture territory, or the like but to satisfy some social need such as revenge or to behave in a manly way. On closer inspection, much of this presumed ritual warfare is really just one phase of an overall warfare pattern, and other phases can be extremely deadly. This does not mean that warfare cannot have a ritual component, as is clearly the case. Conversely, just because warfare has a ritual component or some aspects of it appear formalized and not very deadly does not mean that overall that same warfare cannot be both deadly and biologically and culturally very important. Prior to A.D. 900, southwestern warfare did have its ritual aspects, as seen in the trophy heads, the scalp stretchers, and even the stylized fending sticks, but it was also real, with massacres, destroyed sites, and settlement patterns adapted to long-term needs for defense.

We can summarize the time up to around A.D. 900 in the Southwest as an interval in which warfare was significant but not pervasive. There are locations and sites that are not at all defensive as well as some times and places where there is almost no other evidence for warfare.

The Middle Period

The time interval from around A.D. 900 to 1150 is both the most intriguing and the most difficult to understand in the Southwest. This is the time of the Chaco Interaction Sphere in the eastern Anasazi area, of the Classic Mimbres in the Mogollon region, and of the Sedentary period florescence in the Hohokam area (Crown and Judge 1991; LeBlanc 1983; Lekson 1993; Vivian 1990). The Chaco system seems to reflect the most complex social organization witnessed in the prehistoric Southwest. This Middle period is also the interval for which we have the least evidence for warfare for any time in the Southwest. Despite considerable excavations and extensive survey, there is little evidence for fortresslike sites, no-man's-lands, massive burning of sites, or unburied bodies resulting from massacre.[1] Moreover, the iconography, although limited in extent, does not reflect military imagery. In fact, such terms as *Pax Chaco* have been applied to this time (Lekson 1992).

A depiction of these times as peaceful, however, is not fully accurate. In the Mimbres area, while sites are not defensive and there is little other evidence for warfare, some iconography (unrelated to that of the Early period) does point to human sacrifice or trophy taking. Several Mimbres bowls show such events, and another, unfortunately incomplete, shows actual warfare (see LeBlanc 1999). Archaeological support for these scenes includes a number of bodies without heads and skulls without bodies found (Anyon and LeBlanc 1984). However, the real anomalous situation comes from the Chaco Interaction Sphere. Several Chaco great houses are on high points that form a sig-naling network over a considerable area. Straight roads connect some of the great houses. As we would expect signaling to be for defense and as straight roads tend to be for military purposes, this evidence suggests there was warfare that is harder to recognize than at other times in the Southwest.

It has also recently become clear that there are a number of instances of treating some members of this society as "subhuman." Bodies are thrown in trash dumps, stuffed head first down pits, and so on. Other people, especially but not exclusively women, were bat-tered but not killed (Martin 1997). And, most surprisingly, more than thirty cases of humans either being consumed or their bodies being butchered are known (Turner and Turner 1999). Such cases of what is possibly cannibalism are not a normal southwestern practice but are almost completely restricted to the time and area of the Chaco Interac-tion Sphere. Most instances of butchering are of multiple individuals, approximately eight or so individuals being the typical number butch-ered in a single event, but some events represent more than thirty indi-viduals.

At first glance, these types of evidence would seem to argue for warfare during Chacoan times, and some (such as Wilcox 1993) have made such an argument. However, the lack of many other indepen-dent lines of evidence we would expect to find if warfare were com-mon, such as the large number of very indefensible sites, the lack of burned sites, the absence of no-man's-lands, and so on, would argue against such models. Moreover, while straight roads can be consid-ered military roads, just like in the Yucatán and at La Quemada, many roads in the Chaco Sphere are short and seem ritually based. Overall, violent behavior within a single polity seems more likely than between-polity warfare as an explanation for this evidence. However, as is discussed later in this chapter, the possibility of Mesoamerican involvement, perhaps nonpeaceful involvement, in the Chaco Sphere needs to be considered.

There is evidence that this relative "peace" (or whatever it was) began to break down toward the end of the Middle period when building activity enclosed previously open sides of many of the Chaco great houses, making them quite defensible. At the end of the Middle period, burning and concurrent site abandonment occurred, as did the formation of no-man's-lands beginning at this time in the Hohokam area (Wilcox 1989), a trend that accelerated in the subsequent period.

The Late Period

By the early to mid-1200s, evidence for increased conflict is widespread in the Southwest. The initial response to this escalation of warfare was for the population to agglomerate while still remaining in discrete housing units. Groups of small and medium-size pueblos become common, and the formation of no-man's-lands begins. The population of these aggregates often numbered in the several hundreds. There is evidence that many of these agglomerated but not defensible communities were attacked and burned and soon were replaced by large, defensible communities. The latter communities formed tight clusters with ever increasing no-man's-lands between them. At some point between A.D. 1276 and 1325, there were about twenty-seven site clusters in the northern and central Southwest, with an as yet not clearly determined number of additional groupings in the more southern areas. In addition, tight groupings of sites formed in the Rio Grande area.

The northern clusters contained from two to eighteen separate communities, usually spaced about three miles apart. Such groups of sites were separated by about twenty miles from other groups, a separation that increased over time. Over the next century, most of these groups of sites declined and disappeared, leaving vast areas depopulated. In the area that previously held the twenty-seven site clusters, only three remained, the historically known Hopi, Zuni, and Acoma. In the Rio Grande, the number of sites and the number of clusters also declined but not as dramatically. At some point, people linguistically related to Acoma moved into the center of the Rio Grande, perhaps occupying a no-man's-land that opened up between other site clusters. In all these cases, the communities in each group of sites were located so close together that they must have formed alliances of some type (which is borne out by their high degree of ceramic and architectural similarity), but exactly what the nature of the social integration was among them is not clear. Alliances also formed between site clusters, but these alliances were apparently much more ephemeral and not of the same type as the relationships maintained among the sites within clusters.

Interestingly, trade and interaction (evidenced primarily by ceramics) between these community clusters both increased and decreased at the same time. Uneven patterns of interaction suggest that alliances formed between clusters. However, most alliances seem to have been short lived, as many of the clusters died out. If one did not have the fine-grained temporal control available in the Southwest, scholars might assume that everyone in the Late period was interacting with everyone else, but this was not the case, and interaction rapidly shifted (LeBlanc 2000).

The communities were rendered defensible by several means. Some were built in cave overhangs well known as cliff dwellings. Most, however, were pueblos of many hundreds of rooms built with high exterior walls formed by an outer row of two-storied rooms with large central plazas. Some pueblos were situated on high landforms for additional protection, and others were very near domestic water sources, sometimes with walk-in wells in the plazas. Despite the defensive nature of these towns, many were attacked and destroyed, with massive burning and unburied bodies.

During the Late period, there was considerable movement of people over both long and short distances, based on architectural and ceramic links to distant areas (Haury 1958; LeBlanc 1998; Lindsay 1987; Mills 1995; Woodson 1995). One motivation for this movement was probably to maintain the numbers of people required for a pueblo to be large enough to survive attack. Despite the efforts to survive in this difficult time, the population declined precipitously, perhaps to a fifth of its previous maximum (see Dean et al. 1994). This population decline was probably due to a combination of starvation, poor nutrition, and actual deaths due to warfare. The *kachina* cult developed and rapidly spread at this time (Adams 1991). Its focus on rain and fertility was perhaps a response to the difficult times and its integrating social mechanism a response to the much greater numbers of people living in close proximity in massive buildings.

As mentioned, one measure of the relationship between allied or competing polities is the nature of trade. Long-distance trade items in the Southwest included shell, turquoise, copper bells, parrots and parrot feathers, and ceramics. Other goods, such as textiles and salt, were probably also important but are too rare archaeologically to evaluate. Up to around A.D. 1150, much of this trade was organized along north–south lines, with parrots, copper, and shell coming from the south and turquoise going back. When warfare intensifies in the Late period, we see a decline in the trade of copper bells, shell, and parrots in northern parts of the Southwest (these goods continue to some degree in the southern areas). However, ceramic trade seems to intensify, and trade links seem to take on a more east–west aspect (Upham 1982). The polities that formed in the Late period would have been under pressure to develop and maintain alliances with other polities. Exchange in ceramics may have been a means to strengthen and demonstrate these alliances. Moreover, access to buffalo hides may have been important if the hides were being used for shields. Thus, east–west trade would have linked western groups to the eastern plains and the buffalo products. Thus, warfare may have required new trade links to obtain weaponry-related materials. If traded items were used to signal alliances, trade may have intensified when warfare intensified. While trade items may have been treated as prestige goods, they may be better understood as functioning within a military alliance milieu.

In summary, the Late period warfare started with slightly defensive sites and rapidly intensified with much more defensible sites, no-man's-lands, and alliances. Within a century, many sites had been destroyed, large areas had been abandoned, and the region's population declined markedly. The Southwest never fully recovered from these events. Interestingly, this sequence of events, as well as their consequences, closely matches that found in the Petexbatun area of the Yucatán during the Late Classic, although the dating and causes do not seem to be related (Demarest et al. 1997).

Overall Considerations of Southwestern Warfare

In summary, evidence for warfare in the Southwest is panregional, and climatic change had an impact on the intensity of warfare. It is hard to correlate changes in intensity in warfare with climate prior to A.D. 900 because of a paucity of data, while the correlation is clearer for the later periods. Around A.D. 900, the Southwestern climate seems to have improved, as it did in Europe at this time, which is known there as the Medieval Warm period. In the Southwest, the population seems to have increased about fivefold (Dean et al. 1994). This interval was followed by a deteriorating climate. By A.D. 1300, the increased cold is considered to be the beginning of the Little Ice Age (Grove 1990; Lamb 1995; Peterson 1988, 1994). Thus, we have an improved climate, increasing population, and a decrease in warfare, followed by deteriorating climate, increasing warfare, and a population crash. It is difficult not to view the increase in warfare in the Late period as a consequence of the climatic changes. A similar case can be made for the Midwest, the Southeast, the Northwest coast, and the Northeast regions of North America at this same time (summarized in LeBlanc 1999).

Did the same sequence take place in Mesoamerica? We would expect that climate change would have less of an impact in Mesoamerica than in North America. There is no reason why conditions that led to deteriorating climate in North America would have also been deleterious in Mesoamerica. It is possible that the Medieval Warm interval had negative effects on parts of Mesoamerica, the opposite of what occurred in the north. It is also possible that the contraction of the northern boundary of Mesoamerican cultural area was a consequence of the Little Ice Age in parallel with events in North America. No particular set of consequences is being proposed here. It seems unlikely, however, that if these climate changes had such an impact in North America and elsewhere, that Mesoamerica would not have been affected in some way. At this point, there seems to be little evidence one way or the other. There is evidence from lake sediments of a distinct dry period that just precedes the Medieval Warm interval in the Yucatán that coincides with the end of the Classic and may be involved (Hodell et al. 1995), although Demarest (1997b) points out that the intense warfare resulting in political and demographic collapse in the Petexbatun region preceded this event. Conversely, the time intervals that represent the Medieval Warm and the Little Ice Age elsewhere in the world show no strong evidence for either particularly wet or dry climates in the Yucatán and look quite similar.

Another important aspect of southwestern warfare is that it was serious. A considerable number of individuals were being killed, and at times both the settlement locations, settlement configurations, and social systems were being affected by warfare. This fits with Keeley's (1996) argument that nonstate warfare was not insignificant or "ritual" behavior that looked like warfare but where few individuals were killed and there were no real consequences. Warfare was having a major impact on these societies, and this impact must be considered in trying to understand them.

A Southwestern View of Mesoamerican Warfare

Having briefly summarized events in the Southwest, it now is possible to contrast it with Mesoamerica. First, one is struck by how much evidence and discussion there is about Classic period and later warfare in Mesoamerica in contrast to the Formative period. Very little Early and Middle Formative evidence for warfare has been recognized with a few notable exceptions. The case for Middle Formative warfare in Oaxaca is well laid out (Marcus and Flannery 1996). There is also good evidence of warfare in the Middle Formative Maya at the site of Blackman Eddy, Belize (Brown and Garber, chapter 6 in this volume). Heads without bodies and bodies without heads were found in Early Formative contexts at Chalcatzingo (Grove 1987). Coe and Diehl (1980) suggest evidence for cannibalism during the Early Formative at San Lorenzo Tenochtitlán that is related to warfare, while Reilly and Garber (chapter 8 in this volume) also see considerable iconographic evidence for warfare in the Olmec area during the Early and Middle Formative. In the Valley of Mexico, the Middle Formative site of Tlatelcomila also has evidence of cannibalism that may relate to warfare (Pijoan and Lory 1997; Pijoan et al. 1989; Turner and Turner 1999). Similar evidence has been reported for Early Formative contexts at Tlatilco (Faulhaber 1965) and Tlapacoya-Zohapilco (Niederberger 1987). Webster (1975, 1977) discusses evidence for Late Formative warfare in the Maya lowlands. The problem with many of these pieces of evidence is that they are isolated and tell us little about the nature of warfare at these times, and rarely are there multiple lines of evidence from the same area and time span.

Similarly, one is struck by the paucity of evidence for no-man's-lands, visual links between sites, and the rarity of defensive communities prior to the Postclassic. This does not mean that empty zones or fortified sites are not known earlier (clearly they are), but they seem to be relatively rare. Additionally, while Hassig (1992a) discusses the evolution of weaponry over time, this seems to be underappreciated, as does the role of warfare in exchange of utilitarian and elite goods. Each of these topics is considered in more detail here.

One important question regarding early Mesoamerican warfare concerns the spread of agriculture. Agriculture independently developed in highland Mesoamerica. However, as in much of the rest of the world, agriculture spread by diffusion or the movement of farmers to lowland Mesoamerica (including the Maya area) to western Mexico and to northern Mesoamerica, including the Southwest (Cobb et al. 1999). Such spreads were not a peaceful process in other parts of the world (Keeley 1988, 1996), nor do they appear peaceful in the Southwest. Is it likely that the spread of agriculture throughout greater Mesoamerica was peaceful in all these instances except in the Southwest?

Is it really possible that from at least 1500 B.C., if not before, parts of Mesoamerica had agricultural villages with larger populations than those of the Southwest yet little evidence for warfare for almost the next 1,000 years? Most likely, so little is known about the Early and Middle Formative that evidence for warfare has gone unrecognized (see Brown and Garber, chapter 6 in this volume; Reilly and Garber, chapter 8 in this volume). If warfare did not exist during this time, its absence is of considerable theoretical interest.

A second important question concerns alliance building and the presence of no-man's-lands. When warfare intensified in the Southwest, polities formed with broad no-man's-lands between them, as has been discussed. Is this a behavior particular to tribally organized groups, or should we also expect empty zones with chiefdoms and states? Again, the excellent data from Oaxaca and surrounding areas show empty zones both prior to and after the founding of Monte Albán (Marcus and Flannery 1996; Redmond 1983), but there seems to be little in the published literature for other areas that demonstrates the existence of such zones. The Maya area is particularly intriguing. Alliances (or hegemonic states) seem to have formed both in the southern lowlands (A. Chase and D. Chase 1998a; Chase and Chase, chapter 10 in this volume) and in the north. One can see an alliance (or state) centered on Cobá that was in competition with Chichén Itzá, which was also in competition with a Puuc alliance that included Uxmal, Sayil, and Kabah (Ambrosino et al., chapter 7 in this volume; Freidel 1992). This information is based on inscriptions, iconography, ceramics, and architecture including defensive walls and causeways (*sacbeob*). Yet to date, line-of-sight links between the various cities in these alliances have not been shown to exist or not exist, nor have surveys shown whether there were empty zones between the polities. It must be admitted that survey in a tropical rainforest is much harder than the arid Southwest, and it may take many more years of work to find such evidence even if it exists. One would expect that if warfare included large groups of men, including nonelites, that signaling and empty zones would be more likely. If warfare was small scale between elites, the peasants may have been irrelevant, and no empty zones would form. Moreover, signaling for aid from one center to another may not have been useful if swift raids were the norm. Thus, a better understanding of the nature of the warfare and defenses would presumably provide evidence about the social ramifications of this warfare. However, in all fairness, alliances may have shifted rapidly, as they seem to have done in the Southwest, and any resulting empty zones may have been short lived and thus hard to discern.

Another behavior resulting in empty zones is the rapid coalescing of populations into very large settlements. This is seen in the Southwest, where a few of the site clusters that formed rapidly were much larger than their neighbors. Interestingly, it was these extralarge clusters that survived over time. A similar process, but on a much grander scale, seems to have taken place in Mesoamerica, a step that may be an integral part of the process of state formation. The successful coalescing of people into very large groups would have provided a great military advantage and would probably have led to increased social complexity.

The most dramatic example of this process is the rapid growth of Teotihuacan, but the same process seems to have taken place at Monte Albán and is better understood there. Marcus and Flannery (1996) make a good case that the rapid building of Monte Albán, coupled with the depopulation of much of the valley, was a military as well as political event, enabling one group to dominate the entire Oaxaca Valley and start them on a trajectory of regional control. Is this "domination by coalescing" a more prevalent pattern in Mesoamerica than currently recognized? Is it more common worldwide than currently recognized? I can find no parallels for such rapid population coalescing in the early periods in Peru, but it may have occurred in Mesopotamia (Robert M. Adams, personal communication). Did such massive coalescing take place in the Mesoamerican lowlands? This may have happened at El Mirador in the Late Formative. Other possibilities, such as Mayapán in the Postclassic, are small in scale and follow the collapse of regional polities rather than being part of their initial formulation.

A case can be made that while the *scale* of some of these processes is radically different between the Southwest and Mesoamerica, the *nature* of the processes is quite similar. If this is correct, we would expect to find other instances in both areas. One suspects that cases of no-man's-lands forming and the rapid coalescing of populations into large centers are more common in Mesoamerica than now recognized.

A third question concerning Mesoamerican social systems and warfare can be phrased as the methods and weapons of war. The methods of war, and in particular changes in those methods, should be expected to link directly to the social systems involved and should in turn affect those systems. In addition to issues of technology, there are important topics of how warfare was conducted. For example, to what extent did warfare include large proportions of the polities involved, and to what extent was it restricted to small numbers of specialists? To what extent was force able to be projected over long distances?

Who Was Involved in Warfare

In the Southwest, did escalating warfare increase the social position of successful warriors potentially leading to their attaining some form of social control or dominance? In Mesoamerica, was it ever the case that the elite battled *over* the commoners, or did they battle *with* them? It seems that this question is at the heart of the debate characterized by the differences in the positions of Freidel (1986a) and Webster (1993) although by no means is it restricted to them. Webster accuses many Mayanists of clinging to a tradition of a lack of real war among the Maya (Webster 1993), arguing that lip service is paid to evidence of war but that conflict is seen as ritually based, with inconsequential impact on the social systems. The model is elites fighting with elites almost as a game while the rest of the population is unaffected and uninvolved. Freidel et al. (chapter 11 in this volume) counter that researchers have long recognized warfare in the Maya area and do see it as significant.

Webster makes a good case that much of the discussion of Maya warfare seems to be couched in terms of little more than boys playing games. It is inconceivable that warfare was no more than trying to attain captives for sacrifice. Worldwide, warfare at this level of social complexity can have no short-term territorial gains, and it can be couched in terms of revenge, honor, and the like in the short run. But over the long term, death rates are very high, and resources do change hands. This is one of Keeley's (1996) major points. Once one looks closely, Mesoamerican warfare also involves economic and ecological factors.

There were intensely competing polities, with clear conquest of some polities and repeated suggestions of outsider takeover of other polities. Subsequently, regional abandonments occurred, followed by a decline in social complexity and a decline in regional population. That warfare is not intimately involved as either a cause or a major factor in this process is unlikely. That is, while Freidel and his colleagues and Webster seem to be at odds about how "real" Maya warfare was, no one seems to have characterized how it actually functioned. Until we know that, it is hard to see how it relates to other aspects of the social system.

A critical issue is whether Mesoamerican warfare was restricted to elites fighting with elites. It must be remembered that Homer describes the exploits of the elite during the Trojan War, but large numbers of commoners were involved. A likely scenario for Mesoamerican warfare is that a large segment of society was involved, and the elites were involved as both champion fighters (in the Homeric sense) and military commanders. This model of Mesoamerican warfare would have large numbers of commoners, not trained as professionals, taking part and being killed. Over time, professional soldiers may have developed, but is there any real evidence that armies were comprised almost entirely of professionals? For example, the Aztec army was highly trained and well organized, but it comprised far too many men to have consisted only of elites. Ross Hassig (1992a) touches on these issues, but no coherent, testable model of just who was doing the fighting has yet been put forth. Intriguing relevant evidence comes from the Vanderbilt Petexbatun project (see Demarest 1997b; Demarest et al. 1997). This long-term project focused on warfare more directly than perhaps any in the history of archaeology. They found that there was significant evidence for warfare prior to A.D. 760, but there were no fortifications. They were then rapidly implemented (initially with a noticeable lack of skill). They were so extensive that they could not have been defended by just the elite. The implication is that prior to A.D. 760, warfare did not involve attacking political centers and may well have been elite based, champion-type fighting, but after A.D. 760, the nature of the warfare changed, and everyone became involved. Despite such tantalizing evidence, the lack of knowledge of who was doing the fighting would seem to be the most glaring gap in our understanding of Mesoamerican warfare and one that has the most serious implications for the Southwest, as is considered next.

Weapons

One aspect of both Southwestern and Mesoamerican warfare that is traditionally almost completely ignored is the impact of new weapons technology (although Hassig [1992a] touches tangentially on this topic). In Europe (and China), new technologies had significant impact on warfare and society. Examples include bronze technology, the chariot, horses, and so on. Are there parallels in Mesoamerica and the Southwest, and if not, why not? The impact of metallurgy on warfare is an interesting topic but is not considered here. Instead, there were several important changes in weaponry in the Southwest that should have impacted Mesoamerica. Particularly interesting is the spread of bow-and-arrow technology.

All indications are that the bow and arrow were not independently invented in the Americas (Blitz 1988). The bow seems to come into the Americas from Asia, working its way south beginning around 0 A.D., although claims for earlier appearance have been made (Mabry 1997; Nassaney and Pyle 1999). The current estimate has it reaching the northern Southwest in the period A.D. 200–300 but not reaching the present U.S.–Mexican border until about A.D. 500. This bow was the self bow, one that was not terribly powerful and probably more useful for hunting than for warfare. Nevertheless, it seems to have soon almost completely replaced the atlatl in the Southwest.[2] The self bow spread throughout Mesoamerica prior to the Spanish conquest, although the timing is far from clear. Using the rate it took the bow to disperse over North America, it is unlikely the bow reached the Valley of Mexico until after A.D. 600 and the Yucatán until after A.D. 800. Sheets (chapter 15 in this volume) implies that the bow was in El Salvador by around A.D. 800. Clearly, simply using a guess date based on diffusion rates is of limited use. However, no synthetic consensus-based discussion of the spread and adoption of the bow in Mesoamerica seems to exist.

One can argue that the atlatl required considerable skill and practice to use, and because few atlatl darts could be carried, it could not be used as an area weapon.[3] Both the bow and the sling are more suited for area weapons. The use of an area weapon requires less skill than a personnel weapon. All you need to do is shoot or throw in the right direction. This means that the widespread adoption of a possible area weapon, such as the bow, could have had profound implications for the nature of warfare.

In particular, it is possible that atlatl-based warfare in the highlands and thrusting spear–based warfare in the Maya area focused on elites with few commoners involved. I am suggesting not that it was that way but that it could have been that way. Arming commoners with the bow, even with little training, could have significantly changed warfare. The elite would have been at great risk from the massed firing of arrows, and armies comprised of many commoners armed with bows could have defeated previously dominant groups who had not adopted the same tactics. The apparent close timing of the introduction of the bow and of the collapse of Teotihuacan around A.D. 600, the decline of Monte Albán, and the end of the Classic Maya around A.D. 800 (assuming that the bow took additional time to reach the Yucatán) seems too coincidental to be unconnected. Could the introduction of the bow have changed the military situation (for example, requiring the need for defensive walls) and in particular decreased the power of the elites so that the systems were destabilized and we see this destabilization archaeologically at the end of the Classic period? The problem with such a scenario is that the timing of the bow and arrow is so poorly known. Unfortunately, the timing of the introduction and spread of the bow in North America does not provide much help answering this question.

An argument against the previously mentioned scenario is the lack of bow-and-arrow depictions in the iconography. However, this objection is not as profound as it might appear. We know that the bow was in use in the Late Postclassic, yet the iconography still depicts the atlatl and sword. It is clear that the elite warriors never accepted the bow as an important or symbolic weapon even when we know it was in use. One argument in favor of the importance of the introduction of the bow is the fact that arrows were a tribute item of the Aztec state (Hassig 1988). If they were militarily irrelevant, why stockpile arrows in large quantities? In fact, the introduction of the bow may have given advantage to those groups that could organize the mass production of arrows and be able to stockpile and distribute them as needed. Again, those people who conservatively stuck with the previous technology, tactics, and utilization of resources may have been disadvantaged.

Of final note, in the Southwest around A.D. 1300–1400, the sinew-backed, recurved bow appears on kiva murals and pottery iconography, and by A.D. 1540, we know that powerful recurved bows were in wide use along with buffalo hide shields. However, the recurved bow never reached Mesoamerica. Given the purported long-distance trade between the areas, why not?

The Implications of Warfare

Accepting the existence of significant warfare in the Southwest or Mesoamerica allows one to see how conflict was intertwined with other aspects of the social systems. The danger is looking at the impact of warfare on other aspects of the social systems rather than having an integrated view that includes the presence of warfare. One little-explored aspect of Southwestern warfare is its role in trade. To what extent was trade used to maintain and signal alliances? How much did trade change in response to changes in warfare? Similar questions seem to be also little developed in Mesoamerica, again with notable exceptions.

Ceramic production and distribution is the best indicator of such interaction because of its ubiquity, preservation, and stylistic variability. Superficially surprising is the fact that warfare does not decrease pottery production or trade. It might be assumed that increased warfare would result in a decline in ceramic quality as well as the distribution of particular types. Fewer resources might be devoted to ceramic production, and disruption of trade would decrease distribution. This turns out to not be the case in Mesoamerica, at least where it has been explicitly examined in the Maya area (Bey, chapter 2 in this volume) or in the Southwest.

A Southwest example of changes in trade and warfare occurs during the increase in warfare around A.D. 1300. We do find some cases of restriction in the distribution of ceramic types. Little outside pottery is found in the Zuni site cluster, and Zuni wares are not widely distributed. However, to the north, some of the highest-quality and most artistically sophisticated pottery ever produced in the Southwest was made in the Hopi site cluster. It is widely traded but not to the Zuni. Some polities received an incredible number of pottery types, and over this entire area a new design style, crosscutting wares, can be found. We have, then, design styles and actual trade pieces moving widely between areas that all other indictors suggest are in vicious competition. While there are a few polities that seem to have become politically isolated, most polities seem to participate more in regional styles and have more actual trade pieces than we find previously, and some pottery increases in quality. I have argued elsewhere (LeBlanc 1999, 2000) that these distributions represent efforts to maintain alliances between polities. Despite the difficulty of these times, ceramic trade was not curtailed, nor was the sharing of design styles diminished by warfare.

Much the same seems to be the case for the Maya area. When warfare intensifies, there are some cases of decline in quality (Foias and Bishop 1997), the replacement of types when one polity conquers another (Ardren et al. 1998), and increased regionalization of styles (Ball 1993). These examples are all considered in more detail by Bey (chapter 2 in this volume). However, at the same time, elite pottery, especially cylinder vases, seem to be widely traded and may have been used as emblems of alliances (Reents-Budet 1994; Schele and Miller 1986).

Conclusions

The American Southwest and Mesoamerica are quite similar in terms of how archaeologists have dealt with warfare. In each area, there were periods of acceptance of warfare, then denial, and finally the beginnings of serious attempts to integrate warfare into model building. Differences between the two regions seem related more to the nature of the information currently available and the greater social complexity of Mesoamerica than to more fundamental ideological or environmental factors.

Of particular interest is the lack of congruence between social complexity and warfare between the two areas. In Mesoamerica, from around 2500 B.C. to around 700 B.C., there was a sequence of villages, then simple chiefdoms (complex chiefdoms and even states follow soon thereafter but not in the Southwest). Offset some 1,000 to 1,500 years, we find much the same trajectory of social complexity in the Southwest. In Mesoamerica, this time is seen as having little warfare, yet there is considerable warfare in the Southwest. Also of interest is that in the Southwest one can correlate increases and decreases in warfare with climate change but apparently not in Mesoamerica. How real are these differences between areas? I believe that they are not as different as currently perceived. It would seem worthwhile for Meso-american archaeologists to look more carefully for climate-related changes and the intensity of warfare, as such correlations occur not only in the Southwest but in the rest of North America as well.

There is also the potential for a domino effect in our understanding of warfare and its consequences. If we could better understand Maya warfare, we might be able to better understand highland Meso-america warfare (based on the assumption that the superior textual information from the Maya area will enable us to obtain a more refined understanding of the Maya case). This in turn will potentially enable us to understand whether highland Mesoamerican warfare could have been impacting the Southwest. Thus, a better understanding of Mesoamerican warfare may enable us to place the Southwest in its overall Mesoamerican context. Conversely, the fine-grained analysis of warfare potentially available for the Southwest may help develop models of exchange, alliance formation, and the evolution of no-man's-lands useful for studying Mesoamerica.

Notes

1. For almost the entire period, Chaco great houses had high back sides with rooms stepping down to a plaza area that was open on at least one side.

Despite the multistoried aspect of the buildings, if they had been built for defense, the open plazas would have been enclosed. Most artist reconstructions and ground plans of Chaco great houses show them at their final stage of building late in the period when the plazas were finally enclosed and therefore are potentially misleading.

2. The evolution of southwestern weapons has been described in greater detail elsewhere (LeBlanc 1997, 1999). The first tool kit consisted of atlatls and fending sticks. Fending sticks are clearly used with atlatls as a defensive weapon (Geib 1990; Heizer 1942) over much of the west prior to A.D. 200. For reasons that do not seem clear Hassig (1992a) rejects what appear to be representations of a similar weapon in Mesoamerica as fending sticks. Both the atlatl and fending sticks disappear from the Southwest with the introduction of the bow, which is soon accompanied by wicker shields. When the recurved bow is introduced, the wicker shields are replaced by buffalo hide shields. There must have been profound changes in tactics associated with the new weapons. Greater specialization in warfare and changes in trade may also have accompanied these technological shifts.

3. The military define two classes of weapons or uses of weapons. An *area* weapon is used to saturate an area with arrows, artillery shells, or sling missiles. The point is not to aim for an individual; instead, if enough projectiles are sent to a given area, a considerable number of people in that area will get hit. Conversely, a *personnel* weapon is one that is actually aimed at someone. While an atlatl dart certainly can be used as an area weapon, the inability to carry many projectiles limits its use in that way.

Chapter Fifteen

Warfare in Ancient Mesoamerica: A Summary View

Payson D. Sheets

This chapter focuses on warfare in ancient Mesoamerica rather than violence or conflict. The latter two may occur on the interpersonal or interfamilial level and often do not preserve well archaeologically. However, warfare as a socially sanctioned and planned aggressive activity can be preserved reasonably well, especially in a society with considerable architecture as well as writing and art in various media. The objective of this chapter is to briefly consider the history of Meso-american warfare (see also LeBlanc, chapter 14, and Stanton and Brown, chapter 1 in this volume), to review the principal accomplishments of this volume's chapters, and to comment on the current status of Mesoamerican warfare in general. It is refreshing for me to summa-rize and comment on a book on Mesoamerican warfare not written by the traditional "big gun" distinguished scholars but by the next generation of archaeologists exploring the nature and implications of war with new data and ideas.

Overview of Mesoamerican Warfare Studies

The first European contact with a New World civilization was in war, as the Spanish and their Tlaxcalan and other allies conquered the

Aztec capital Tenochtitlán. As the Spanish expanded their contacts and attempted to establish control in the sixteenth century, they chronicled warfare and sacrifice throughout Mesoamerica. Despite Spanish documentation of Contact period indigenous warfare, scholars in the early and middle part of the twentieth century often depicted ancient civilizations as peaceful. As scholars have depicted societies as bellicose or peaceful or as they have explored the reasons for warfare, they often have revealed more about their own assumptions and desires than the subject matter under study.

As reflected in this volume, Mesoamerican scholars in recent years have recognized the abundant and wide range of material correlates that warfare has left in the archaeological record. Those material correlates range from the instruments of warfare and fortifications through artistic depictions to textual statements of warfare and its consequences. Certainly, warfare was initiated as a means to capture sacrificial victims for largely religious purposes on occasion, but even then can this be divorced from a function of bolstering political authority? As the evidence for warfare in Mesoamerica accumulates, we must also consider that warfare was an integral component to the emergence of middle range and complex societies throughout the Formative, Classic, and Postclassic.

Warfare in pre-Columbian Oaxaca has been studied for more than half a century, beginning with Caso (1947) at Monte Albán. Marcus and Flannery (1996) have broadened and deepened our understanding of conflict within and surrounding the Oaxaca Valley, including some evidence of warfare prior to the founding of Monte Albán about 500 B.C. Redmond and Spencer (1983) convincingly documented the conquest of the Cuicatlán Cañada north of the Oaxaca Valley by Monte Albán. However, as Joyce argues in this volume (chapter 4), the claims of militarism from Monte Albán may have been exaggerated. He searched the lower Verde Valley for evidence of Monte Albán conquest in the Late Formative and found little. Ironically, he did find evidence for a strong presence of a different foreign polity a few centuries later that could have had military aspects. Teotihuacan entered the area in a major way in the Early Classic, as evidenced by the lower Verde area having the highest percentage of green Pachuca obsidian of any area outside the Basin of Mexico, along with some settlement shifts to defensible locations and some ceramic changes. Judging from present evidence, if this area had been conquered, it was more likely by Teotihuacan than Monte Albán.

These issues in Oaxaca are exemplary of deeper questions in

Mesoamerican archaeology. Often we ask, Was the expansion of society X of an economic nature, or was it theocratic, or was it political? The issues are often simplified to a prime motivator for expansion that can focus on mercantile objectives versus religious conversion or conquest and domination. However, what many of these essays indicate to me is that our Western categories may be useful for initial heuristic purposes but may be misleading if they are allowed to stand unchallenged in the final analysis. Most expansions involved what we would categorize as economic, political, and religious phenomena in deeply intertwined manners.

The recognition of the centrality of warfare to the Classic Maya has been a long time coming. Thompson (1970), the great mid-twentieth-century Mayanist, did acknowledge that warfare existed, but he emphasized warfare in Postclassic and historic times. In his magnum opus *The Rise and Fall of Maya Civilization* (1st ed. 1954, 2nd ed. 1966), he argued that all Mesoamerican warfare originated in the need to obtain captives for the sacrifices needed to nurture the deities (Thompson 1966:113). He viewed the Mexicans as more warlike than the Maya, a trend that culminated with the Aztecs.

Thompson (1970:293) did refer to the jaguar and eagle as war gods, which was a step toward the current recognition of the two warrior orders, of eagle and jaguar knights, that were at Teotihuacan and were adopted by the Maya at Tikal and other areas. They become common in the Late Classic (at Bonampak) and Epiclassic (at Cacaxtla) as well as the Early Postclassic (at Tula; but for an Epiclassic dating, see Ringle et al. 1998) and Late Postclassic (at Tenochtitlán). In Aztec mythology, the opposition of jaguar and eagle knights represented the earth and the sky and thus femaleness and maleness. Not only did the warrior orders operate in military campaigns, but they figured prominently in public performances while presenting their captive victims to ensure the proper working of the cosmos.

As early as 1940, Means (1940:438) perceived a fundamental difference between Andean and Middle American warfare. He saw Inka warfare directed toward conquest and acculturation, to bring other peoples into Inka civilization. In contrast, he, like Thompson, viewed Middle American warfare as oriented toward capturing opposing warriors to sacrifice them to provide sustenance for their deities. I believe the fact that it is the only reference to warfare in the Maya area in the index of that entire synthesis volume *The Maya and Their Neighbors* indicates how unimportant warfare was considered by the principal scholars of those decades (Hay et al. 1940).

One discovery that made scholars rethink the "peaceful Maya" were the huge ditch-and-parapet fortifications constructed in the Late Formative by Tikal to protect them from Uaxactún (Puleston and Callender 1967). After Tikal apparently conquered Uaxactún, the earthworks no longer served any purpose, and they fell into disrepair. The discovery a decade later of defensive fortifications around Becán indicated the threat of warfare was more widespread among the Maya (Webster 1977). More recently, Demarest (1997b) and Inomata (1997) have shown the intensity and social consequences of warfare in the Petexbatun region that led to the end of civilization as the Classic Maya knew it in that area.

Artistic evidence of warfare has also accumulated in the nineteenth and twentieth centuries, as stela scenes and painted evidence from ceramics and murals have become available and are better understood. Hieroglyphic evidence has accumulated more in the "punctuated equilibrium" model rather than a "uniformitarian" accumulation. Throughout most of the past two centuries, epigraphic evidence of warfare grew very slowly, but that changed dramatically with the decipherment of the "shell/star" hieroglyph for warfare and the linking of it with the Venus cycle, captives, and Tlaloc-Venus warfare (Schele and Freidel 1990) and numerous hieroglyphic decipherments, particularly in the southern Maya lowlands.

Warfare was woven deeply into the social fabric of most Formative and all Classic and Postclassic Mesoamerican civilizations. It appears that all levels of those societies, from commoners to elites, believed that sacrifice was essential for the proper functioning of the cosmos. Based on the core belief that one does not receive something for nothing, people would offer sacrifices in various forms to receive rain, a good crop harvest, a propitious marriage, recovery from disease, or other anxious need. The sacrifice could take the form of bloodletting, sacrificing food or drink, or the sacrifice of a person. Sacrifice of a person captured in warfare became very common in the Classic and Postclassic. Sacrifice in general and human sacrifice in particular probably had deep roots in the Formative period, with origins possibly in the Archaic or earlier, but it is not until the Late Formative that sacrifice is commonly preserved in the archaeological record.

Evidence of Warfare in Mesoamerica

One of the advantages of studying Mesoamerican warfare is that a wider range of phenomena is available to the scholar than in other pre-Columbian culture area of the New World. I note a dozen of them here with the objective of encouraging future scholars to spread a wide net in their studies.

Fortifications. Site fortification is prima facie evidence of fear of attack, and in many cases one can identify from whom that fear developed. The Tikal ditch-and-embankment (Puleston and Callendar 1967) built in fear of Uaxactún is a good example. As that feature seems to have no other function than defense, it is unusually unequivocal evidence. In contrast, the apparent fortifications of sites such as Becán, Cacaxtla, Xochicalco, and Monte Albán could also have had residential and/or agricultural functions.

Art and iconography. The prominent display of trophy heads in skull racks or display of them in sculpture or other forms of art are generally the result of opposing warriors being captured in battle and brought into the victorious settlement for sacrifice. The five-point star is now widely recognized as indicating Venus and the need to capture victims for sacrifice in the Classic and Postclassic of Mesoamerica. Headrick (chapter 9 in this volume) provides a good example of the iconography of aggression.

Weapons. The discovery of weapons of war in sites and the depiction of war weapons in art are reasonably reliable indicators of warfare. McCafferty (chapter 12 in this volume) notes a large number of dart points associated with Structure 1 at Cholula that, combined with other evidence, indicates warfare activity. However, the presence of items that *could* be used in war does not mean that they *were* used in war because such implements can be used in hunting or in art as mythology or as symbolic of hunting, war, aggression, or defense. A technology that could have been used in war but evidently was much more important in hunting is illustrated by the bow and arrow coming into ancient El Salvador in the Terminal Classic (ca. A.D. 800). The evidence is the ubiquity of the small projectile points made from snapped prismatic blade sections (Sheets 1978). They must be arrow points, as they are too small and fragile to be atlatl dart points or spear points. They commonly are found in the most mountainous of terrain, far from any human settlements (Sheets 1983), and evidently were used for hunting, particularly of deer. The rarity of other indicators for warfare in pre-Columbian El Salvador further substantiates the argument that these artifacts were not used for intraspecies purposes.

The weapons depicted in sculptures, such as the atlatls and darts in the hands of the atlantid figures at Tula, are unequivocal. Equally convincing are the weapons depicted in aggressive murals at Chichén

Itzá and other Classic and Postclassic sites. In addition to bows and arrows and atlatls and darts, spears and clubs were used in war. The latter, resembling a baseball bat but with obsidian or occasionally chert prismatic blade segments inserted longitudinally, must have had a horrific impact, as the lithics shattered on impact, macerating tissue and causing massive hemorrhaging. Such a club is illustrated on Stela 5 at Uaxactún (Schele and Freidel 1990:146). These clubs with lithic inserts would be useful only in warfare and not in hunting or other uses. As LeBlanc (chapter 14 in this volume) notes, the sling is useful to herding peoples and as an implement of war. It is also useful to agriculturalists to discourage herbivory by birds in maize fields.

Epigraphy. It has taken Mayanists a long time to get past their suspicions about the possible reliability of the written record of the Classic period. We all learned at an early age what liars the Aztecs were, deliberately rewriting their history for self-aggrandizement to look eminently civilized in the finest aggressive Mesoamerican sense. Fortunately, it turns out that the Maya texts are generally reliable. Thus, the Maya text describing a battle, a capture, or a decapitation should be taken seriously. The texts are often limited to the victor proclaiming the outcome, with no details about the scale of battle, the reasons for it, and the planning for it.

Osteology. Skeletal analyses can divulge evidence of trauma. An occasional broken bone is not reliable evidence of warfare, but a high frequency of parry fractures in the radius and ulna of young adult males is a good indicator. Skull fracture patterns can also be evidence of warfare, as can simultaneous multiple burials. Decapitations can be indirect indications, after a captive was hauled into the victorious polity and sacrificed.

Artifacts. Warfare, especially toward the severe end of the spectrum, can result in abrupt changes in artifact or architectural styles or frequencies. However, it is risky to argue in the other direction, of artifactual changes indicating warfare in the absence of supporting data, as so many ecologic, economic, religious, demographic, social, adaptive, or political phenomena can also spread or suppress artifact styles and technologies.

Assimilation or elimination. Warfare can cause a functioning polity to disappear rapidly, but so can other factors. A sudden change in upper-level administration, as apparently occurred in the Early Classic period in Uaxactún, can be evidence of a conquest.

Language and cognition. The terms and concepts used by a society either at the time when warfare is being studied or perhaps later among members of the same ethnic-linguistic group can provide extraordinary insight into warfare. This category provides a hearty dose of *their* view, of the emic perspective. Many other indicators here discussed are our interpretive impositions on the archaeological record, with all the dangers inherent in that. Those dangers include the fact that so often we see what we are trained to see and want to see in the archaeological record. Thus, their cognitive categories act as an antidote to exclusively relying on our etic categories. At least knowing their categories helps us be aware of our projecting our own biases onto the archaeological record.

As Chase and Chase describe in chapter 10 of this volume, the Classic Maya had four distinct linguistic categories of warfare. *Chuc'ah*, or "capture," warfare involves the planning of a battle, a successful encounter with the opposition, and the capture of at least one opposing warrior. Both sides could win, each by capturing someone from the other side. The capture of a person can symbolically extend to the defeat of the opposing polity, but this obviously is not a defeat in warfare as conceptualized in the modern Western world. A *ch'ak*, or "axe," event is similar to the capture event, but the person captured is an elite. The capture of 18 Rabbit from Copán by Quirigua and his subsequent decapitation is the best-known example. A *hubi*, or "destruction," is of greater societal consequence and is more similar to warfare as practiced by modern "civilizations." The most severe form of warfare was the "shell-star" battle, where a polity can conquer and assimilate another, resulting in the long-term or even permanent suppression of political and economic independence. Certainly an important endeavor by Maya archaeologists would be to identify the material correlates of each of these emic types of warfare and see how they change through time or vary among contemporary polities.

Ethnohistory and history. The Spanish in the sixteenth century recorded warfare throughout Mesoamerica. Their recording of chronic warfare among pre-Columbian societies should be taken with a grain of salt. For instance, the Aztec claims of their military struggles with Tlaxcala seem exaggerated, and I suspect the Aztecs completely surrounded Tlaxcala with conquered peoples and maintained Tlaxcala as a convenient nearby hunting preserve where their youths could prove themselves in battle and bring captives back to Tenochtitlán. I would not call Tlaxcala an independent polity. And it was to the advantage of the Mexican warrior who brought back a Tlaxcalan captive to believe and act as if he was obtained from an enemy warring state rather than from a hunting preserve. If this interpretation is correct, the Tlaxcalans were subjugated more profoundly by their being maintained as a hunting preserve than were many societies that were militarily conquered by the Aztec war machine and only loosely assimilated into their empire. McCafferty's chapter further underscores the inconsistencies of the ethnohistoric record and illustrates the need for archaeological evidence in conjunction with the written record to provide a more complete picture.

Oral history, mythology, and religion. Sources such as the Chilam Balam, Popol Vuh, Mixtec codices, and the Florentine Codex provide insights on competition, sacrifice, and warfare.

Settlement patterns. The finding of contested zones, of "no-man's-lands" between polities, can be indications of protracted hostilities. They can occur between states, between city states, or between chiefdoms, as illustrated by the uninhabited zones between the Barriles chiefdoms in western Panama (Linares et al. 1975).

Desecratory termination rituals. Several chapters in this volume make significant progress in identifying deposits that may often represent the result of warfare in the deliberate termination of buildings and the supernatural powers in them, as different from dedicatory and reverential termination rituals. One key difference is the scale and intensity of architectural destruction, and the term *desecration* is appropriate here. And it is important to note that if these identifications are correct, Brown and Garber in chapter 6 have moved the earliest identification of warfare in the Maya area into the Middle Formative period. Their estimated date of about 650 B.C. is slightly earlier than the time that Marcus and Flannery (1996) see the earliest warfare in the Oaxaca Valley. The differences between dedication, desecration, and reverential termination rituals are subtle, yet they are of great importance and deserve considerable research attention to improve our understanding of warfare.

Several studies in this volume successfully combine several lines of evidence to better illuminate our understanding of ancient Mesoamerican warfare. In particular, chapter 11, by Freidel and colleagues, provides an excellent example of how to closely examine epigraphic, architectural, sculptural, artistic, and artifactual evidence to distinguish conquest of one polity by another versus internal strife and usurpation of power. These authors suggest that the Maya rules of dynastic succession at Tikal were magically manipulated by Nuun Yax Ain (Curl-Snout), who took the Tikal throne from Toh-Chak-Ich'ak (Great-Jaguar-Paw) with the assistance of Siyah K'ak' (Smoking Frog). They suggest that Nuun Yax Ain performed magical rituals that legitimated his place in the Tikal dynastic sequence. What actually happened at Tikal, two-thirds of the way through the fourth century, is far from being well understood. However, I am optimistic that by conjoining multiple lines of evidence and analyzing them carefully, Mayanists might convince even a jury in Los Angeles.

It is instructive to review the history of studies of Mesoamerican warfare to see the changes in assumptions and understandings as twentieth-century archaeologists have explored the topic. One of the most important recent changes is the combination of field archaeology with epigraphy and iconography, which has combined emic with etic approaches. I believe one area that needs further development is for archaeologists to move beyond the assumption that warfare occurred just on the battlefield at a distance from the city. I suggest that at the first stages of preparation for warfare, the action in fact did occur at a distance (such as setting the field of battle with the battle standards). I suspect a participant in the battle might emphasize the more important battle was occurring in the supernatural realm. And the end of the battle is not the end of the story. Perhaps we can learn more about Mesoamerican warfare by studying the next steps, of bringing the captives back, of creation of "stage space" in which to reenact battles, in which the captives shed blood and lose their lives in order that the cosmos may continue functioning. The Western view of war emphasizes the field of battle, body counts, and equipment destroyed, but to understand Mesoamericans we must also emphasize the public performances within the city before and especially after the battle was completed. Mesoamerican city planning not only took into account the cardinal-cosmological directions but also built stage space in overt ways to render visible and audible the enactments of battles and communications with the supernatural realm. Maya stage space in their cities certainly was not a proscenium stage.

Warfare should not be seen as a monolithic repetitive entity among Mesoamerican societies. Rather, warfare varied considerably, depending on factors such as the degree of political centralization, presence or absence of competitive nearby polities, demographic and ecologic processes, ritualization of warfare, resource unpredictability, and economic and technological changes. Hassig (1992a) deals with some of these factors, and I anticipate that future warfare research will both broaden and deepen them. Are there correlations between the degree of political centralization and the nature of warfare? In a general sense, there is a relationship, as both of the most highly urbanized and centralized civilizations, Teotihuacan and the Aztecs, waged war

with standing armies against external polities. Hassig (1992a) characterizes Teotihuacan and the Aztecs as meritocratic states with some
social mobility for individuals based on their military successes. Both
states were relatively innovative in military techniques and technology, and both developed large standing armies that expanded over
much of Mesoamerica, but neither society lasted for a long time. In
contrast, the Maya waged aristocratic wars, were more conservative,
avoided having large standing armies of commoners, and as a result
were less expansionistic and in the long run more stable. I believe that
we can include the Olmec with the Maya in these characteristics.
Additionally, I believe that the Zapotecs more closely resemble the
Maya than the Basin of Mexico states. Occasional incorporations of the
Basin of Mexico style of dispersed leadership occurred in the Maya
area in the very Late Classic at Seibal and at about the same time at
Chichén Itzá. I believe that Hassig underestimates the degree to which
religion permeated Mesoamerican warfare, particularly in those societies that waged aristocratic wars, but his distinctions are significant
and bear further scrutiny. That Teotihuacan and, to a lesser degree,
the Aztecs avoided the cult of the king and avoided prominent public
depictions of supreme rulers is an important symptom of the significant differences in internal organizational principles among Mesoamerican states.

Overview of Chapters in This Volume

Following are comments on the chapters of this volume that have not
been discussed already in previous sections of this chapter. Stanton
and Brown begin this volume with an overview of the general themes
of the volume and provide pertinent background information related
to these themes. The major themes of the book include spatial boundaries, ritualized warfare, iconography and epigraphy of war, and the
use of the ethnohistoric and ethnographic records in warfare studies.
From the latter approach, much knowledge has been gained about
Aztec warfare, yet the disagreements continue regarding military
practices, contexts, objectives, and underlying causes. Some scholars
have minimized Aztec warfare by emphasizing its defensive nature or
its religious/ideological nature. Others have emphasized the economic or political underpinnings of Aztec warfare. The nature of warfare at Tula and Teotihuacan is less clear than it is with the Aztecs. In
part that is explained by their greater antiquity and lack of ethnohistoric records, but at Teotihuacan warfare was depicted indirectly.

And even less clear than Teotihuacan is warfare among the Olmec in the tropical lowlands. The mutilation of carved stone monuments perhaps resulted from battles lost, but they could have also have been termination rituals that removed a powerful entity after its purposes were served. Hassig (1992a) mentions possible cannibalism of captive victims and weapons such as thrusting spears, clubs, and maces. His suggestion of the need to protect trading caravans is reasonable, and Olmec warfare may have been more defensive than offensive. So few of the previously mentioned warfare indicators have been clearly demonstrated among the Olmec that it was difficult to see war as common or intense in that culture until Reilly and Garber (chapter 8 in this volume) started looking closely. It does appear that the Olmec were similar to Teotihuacan in depicting warfare covertly by emphasizing its supernatural aspect. Both avoided the Bonampak-style battlefield depictions in favor of symbolism, simile and metaphor, and mythology. Both avoided personalizing warfare as a part of kingly centralization of power, in contrast to the Maya, Aztec, and Zapotec use of warfare for internal propaganda and ruler aggrandizement. But this is not to deny the role of militarism in elite power. I suspect that as Olmec scholars distinguish between desecratory and reverential termination rituals, they will find more evidence of warfare than hitherto had been believed.

In chapter 14, LeBlanc provides a stimulating comparison and contrast of warfare in Mesoamerica and what he sees as the northern Mesoamerican extension that most archaeologists call the Southwest. His observation that it appears that warfare was more intense in simpler southwestern societies than with comparable Mesoamerican societies (Early and Middle Formative periods) is a clarion call for research. Might the greater frost hazards and intermittent moisture deficits of the Southwest been stimuli for warfare? The great drought of the ninth century (Hodell et al. 1995) in the southern Maya lowlands must have been an additional stressor on the Terminal Classic Maya, but did it lead to the intensification of warfare, analogous to drought stress and warfare intensification in the Southwest? Or are unpredictable resources scarcities more a cause of warfare than chronic and predictable environmental stresses such as long-lasting droughts?

A few centuries later than the Olmec but still in the Formative, the major Maya sites of El Mirador (Dahlin 1984), Tikal (Puleston and Callendar 1967), and Becán (Webster 1977) were fortified. An important contribution of this volume is the pervasiveness of warfare throughout most of Mesoamerica in the Formative, Classic, and Postclassic, yet how differently it was waged and depicted by the various civilizations.

In chapter 3, Golden takes an avowedly political approach to war by emphasizing the maintenance or extensions of authority, and he focuses on the relationship of Bird Jaguar at Yaxchilán with the secondary elite ruler Tilo:m at La Pasadita. His chapter forcefully adds the political dimension while not superseding or minimizing economic and religious interpretations in my view. One wonders why El Cayo is located on the river if the inland portage was so important because the rapids made the river nonnavigable. He effectively undermines the relevance of the "weak state" models, such as segmentary states or galactic polities, to the Classic Maya.

Chapter 7 by Ambrosino and colleagues on Yaxuná is an impressive demonstration of the subtleties that can be considered in the context of a well-researched site. As they note, the northern lowlands have contributed much less to our knowledge of Maya warfare than their southern counterpart. The amount of information on war at Yaxuná, however, is astounding and demonstrates the quality of data one can obtain when excavation objectives are clear. The authors even are able to identify the likely perpetrators by close ceramic analyses connected to desecratory architectural terminations. Their ambitious objective, to understand how commoners were affected by war, was partially achieved. The changes in ceramics outside the site core do give some indications of changes for commoners. However, the direct data on structure terminations are all from elite "downtown" Yaxuná. It is hoped other scholars will take on this important charge, to explore the implications of warfare for the entire range of social components.

In chapter 11, Freidel and colleagues explore Early Classic texts and the archaeological record for evidence of conquest and dynastic succession, focusing on Tikal and Yaxuná. More specifically, they examine the magical manipulation of dynastic succession by hostile individuals. They explore the assertion that Teotihuacan conquered Tikal and placed Curl-Snout (Nuun Yax Ain) on the throne in A.D. 378. However, they suggest that a more plausible explanation was that local factions affiliated with Teotihuacan disrupted the dynastic sequence and placed Nuun Yax Ain on the throne. Through magical rituals, Nuun Yax Ain was legitimately incorporated into the dynastic sequence of Tikal. I agree that the likelihood that Teotihuacan conquered Tikal is declining as more detailed data are acquired.

In chapter 13, Mock provides informal views of conflict dramas at various times throughout the Maya area. She takes a step in a direction of inquiry that I have long thought has been underdeveloped. That is, it would be illuminating to explore stage spaces in Mesoamerican sites. Many public areas, as well as semiprivate areas, were crucial to the belief/behavioral aspects of Mesoamerican culture. Maya elites created stage spaces in which the dynamic ambiguities of reality could be enacted—the performances that demonstrated the cosmos as benefit and as hazard that showed the opposition and integration of sky and earth, of male and female, of dark and light, and so forth. Ultimately, such dramas served educational purposes along with propaganda, enculturation, rejuvenation, verification of authority, and supernatural access.

In chapter 10, Chase and Chase provide a shining example of the benefits of "throwing a broad net" while studying warfare. They do not prematurely limit themselves but rather use all sources of information to rather convincingly interpret Caracol's political, economic, demographic, and military history with adjoining areas in the southern Maya lowlands. Their research, with others, that has identified four different kinds of warfare is of immense importance, as this is an emic view that is rarely available to New World archaeologists. As they note, there is much to be done to refine the variation in warfare, but the kinds range from largely ritually prescribed to the kind of all-out warfare that has become all too common in our modern world. The variation in warfare ranges from forms that affect largely only the elite to forms that have consequences for most or all residents of defeated and victorious polities. It is clear that combining epigraphic, artistic, and field archaeological research into Mesoamerican warfare research will contribute exciting breakthroughs and understandings in the next few decades.

Headrick deepens our understanding of the relationships of art, gender, symbolism, propaganda, and cosmology in chapter 9, on butterflies and war at Teotihuacan. She convincingly shows how butterfly symbolism, with the belief system underlying it, encouraged able-bodied Teotihuacan males to enter the battlefield with an optimistic mentality. If they flitted about the battlefield and captured an opposing warrior, they could bring him back to Teotihuacan for sacrifice. Or if they were killed in battle, they were assured a glorious afterlife, and their souls could return to earth as butterflies. Despite the dangers of such an approach, this probably is an instance where Aztec ethnohistory can help illuminate Teotihuacan belief and practice. I suspect that the "anonymity" of Teotihuacan warfare and in rulership may have common roots. It may have been deliberate policy to avoid the cult of the named semidivine ruler aggrandizing himself with personal portraiture and battle victories. The Teotihuacanos said *"basta"* to Ozymandias.

In a very important chapter, Reilly and Garber argue that the Olmec were the first Mesoamerican civilization to integrate warfare with fertility in belief and in practice. This deeply Mesoamerican ethos certainly pervaded the Classic and Postclassic, and I think they have succeeded in demonstrating its presence 3,000 years ago. Although the other indicators of warfare listed earlier are largely missing from the Olmec, the human dominated by the jaguar motif and other elements probably do indirectly argue for warfare in the Middle and Late Formative.

In chapter 12, McCafferty contrasts ethnohistoric documents with the archaeological record in the Puebla/Tlaxcala Valley of Central Mexico, focusing primarily on the famous site of Cholula. He examines three possible episodes of conflict. The first possible warfare event involves interaction with the Olmeca-Xicallanca and the local population in the area. Historic documents indicate a violent invasion; however, archaeological data from Cholula suggest a more gradual integration of the two populations. The archaeological evidence for the second episode is more conclusive and points toward a volatile situation when the Tolteca-Chichimeca arrived at Cholula around A.D. 1200. McCafferty also illustrates contradictions within several ethnohistoric documents related to the famous "Cholula Massacre" indicating different political agendas of the writers. Archaeological evidence seemingly contradicts several versions of this historic event as well, further emphasizing the political agenda of the historic chroniclers.

Conclusions

Many scholars have studied warfare in Mesoamerica. In retrospect, the way research questions have been phrased has often overly focused the domain under consideration. The scholars who argue about what was the "real" nature of war among Mesoamerican societies may have prematurely limited their answers because in the two societies where war is better understood, the Aztec and the Maya, there were quite different kinds of warfare practiced, with markedly different tactics and societal implications. Thus, the scholars who argue that one kind of war is the "true" warfare can be as correct as the scholars who argue a different kind of war is the "true" form.

Thus, we need not a leveling of the playing field but rather an acknowledged broadening of the playing field.

It is my opinion that the debate over whether warfare in Mesoamerican societies was motivated primarily by political, economic, religious, or demographic-ecologic factors is healthy and eminently worthwhile. And I am confident that the debate will go on indefinitely because thorough and precise knowledge of the cause(s) of warfare is not attainable. Even under the ideal circumstances for warfare scholarship, having unrestricted access to a recent and historically documented war and to participants in that war, it is not possible to accurately know the role of all factors. The factors vary with different participants in the war and even with a particular participant over time. But that is not cause for paleo-despair, as debate and skepticism can stimulate better scholarship to move us slightly closer to understanding the behaviors and beliefs of warfare, some of the instigating pressures, and occasionally something about the motivations of ancient wars.

I also look forward to Mesoamerican archaeologists incorporating the research of cultural anthropologists. For instance, Ember and Ember (1992) conducted a detailed multivariate study of 186 preindustrial societies to explore the reasons why they went to war. The Embers found that the single highest predictor of warfare is a society's fear of resource unpredictability, often due to apparently capricious natural disasters that destroy food resources. Predictable, chronic natural disasters, such as long-term drought, are less causative of warfare. Unless a society is already greatly stressed, it can accommodate to a long-term drought by such means as intensifying water control. I suspect that the migration of the Anasazi from the Mesa Verde region to the middle Rio Grande was such an accommodation to the long drought of the late thirteenth century in the Southwest. The fear of future sustenance loss or loss of other resources rather than actual deprivation seems to be the strongest motivator for warfare according to the Embers. The second-strongest predictor, about half as strong as resource unpredictability, is a society socializing their members for mistrust of the "other." These two strongest factors certainly are far from being mutually exclusive, and when a society fears an unpredictable nature and foments distrust and hatred for "outside" societies, warfare is a common result. Although many societies in their sample are not state level, these results are intriguing and eminently researchable among Mesoamerican societies from the Formative through the

Postclassic. I look forward to explorations to see how fear of an unpredictable nature and fear of others may have underlain Mesoamerican warfare and how a range of coping mechanisms ranging from extending water control through fortifications to developing supernatural access may have been involved.

Bibliography

Acosta, Jorge R.
  1956–1957   Interpretación de Algunos Datos Obtenidos en Tula Relativos a la Época Tolteca. *Revista Mexicana de Estudios Antropológicos* 14:75–110.
  1970   El Altar 1. In *Proyecto Cholula,* ed. I. Marquina, pp. 93–102. Serie Investigaciones 19, Instituto Nacional de Antropología e Historia, México, D.F.
Adams, E. Charles
  1991   *The Origin and Development of the Pueblo Katsina Cult.* University of Arizona Press, Tucson.
Adams, R. E. W.
  1973   Maya Collapse: Transformation and Termination in the Ceramic Sequence at Altar de Sacrificios. In *The Classic Maya Collapse,* ed. T. P. Culbert, pp. 133–63. University of New Mexico Press, Albuquerque.
  1995   The Programme for Belize Regional Archaeological Project: 1994 Interim Report, Introduction. In *The Programme for Belize Archaeological Project: 1994 Interim Report,* ed. Richard E. W. Adams and Fred Valdez Jr., pp. 1–15. Center for Archaeology and Tropical Studies and University of Texas, San Antonio.
Algaze, G.
  1993   Expansionary Dynamics of Some Early Pristine States. *American Anthropologist* 95:304–33.
Altshuler, Milton
  1958   On the Environmental Limitations of Maya Cultural Development. *Southwestern Journal of Anthropology* 14:189–98.
Alvarado Tezozomoc, Hernando
  1975   Crónica Mexicana. In *Crónica Mexicana—Códice Ramírez,* ed. M. Orozco and Berra, pp. 223–701. Porrúa, México.

Ambrosino, James N.
  1995 Excavations at Structure 6F-68 and the Southwest Corner of Structure 6F-4. In *The Selz Foundation Yaxuna Project: Final Report of the 1994 Field Season,* ed. J. N. Ambrosino, D. A. Freidel, D. Johnstone, and C. K. Suhler, pp. 11–17. Manuscript on file, Department of Anthropology, Southern Methodist University, Dallas.
  1996 Excavations at Structures 6F-4, 6F-68, and 6F-72. In *The Selz Foundation Yaxuna Project: Final Report of the 1995 Field Season,* ed. J. N. Ambrosino, D. A. Freidel, D. Johnstone, J. M. Shaw, and C. K. Suhler, pp. 23–40. Manuscript on file, Department of Anthropology, Southern Methodist University, Dallas.
  1997 *A Desecrated Burial from Yaxuná, Yucatán and Its Implications for Maya Governance and Warfare.* Paper presented at the 62nd annual meeting of the Society for American Archaeology.
  2003 Context and Pattern in the Archaeological Deposit Associated with a Puuc Palace at Yaxuna, Yucatan. In *Maya Palaces and Elite Residences,* ed. J. Christie. University of Texas Press, Austin.
Ambrosino, James N., Traci Ardren, and Kam Manahan
  2001 Fortificaciones Defensives en Yaxuná, Yucatán. In *Yucatán a Traves de los Siglos,* ed. R. Gubler and P. Martel, pp. 49–66. Universidad Autonoma de Yucatán, Mérida.
Andrews, Anthony P., and Fernando Robles C.
  1985 Chichen Itza and Coba: Itza Maya Standoff in Early Postclassic Yucatan. In *The Lowland Maya Postclassic,* ed. A. F. Chase and P. M. Rice, pp. 62–72. University of Texas Press, Austin.
Andrews, E. Wyllys, V, and Barbara W. Fash
  1992 Continuity and Change in a Royal Maya Residential Complex at Copan. *Ancient Mesoamerica* 3:63–88.
Angulo V., Jorge
  1987 The Chalcatzingo Reliefs: An Iconographic Analysis. In *Ancient Chalcatzingo,* ed. D. C. Grove, pp. 132–58. University of Texas Press, Austin.
Anyon, Roger, and Steven A. LeBlanc
  1984 *The Galaz Ruin: A Prehistoric Mimbres Village in Southwestern New Mexico.* University of New Mexico Press, Albuquerque.
Ardren, Traci
  1994 Operation 67. In *The Selz Foundation Yaxuna Project: Final Report of the 1993 Field Season,* ed. T. Ardren, S. Bennett, D. A. Freidel, D. Johnstone, and C. K. Suhler, pp. 70–73. Manuscript on file, Department of Anthropology, Southern Methodist University, Dallas.
  1997 *The Politics of Place: Architecture and Cultural Change at the Xkanha Group, Yaxuná, Yucatán, México.* Unpublished Ph.D. dissertation, Yale University, New Haven, Conn.
  2002 Death Became Her: Images of Female Power from Yaxuna Burials. In

Ancient Maya Women, ed. T. Ardren, pp. 68–88. AltaMira Press, Walnut Creek, Calif.

Ardren, Traci, Charles K. Suhler, and David Johnstone
1998   *Evidence for Late Classic Conflict at Yaxuna: Warfare at the Borderlands.* Paper presented at the 63rd annual meeting of the Society for American Archaeology.

Armillas, Pedro
1944   Oztuma, Gro., Fortaleza de los Mexicanos en la Frontera de Michoacan. *Revista Mexicana de Estudios Antropologicos* 6:165–75.
1946   Los Olmeca-Xicalanca y los Sitios Arqueologicas del Suroeste de Tlaxcala. *Revista Mexicana de Estudios Antropologicos* 8:137–46.
1948   Fortalezas Mexicanas. *Cuadernos Americanos* 7:143–63.
1950   Teotihuacán, Tula, y los Toltecas: Las Culturas Post-Arcáicas y Preaztecas del Centro de México: Excavaciones y Estudios, 1922–1950. *Runa* 3:37–70.
1951   Mesoamerica Fortifications. *Antiquity* 25:77–86.

Arnold, Phillip J.
1999   On Typologies, Selection, and Ethnoarchaeology in Ceramics Production Studies. In *Material Meanings: Critical Approaches to the Interpretation of Material Culture,* ed. E. S. Chilton, pp. 103–17. The University of Utah Press, Salt Lake City.

Arnold, P. J., C. A. Pool, R. R. Kneebone, and R. S. Santley
1993   Intensive Ceramic Production and Classic-Period Political Economy in the Sierra de los Tuxtlas, Veracruz, Mexico. *Ancient Mesoamerica* 4:175–91.

Ashmore, Wendy
1980   Discovering Early Classic Quirigua. *Expedition* 23:35–44.

Awe, Jaime J.
1992   *Dawn in the Land between the Rivers: Formative Occupation at Cahal Pech, Belize and Its Implications for Preclassic Development in the Maya Lowlands.* Unpublished Ph.D. dissertation, Institute of Archaeology, University of London, London.

Ayala Falcón, Maricela
1987   La Estela 39 de Tikal, Mundo Perdido. In *Memorias de Primer Coloquio Internacional de Mayistas, 5–10 de Augosto de 1985,* ed. M. de la Garza et al., pp. 599–654. Universidad Nacional Autónoma de México, Centro de Esudios Mayas, México.

Baird, Ellen T.
1989   Stars and Wars at Cacaxtla. In *Mesoamerica after the Decline of Teotihuacan, A.D. 700–900,* ed. R. A. Diehl and J. C. Berlo, pp. 105–22. Dumbarton Oaks Research Library and Collection, Washington, D.C.

Balkansky, A. K.
1997   *Archaeological Settlement Patterns of the Sola Valley, Oaxaca, Mexico.* Ph.D. dissertation, Department of Anthropology, University of Wisconsin, Madison. University Microfilms, Ann Arbor, Mich.

1998   Origin and Collapse of Complex Societies in Oaxaca (Mexico): Eval-
        uating the Era from 1965 to the Present. *Journal of World Prehistory*
        12:451–93.
2001   On Emerging Patterns in Oaxaca Archaeology. *Current Anthropology*
        42:559–61.
Ball, Joseph W.
1974   A Coordinate Approach to Northern Maya Prehistory: A.D. 700–
        1200. *American Antiquity* 39:85–93.
1983   Teotihuacan, the Maya, and Ceramic Interchange: A Contextual Per-
        spective. In *Highland-Lowland Interaction in Mesoamerica: Interdisci-
        plinary Approaches*, ed. A. G. Miller, pp. 125–45. Dumbarton Oaks
        Research Library and Collections, Washington, D.C.
1993   Pottery, Potters, and Polities: Some Socioeconomic and Political
        Implications of Late Classic Maya Ceramic Industries. In *Lowland
        Maya Civilization in the Eighth Century* A.D., ed. J. A. Sabloff and J. S.
        Henderson, pp. 243–72. Dumbarton Oaks Research Library and Col-
        lection, Washington, D.C.
Ball, Joseph W., and Jennifer T. Taschek
2003   Reconsidering the Belize Valley Preclassic: A Case for Multiethnic
        Interactions in the Development of a Regional Culture Tradition.
        Ancient Mesoamerica 14(2).
Barrera Vasquez, Alfredo
1965   *El Libro de las Cantares de Dzitbalche*. Instituto Nacional de Antropo-
        logia e Historia Series Investigaciones 9, D.F.
Barth, Fredrik
1969   Introduction. In *Ethnic Groups and Boundaries: The Social Organization
        of Culture Difference*, ed. F. Barth, pp. 1–38. Universitetsforlaget, Oslo,
        Norway.
Baudez, Claude F., and Peter Mathews
1978   Capture and Sacrifice at Palenque. In *Tercera Mesa Redonda de Palen-
        que, Vol. IV*, ed. M. Greene Robertson and D. C. Jeffers, pp. 31–40.
        Pre-Columbian Art Research, Herald Printers, Monterey.
Beaudry, Marilyn P., and David B. Tucker
1989   Household 1 Area Excavations. In *1989 Archaeological Investigations
        at the Ceren Site, El Salvador: A Preliminary Report*, ed. P. D. Sheets and
        B. R. McKee, pp. 29–40. Report on file, Department of Anthropology,
        University of Colorado, Boulder.
Beekman, Christopher S.
1996   *The Long-Term Evolution of a Political Boundary: Archaeological Research
        in Jalisco Mexico*. Unpublished Ph.D. dissertation, Vanderbilt Univer-
        sity, Nashville.
Bennett, Sharon
1993   1992 Burials from Yaxuna, Yucatan. In *The Selz Foundation Yaxuna
        Project: Final Report of the 1992 Field Season*, ed. C. K. Suhler and D. A.

Freidel, pp. 144–64. Manuscript on file, Department of Anthropology, Southern Methodist University, Dallas.

Berdan, Frances F.
1978   Ports of Trade in Mesoamerica: A Reappraisal. In *Cultural Continuity in Mesoamerica*, ed. D. L. Browman, pp. 179–98. Mouton, Paris.

Berdan, F. F., R. E. Blanton, E. H. Boone, M. G. Hodge, M. E. Smith, and E. Umberger
1996   *Aztec Imperial Strategies*. Dumbarton Oaks Research Library and Collection, Washington, D.C.

Berlin, Heinrich
1958   El Glifo "Emblema" en las Inscripciones Mayas. *Journal de la Societé des Américanistes* 47:111–19.

Berlo, Janet C.
1983   The Warrior and the Butterfly: Central Mexican Ideologies of Sacred Warfare and Teotihuacan Iconography. In *Text and Image in Pre-Columbian Art*, ed. J. C. Berlo, pp. 179–217. BAR International Series 180, Oxford, U.K.
1984   *Teotihuacan Art Abroad: A Study of Metropolitan Style and Provincial Transformation in Incensario Workshops*. BAR International Series 199, Oxford, U.K.
1992   Icons and Ideologies at Teotihuacan: The Great Goddess Reconsidered. In *Art, Ideology, and the City of Teotihuacan*, ed. J. C. Berlo, pp. 129–68. Dumbarton Oaks Research Library and Collection, Washington, D.C.

Bernal, Ignacio
1969   *The Olmec World*. University of California Press, Berkeley.

Berrin, Kathleen, and Esther Pasztory (eds.)
1993   *Teotihuacan: Art from the City of the Gods*. Thames and Hudson, Fine Arts Museums of San Francisco, London.

Bey, George J., III, Craig A. Hanson, and William M. Ringle
1997   Classic to Postclassic at Ek Balam: Architectural and Ceramic Evidence for Defining the Transition. *Latin American Antiquity* 8:237–54.

Beyer, Hermann
1965   La Mariposa en el Simbolismo Azteca. *El México Antiguo* 10:465–69.

Binford, Lewis R.
1962   Archaeology as Anthropology. *American Antiquity* 28:217–25.

Bittman Simons, Bente
1968a   The Codex of Cholula: A Preliminary Study. *Tlalocan* 5:267–88.
1968b   The Codex of Cholula: A Preliminary Study, Part II. *Tlalocan* 5:289–339.

Blitz, John H.
1988   Adoption of the Bow in Prehistoric North America. *North American Archaeologist* 9:123–45.

Bond, T. M., W. M. Ringle, G. J. Bey, and J. G. Smith

1999   *Ceramics from Ichmul de Morley, Yucatan, Mexico.* Paper presented at the 64th annual meeting of the Society for American Archaeology.

Bonfil Batalla, Guillermo
   1973   *Cholula: La Ciudad Sagrada en la Era Industrial.* Instituto de Investigaciones Historicas, Universidad Nacional Autonoma de Mexico, Mexico, D.F.

Boone, Elizabeth H. (ed.)
   1984   *Ritual Human Sacrifice in Mesoamerica.* Dumbarton Oaks Research Library and Collection, Washington, D.C.

Bové, Frederick J.
   1991   The Teotihuacan-Kaminaljuyú-Tikal Connection: A View from the South Coast of Guatemala. In *The Sixth Palenque Roundtable, 1986,* ed. M. Greene Robertson and V. Fields, pp. 135–42. University of Oklahoma, Norman.

Brainerd, George W.
   1958   *The Archaeological Ceramics of Yucatan.* University of California Anthropological Records, Volume 19, Berkeley.

Brandes, Stanley
   1998   Iconography in Mexico's Day of the Dead: Origins and Meaning. *Ethnohistory* 45:180–221.

Brasderfer, Fernando G.
   1981   Hallazgos Recientes en Coba, Quintana Roo. *Boletin de la Escuela de Ciencias Antropologicas de la Universidad de Yucatan* 9(50–51):52–59.

Bray, Warwick
   1968   *Everyday Life of the Aztecs.* G. P. Putman's Sons, New York.

Bricker, Victoria R.
   1973   *Ritual Humor in Highland Chiapas.* University of Texas Press, Austin.
   1981   *The Indian Christ, the Indian King: The Historical Substrate of Maya Myth and Ritual.* University of Texas Press, Austin.

Brockington, D. L.
   1983   The View from the Coast: Relationships between the Coast and Valley of Oaxaca. *Notas Mesoamericanas* 9:24–31.
   1987   El Clásico en la Costa de Oaxaca. In *El Auge y la Caída del Clásico en el México Central,* ed. J. Mountjoy and D. L. Brockington, pp. 225–35. Universidad Nacional Autónoma de México, México.

Brown, Kenneth L.
   1977   The Valley of Guatemala: A Highland Port of Trade. In *Kaminaljuyu and Teotihuacan: A Study in Prehistoric Culture Contact,* ed. W. T. Sanders and J. W. Michels, pp. 205–395. Pennsylvania State University Press Monograph Series on Kaminaljuyu, State College.

Brown, M. Kathryn, and James F. Garber
   1998   *The Origin and Function of Mask Facades in the Maya Lowlands.* Paper pesented at the 63rd annual meeting of the Society for American Archaeology.

Brown, M. Kathryn, and James F. Garber
1999 Evidence of Conflict during the Middle Preclassic in the Maya Low-lands: A View from Blackman Eddy, Belize. In *The Belize Valley Archaeological Project: Results of the 1998 Field Season,* ed. J. F. Garber and M. K. Brown, pp. 5–21. Report on file, Department of Archaeology, Belmopan, Belize.

Brown, M. Kathryn, James F. Garber, and Christopher J. Hartman
1998 A Middle Preclassic Mask, Triadic Architectural Arrangement, and Early Ritual Deposits at Blackman Eddy: Implications for Social Complexity during the Middle Formative. In *The Belize Valley Archaeology Project: Results of the 1997 Field Season,* ed. J. F. Garber and D. J. Glassman, pp. 33–48. Report on file, Department of Archaeology, Belize.
1999 *Middle Preclassic Ritual in the Maya Lowlands: An Example from the Site of Blackman Eddy, Belize.* Paper presented at the 64th annual meeting of the Society for American Archaeology.

Brumfiel, Elizabeth
1991 Weaving and Cooking: Women's Production in Aztec Mexico. In *Engendering Archaeology: Women and Prehistory,* ed. J. M. Gero and M. W. Conkey, pp. 224–51. Basil Blackwell, Oxford, U.K.

Brundage, Burr C.
1972 *A Rain of Darts: The Mexica Aztecs.* University of Texas Press, Austin.

Bullard, William R., Jr.
1960 Maya Settlement Pattern in Northeastern Peten, Guatemala. *American Antiquity* 41:465–77.

Burkhart, Louise M.
1989 *The Slippery Earth: Nahua-Christian Moral Dialogue in Sixteenth-Century Mexico.* University of Arizona Press, Tucson.

Byland, Bruce E., and M. D. Pohl John
1990 Alianza y Conflicto de los Estados Mixtecos: El Caso de Tilantongo. In *Lecturas Históricas del Estado de Oaxaca, Vol. I,* ed. M. Winter, pp. 379–90. Instituto Nacional de Antropología e Historia, Gobierno del Estado de Oaxaca, México.
1994 Political Factions in the Transition from Classic to Postclassic in the Mixteca Alta. In *Factional Competition and Political Development in the New World,* ed. E. M. Brumfiel and J. W. Fox, pp. 117–26. Cambridge University Press, Cambridge, U.K.

Campbell, Lyle, and Terrance Kaufman
1976 A Linguistic Look at the Olmec. *American Antiquity* 41:80–89.

Carlsen, Robert, and Martin Prechtel
1997 The Flowering of the Dead: An Interpretation of Highland Maya Culture. *Man* 26:23–42.

Carlson, John B.
1991 *Venus-Regulated Warfare and Ritual Sacrifice in Mesoamerica: Teotihua-*

can and the Cacaxtla "Star Wars" Connection. Center for Archaeoastronomy, Technical Publication No. 7, University of Maryland, College Park.

Carneiro, Robert L.
1970   A Theory of the Origin of the State. *Science* 169:733–39.
1981   The Chiefdom: Precursor of the State. In *The Transition to Statehood in the New World,* ed. G. D. Jones and R. R. Kautz, pp. 37–79. Cambridge University Press, Cambridge, U.K.
1990   Chiefdom-Level Warfare as Exemplified in Fiji and the Cauca Valley. In *The Anthropology of War,* ed. J. Haas, pp. 190–211. Cambridge University Press, Cambridge, U.K.
1994   War and Peace: Alternating Realities in Human History. In *Studying War: Anthropological Perspectives, War and Society, Vol. 2,* ed. S. P. Reyna and R. E. Davis, pp. 3–27. Gordon and Breach Science Publishers, Langhorne, Pa.

Carr, Christopher, and Jill E. Neitzel (eds.)
1995   *Style, Society, and Person: Archaeological and Ethnological Approaches.* Plenum Press, New York.

Carrasco, Pedro
1971   Los Barrios Antiguos de Cholula. *Estudios y Documentos de la Región de Puebla-Tlaxcala* 3:9–87.

Caso, Alfonso
1938   *Exploraciones en Oaxaca, Quinta y Sexta Temporadas, 1936–1937.* Instituto Panamericano de Geografía e Historia, Publicación 34, México.
1942   El Paraiso Terrenal en Teotihuacan. *Cuadernos Americanos* 6:127–36.
1947   Calendario y Escritura de las Antiguas Culturas de Monte Albán. *Obras Completas de Miguel Othón de Mendizábal* 1:116–43.

Caso, A., I. Bernal, and J. R. Acosta
1967   *La Cerámica de Monte Albán.* Memorias del Instituto Nacional de Antropología e Historia No. 13, México.

Castro Morales, Efrain, and Roberto Garcia Moll
1972   Un Entierro Colectivo en la Ciudad de Cholula, Puebla. In *Religión en Mesoamerica,* ed. J. Litvak King and N. Castillo Tejero, pp. 381–84. Sociedad Mexicana de Antropología, México, D.F.

Chadwick, Robert E. L.
1966   The "Olmeca-Xicallanca" of Teotihuacan: A Preliminary Study. *Mesoamerican Notes* 7–8:1–23.

Chapman, Anne C.
1957   Port of Trade Enclaves in Aztec and Maya Civilizations. In *Trade and Market in the Early Empires,* ed. K. Polanyi, C. Arensberg, and H. W. Pearson, pp. 114–53. The Free Press, New York.

Chase, Arlen F.
1985   Troubled Times: The Archaeology and Iconography of the Terminal Classic Southern Lowland Maya. In *Fifth Palenque Round Table, 1983,*

Vol. 7, ed. M. Greene Robertson and V. M. Fields, pp. 103–14. Pre-Columbian Art Research Institute, San Francisco.

1991   Cycles of Time: Caracol in the Maya Realm. In *Sixth Palenque Round Table, 1986,* ed. M. Greene Robertson and V. M. Fields, pp. 32–42. University of Oklahoma Press, Norman.

1992   Elites and the Changing Organization of Classic Maya Society. In *Mesoamerican Elites: An Archaeological Assessment,* ed. D. Z. Chase and A. F. Chase, pp. 30–49. University of Oklahoma Press, Norman.

1994   A Contextual Approach to the Ceramics of Caracol, Belize. In *Studies in the Archaeology of Caracol, Belize,* ed. D. Z. Chase and A. F. Chase, pp. 157–82. Monograph 7, Pre-Columbian Art Research Institute, San Francisco.

1998   Planeacion Civica e Integracion de Sitio en Caracol, Belice: Definiendo una Economia Administrada del Period Clasico Maya. *Los Investigadores de la Cultura Maya* 6:26–44.

Chase, Arlen F., and Diane Z. Chase

1987   *Investigations at the Classic Maya City of Caracol, Belize: 1985–1987.* Pre-Columbian Art Research Institute, San Francisco.

1989   The Investigation of Classic Period Maya Warfare at Caracol, Belice. *Mayab* 5:5–18.

1992   El Norte y el Sur: Politica, Dominios, y Evolucion Cultural Maya. *Mayab* 8:134–49.

1994a   Details in the Archaeology of Caracol, Belize: An Introduction. In *Studies in the Archaeology of Caracol, Belize,* ed. D. Z. Chase and A. F. Chase, pp. 1–11. Monograph 7, Pre-Columbian Art Research Institute, San Francisco.

1994b   Maya Veneration of the Dead at Caracol, Belize. In *Seventh Palenque Round Table, 1989,* ed. M. Greene Robertson and V. M. Fields, pp. 55–62. Pre-Columbian Art Research Institute, San Francisco.

1996a   A Mighty Maya Nation: How Caracol Built an Empire by Cultivating Its "Middle Class." *Archaeology* 49:66–72.

1996b   More Than Kin and King: Centralized Political Organization among the Ancient Maya. *Current Anthropology* 37:803–10.

1996c   The Organization and Composition of Classic Lowland Maya Society: The View from Caracol, Belize. In *Eighth Palenque Round Table, 1993,* ed. M. J. Macri and J. McHargue, pp. 213–22. Pre-Columbian Art Research Institute, San Francisco.

1998a   Late Classic Maya Political Structure, Polity Size, and Warfare Arenas. In *Anatomia de una Civilizacion: Aproximaciones Interdisciplinarias a la Cultura Maya,* ed. A. C. Ruiz, Y. F. Marquinez, J. M. G. Campillo, J. I. Ponce de Leon, A. L. Garcia-Gallo, and L. T. Sanz Castro, pp. 11–29. Sociedad Espanola de Estudios Mayas, Madrid.

1998b   Scale and Intensity in Classic Period Maya Agriculture: Terracing and Settlement at the "Garden City" of Caracol, Belize. *Culture and Agriculture* 20:60–67.

2001   The Royal Court of Caracol, Belize: Its Palaces and People. In *Royal Courts of the Ancient Maya: Volume 2: Data and Case Studies*, ed. T. Inomata and S. D. Houston, pp. 102–37. Westview Press, Boulder, Colo.

Chase, Arlen F., Nikolai Grube, and Diane Z. Chase
1991   *Three Terminal Classic Monuments from Caracol, Belize*. Research Reports on Ancient Maya Writing, Center for Maya Research, Washington, D.C.

Chase, Diane Z.
1986   Social and Political Organization in the Land of Cacao and Honey: Correlating the Archaeology and Ethnohistory of the Postclassic Lowland Maya. In *Late Lowland Maya Civilization*, ed. J. A. Sabloff and E. W. Andrews V, pp. 347–77. University of New Mexico Press, Albuquerque.
1998   Albergando a Los Muertos en Caracol, Belice. *Los Investigadores de la Cultura Maya* 6:26–44.

Chase, Diane Z., and Arlen F. Chase
1996   Maya Multiples: Individuals, Entries, and Tombs in Structure A34 of Caracol, Belize. *Latin American Antiquity* 7:61–79.
1998   The Architectural Context of Caches, Burials, and Other Ritual Activities for the Classic Period Maya (as Reflected at Caracol, Belize). In *Functions and Meaning in Classic Maya Architecture*, ed. S. D. Houston, pp. 299–332. Dumbarton Oaks Research Library and Collection, Washington, D.C.
2000   La Guerra Maya del Periodo Clasico desde la Perspectiva de Caracol, Belice. *La Guerra Entre Los Antiguos Mayas*, ed. S. Trejo, pp. 53–72. Instituto Nacional de Antropologia e Historia and Consejo Nacional para la Cultura y las Artes, Mexico.

Chase, Diane Z., and Arlen F. Chase (eds.)
1994   *Studies in the Archaeology of Caracol, Belize*. Monograph 7, Pre-Columbian Art Research Institute, San Francisco.

Chase, D. Z., A. F. Chase, C. White, and W. Giddens
1998   *Human Skeletal Remains in Archaeological Context: Status, Diet, and Household at Caracol, Belize*. Paper presented at the 14th International Congress of Anthropological and Ethnological Sciences.

Child, Mark B.
1999   *Classic Maya Warfare and Its Sociopolitical Implications*. Paper presented at the 98th annual meeting of the American Anthropological Association.

Clark, John E.
1986   From Mountains to Molehills: A Critical Review of Teotihuacan's Obsidian Industry. In *Economic Aspects of Prehispanic Highland Mexico*, ed. B. L. Isaac, pp. 23–74. Research in Economic Anthropology, Supplement 2, JAI Press, Greenwich, Conn.

Cobb, Charles R., Jeffrey Maymon, and Randall H. McGuire
1999   Feathered, Horned, and Antlered Serpents: Mesoamerican Connec-

tions with the Southwest and Southeast. In *Great Towns and Regional Polities in the Prehistoric American Southwest and Southeast,* ed. J. E. Neitzel, pp. 165–81. University of New Mexico Press, Albuquerque.

Coe, Michael D.

1965a *The Jaguar's Children: Pre-Classic Central Mexico.* Museum of Primitive Art, New York.

1965b The Olmec Style and Its Distribution. *Archaeology of Southern Mesoamerican, Part Two,* ed. G. R. Willey, pp. 739–75. Handbook of Middle American Indians, Vol. 3, University of Texas Press, Austin.

1967 Solving a Monumental Mystery. *Discovery* 3:21–26.

1968 San Lorenzo and the Olmec Civilization. In *Dumbarton Oaks Conference on the Olmec,* ed. E. P. Benson, pp. 41–71. Dumbarton Oaks Research Library and Collection, Washington, D.C.

1972 Olmec Jaguars and Olmec Kings. In *The Cult of the Feline: A Conference on Pre-Columbian Iconography,* ed. E. P. Benson, pp. 1–18. Dumbarton Oaks Research Library and Collection, Washington, D.C.

1976 Early Steps in the Evolution of Maya Writing. In *Origins of Religious Art and Iconography in Preclassic Mesoamerica,* ed. H. B. Nicholson, pp. 107–22. UCLA Latin American Center Publications, Los Angeles.

1977 Olmec and Maya: A Study in Relationships. In *The Origins of Maya Civilization,* ed. R. E. W. Adams, pp. 183–95. University of New Mexico Press, Albuquerque.

Coe, Michael D., and Richard A. Diehl

1980 *In the Land of the Olmec: The Archaeology of San Lorenzo Tenochtitlán.* University of Texas Press, Austin.

Coe, Michael D., and Mark Van Stone

2001 *Reading the Maya Glyphs.* Thames and Hudson, London.

Coe, William R.

1959 *Piedras Negras Archaeology: Artifacts, Caches, and Burials.* Museum Monographs, The University Museum, University of Pennsylvania, Philadelphia.

1990 *Excavations in the Great Plaza, North Terrace, and North Acropolis of Tikal.* Tikal Report, No. 14, University of Pennsylvania, University Museum, Philadelphia.

Coggins, Clemency C.

1976 *Painting and Drawing Styles at Tikal: An Historical and Iconographic Approach.* Unpublished Ph.D. dissertation, Harvard University, Cambridge, Mass.

1979 A New Order and the Role of the Calendar: Some Characteristics of the Middle Classic Period at Tikal. In *Maya Archaeology and Ethnohistory,* ed. N. Hammond and G. R. Willey, pp. 38–50. University of Texas Press, Austin.

Cohadas, Marvin

1991 Ballgame Imagery of the Maya Lowlands: History and Iconography.

In *The Mesoamerican Ballgame*, ed. V. Scarborough and D. Wilcox, pp. 251–88. University of Arizona Press, Tucson.

Cohen, Ronald
1984 Warfare and State Formation: Wars Make States and States Make Wars. In *Warfare, Culture, and Environment*, ed. R. B. Ferguson, pp. 329–58. Academic Press, New York.

Cole, Sally J.
1993 Basketmaker Rock Art at the Green Mask Site, Southeastern Utah. In *Anasazi Basketmaker: Papers from the 1990 Wetherhill-Grand Gulch Symposium*, ed. V. M. Atkins, pp. 193–222. Cultural Resource Series 24, Bureau of Land Management, Salt Lake City.

Conkey, Margaret W., and Christine A. Hastorf (eds.)
1990 *The Uses of Style in Archaeology*. Cambridge University Press, Cambridge, U.K.

Conrad, Geoffery W., and Arthur A. Demarest
1984 *Religion and Empire: The Dynamics of Aztec and Inca Expansion*. Cambridge University Press, Cambridge, U.K.

Contreras, Eduardo
1970 El Altar 3. In *Proyecto Cholula*, ed. I. Marquina, pp. 111–18. Serie Investigaciones 19. Instituto Nacional de Antropología e Historia, Mexico, D.F.

Cordell, Linda S.
1997 *Archaeology of the Southwest*. Academic Press, Orlando.

Cortés, Hernán
1986 *Letter from Mexico*. Trans. and ed. A. Pagden. Yale University Press, New Haven, Conn.

Cowgill, George L.
1997 State and Society at Teotihuacan, Mexico. *Annual Review of Anthropology* 26:129–61.

Crotty, Helen Koefoed
1995 *Anasazi Mural Art of the Pueblo IV Period, A.D. 1300–1600: Influences, Selective Adaptation, and Cultural Diversity in the Prehistoric Southwest*. Unpublished Ph.D. dissertation, Department of Art History, University of California, Los Angeles.

Crown, Patricia L., and W. James Judge (eds.)
1991 *Chaco & Hohokam: Prehistoric Regional Systems in the American Southwest*. School of American Research Press, Santa Fe, N.M.

Culbert, T. Patrick
1991a Maya Political History and Elite Interaction: A Summary View. In *Classic Maya Political History: Hieroglyphic and Archaeological Evidence*, ed. T. P. Culbert, pp. 311–46. Cambridge University Press, Cambridge, U.K.
1995 Warfare and the Segmentary State. *Pre-Columbian Art Research Institute Newsletter* 21:6–9.

Culbert, T. Patrick (ed.)
1991b *Classic Maya Political History: Hieroglyphic and Archaeological Evidence.* Cambridge University Press, Cambridge, U.K.

Cyphers, Ann
1993 Escenas Escultóricas Olmecas. *Antropológicas* 6:47–57.
1996 Recent Discoveries at San Lorenzo, Veracruz. In *Olmecs*, pp. 56–59. Arqueología Mexicana, México.
1997 Los Felinos de San Lorenzo. In *Poblacion, Subsistencia, y Medio Ambiente en San Lorenzo Tenochtitlán*, ed. A. Cyphers, pp. 195–226. Universidad Nacional Autonoma de México, Instituto de Investigaciones Antropológicas, México.

Dahlin, Bruce H.
1984 A Colossus in Guatemala: The Preclassic City of El Mirador. *Archaeology* 37:18–25.

D'Altroy, T. N.
1992 *Provincial Power in the Inka Empire.* Smithsonian Institution Press, Washington, D.C.

Davies, Nigel
1974 *The Aztecs: A History.* G. P. Putnam's Sons, New York.
1977 *The Toltecs Until the Fall of Tula.* University of Oklahoma Press, Norman.
1987 *The Aztec Empire: The Toltec Resurgence.* University of Oklahoma Press, Norman.

Davis, Whitney
1978 The So-Called Jaguar-Human Copulation Scenes in Olmec Art. *American Antiquity* 43:453–57.

Deal, Michael
1985 Household Pottery Disposal in the Maya Highlands: An Ethnoarchaeological Interpretation. *Journal of Anthropological Archaeology* 4:243–91.

Deal, Michael, and Melissa B. Hagstrum
1995 Ceramic Reuse Behavior among the Maya and Wanka. In *Expanding Archaeology*, ed. J. M. Skibo, W. H. Walker, and A. E. Nielson, pp. 111–25. University of Utah Press, Salt Lake City.

Dean, Jeffrey S., William H. Doelle, and Janet D. Orcutt
1994 Adaptive Stress, Environment, and Demography. In *Themes in Southwest Prehistory*, ed. G. J. Gumerman, pp. 33–86. School of American Research Press, Santa Fe, N.M.

DeCicco, G., and D. L. Brockington
1956 *Reconocimiento Arqueológico en el Suroeste de Oaxaca.* Informe No. 6, Dirección de Monumentos Prehispánicos, Instituto Nacional de Antropología e Historia, México.

Demarest, Arthur A.
1978 Interregional Conflict and "Situational Ethics" in Classic Maya War-

fare. In *Codex Wauchope: A Tribute Roll,* ed. M. Giardino, B. Edmonson, and W. Creamer, pp. 101–11. Bureau of Administrative Services, Tulane University, New Orleans.

1992 Ideology in Ancient Maya Cultural Evolution: The Dynamics of Galactic Polities. In *Ideology and Pre-Columbian Civilizations,* ed. A. A. Demarest and G. W. Conrad, pp. 135–57. School of American Research Press, Santa Fe, N.M.

1993 The Violent Saga of a Maya Kingdom. *National Geographic* 183:94–111.

1997a War, Peace, and the Collapse of a Native American Civilization: Lessons for Contemporary Systems of Conflict. In *A Natural History of Peace,* ed. T. Gregor, pp. 215–48. Vanderbilt University Press, Nashville.

1997b The Vanderbilt Petexbatun Regional Archaeological Project: 1989–1994: Overview, History, and Major Results of a Multidisciplinary Study of the Classic Maya Collapse. *Ancient Mesoamerica* 8:209–27.

Demarest, A. A., M. O'Mansky, C. Wolley, D. Van Tuerenhout, T. Inomata, J. Palka, and H. Escobedo

1997 Classic Maya Defensive Systems and Warfare in the Petexbatun Region. *Ancient Mesoamerica* 8:229–53.

Díaz del Castillo, Bernal

1956 *The Discovery and Conquest of Mexico.* Farrar, Straus, and Cudahy, New York.

1963 *The Conquest of New* Spain. Trans. J. M. Cohen. Penguin Books, Harmondsworth, U.K.

Diehl, Richard A.

1983 *Tula: The Toltec Capital of Ancient Mexico.* Thames and Hudson, New York.

Dietler, Michael, and Ingrid Herbich

1989 Tich Matek: The Technology of Luo Pottery Production and the Definition of Ceramic Style. *World Archaeology* 21:148–64.

Dobres, Marcia-Anne

1995 Gender and Prehistoric Technology: On Social Agency of Technical Strategies. *World Archaeology* 27:25–49.

Driver, David W., and Jennifer McWilliams

1995 Excavations at the Ontario Village Site. In *The Belize Valley Archaeological Project: Results of the 1994 Field Season,* ed. J. F. Garber and D. J. Glassman, pp. 26–57. Report on file, Department of Archaeology, Belmopan, Belize.

Dudek, Martin G.

1993 *The Cholulan Massacre Accounts: Processes and Influences in the Formation of History.* Paper presented at the International Congress of Anthropological and Ethnological Sciences, Mexico City.

Durán, Diego
1967 *Historia de las Indias de Nueva España e Islas de la Tierra Firme.* Porrúa, Mexico.
1971 *The Book of the Gods and Rites and the Ancient Calendar.* Trans. and ed. F. Horcasitas and D. Heyden, with foreword by M. Leon-Portilla. University of Oklahoma Press, Norman.
1994 *The History of the Indies of New Spain.* Trans., annot., and intro. D. Heyden. University of Oklahoma Press, Norman.
Earle, Timothy K.
1987 Chiefdoms in Archaeological and Ethnohistorical Perspective. *Annual Review of Anthropology* 16:279–304.
Ember, Carol, and Melvin Ember
1992 Resource Unpredictability, Mistrust, and War. *Journal of Conflict Resolution* 36:242–62.
Fahsen, Federico
1988 *A New Early Classic Text from Tikal.* Research Reports on Ancient Maya Writing 17, Center for Maya Research, Washington, D.C.
Fash, William L.
1989 The Sculptural Facade of Structure 9N-82: Content, Form, and Significance. In *The House of the Bacabs, Copan, Honduras,* ed. D. L. Webster, pp. 41–72. Dumbarton Oaks Research Library and Collection, Washington, D.C.
1991 *Scribes, Warriors, and Kings: The City of Copan and the Ancient Maya.* Thames and Hudson, London.
Fash, William L., and Robert J. Sharer
1991 Sociopolitical Developments and Methodological Issues at Copan, Honduras: A Conjunctive Approach. *Latin American Antiquity* 2:166–87.
Fash, William L., and David S. Stuart
1991 Dynastic History and Cultural Evolution at Copan, Honduras. In *Classic Maya Political History: Hieroglyphic and Archaeological Evidence,* ed. T. P. Culbert, pp. 147–79. Cambridge University Press, Cambridge, U.K.
Faulhaber, J.
1965 La Poblacion de Tlatilco, Mexico, Caracterizada por Sus Entierros. In *Homenaje a Juan Comas en su 65 Aniversario, Volume II,* pp. 83–121. Editorial Libros de México, México.
Feinman, G. M., and L. M. Nicholas
1990 At the Margins of the Monte Albán State: Settlement Patterns in the Ejutla Valley, Oaxaca, México. *Latin American Antiquity* 1:216–46.
1991 The Monte Albán State: A Diachronic Perspective on an Ancient Core and its Periphery. In *Core/Periphery Relations in Precapitalist Worlds,* ed. C. Chase-Dunn and T. D. Hall, pp. 240–76. Westview Press, Boulder, Colo.

1993   Shell-Ornament Production in Ejutla: Implications for Highland-Coastal Interaction in Ancient Oaxaca. *Ancient Mesoamerica* 4:103–19.

Ferguson, R. Brian
1984   Introduction: Studying War. In *Warfare, Culture, and Environment*, ed. R. B. Ferguson, pp. 111–40. Academic Press, New York.
1990   Explaining War. In *The Anthropology of War*, ed. J. Haas, pp. 26–55. Cambridge University Press, Cambridge, U.K.
1994   The General Consequences of War: An Amazonian Perspective. In *Studying War: Anthropological Perspectives, War and Society*, Vol. 2, ed. S. P. Reyna and R. E. Davis, pp. 85–111. Gordon and Breach Science Publishers, Langhorne, Pa.

Fields, Virginia M.
1989   *The Divine Origin of Kingship among the Lowland Classic Maya.* Unpublished Ph.D. dissertation, University of Texas, Austin.
1991   The Iconographic Heritage of the Maya Jester God. *Sixth Palenque Round Table 1986,* ed. M. Greene Robertson, pp. 167–74. University of Oklahoma Press, Norman.

Finsten, Laura
1996   Periphery and Frontier in Southern Mexico: The Mixteca Sierra in Highland Oaxaca. In *Pre-Columbian World Systems*, ed. P. N. Peregrine and G. M. Feinman, pp. 77–95. Monographs in World Archaeology No. 26, Prehistory Press, Madison, Wis.

Flannery, Kent V.
1983a Zapotec Warfare: Archaeological Evidence for the Battles of Huitzo and Guiengola. In *The Cloud People: Divergent Evolution of the Zapotec and Mixtec Civilizations*, ed. K. V. Flannery and J. Marcus, pp. 318–22. Academic Press, New York.
1983b Monte Negro: A Reinterpretation. In *The Cloud People: Divergent Evolution of the Mixtec and Zapotec Civilizations*, ed. K. V. Flannery and J. Marcus, pp. 99–102. Academic Press, New York.

Flannery, Kent V., and Joyce Marcus
1983a An Editorial Opinion on the Mixtec Impact. In *The Cloud People: Divergent Evolution of the Zapotec and Mixtec Civilizations*, ed. K. V. Flannery and J. Marcus, pp. 277–79. Academic Press, New York.

Flannery, Kent V., and Joyce Marcus (eds.)
1983b *The Cloud People: Divergent Evolution of the Zapotec and Mixtec Civilizations.* Academic Press, New York.

Foias, Antonia, and Ronald L. Bishop
1997   Changing Ceramic Production and Exchange in the Petexbatun Region, Guatemala: Reconsidering the Classic Maya Collapse. *Ancient Mesoamerica* 8:275–92.

Folan, W. J., J. Marcus, S. Pincemin, M. Carrasco, L. Fletcher, and A. Lopez
1995   Calakmul: New Data from an Ancient Maya Capital in Campeche, Mexico. *Latin American Antiquity* 6:310–34.

Foncerrada de Molina, Marta
  1976   La Pintura Mural de Cacaxtla, Tlaxcala. *Anales del Instituto de Investi-
          gaciones Esteticas* 56:5–20.
  1980   Mural Painting in Cacaxtla and Teotihuacan Cosmopolitism. In *Third
          Palenque Round Table, 1978, Part 2,* ed. M. Greene Robertson, pp. 183–
          98. University of Texas Press, Austin.
Fowler, William R., Jr.
  1989   *The Evolution of Ancient Nahua Civilizations: The Pipil-Nicarao of Cen-
          tral America.* University of Oklahoma Press, Norman.
Fox, John W.
  1978   *Quiche Conquest: Centralism and Regionalism in Highland Guatemalan
          State Development.* University of New Mexico Press, Albuquerque.
  1981   The Late Postclassic Eastern Frontier of Mesoamerica: Innovation
          along the Periphery. *Current Anthropology* 22:322–44.
  1987   *Maya Postclassic State Formation: Segmentary Lineage Migration in
          Advancing Frontiers.* Cambridge University Press, Cambridge, U.K.
Fox, Richard G.
  1977   *Urban Anthropology: Cities in Their Cultural Settings.* Prentice Hall,
          Englewood Cliffs, N.J.
Fried, M. H., M. Harris, and R. Murphy (eds.)
  1968   *War: The Anthropology of Armed Conflict and Aggression.* The Natural
          History Press, Garden City, N.Y.
Freidel, David A.
  1986a   Maya Warfare: An Example of Peer Polity Interaction. In *Peer Polity
          Interaction and Socio-Political Change,* ed. C. Renfrew and J. F. Cherry,
          pp. 93–108. Cambridge University Press, Cambridge, U.K.
  1986b   The Monumental Architecture. In *Archaeology at Cerros Belize, Central
          America, Volume I: An Interim Report,* ed. D. A. Freidel and R. A. Rob-
          ertson, pp. 1–22. Southern Methodist University Press, Dallas.
  1987   *Yaxuna Archaeological Survey: A Report of the 1986 Field Season.* Manu-
          script on file, Department of Anthropology, Southern Methodist
          University, Dallas.
  1989   *The Maya War Jaguar: Historical Invention and Structural Transforma-
          tion.* Paper presented at the 54th annual meeting of the Society for
          American Archaeology.
  1990   The Jester God: The Beginning and End of a Maya Royal Symbol. In
          Vision and Revision in Maya Studies, ed. F. S. Clancy and P. D. Har-
          rison, pp. 67–78. University of New Mexico Press, Albuquerque.
  1992   Children of First Father's Skull: Terminal Classic Warfare in the
          Northern Maya Lowlands. In *Mesoamerican Elites: An Archaeological
          Assessment,* ed. D. Z. Chase and A. F. Chase, pp. 99–117. University
          of Oklahoma Press, Norman.
  1999   Introduction. In *Final Report of the 1997 Season with Collected Papers:
          The Selz Foundation Yaxuna Project,* ed. J. M. Shaw and D. A. Freidel,

pp. 1–6. Manuscript on file, Department of Anthropology, Southern Methodist University, Dallas.

Freidel, David A., and Linda Schele
1989   Dead Kings and Living Temples. In *Word and Image in Maya Culture: Explorations in Language, Writing, and Representation,* ed. W. F. Hanks and D. S. Rice, pp. 233–43. University of Utah Press, Salt Lake City.

Freidel, David A., Linda Schele, and Joy Parker
1993   *Maya Cosmos: Three Thousand Years on the Shaman's Path.* William Morrow, New York.

Freidel, David A., and Charles K. Suhler
1998   Visiones Serpentinas y Laberintos Mayas. *Arqueologia Mexicana* 6(34):28–37.

Freidel, David A., Charles K. Suhler, and Rafael Cobos P.
1998   Termination Ritual Deposits at Yaxuna: Detecting the Historical in Archaeological Contexts. In *The Sowing and the Dawning: Termination, Dedication, and Transformation in the Archaeological and Ethnographic Record of Mesoamerica,* ed. S. B. Mock, pp. 135–44. University of New Mexico Press, Albuquerque.

Fulford, M.
1992   Territorial Expansion and the Roman Empire. *World Archaeology* 23:294–305.

Furst, Peter T.
1968   The Olmec Were-Jaguar Motif in the Light of Ethnographic Reality. In *Dumbarton Oaks Conference on the Olmec,* ed. E. P. Benson, pp. 143–78. Dumbarton Oaks Research Library and Collection, Washington, D.C.
1974   Morning Glory and Mother Goddess at Tepantitla, Teotihuacan: Iconography and Analogy in Pre-Columbian Art. In *Mesoamerican Archaeology: New Approaches,* ed. N. Hammond, pp. 187–215. University of Texas Press, Austin.
1995   Shamanism, Transformation, and Olmec Art. In *The Olmec World: Ritual and Rulership,* pp. 69–81. The Art Museum, Princeton University, Princeton, N.J.

Garber, James F.
1981   *Material Culture and Patterns of Artifact Consumption and Disposal at the Maya Site of Cerros in Northern Belize.* Unpublished Ph.D. dissertation, Southern Methodist University, Dallas.
1983   Patterns of Jade Consumption and Disposal at Cerros, Northern Belize. *American Antiquity* 48:800–7.
1986   The Artifacts. In *Archaeology at Cerros, Belize, Central America, Volume I: An Interim Report,* ed. D. A. Freidel and R. A. Robertson, pp. 117–26. Manuscript on file, Department of Anthropology, Southern Methodist University Press, Dallas.
1989   *Archaeology at Cerros, Belize, Central America, Volume II: The Artifacts.* Southern Methodist University Press, Dallas.

1993   The Cultural Context of Jade Artifacts from the Maya Site of Cerros, Belize. In *Precolumbian Jade: New Geological and Cultural Interpretations,* ed. F. W. Lange, pp. 166–72. University of Utah Press, Salt Lake City.

Garber, James F., M. Kathryn Brown, and Christopher J. Hartman
1998   Middle Preclassic Public Architecture: The Blackman Eddy Example. In *The Belize Valley Archaeology Project: Results of the 1997 Field Season,* ed. J. F. Garber and D. J. Glassman, pp. 5–31. Report on file, Department of Archaeology, Belmopan, Belize.

Garber, James F., Christopher J. Hartman, and Tania Wildman
1996   Excavations on Structure B1 at Blackman Eddy: Results of the 1995 Field Season. In *The Belize Valley Archaeological Project: Results of the 1995 Field Season,* ed. J. F. Garber and D. J. Glassman, pp. 6–34. Report on file, Department of Archaeology, Belmopan, Belize.

Garciagodoy, Juanita
1998   *Digging the Days of the Dead.* University Press of Colorado, Niwot, Colo.

Gaxiola, M.
1984   *Huamelulpan: Un Centro Urbano de la Mixteca Alta.* Colección Científica, Instituto Nacional de Antropología e Historia, México.

Geertz, Clifford
1973   *The Interpretation of Cultures.* Basic Books, New York.
1980   *Negara: The Theater State in Nineteenth-Century Bali.* Princeton University Press, Princeton, N.J.

Geib, Phil R.
1990   A Basketmaker II Wooden Tool Cache from Lower Glen Canyon. *The Kiva* 55:265–77.

Gerhardt, Juliette C., and Norman Hammond
1991   The Community of Cuello: The Ceremonial Core. In *Cuello: An Early Maya Community in Belize,* ed. N. Hammond, pp. 98–117. Cambridge University Press, Cambridge, U.K.

Gerstle, Andrea I.
1989   Excavation at Structure 3, Ceren 1989. In *1989 Archaeological Investigations at the Ceren Site, El Salvador: A Preliminary Report,* ed. P. D. Sheets and S. E. Simmons, pp. 46–90. Report on file, Department of Anthropology, University of Colorado, Boulder.
1993   Excavations at Structure 10, Joya de Ceren (Operation 8). In *Preliminary Report of the Ceren Research Project, 1993 Season,* ed. P. D. Sheets and S. E. Simmons, pp. 46–90. Report on file, Department of Anthropology, University of Colorado, Boulder.

Giddens, Wendy
1997   *Animal Utilization in a Growing City: Vertebrate Exploitation at Caracol, Belize.* Paper presented at the 62nd annual meeting of the Society for American Archaeologists.

Givens, R. Dale, and Martin Nettleship (eds.)
  1976   *Discussions on War and Human Aggression.* Mouton, Paris.
González L., Ernesto, and Lourdes Márquez M.
  1995   La Zona Oaxaqueña en el Posclásico. In *Historia Antigua de México, Volumen III: El Horizonte Posclásico y Algunos Aspectos Intelectuales de las Culturas Mesoamericanas,* ed. L. Manzanilla and L. López L., pp. 55–86. Instituto Nacional de Antropología e Historia, México.
Gonzalez L., Rebecca
  1988   Proyecto Arqueologico La Venta. *Arqueologica* 4:121–65.
Gorenstein Shirley
  1973   *Tepexi el Viejo: A Postclassic Fortified Site in the Mixteca-Puebla Region of Mexico.* Transactions of the American Philosophical Society, Vol. 63, Pt. 1, Philadelphia.
Gorenstein, Shirley, and Helen P. Pollard
  1991   Xanhari: Protohistoric Tarascan Routes. In *Ancient Road Networks and Settlement Hierarchies in the New World,* ed. C. D. Trombold, pp. 170–85. Cambridge University Press, Cambridge, U.K.
Gossen, Gary H.
  1986   Mesoamerican Ideas as a Foundation for Regional Synthesis. In *Symbol and Meaning beyond the Closed Community: Essays in Mesoamerican Ideas,* ed. G. H. Gossen, pp. 1–8. Institute for Mesoamerican Studies, Albany, N.Y.
Graham, Ian
  1967   *Archaeological Explorations of El Petén, Guatemala.* Middle American Research Institute, Publication 33, Tulane University, New Orleans.
Graham, John A.
  1990   *Monumental Sculpture and Hieroglyphic Inscriptions.* Memoirs of the Peabody Museum of Archaeology and Ethnology, Vol. 16, No. 1, Harvard University, Cambridge, Mass.
Griffin, Gillette G.
  1967   Cave Trip Discloses Earliest American Art. *Princeton Quarterly* 34:6–9.
Grove, David C.
  1968   Chalcatzingo, Morelos, Mexico: A Reappraisal of the Olmec Rock Carvings. *American Antiquity* 33:486–91.
  1972   Olmec Felines in Highland Central Mexico. In *The Cult of the Feline,* ed. E. P. Benson, pp. 153–64. Dumbarton Oaks Research Library and Collection, Washington, D.C.
  1981   Olmec Monuments: Mutilation as a Clue to Meaning. In *The Olmec and Their Neighbors,* ed. E. P. Benson, pp. 49–68. Dumbarton Oaks Research Library and Collections, Washington, D.C.
  1984   *Chalcatzingo: Excavations on the Olmec Frontier.* Thames and Hudson, London.
  1988   *Archaeological Investigations on the Pacific Coast of Oaxaca, Mexico,*

1986. Report submitted to the National Geographic Society, Washington, D.C.

Grove, David C. (ed.)
1987   *Ancient Chalcatzingo.* University of Texas Press, Austin.

Grove, David C., and Jorge Angulo V.
1987   A Catalog and Description of Chalcatzingo's Monuments. In *Ancient Chalcatzingo,* ed. D. C. Grove, pp. 110–31. University of Texas Press, Austin.

Grove, Jean
1990   *The Little Ice Age.* Routledge, London.

Grube, Nikolai
1994   Epigraphic Research at Caracol, Belize. In *Studies in the Archaeology of Caracol, Belize,* ed. D. Z. Chase and A. F. Chase, pp. 83–122. Monograph 7, Pre-Columbian Art Research Institute, San Francisco.

Grube, Nikolai, and Simon Martin
1998   Deciphering Maya Politics. In *Notebook for the XXIInd Maya Hieroglyphic Forum at Texas.* Department of Art and Art History, the College of Fine Arts, and the Institute of Latin American Studies, University of Texas, Austin.

Guderjan, Thomas H., and James F. Garber (eds.)
1995   *Maya Maritime Trade, Settlement, and Populations on Ambergris Cay, Belize.* Maya Research Program and Labyrinthos, San Antonio, Tex.

Guy, Carlo T. E.
1967   Oldest Painting in the New World. *Natural History* 76:28–35.

Haas, Jonathan, and Winifred Creamer
1993   *Stress and Warfare among the Kayenta Anasazi of the 13th Century* A.D. Field Museum of Natural History, Chicago.
1997   Warfare among the Pueblos: Myth, History, and Ethnology. *Ethnohistory* 44:235–61.

Hammond, Norman
1991   Inside the Black Box: Defining Maya Polity. In *Classic Maya Political History: Hieroglyphic and Archaeological Evidence,* ed. T. P. Culbert, pp. 253–84. Cambridge University Press, Cambridge, U.K.
1999   The Genesis of Hierarchy: Mortuary and Offertory Ritual in the Pre-Classic at Cuello, Belize. In *Social Patterns in Pre-Classic Mesoamerica,* ed. D. C. Grove and R. A. Joyce, pp. 49–66. Dumbarton Oaks Research Library and Collection, Washington, D.C.

Hansen, Richard D.
1992   *The Archaeology of Ideology: A Study of Maya Preclassic Architectural Sculpture at Nakbe, Peten, Guatemala.* Unpublished Ph.D. dissertation, University of California, Los Angeles.
1993   *Investigaciones Arqueológicas en Nakbé, Petén: El Resumen de la Temporada de Campo de 1993.* University of California, Los Angeles.

Harris, John F., and Stephen K. Sterns
   1997   *Understanding Maya Inscriptions: A Hieroglyphic Handbook.* The University of Pennsylvania Museum, Philadelphia.
Hartman, C. J., M. K. Brown, J. B. Pagliaro, and J. McWilliams
   1999   The 1998 Excavations on Structure B1 at the Site of Blackman Eddy: Results of Excavations in Operations 15n, 18a, and 19a. In *The Belize Valley Archaeological Project: Results of the 1998 Field Season,* ed. J. F. Garber and M. K. Brown, pp. 68–91. Report on file, Department of Archaeology, Belmopan, Belize.
Hartman, Christopher J., and Jonathan Pagliaro
   2000   The 1999 Excavations in Operations 19a, 19b, and 19c at the Site of Blackman Eddy, Belize. In *The Belize Valley Archaeological Project: Results of the 1999 Field Season,* ed. J. F. Garber and M. K. Brown, pp. 26–46. Report on file, Department of Archaeology, Belmopan, Belize.
Hassig, Ross
   1988   *Aztec Warfare: Imperial Expansion and Political Control.* University of Oklahoma Press, Norman.
   1992a *War and Society in Ancient Mesoamerica.* University of California Press, Berkeley.
   1992b Aztec and Spanish Conquest in Mesoamerica. In *War in the Tribal Zone: Expanding States and Indigenous Warfare,* ed. R. B. Ferguson and N. L. Whitehead, pp. 83–102. School of American Research Press, Santa Fe, N.M.
Haury, Emil W.
   1958   Evidence at Point of Pines for a Prehistoric Migration from Northern Arizona. In *Migrations in New World Culture History,* ed. R. H. Thompson, pp. 1–8. University of Arizona Bulletin 29, University of Arizona Press, Tucson.
Haviland, William A.
   1994   Star Wars at Tikal or Did Caracol Do What the Glyphs Say They Did? In *Anthropology,* ed. W. A. Haviland, pp. 266–70. Holt, Reinhart, and Winston, New York.
Haviland, W. A., M. J. Becker, A. Chowning, K. A. Dixon, and K. Heider
   1985   *Excavations in Small Residential Groups of Tikal: Groups 4F-1 and 4F-2.* Tikal Report, No. 19, University Museum Monograph 58, University of Pennsylvania, Philadelphia.
Hay, C. L., R. L. Linton, S. K. Lothrop, H. L. Shapiro, and G. C. Valliant
   1940   *The Maya and Their Neighbors: Essays on Middle American Anthropology and Archaeology.* D. Appleton-Century, New York.
Hayden, Brian D.
   1979   Material Culture in the Maya Highlands: A Preliminary Study. In *Settlement Pattern Excavations at Kaminaljuyu, Guatemala,* ed. J. W. Michels, pp. 183–222. Monograph Series on Kaminaljuyu, Pennsylvania State University Press, State College.

Hayden, Brian D., and Aubrey Cannon
  1983   Where the Garbage Goes: Refuse Disposal in the Maya Highlands. *Journal of Anthropological Archaeology* 2:117–63.
Headrick, Annabeth
  1996   *The Teotihuacan Trinity: unMASKing the Political Structure.* Ph.D. dissertation, Department of Art History, University of Texas, Austin. University Microfilms, Ann Arbor, Mich.
  1999   The Street of the Dead . . . It Really Was: Mortuary Bundles at Teotihuacan. *Ancient Mesoamerica* 10:1–17.
Healan, Dan M., Robert H. Cobean, and Richard A. Diehl
  1989   Synthesis and Conclusions. In *Tula of the Toltecs: Excavations and Survey,* ed. D. M. Healan, pp. 239–51. University of Iowa Press, Iowa City.
Heizer, Robert F.
  1942   Ancient Grooved Clubs and Modern Rabbit-Sticks. *American Antiquity* 8:41–56.
  1960   Agriculture and the Theocratic State in Lowland Southeastern Mexico. *American Antiquity* 26:215–22.
Hicks, Frederic
  1979   "Flowery War" in Aztec History. *American Ethnologist* 6:87–92.
Hirth, Kenneth G.
  1978   Teotihuacan Regional Population Administration in Eastern Morelos. *World Archaeology* 9:320–33.
  1980   *Eastern Morelos and Teotihuacan: A Settlement Survey.* Vanderbilt University Publications in Anthropology, No. 25, Nashville.
  1989   Militarism and Social Organization at Xochicalco, Morelos. In *Mesoamerica after the Decline of Teotihuacan,* A.D. 700–900, ed. R. A. Diehl and J. C. Berlo, pp. 69–81. Dumbarton Oaks Research Library and Collection, Washington, D.C.
  1995   Urbanism, Militarism, and Architectural Design: An Analysis of Epiclassic Sociopolitical Structure at Xochicalco. *Ancient Mesoamerica* 6:237–50.
Hirth, Kenneth G., and Jorge Angulo V.
  1981   Early State Expansion in Central Mexico: Teotihuacan in Morelos. *Journal of Field Archaeology* 8:135–50.
Historia Tolteca-Chichimeca
  1976   *Historia Tolteca-Chichimeca.* Ed. and Trans. P. Kirchhoff, L. Odena G., and L. Reyes G. Instituto Nacional de Antropología e Historia, México, D.F.
Hodder, Ian
  1991   Interpretive Archaeology and Its Role. *American Antiquity* 56:7–18.
Hodell, David A., Jason H. Curtis, and Mark Brenner
  1995   Possible Role of Climate in the Collapse of Classic Maya Civilization. *Nature* 375:391–94.

Holley, George R.
  1983   *Ceramic Change at Piedras Negras, Guatemala.* Unpublished Ph.D. dissertation, Southern Illinois University, Carbondale.
Hohmann, Bobbi
  2002   *Preclassic Maya Shell Ornament Production in the Belize Valley, Belize.* Unpublished Ph.D. dissertation, University of New Mexico, Albuquerque.
Houk, Brett A.
  1996   *The Archaeology of Site Planning: An Example from the Maya Site of Dos Hombres, Belize.* Unpublished Ph.D. dissertation, Department of Anthropology, University of Texas, Austin.
Houston, Steven D.
  1991   Appendix: Caracol Altar 21. In *Sixth Palenque Round Table, 1986,* ed. M. Greene Robertson and V. M. Fields, pp. 38–41. University of Oklahoma Press, Norman.
  1992   A Name Glyph for Classic Maya Dwarfs. In *The Maya Vase Book, Vol. 3,* ed. J. Kerr, pp. 526–31. Kerr and Associates, New York.
  1993   *Hieroglyphs and History at Dos Pilas: Dynastic Politics of the Classic Maya.* University of Texas Press, Austin.
Houston, S. D., H. Escobedo, Mark Child, C. Golden, R. Muñoz, and M. Urquizú
  1998   Monumental Architecture at Piedras Negras, Guatemala: Time, History, and Meaning. *Mayab* 11:40–56.
Houston, Stephen D., and Peter Mathews
  1985   *The Dynastic Sequence of Dos Pilas, Guatemala.* Monograph 1, Pre-Columbian Art Research Institute, San Francisco.
Houston, Stephen D., and David Stuart
  1989   *The Way Glyph: Evidence for "Co-Essences" among the Classic Maya.* Research Reports on Ancient Maya Writing 30, Center for Maya Research, Washington, D.C.
  1996   Of Gods, Glyphs, and Kings: Divinity and Rulership among the Classic Maya. *Antiquity* 70:289–312.
  1998   The Ancient Maya Self: Personhood and Portraiture in the Classic Period. *RES* 33:72–101.
  2000   Into the Minds of Ancients: Advances in Maya Glyph Studies. *Journal of World Prehistory* 14:121–201.
  2001   Peopling the Classic Maya Court. In *Royal Courts of the Ancient Maya: Volume 1,* ed. T. Inomata and S. D. Houston, pp. 54–83. Westview Press, Boulder, Colo.
Howard, Julie, and Joel C. Janetski
  1992   Human Scalps from Eastern Utah. *Utah Archaeology* 5:125–32.
Huckell, Bruce B.
  1995   *Of Marshes and Maize: Preceramic Agricultural Settlements in the Cienega Valley, Southeastern Arizona.* Anthropology Papers of the University of Arizona, No. 59, University of Arizona Press, Tucson.

Hurst, Winston B., and Christy G. Turner II
  1993   Rediscovering the "Great Discovery": Wetherill's First Cave 7 and Its
          Record of Basketmaker Violence. In *Anasazi Basketmaker: Papers from
          the 1990 Wetherill-Grand Gulch Symposium*, ed. V. M. Atkins, pp. 143–
          91. Bureau of Land Management, Cultural Resource Series No. 24,
          Salt Lake City.
Hutson, Scott R., and Travis W. Stanton
  2001   *Espacios Domesticos y la Vida Cotidiana del Sitio Arqueológico de Chun-
          chucmil, Yucatán.* Paper presented at the Congreso Internacional de
          Cultura Maya, Mérida.
Hyslop, John
  1976   The Frontier between Michoacan and the Culhua Mexica. In *The
          Aztec-Tarascan Frontier: The Acambaro Focus*, ed. S. Gorenstein, pp.
          1–35. Department of Anthropology/Sociology, Rensselaer Polytech-
          nic Institute, Troy, N.Y.
Inomata, Takeshi
  1997   The Last Days of a Fortified Classic Maya Center: Archaeological
          Investigations at Aguateca, Guatemala. *Ancient Mesoamerica*
          8:337–51.
  2001   King's People: Classic Maya Courtiers in a Comparative Perspective.
          In *Royal Courts of the Ancient Maya: Volume I*, ed. T. Inomata and S.
          D. Houston, pp. 27–53. Westview Press, Boulder, Colo.
Isaac, Barry L.
  1983a   The Aztec "Flowery War": A Geopolitical Explanation. *Journal of
          Anthropological Research* 39:415–23.
  1983b   Aztec Warfare: Goals and Battlefield Comportment. *Ethnology*
          22:121–31.
Ixtlilxochitl, Fernando de Alva
  1975–1977   *Obras Históricas.* Ed. and intro. E. O'Gorman. Instituto de
          Investigaciones Históricas, Universidad Nacional Autonoma de Méx-
          ico, D.F.
Jacobs, David
  1998   *Iconography of Warfare?* Paper presented at the 63rd annual meeting
          of the Society for American Archaeology.
Jaeger, Susan L.
  1987   Appendix 3: The Conchita Causeway and Associated Settlement. In
          Investigations at the Classic Maya City of Caracol, Belize: 1985–1987, ed.
          A. F. Chase and D. Z. Chase, pp. 101–5. Monograph 3, Pre-Colum-
          bian Art Research Institute, San Francisco.
  1991   *Settlement Pattern Research at Caracol, Belize: The Social Organization of
          a Classic Period Maya Site.* Unpublished Ph.D. dissertation, Southern
          Methodist University, Dallas.
  1994   The Conchita Causeway Settlement Subprogram. In *Studies in the
          Archaeology of Caracol, Belize*, ed. D. Z. Chase and A. F. Chase, pp.

47–63. Monograph 7, Pre-Columbian Art Research Institute, San Francisco.

Jiménez M., Wigberto
1966 Mesoamerica Before the Toltecs. In *Ancient Oaxaca*, ed. J. Paddock, pp. 3–82. Stanford University Press, Stanford, Calif.

Johnson, James T.
1997 *The Holy War Idea in Western and Islamic Traditions*. Pennsylvania State University Press, University Park.

Johnstone, David
1994 Residential Excavations. In *The Selz Foundation Yaxuna Project: Final Report of the 1993 Field Season*, ed. T. Ardren, S. Bennett, D. A. Freidel, D. Johnstone, and C. K. Suhler, pp. 83–88. Manuscript on file, Department of Anthropology, Southern Methodist University Press, Dallas.
2001 *The Ceramics of Yaxuna, Yucatan*. Unpublished Ph.D. dissertation, Southern Methodist University, Dallas.

Jones, Christopher
1991 Cycles of Growth at Tikal. In *Classic Maya Political History*, ed. T. P. Culbert, pp. 102–27. Cambridge University Press, Cambridge, U.K.

Jones, Christopher, and Linton Satterthwaite
1982 *The Monuments and Inscriptions of Tikal: The Carved Monuments*. Tikal Report, No. 33, Pt. A, The University Museum, University of Pennsylvania, Philadelphia.

Joyce, Arthur A.
1991a *Formative Period Occupation in the Lower Río Verde Valley, Oaxaca, Mexico: Interregional Interaction and Social Change*. Ph.D. dissertation, Department of Anthropology, Rutgers University, New Brunswick, N.J. University Microfilms, Ann Arbor, Mich.
1991b Formative Period Social Change in the Lower Rio Verde Valley, Oaxaca, Mexico. *Latin American Antiquity* 2:126–50.
1993a Interregional Interaction and Social Development on the Oaxaca Coast. *Ancient Mesoamerica* 4:67–84.
1993b *The Interregional Impact of State Formation in Oaxaca*. Report submitted on research activities performed as a 1992–1993 Kalbfleisch fellow. American Museum of Natural History, New York.
1994a Monte Albán en el Contexto Pan-Regional. In *Monte Albán: Estudios Recientes*, ed. M. Winter, pp. 63–76. Contribución No. 2 del Proyecto Especial Monte Albán 1992–1994, Oaxaca, México.
1994b Late Formative Community Organization and Social Complexity on the Oaxaca Coast. *Journal of Field Archaeology* 21:147–68.
2000 The Founding of Monte Alban: Sacred Propositions and Social Practices. In *Agency in Archaeology*, ed. M.-A. Dobres and J. E. Robb, pp. 71–91. Routledge Press, London.

Joyce, Arthur A. (ed.)
1999 *El Proyecto Patrones de Asentamiento del Río Verde*. Report submitted

to the Consejo de Arqueología, Instituto Nacional de Antropología e Historia, México.

Joyce, A. A., J. M. Elam, M. D. Glascock, H. Neff, and M. Winter
1995   Exchange Implications of Obsidian Source Analysis from the Lower Rio Verde Valley, Oaxaca, Mexico. *Latin American Antiquity* 6:3–15.

Joyce, Arthur A., and Marcus Winter
1989   Investigaciones Arqueológicas en la Cuenca del Río Verde Inferior, 1988. *Notas Mesoamericanas* 11:249–62.
1996   Ideology, Power, and Urban Society in Pre-Hispanic Oaxaca. *Current Anthropology* 37:33–47.

Joyce, A. A., M. Winter, and R. G. Mueller
1998   *Arqueología de la Costa de Oaxaca: Asentamientos del Periodo Formativo en el Valle del Río Verde Inferior.* Estudios de Antropología e Historia No. 40, Centro INAH Oaxaca, México.

Joyce, A. A., R. N. Zeitlin, J. F. Zeitlin, and J. Urcid
2000   On Oaxaca Coast Archaeology: Setting the Record Straight. *Current Anthropology* 41(4):623–25.

Kappelman, Julia
1997   *Of Macaws and Men: Late Preclassic Cosmology and Political Ideology in Izapan-Style Monuments.* Unpublished Ph.D. dissertation, University of Texas, Austin.

Kappelman, Julia, and F. Kent Reilly III
1999   Paths to Heaven, Ropes to Earth: Birds, Jaguars, and Cosmic Cords in Formative Period Mesoamerica. *Ancient America* 3:33–52.

Kartunnen, Frances
1994   *Between Worlds: Interpreters, Guides, and Survivors.* Rutgers University Press, New Brunswick, N.J.

Keeley, Lawrence H.
1988   Hunter-Gatherer Economic Complexity and Population Pressure: A Cross-Cultural Analysis. *Journal of Anthropological Archaeology* 7:373–411.
1996   *War before Civilization.* Oxford University Press, Oxford, U.K.

Kepecs, Susan
1998   Diachronic Ceramic Evidence and Its Social Implications in the Chikinchel Region, Northeastern Yucatan, Mexico. *Ancient Mesoamerica* 9:121–35.

Kerr, Justin
1989   *The Maya Vase Book, Volume l.* Kerr and Associates, New York.

Kidder, Alfred V., Jesse D. Jennings, and Edwin M. Shook
1946   *Excavations at Kaminaljuyu, Guatemala.* Carnegie Institution of Washington, Publication 561, Washington, D.C.

Klein, Cecilia
1988   Rethinking Cihuacoatl: Aztec Political Imagery of the Conquered Woman. In *Smoke and Mist: Mesoamerican Studies in Memory of Thelma*

D. *Sullivan,* ed. J. K. Josserand and K. Dakin, pp. 237–77. BAR International Series, Oxford, U.K.

1991 Snares and Entrails: Mesoamerican Symbols of Sin and Punishment. *RES* 19/20:81–104.

Knight, Vernon J., Jr.
1986 The Institutional Organization of Mississippian Religion. *American Antiquity* 51:675–86.

Kubler, George
1985 The Iconography of the Art of Teotihuacan. In *Studies in Ancient American and European Art: The Collected Essays of George Kubler,* ed. T. F. Reese, pp. 263–74. Yale University Press, New Haven, Conn.

Kurjack, Edward B., and E. Wyllys Andrews V
1976 Early Boundary Maintenance in Northwest Yucatan, Mexico. *American Antiquity* 41:318–25.

Lamb, Hubert H.
1995 *Climate, History and the Modern World.* Routledge, London.

Langley, James C.
1986 *Symbolic Notation of Teotihuacan: Elements of Writing in a Mesoamerican Culture of the Classic Period.* BAR International Series 313, Oxford, U.K.

Laporte, Juan Pedro
1994 *Ixtonton, Dolores, Peten: Entidad Politica del Noroeste de las Montanas Mayas.* Atlas Arqueologico de Guatemala No. 2, Instituto de Antropologia e Historia, Guatemala.

Laporte, Juan Pedro, and Vilma Fialko C.
1990 New Perspectives on Old Problems: Dynastic References for the Early Classic at Tikal. In *Vision and Revision in Maya Studies,* ed. F. S. Clancy and P. D. Harrison, pp. 33–66. University of New Mexico Press, Albuquerque.
1995 Un Reencuentro con Mundo Perdido, Tikal, Guatemala. *Ancient Mesoamerica* 6:41–94.

Laporte, J. P., B. Hermes, L. de Zea, and M. J. Iglesias
1992 Nuevos Entierros y Escondites de Tikal, Subfases Manik 3a y 3b. *Cerámica de Cultura Maya* 16:30–67.

Laporte, Juan Pedro, Rolando Torres, and Bernard Hermes
1989 Ixtonton: Evolucion de un Asentamiento en el alto Mopan, Peten, Guatemala. *Mayab* 5:19–29.

Las Casas, Bartolomé de
1992 *A Short Account of the Destruction of the Indies.* Ed. and trans. Nigel Griffin. Penguin Classics, London.

Laughlin, Robert M. (comp. and trans.)
1988 *Mayan Tales from Zinacantan: Dreams and Stories from the People of the Bat.* Smithsonian Institution Press, Washington, D.C.

LeBlanc, Steven A.
  1983   *The Mimbres People: Ancient Painters of the American Southwest.*
         Thames and Hudson, London.
  1997   Modeling Warfare in Southwestern Prehistory. *North American
         Archaeologist* 18:235–76.
  1998   Settlement Consequences of Warfare during the Late Pueblo III and
         Pueblo IV Period. In *Migration and Reorganization: The Pueblo IV
         Period in the American Southwest,* ed. K. A. Spielmann, pp. 115–35.
         Arizona State University Anthropology Papers, No. 51, Tempe.
  1999   *Prehistoric Warfare in the American Southwest.* University of Utah
         Press, Salt Lake City.
  2000   The Impact of Warfare on Southwestern Regional Systems after AD
         1250. In *The Archaeology of Regional Interaction in the American South-
         west,* ed. M. Hegmon, pp. 41–70. University of Colorado Press,
         Boulder.
Lekson, Stephen H.
  1992   *Scale and Process in the Southwest.* Paper presented at the Third South-
         western Symposium.
  1993   Chaco, Hohokam and Mimbres: The Southwest in the 11th and 12th
         Centuries. *Expedition* 35:44–52.
León-Portilla, Miguel (ed.)
  1992   *The Broken Spears: The Aztec Account of the Conquest of Mexico.* Beacon
         Press, Boston.
Leone, Mark P., Parker B. Potter Jr., and Paul A. Shackel
  1987   Toward a Critical Archaeology. *Current Anthropology* 28:283–302.
Levine, Marc N.
  2002   *Ceramic Change and Continuity in the Lower Río Verde Region of Oaxaca,
         Mexico: The Late Formative to Early Terminal Formative Transition.*
         Unpublished M.A. thesis, University of Colorado at Boulder,
         Boulder.
LeVine, Robert A., and Donald T. Campbell
  1972   *Ethnocentrism: Theories of Conflict, Ethnic Attitudes, and Group Behav-
         ior.* John Wiley & Sons, New York.
Lienzo de Tlaxcala
  1979   *El Lienzo de Tlaxcala.* Commentary by A. Chavero [1892]. Editorial
         Cosmos, D.F., Mexico.
Linares, O., P. D. Sheets, and J. Rosenthal
  1975   Prehistoric Agriculture in Tropical Highlands. *Science* 187:137–45.
Lind, M.
  1987   *The Sociocultural Dimensions of Mixtec Ceramics.* Vanderbilt University
         Publications in Anthropology No. 36, Nashville.
Lindsay, Alexander, Jr.
  1987   Anasazi Population Movements to Southeastern Arizona. *American
         Archaeology* 6:190–98.

Linné, S.
  1934   *Archaeological Researches at Teotihuacan, Mexico.* Ethnographic Museum of Sweden, New Series, Publication 1, Stockholm.
  1942   *Mexican Highland Cultures: Archaeological Researches at Teotihuacan, Calpulalpan and Chalchicomula in 1934/35.* Ethnographic Museum of Sweden, New Series, Publication 7, Stockholm.
Litvak King, Jaime
  1971   Investigaciones en la Valle de Xochicalco, 1569–1970. *Anales de Antropologia* 7:102–24.
Long, J. R., and D. L. Brockington
  1974   Stone Tools. In *The Oaxaca Coast Project Reports: Part 1,* ed. D. L. Brockington, M. Jorrín, and J. R. Long, pp. 83–97. Vanderbilt University Publications in Anthropology No. 8, Nashville.
López Alonso, Sergio, Zaid Lagunas R., and Carlos Serrano
  1976   *Enterramientos Humanos de la Zona Arqueológica de Cholula, Puebla.* Colección Científica 44, Departmento de Antropología Física, SEP-INAH, Mexico, D.F.
López de Gómara, Francisco
  1964   *Cortéz: The Life of the Conqueror by His Secretary.* Trans. and ed. L. B. Simpson. University of California Press, Berkeley.
López de Molina, Diana
  1981   Un Informe Preliminár sobre la Cronología de Cacaxtla. In *Interacción Cultural en México Central,* ed. E. C. Rattray, J. Litvak King, and C. Diaz O., pp. 169–73. Universidad Nacional Autonoma de México, D.F.
López de Molina, Diana, and Daniel Molina F.
  1986   Arqueología. In *Cacaxtla: El Lugar Donde Muere la Lluvia en la Tierra,* ed. S. Lombardo de Ruiz, D. López de Molina, and D. Molina F., pp. 11–208. Instituto Nacional de Antropología e Historia, Gobierno del Estado de Tlaxcala, México.
López Luján, Leonardo
  1998   Recreating the Cosmos: Seventeen Aztec Dedication Caches. In *The Sowing and the Dawning: Termination, Dedication, and Transformation in the Archaeological and Ethnographic Record of Mesoamerica,* ed. S. B. Mock, pp. 177–87. University of New Mexico Press, Albuquerque.
Lopez V., Sandra L.
  1989   *Análisis y Clasificación de la Cerámica de un Sitio Maya del Clásico: Yaxchilán, México.* BAR International Series 535, Oxford, U.K.
Lounsbury, Floyd G.
  1982   Astronomical Knowledge and Its Uses at Bonampak, Mexico. In *Archaeoastronomy in the New World,* ed. A. F. Aveni, pp. 143–68. Cambridge University Press, Cambridge, U.K.
Lowe, Gareth W.
  1977   The Mixe-Zoque as Competing Neighbors of the Early Lowland

Maya. In *The Origins of Maya Civilization*, ed. R. E. W. Adams, pp. 197–248. University of New Mexico Press, Albuquerque.

Mabry, Jonathan B.
1997   *Archaeological Investigations of Early Village Sites in the Middle Santa Cruz Valley: Descriptions of the Santa Cruz Bend, Square Hearth, Stone Pipe, and Canal Sites.* Anthropological Papers No. 18, Center for Desert Archaeology, Tucson, Ariz.

MacKie, Euan W.
1985   *Excavations at Xunantunich and Pomona, Belize, in 1959–60.* BAR International Series 251, Oxford, U.K.

Manzanilla, Linda
1993   *Anatomía de un Conjunto Residencial Teotihuacano en Oztoyahualco.* UNAM y INAH, México.

Manzanilla, Linda, and Emilie Carreón
1989   Un Incensario Teotihuacano en Contexto Doméstico: Restauración e Interpretación. *Antropológicas* 4:5–18.

Marcus, Joyce
1974   The Iconography of Power among the Classic Maya. *World Archaeology* 6:83–94.
1976   The Iconography of Militarism at Monte Alban and Neighboring Sites in the Valley of Oaxaca. In *Origins of Religious Art and Iconography in Preclassic Mesoamerica*, ed. H. B. Nicholson, pp. 123–39. UCLA Latin American Center Publications, Los Angeles.
1983   The Conquest Slabs of Building J, Monte Albán. In *The Cloud People: Divergent Evolution of the Zapotec and Mixtec Civilizations*, ed. K. V. Flannery and J. Marcus, pp. 106–8. Academic Press, New York.
1992a *Ancient Mesoamerican Writing Systems: Propaganda, Myth, and History in Four Ancient Civilizations.* Princeton University Press, Princeton, N.J.
1992b Political Fluctuations in Mesoamerica. *National Geographic Research & Exploration* 8:392–411.
1999   Men's and Women's Ritual in Formative Mesoamerica. In *Social Patterns in Pre-Classic Mesoamerica*, ed. D. C. Grove and R. A. Joyce, pp. 67–96. Dumbarton Oaks Research Library and Collection, Washington, D.C.

Marcus, Joyce, and Kent V. Flannery
1996   *Zapotec Civilization: How Urban Society Evolved in Mexico's Oaxaca Valley.* Thames and Hudson, London.

Markman, C. W.
1981   *Prehispanic Settlement Dynamics in Central Oaxaca, Mexico: A View from the Miahuatlán Valley.* Vanderbilt University Publications in Anthropology No. 26. Nashville.

Marquina, Ignacio
1970   Pirámide de Cholula. In *Proyecto Cholula*, ed. I. Marquina, pp. 31–46.

Serie Investigaciones 19, Instituto Nacional de Antropología e Historia, D.F.

Martin, Debra L.
1997   Violence against Women in the La Plata River Valley (A.D. 1000–1300). In *Troubled Times: Violence and Warfare in the Past*, ed. D. L. Martin and D. W. Frayer, pp, 45–75. Gordon and Breach Publishers, Amsterdam.

Martin, Richard C.
1991   The Religious Foundations of War, Peace, and Statecraft in Islam. In *Just War and Jihad: Historical and Theoretical Perspectives on War and Peace in Western and Islamic Traditions*, ed. J. Kelsay and J. T. Johnson, pp. 91–117. Greenwood Press, Westport, Conn.

Martin, Simon, and Nikolai Grube
1995   Maya Superstates: How a Few Powerful Kingdoms Vied for Control of the Maya Lowlands during the Classic Period (A.D.). *Archaeology* 48:41–47.

2000   *Chronicle of the Maya Kings and Queens: Deciphering the Dynasties of the Ancient Maya.* Thames and Hudson, New York.

Massey, Virginia
1989   *The Human Skeletal Remains from a Terminal Classic Skull Pit at Colha, Belize.* Papers of the Colha Project 3. Texas Archaeological Research Laboratory at the University of Texas, Austin, and Texas A&M University.

1994   Osteological Analysis of the Skull Pit Children. In *Continuing Archaeology at Colha, Belize*, ed. T. R. Hester, H. J. Shafer, and J. D. Eaton, pp. 209–20. Studies in Archaeology, 16, Texas Archaeological Research Laboratory, University of Texas, Austin.

Matheny, Ray T.
1970   *The Ceramics of Aguacatal, Campeche, Mexico.* Papers of the New World Archaeological Foundation No. 27, Brigham Young University, Provo, Utah.

Mathews, Peter
1985   Maya Early Classic Monuments and Inscriptions. In *A Consideration of the Early Classic Period in the Maya Lowlands*, ed. G. W. Willey and P. Mathews, pp. 5–54. Institute for Mesoamerican Studies, State University of New York at Albany, Publication 10, Albany.

1988   *The Sculpture of Yaxchilán.* Unpublished Ph.D. dissertation, Yale University, New Haven, Conn.

2000   Guerra en los Tierras Bajas Occidentales Mayas. In *Guerra Entre los Antiguos Maya*, ed. S. Trejo, pp. 125–55. Primera Mesa Redonda de Palenque, INAH, Mexico.

Mathews, Peter, and Linda Schele
1974   Lords of Palenque: The Glyphic Evidence. In *Primera Mesa Redonda de Palenque, Part I*, ed. M. Greene Robertson, pp. 63–75. The Robert Louis Stevenson School, Pebble Beach, Calif.

Matson, R. G.
  1991   *The Origins of Southwestern Agriculture.* University of Arizona Press, Tucson.

Matthews, Paul
  1994   *Ch'akah U Tz'ibal: The Axing of History at Seibal.* Texas Notes on Precolumbian Art, Writing, and Culture, No. 65, Center for the History and Art of Ancient American Culture, University of Texas, Austin.

Maudslay, Alfred P., and A. C. Maudslay
  1899   *A Glimpse at Guatemala, and Some Notes on the Ancient Monuments of Central America.* N.p., London.

Mayhall, Marguerite
  1991   *The Butterfly Complex at Teotihuacan: Blood, War, and Transformation.* Art History Seminar Paper (manuscript in possession of author).

McAnany, Patricia A.
  1992   A Theoretical Perspective on the Elites and the Economic Transformation of Classic Period Maya Households. In *Understanding Economic Process,* ed. S. Ortiz and S. Lees, pp. 85–103. Monographs in Economic Anthropology, No. 10, University Press of America, Lanham, Md.
  1998   Ancestors and the Classic Maya Built Environment. In *Function and Meaning in Classic Maya Architecture,* ed. S. D. Houston, pp. 271–98. Dumbarton Oaks Research Library and Collection, Washington, D.C.

McCafferty, Geoffrey G.
  1992   *The Material Culture of Postclassic Cholula, Mexico: Contextual Analysis of the UA-1 Domestic Compounds.* Unpublished Ph.D. dissertation, Department of Anthropology, State University of New York at Binghamton, Binghamton.
  1994   The Mixteca-Puebla Stylistic Tradition at Early Postclassic Cholula. In *Mixteca-Puebla: Discoveries and Research in Mesoamerican Art and Archaeology,* ed. H. B. Nicholson and E. Quiñones Keber, pp. 53–78. Labyrinthos Press, Culver City, Calif.
  1996a The Ceramics and Chronology of Cholula, Mexico. *Ancient Mesoamerica* 7:299–323.
  1996b Reinterpreting the Great Pyramid of Cholula, Mexico. *Ancient Mesoamerica* 7:1–17.
  1997   Giants, Tyrants, and Toltecs: Ethnic Change in Classic/Postclassic Cholula. In *Liminal States: Central Mesoamerica during the Classic/Postclassic Transition,* comp. R. Koontz and G. McCafferty. Workbook for a special session of the University of Texas Maya Meetings, Austin.
  1998   *Nuevas (y Viejas) Ideas Sobre el Epiclásico en Cholula.* Paper presented at the Congress of the Sociedad Mexicana de Antropología, San Luis Potosi.
  2000a The Cholula Massacre: Factional Histories and Archaeology of the

Spanish Conquest. In *The Entangled Past: Integrating History and Archaeology*, ed. M. Boyd, J. C. Erwin, and M. Hendrickson, pp. 347–59. Proceedings of the 30th Annual Chacmool Conference, University of Calgary, Calgary.

2000b Tollan Cholollan and the Legacy of Legitimacy during the Classic-Postclassic Transition. In *Mesoamerica's Classic Heritage: From Teotihuacan to the Aztecs*, ed. D. Carrasco, L. Jones, and S. Sessions, pp. 341–67. University of Colorado Press, Boulder.

2001 Mountain of Heaven, Mountain of Earth: The Great Pyramid of Cholula as Sacred Landscape. In *Landscape and Power in Ancient Mesoamerica*, ed. R. Koontz, K. Reese-Taylor, and A. Headrick, pp. 279–316. Westview Press, Boulder, Colo.

McCafferty, Geoffrey G., and Sergio Suárez C.

1995 *The Classic/Postclassic Transition at Cholula: Recent Investigations at the Great Pyramid.* Paper presented at the annual meeting of the Society for American Archaeology, Minneapolis.

McCafferty, Sharisse D., and Geoffrey G. McCafferty

1994 The Conquered Women of Cacaxtla: Gender Identity or Gender Ideology? *Ancient Mesoamerica* 5:159–72.

2003 Weaving Space: Textile Imagery and Landscape in the Mixtec Codices. *2001: An Odyssey of Space*, ed. E. Robertson, D. Fernandez, and M. Zender. Proceedings of the 35th Annual Chacmool Conference, University of Calgary, Calgary.

McIntosh, Susan K. (ed.)

1999 *Beyond Chiefdoms: Pathways to Complexity in Africa.* Cambridge University Press, Cambridge, U.K.

McKee, Brian R.

1989 Excavations at Structure Complex 2. In *1989 Archaeological Investigations at the Ceren Site, El Salvador: A Preliminary Report*, ed. P. D. Sheets and B. R. McKee, pp. 41–57. Report on file, Department of Anthropology, University of Colorado, Boulder.

1993 Archaeological Investigations at Operation 2. In *Preliminary Report of the Ceren Research Project, 1993 Season*, ed. P. D. Sheets and S. E. Simmons, pp. 125–37. Report on file, Department of Anthropology, University of Colorado, Boulder.

McVicker, Donald

1985 The "Mayanized" Mexicans. *American Antiquity* 50:82–101.

Means, Philip A.

1940 The Philosophic Interrelationship between Middle American and Andean Religions. In *The Maya and Their Neighbors: Essays on Middle American Anthropology and Archaeology*, ed. C. L. Hay, R. L. Linton, S. K. Lothrop, H. L. Shapiro, and G. C. Valliant, pp. 430–40. D. Appleton-Century, New York.

Messinger Cypress, Sandra
1991   *La Malinche in Mexican Literature: From History to Myth.* University of
        Texas Press, Austin.
Miller, Arthur G.
1973   *The Mural Painting of Teotihuacan.* Dumbarton Oaks Research Library
        and Collection, Washington, D.C.
Miller, Mary E.
1986   *The Murals of Bonampak.* Princeton University Press, Princeton, N.J.
1993   On the Eve of Collapse: Maya Art of the Eighth Century. In *Lowland
        Maya Civilization in the Eighth Century* A.D., ed. J. A. Sabloff and J. S.
        Henderson, pp. 355–413. Dumbarton Oaks Research Library and
        Collection, Washington, D.C.
1998   A Design for Meaning in Maya Architecture. In *Function and Mean-
        ing in Classic Maya Architecture,* ed. S. D. Houston, pp. 187–222.
        Dumbarton Oaks Research Library and Collection, Washington,
        D.C.
2001   Life at Court: The View from Bonampak. In *Royal Courts of the
        Ancient Maya: Volume 2,* ed. T. Inomata and S. D. Houston, pp. 201–
        22. Westview Press, Boulder, Colo.
Miller, Virginia E.
1985   The Dwarf Motif in Classic Maya Art. In *Fourth Palenque Round Table,*
        ed. E. P. Benson, pp. 141–53. Pre-Columbian Art Research Institute,
        San Francisco.
Millon, Clara
1973   Painting, Writing, and Polity at Teotihuacan, Mexico. *American
        Antiquity* 38:294–314.
1988   A Reexamination of the Teotihuacan Tassel Headdress Insignia. In
        Feathered Serpents and Flowering Tress, ed. K. Berrin, pp. 114–34. Fine
        Arts Museums of San Francisco, San Francisco.
Millon, René
1981   Teotihuacan: City, State, and Civilization. In *Supplement to the Hand-
        book of Middle American Indians,* ed. V. R. Bricker and J. A. Sabloff, pp.
        189–243. University of Texas Press, Austin.
1988   The Last Years of Teotihuacan Dominance. In *The Collapse of Ancient
        States and Civilizations,* ed. N. Yoffee and G. L. Cowgill, pp. 102–64.
        University of Arizona Press, Tucson.
Mills, Barbara J.
1995   *Reconsidering Migration, Integration, and Aggregation in the Silver Creek
        Area of East-Central Arizona.* Paper presented at the fall meeting of
        the Arizona Archaeological Council.
Minc, Leah D., Mary G. Hodge, and M. James Blackman
1994   Stylistic and Spatial Variability in Early Aztec Ceramics: Insights
        into Pre-Imperial Exchange Systems. In *Economies and Polities in the
        Aztec Realm,* ed. M. G. Hodge and M. E. Smith, pp. 133–73. Studies

on Culture and Society, Volume 6, Institute for Mesoamerican Studies, State University of New York at Albany, Albany.

Mock, Shirley B.

1994a Destruction and Denouement during the Late-Terminal Classic: The Colha Skull Pit. In *Continuing Archaeology at Colha, Belize, Studies in Archaeology 16*, ed. T. R. Hester, H. J. Shafer, and J. D. Eaton, pp. 221–31. Texas Archaeological Research Laboratory, University of Texas, Austin.

1994b *The Northern River Lagoon Site (NRL): Late to Terminal Classic Maya Settlement, Saltmaking, and Survival on the Northern Belize Coast.* Unpublished Ph.D. dissertation, University of Texas, Austin.

1997 Monkey Business at Northern River Lagoon: A Coastal-Inland Interaction Sphere in Northern Belize. *Ancient Mesoamerica* 8:165–83.

1998a Prelude. In *The Sowing and the Dawning: Termination, Dedication, and Transformation in the Archaeological and Ethnographic Record of Mesoamerica*, ed. S. B. Mock, pp. 3–18. University of New Mexico Press, Albuquerque.

1998b The Defaced and the Forgotten: Decapitation and Flaying/Mutilation as a Termination Event at Colha, Belize. In *The Sowing and the Dawning: Termination, Dedication, and Transformation in the Archaeological and Ethnographic Record of Mesoamerica*, ed. S. B. Mock, pp. 113–23. University of New Mexico Press, Albuquerque.

1999 *The Terminal Classic-Postclassic Ceramics from Coastal Lagoons in Northern Belize.* Paper presented at the 64th annual meeting of the Society for American Archaeology.

Monagan, John

1998 Dedication: Ritual or Production? In *The Sowing and the Dawning: Termination, Dedication, and Transformation in the Archaeological and Ethnographic Record of Mesoamerica*, ed. S. B. Mock, pp. 47–52. University of New Mexico Press, Albuquerque.

Monjarás-Ruiz, Jesús

1976 Panorama General de la Guerra Entre los Aztecas. *Estudios de Cultura Nahuatl* 12:241–64.

Monks, Sarah, and Richard Osgood

2000 Introduction. In *Bronze Age Warfare*, ed. R. Osgood, S. Monks, and J. Toms, pp. 1–8. Sutton Publishing, Gloucestershire, U.K.

Morley, Sylvanus G.

1946 *The Ancient Maya.* Stanford University Press, Stanford, Calif.

Muñoz Camargo, Diego

1966 *Historia de Tlaxcala.* Ed. A. Chavero. Tipográfica de Secretaría de Fomento, México.

Nagao, Debra

1989 Public Proclamation in the Art of Cacaxtla and Xochicalco. In *Mesoamerica after the Decline of Teotihuacan, A.D. 700–900*, ed. R. A. Diehl and J. C. Berlo, pp. 83–104. Dumbarton Oaks Research Library and Collection, Washington, D.C.

Nahm, Werner
1994 Maya Warfare and the Venus Year. *Mexicon* 16:6–10.

Nassaney, Michael S., and Kendra Pyle
1999 The Adoption of the Bow and Arrow in Eastern North America: A View from Central Arkansas. *American Antiquity* 62:243–63.

Nelson, Ben A., J. Andrew Darling, and David A. Kice
1992 Mortuary Practices and the Social Order at La Quemada, Zacatecas, Mexico. *Latin American Antiquity* 3:298–315.

Nettleship, Martin A.
1975 Definitions. In *War, Its Causes and Correlates*, ed. M. A. Nettleship, R. D. Givens, and A. Nettleship, pp. 73–90. Mouton, Paris.

Nicholson, Henry B.
1960 The Mixteca-Puebla Concept in Mesoamerican Archaeology: A Re-Examination. In *Men and Cultures: Selected Papers from the Fifth International Congress of Anthropological and Ethnological Sciences, Philadelphia, September 1–9, 1956*, ed. A. F. C. Wallace, pp. 612–17. University of Pennsylvania, Philadelphia.
1982 The Mixteca-Puebla Concept Re-Visited. In *The Art and Iconography of Late Post-Classic Central Mexico*, ed. E. H. Boone, pp. 227–54. Dumbarton Oaks Research Library and Collection, Washington, D.C.

Niederberger, B. C.
1987 *Paleopaysages et Archaeologie Pre-Urbaine du Basin de México: Tome II*. Centre d'Etudes Mexicaines et Centroamericaines, Mexico.

Noguera, Eduardo
1937 *El Altar de los Craneos Esculpidos de Cholula*. Talleres Gráficos de la Nación, D.F.

O'Brien, M. J., and D. E. Lewarch
1992 Regional Analysis of the Zapotec Empire, Valley of Oaxaca, Mexico. *World Archaeology* 23:264–82.

Olivera, Mercedes
1970 La Importancia Religiosa de Cholula. In *Proyecto Cholula*, ed. I. Marquina, pp. 211–42. Serie Investigaciones 19, Instituto Nacional de Antropología e Historia, México.

Olivera de V., Mercedes, and Cayetano Reyes
1969 Los Choloques y los Cholultecas: Apuntes sobre las Relaciones Étnicas en Cholula hasta el Siglo XVI. *Anales del INAH* 1:247–74.

Otterbein, Karl F.
1973 The Anthropology of War. In *Handbook of Social and Cultural Anthropology*, ed. J. Honigmann, pp. 923–58. Rand McNally, Chicago.

Pagliaro, J. B., J. F. Garber, D. M. Glassman, and M. K. Brown
1998 *Defining Maya Termination Deposits: Examples from the Belize River*

Valley. Paper presented at the 63rd annual meeting of the Society for American Archaeology.

Parsons, Jeffery R.
1971 *Prehistoric Settlement Patterns in the Texcoco Region, Mexico.* Memoirs of the Museum of Anthropology, University of Michigan, No. 3, Ann Arbor.

Parsons, Mark
1988 *The Iconography of Blood and Sacrifice in the Murals of the White Patio, Atetelco, Teotihuacan.* Unpublished master's thesis, Department of Art and Art History, University of Texas, Austin.

Pasztory, Esther
1974 *The Iconography of the Teotihuacan Tlaloc.* Studies in Pre-Columbian Art and Archaeology 15, Dumbarton Oaks Research Library and Collection, Washington, D.C.

1976 *The Murals of Tepantitla, Teotihuacan.* Garland Publishing, New York.

1988 A Reinterpretation of Teotihuacan and Its Mural Painting Tradition. In *Feathered Serpents and Flowering Trees: Reconstructing the Murals of Teotihuacan,* ed. K. Berrin, pp. 45–77. Fine Arts Museums of San Francisco, San Francisco.

1993 An Image is Worth a Thousand Words: Teotihuacan and the Meanings of Style in Classic Mesoamerica. In *Latin American Horizons,* ed. D. S. Rice, pp. 295–336. Dumbarton Oaks Research Library and Collection, Washington, D.C.

1997 *Teotihuacan: An Experiment in Living.* University of Oklahoma Press, Norman.

Pasztory, Esther (ed.)
1978 *Middle Classic Mesoamerica:* A.D. 400–700. Columbia University Press, New York.

Pendergast, David M.
1969 *The Prehistory of Actun Balam, British Honduras.* Occasional Paper 16, Royal Ontario Museum, Toronto.

1979 *Excavations at Altun Ha, Belize, 1964–1970, Volume 1.* Royal Ontario Museum, Toronto.

1981 Lamanai, Belize: Summary of Excavation Results: 1974–1980. *Journal of Field Archaeology* 8:29–53.

1982 *Excavations at Altun Ha, Belize, 1964–1970, Volume 2.* Royal Ontario Museum, Toronto.

1990 *Excavations at Altun Ha, Belize, 1964–1970, Volume 3.* Royal Ontario Museum, Toronto.

1998 Intercession with the Gods: Caches and Their Significance at Altun Ha and Lamanai, Belize. In *The Sowing and the Dawning: Termination, Dedication, and Transformation in the Archaeological and Ethnographic Record of Mesoamerica,* ed. S. B. Mock, pp. 55–63. University of New Mexico Press, Albuquerque.

Peters, Rudolph
1977 *Jihad in Medieval and Modern Islam.* E. J. Brill, Leiden, Netherlands.
1979 *Islam and Colonialism: The Doctrine of Jihad in Modern History.* Mouton, Paris.
1996 *Jihad in Classical and Modern Islam.* Markus Wiener Publishers, Princeton, N.J.

Peterson, David A., and Z. D. Green
1987 The Spanish Arrival and the Massacre at Cholula. *Notas Mesoamericanas* 10:203–220.

Peterson, K. L.
1988 *Climate and the Dolores River Anasazi.* University of Utah Anthropology Papers 113, University of Utah Press, Salt Lake City.
1994 A Warm and Wet Little Climatic Optimum and a Cold and Dry Little Ice Age in the Southern Rocky Mountains. *Climatic Change* 26:243–69.

Phillips, David A., Jr.
1989 Prehistory of Chihuahua and Sonora, Mexico. *Journal of World Prehistory* 3:373–401.

Pijoan, Carmen Maria, and Josefina Mansilla Lory
1997 Evidence for Human Sacrifice, Bone Modification, and Cannibalism in Ancient Mexico. In *Troubled Times: Violence and Warfare in the Past,* ed. D. L. Martin and D. W. Frayer, pp. 217–39. Gordon and Breach Publishers, Amsterdam.

Pijoan Aguade, Carmen Maria, and Alejandro Pastrana C.
1989 Evidencias de Actividades Rituales en Restos Oseos Humanos en Tlatelcomila, D.F.: El Preclásico ó Formativo. In *Avances y Perspectivas,* pp. 287–307. MNA/INAH, México.

Pohl, John M. D.
1991 *Aztec, Mixtec, and Zapotec Armies.* Men-At-Arms Series, No. 239, Osprey Publishing, London.

Pohl, Mary E. D., and John M. D. Pohl
1994 Cycles of Conflict: Political Factionalism in the Maya Lowlands. In *Factional Competition and Political Development in the New World,* ed. E. M. Brumfiel and J. W. Fox, pp. 138–57. Cambridge University Press, Cambridge, U.K.

Pollard, Helen P.
1994 Ethnicity and Political Control in a Complex Society: The Tarascan State of Prehispanic Mexico. In *Factional Competition and Political Development in the New World,* ed. E. M. Brumfiel and J. W. Fox, pp. 79–88. Cambridge University Press, Cambridge, U.K.

Pollock, H. E. D.
1980 *The Puuc: An Architectural Survey of the Hill Country of Yucatan and Northern Campeche.* Memoirs of the Peabody Museum, Vol. 19, Peabody Museum of Archaeology and Ethnology, Harvard University, Cambridge, Mass.

Porter, J. B.
1989 Olmec Colossal Heads as Recarved Thrones: "Mutilation," Revolution, and Recarving. *RES* 17/18:23–29.
1990 Las Cabezas Colosales Olmecas Como Altares Resculpidos: "Mutilación," Revolución, y Reesculpido. *Arqueología* 3:91–97.
Postgate, J. N.
1992 The Land of Assur and the Yoke of Assur. *World Archaeology* 23:247–63.
Powis, Terry
1996 *Excavations of Middle Formative Period Round Structures at the Tolok Group, Cahal Pech, Belize.* Unpublished master's thesis, Trent University, Peterborough, Ont.
Proskouriakoff, Tatiana
1960 Historical Implications of a Pattern of Dates at Piedras Negras, Guatemala. *American Antiquity* 25:454–75.
1963 Historical Data in the Inscriptions of Yaxchilan, Part I. *Estudios de Cultura Maya* 3:149–67.
1964 Historical Data in the Inscriptions of Yaxchilan, Part II. *Estudios de Cultura Maya* 4:177–201.
1993 *Maya History.* University of Texas Press, Austin.
Puleston, Dennis E.
1974 Intersite Areas in the Vicinity of Tikal and Uaxactun. In *Mesoamerican Archaeology: New Approaches,* ed. N. Hammond, pp. 303–11. University of Texas Press, Austin.
Puleston, Dennis E., and Donald W. Callender
1967 Defensive Earthworks at Tikal. *Expedition* 9:40–48.
Quirarte, Jacinto
1983 Outside Influence at Cacaxtla. In *Highland-Lowland Interaction in Mesoamerica: Interdisciplinary Approaches,* ed. A. G. Miller, pp. 201–21. Dumbarton Oaks Research Library and Collection, Washington, D.C.
Rands, Robert L.
1952 *Some Evidences of Warfare in Classic Maya Art.* Unpublished Ph.D. dissertation, Columbia University, New York.
1973 The Classic Collapse in the Southern Lowlands: Chronology. In *The Classic Maya Collapse,* ed. T. P. Culbert, pp. 43–62. University of New Mexico Press, Albuquerque.
Rathje, William L.
1973 Classic Maya Development and Denouement: A Research Design. In *The Classic Maya Collapse,* ed. T. P. Culbert, pp. 405–54. University of New Mexico Press, Albuquerque.
Redmond, Elsa M.
1983 *A Fuego y Sangre: Early Zapotec Imperialism in the Cuicatlán Cañada, Oaxaca.* Memoirs of the Museum of Anthropology, University of Michigan, No. 16, Ann Arbor.

Redmond, Elsa M., and Charles S. Spencer
1983   The Cuicatlán Cañada and the Period II Frontier of the Zapotec State. In *The Cloud People: Divergent Evolution of the Zapotec and Mixtec Civilizations*, ed. K. V. Flannery and J. Marcus, pp. 117–20. Academic Press, New York.

Reents-Budet, Dorie
1994   *Painting the Maya Universe: Royal Ceramics of the Classic Period*. Duke University Press, Durham, N.C.

Reents-Budet, Dorie, and Ronald Bishop
1989   *The Ik Emblem Glyph Corpus*. Paper and manuscript presented at the Seventh Mesa Redonda de Palenque.

Reese, Kathryn V.
1996   *Narratives of Power: Late Formative Public Architecture and Civic Center Design at Cerros, Belize*. Unpublished Ph.D. dissertation, University of Texas, Austin.

Reilly, F. Kent, III
1989   The Shaman in Transformation Pose: A Study of the Theme of Rulership in Olmec Art. *Record of the Art Museum* 48:4–21.
1991   Olmec Iconographic Influences on the Symbols of Maya Rulership: An Examination of Possible Sources. In *The Sixth Palenque Roundtable, 1986*, ed. M. Greene Robertson and V. Fields, pp. 151–66. University of Oklahoma Press, Norman.
1994   *Visions to Another World: Art, Shamanism, and Political Power in Middle Formative Mesoamerica*. Unpublished Ph.D. dissertation, University of Texas, Austin.
1995   Art, Ritual and Rulership in the Olmec World. In *The Olmec World: Ritual and Rulership*, pp. 27–67. The Art Museum, Princeton University, Princeton, N.J.
1996   The Lazy-S: A Formative Period Iconographic Loan to Maya Hieroglyphic Writing. In *Eighth Palenque Round Table, 1993, Vol. X*, ed. M. Macri and J. McHargue, pp. 413–24. Pre-Columbian Art Research Institute, San Francisco.
1999   Mountains of Creation and Underworld Portals: The Ritual Functions of Olmec Architecture at La Venta, Tabasco. In *Mesoamerican Architecture as a Cultural Symbol*, ed. J. K. Kowalski, pp. 14–39. Oxford University Press, New York.

Renfrew, Colin
1986   Introduction: Peer Polity Interaction and Socio-Political Change. In *Peer Polity Interaction and Socio-Political Change*, ed. C. Renfrew and J. F. Cherry, pp. 1–18. Cambridge University Press, London.

Repetto Tio, B.
1985   *Desarrollo Militar entre los Maya*. Maldonado Editores, INAH-SEP, Yucatán, México.

Reyna, Stephen P.
1994a A Mode of Domination Approach to Organized Violence. In *Study-*

ing War: Anthropological Perspectives, War and Society, Vol. 2, ed. S. P. Reyna and R. E. Davis, pp. 29–65. Gordon and Breach Science Publishers, Langhorne, Pa.

1994b Predatory Accumulation and Religious Conflict in the Early 19th Century Chad Basin. In *Studying War: Anthropological Perspectives, War and Society, Vol. 2*, ed. S. P. Reyna and R. E. Davis, pp. 127–55. Gordon and Breach Science Publishers, Langhorne, Pa.

Rice, Don S., and Prudence M. Rice
1981 Muralla de Leon: A Lowland Maya Fortification. *Journal of Field Archaeology* 8:271–88.

Riches, D.
1991 Aggression, War, Violence: Space/Time and Paradigm. *Man* 26:281–98.

Riese, Berthold
1984 Kriegsberichte de Klassischen Maya. *Baessler-Archiv* 30:255–321.

Ringle, William M., Tomas Gallareta N., and George J. Bey III
1998 The Return of Quetzalcoatl: Evidence for the Spread of a World Religion during the Epiclassic Period. *Ancient Mesoamerica* 9:183–232.

Rivera D., Miguel
1987 *Oxkintok 1*. Misión Arqueológica de España en México, Madrid.

Robertson, Donald
1970 The Tulum Murals: The International Style of the Late Postclassic. In *Verhandlungen des XXXVIII Internationanalen Amerikanistenkongresses. Stuttgart-München*, pp. 77–88. Kommissionsverlag K. Renner, Munich.

1985 The Cacaxtla Murals. In *Fourth Palenque Round Table, 1980*, ed. M. Greene Robertson and E. P. Benson, pp. 291–302. Pre-Columbian Art Research Institute, San Francisco.

Robertson, Robin A.
1983 Functional Analysis and Social Process in Ceramics: The Pottery from Cerros, Belize. In *Civilization in the Ancient Americas: Essays in Honor of Gordon R. Willey*, ed. R. M. Leventhal and A. L. Kolata, pp. 105–42. University of New Mexico Press, Albuquerque.

Robin, Cynthia
1989 *Preclassic Maya Burials at Cuello, Belize*. BAR International Series 480, Oxford, U.K.

Robles C., Fernando
1990 *La Sequencia Cerámica de la Región de Cobá, Quintana Roo*. Instituto Nacional de Antropología e Historia, D.F.

Robles C., Fernando, and Anthony P. Andrews
1986 A Review and Synthesis of Recent Postclassic Archaeology in Northern Yucatan. In *Late Lowland Maya Civilization*, ed. J. A. Sabloff and E. W. Andrews V, pp. 53–98. University of New Mexico Press, Albuquerque.

Rojas, Gabriel de
  1927   Descriptión de Cholula. *Revista Mexicana de Estudios Historicos* 1(6):158–170.
Romero Molina, Javier
  1986   Nuevos Datos Sobre Mutilación Dentaria en Mesoamérica. *Anales de Antropología* 23:349–65.
Roney, John R.
  1996a   *Late Archaic Cerros de Trincheras in Northwestern Chihuahua.* Paper presented at the 61st annual meeting of the Society for American Archeology.
  1996b   *Cerro Juanaquena: A Late Archaic Cerros de Trincheras in Northwestern Chihuahua.* Paper presented at the Archaic Prehistory of the North American Southwest Meetings.
Roper, Marilyn K.
  1975   Evidence of Warfare in the Near East from 10,000–4,300 B.C. In *War, Its Causes and Correlates,* ed. M. A. Nettleship, R. D. Givens, and A. Nettleship, pp. 299–340. Mouton, Paris.
Ross, M. H.
  1986   A Cross-Cultural Theory of Political Conflict and Violence. *Political Psychology* 7:427–69.
Rowlands, Michael J.
  1972   Defense: A Factor in the Organization of Settlements. In *Man, Settlement, and Urbanism,* ed. P. J. Ucko, R. Tringham, and G. W. Dimbleby, pp. 447–62. Duckworth, London.
Roys, Ralph L.
  1933   *The Book of Chilam Balam of Chumayel.* Carnegie Institution of Washington, Publication 438, Washington, D.C.
  1943   *The Indian Background of Colonial Yucatan.* Carnegie Institution of Washington, Publication 548, Washington, D.C.
Ruppert, Karl, J. Eric S. Thompson, and Tatiana Proskouriakoff
  1955   *Bonampak, Chiapas, Mexico.* Carnegie Institution of Washington, Publication 602, Washington, D.C.
Ruz L., Alberto
  1951   Chichen-Itza y Palenque, Ciudades Fortificadas. In *Homenaje al Doctor Alfonso Caso,* pp. 331–42. Imprenta Nueva Mundo, Mexico.
Sabloff, Jeremy A.
  1973   Continuity and Disruption during Terminal Late Classic Times at Seibal: Ceramic and Other Evidence. In *The Classic Maya Collapse,* ed. T. P. Culbert, pp. 107–31. University of New Mexico Press, Albuquerque.
Sabloff, Jeremy A., and Gordon R. Willey
  1967   The Collapse of Maya Civilization in the Southern Lowlands: A Consideration of History and Process. *Southwestern Journal of Anthropology* 23:311–36.

Sahagún, Bernadino de
1950–1982   *General History of the Things of New Spain: Florentine Codex.* Translated by A. J. O. Anderson and C. E. Dibble. University of Utah Press, Salt Lake City.

Salas, Marie Elena, and Carmen Pijoan
1982   *Estudio Osteologico de los Entierros Procedentes de las Exploraciones del Proyecto Nacional Tikal, Temporadas 1980–1982.* Informe, Proyecto Nacional Tikal, Guatemala y Departmento de Antropologia Fisica, Guatemala.

Sanders, William T., and Joseph W. Michels (eds.)
1977   *Teotihuacan and Kaminaljuyu: A Study in Prehistoric Culture Contact.* Pennsylvania State University Press Monograph Series on Kaminaljuyu, State College.

Sanders, William T., Jeffery R. Parsons, and Robert S. Santley
1979   *The Basin of Mexico: Ecological Processes in the Evolution of a Civilization.* Academic Press, New York.

Sanders, William T., and David L. Webster
1988   The Mesoamerican Urban Tradition. *American Anthropologist* 90:521–46.

Santley, Robert S.
1983   Obsidian Trade and Teotihuacan Influence in Mesoamerica. In *Highland-Lowland Interaction in Mesoamerica: Interdisciplinary Approaches,* ed. A. G. Miller, pp. 69–124. Dumbarton Oaks Research Library and Collection, Washington, D.C.
1989   Obsidian Working, Long-Distance Exchange, and the Teotihuacan Presence on the South Gulf Coast. In *Mesoamerican After the Decline of Teotihuacan,* AD 700–900, ed. R. A. Diehl and J. C. Berlo, pp. 131–51. Dumbarton Oaks Research Library and Collection, Washington, D.C.

Santley, R. S., P. Ortiz C., and C. A. Pool
1987   Recent Archaeological Research at Matacapan, Veracruz: A Summary of the Results of the 1982 to 1986 Field Seasons. *Mexicon* 11:41–48.

Satterthwaite, Linton
1958   *The Problem of Abnormal Stela Placements at Tikal and Elsewhere.* Tikal Report, No. 3, The University Museum Press, Philadelphia.

Saul, Frank P., and Julie M. Saul
1991   The Preclassic Population of Cuello. In *Cuello: An Early Maya Community in Belize,* ed. N. Hammond, pp. 134–58. Cambridge University Press, New York.

Schaafsma, Polly
1992   War Imagery and Magic: Petroglyphs at Camanche Gap, Galisteo Basin, New Mexico. In *Archaeology, Art, and Anthropology: Papers in Honor of J. J. Brody,* ed. M. Duran and D. Kirkpatrick, pp. 157–74.

Archaeological Society of New Mexico, No. 18, Albuquerque Archaeological Society, Albuquerque.

Schele, Linda
1982   *Maya Glyphs: The Verbs.* University of Texas Press, Austin.
1984   Human Sacrifice among the Classic Maya. In *Ritual Human Sacrifice in Mesoamerica,* ed. E. H. Boone, pp. 7–48. Dumbarton Oaks Research Library and Collection, Washington, D.C.
1986   *The Tlaloc Heresy: Cultural Interaction and Social History.* Paper presented at "Maya Art and Civilization: The New Dynamics," a symposium sponsored by the Kimball Art Museum, Fort Worth, Tex.
1991a   An Epigraphic History of the Western Maya Region. In *Classic Maya Political History,* ed. T. P. Culbert, pp. 72–101. Cambridge University Press, Cambridge, U.K.
1991b   Another Look at Stela 13. *Copán Note,* 103.
1995   The Olmec Mountain and Tree of Creation in Mesoamerican Cosmology. In *The Olmec World: Ritual and Rulership,* ed. G. Griffin, pp. 105–17. The Art Museum, Princeton University, Princeton, N.J.

Schele, Linda, and David A. Freidel
1990   *A Forest of Kings: The Untold Story of the Ancient Maya.* Quill, New York.

Schele, Linda, and Nikolai Grube
1994   *Notebook for the XVIIIth Maya Hieroglyphic Workshop at Texas, March 12–13, 1994. Tlaloc-Venus Warfare: The Peten Wars 8.17.0.0.0– 9.15.13.0.0,* ed. Timothy Albright. Department of Art and Art History, College of Fine Arts, and the Institutes of Latin American Studies, University of Texas at Austin.

Schele, Linda, and Peter Mathews
1991   Royal Visits and Other Intersite Relationships among the Classic Maya. In *Classic Maya Political History: Hieroglyphic and Archaeological Evidence,* ed. T. P. Culbert, pp. 226–52. Cambridge University Press, Cambridge, U.K.
1998   *The Code of Kings: The Language of Seven Sacred Maya Temples and Tombs.* Scribner's, New York.

Schele, Linda, and Mary Ellen Miller
1986   *The Blood of Kings: Dynasty and Ritual in Maya Art.* Kimball Art Museum, Fort Worth, Tex.

Schiffer, Michael B.
1972   Archaeological Context and Systemic Context. *American Antiquity* 37:156–65.

Schreiber, Katharina J.
1987   Conquest and Consolidation: A Comparison of the Wari and Inka Occupations of a Highland Peruvian Valley. *American Antiquity* 52:266–84.
1992   *Wari Imperialism in Middle Horizon Peru.* Anthropological Paper No. 87, Museum of Anthropology, University of Michigan, Ann Arbor.

Sejourné, Laurette
1959　*Un Palacio en la Ciudad de los Dioses: Teotihuacan.* INAH, México.
1966a　*Arqueología de Teotihuacan: La Cerámica.* Fondo de Cultura Económica, México.
1966b　*Arquitectura y Pintura en Teotihuacan.* Siglo XXI, México.

Seler, Eduard
1990–1998　*Collected Works in Mesoamerican Linguistics and Archaeology.* Labyrinthos, Culver City, Calif.

Serra Puche, Mari Carmen, and J. Carlos Lazcano Arce
1997　Xochitécatl-Cacaxtla en 1 Periodo Epiclásico (650–950 D.C.). *Arqueología* 18:85–102.

Sharer, Robert J.
1978　Archaeology and History at Quirigua, Guatemala. *Journal of Field Archaeology* 5:51–70.
1991　Diversity and Continuity in Maya Civilization: Quirigua as a Case Study. In *Classic Maya Political History: Hieroglyphic and Archaeological Evidence,* ed. T. P. Culbert, pp. 180–98. Cambridge University Press, Cambridge, U.K.

Shaw, Justine M.
1998　*The Community Settlement Patterns and Community Architecture of Yaxuna from* A.D. *600–1400.* Unpublished Ph.D. dissertation, Southern Methodist University, Dallas.

Sheets, Payson D.
1978　Artifacts. In *The Prehistory of Chalchuapa, El Salvador, Volume II,* ed. R. J. Sharer, pp. 1–131. University of Pennsylvania Press, Philadelphia.
1992　*The Ceren Site: A Prehistoric Village Buried by Volcanic Ash in Central America.* Case Studies in Archaeology Series, Harcourt Brace College Publishers, Fort Worth, Tex.

Sheets, Payson D. (ed.)
1983　*Archeology and Volcanism in Central America: The Zapotitan Valley of El Salvador.* University of Texas Press, Austin.

Shelby, Charmion (trans.)
1993　La Florida by Garcilaso de la Vega, the Inca. In *The De Soto Chronicles: The Expedition of Hernando de Soto to North America in 1539–1543,* ed. Lawrence A. Clayton, Vernon J. Knight Jr., and Edward C. Moore, pp. 25–559. University of Alabama Press, Tuscaloosa.

Shook, Edwin M.
1952　*The Great Wall of Mayapan.* Current Reports No. 2, Carnegie Institution of Washington, Washington, D.C.
1958　*Field Director's Report: The 1956 and 1957 Seasons.* Tikal Report, No. 1, The University Museum Press, Philadelphia.
1998　Excerpt from Edward Shook's Field Notebook, June 1937. *Pre-Columbian Art Research Institute Newsletter* 25:13–16.

Sinopoli, Carla M.
   1994   Political Choices and Economic Strategies in the Vijayanagara
          Empire. In *Economic Anthropology and the State,* ed. E. M. Brumfiel,
          pp. 223–42. Monographs in Economic Anthropology, No. 11, Uni-
          versity Press of America, Lanham, Md.
Smith, A. Ledyard
   1950   *Uaxactun, Guatemala: Excavations of 1931–1937.* Carnegie Institution
          of Washington, Publication 588, Washington, D.C.
Smith, J. Gregory
   1998   *Molcajetes at Ichmul de Morley, Yucatan: A Multi-Interpretive Approach.*
          Paper Presented at the 97th annual meeting of the American
          Anthropological Association.
Smith, Michael E.
   1987   The Expansion of the Aztec Empire: A Case Study in the Correlation
          of Diachronic Archaeological and Ethnohistorical Data. *American
          Antiquity* 52:37–54.
   1996   *The Aztecs.* Blackwell, Oxford, U.K.
Smith, Michael E., and Frances F. Berdan
   1992   Archaeology of the Aztec Empire. *World Archaeology* 23:353–67.
Smith, Michael E., and Cynthia M. Heath-Smith
   1980   Waves of Influence in Postclassic Mesoamerica? A Critique of the
          Mixteca-Puebla Concept. *Anthropology* 4(2):15–50.
Smith, Michael E., and L. Montiel
   2001   The Archaeological Study of Empires and Imperialism in Prehis-
          panic Central Mexico. *Journal of Anthropological Archaeology*
          20:245–84.
Smith, Robert E.
   1971   *The Pottery of Mayapan.* Papers of the Peabody Museum of Archaeol-
          ogy and Ethnology, Harvard University, Vol. 66, Cambridge, Mass.
Sosa, John R., and Dorie J. Reents
   1980   Glyphic Evidence for Classic Maya Militarism. *Belizean Studies*
          8:2–11.
Soustelle, Jacques
   1970   *Daily Life of the Aztecs on the Eve of the Spanish Conquest.* Stanford Uni-
          versity Press, Stanford, Calif.
Southall, Aidan
   1988   The Segmentary State in Africa and Asia. *Comparative Studies in Soci-
          ety and History* 30:52–82.
Spencer, Charles S.
   1982   *The Cuicatlán Cañada and Monte Albán: A Study of Primary State Forma-
          tion.* Academic Press, New York.
Spencer, Charles S., and Else M. Redmond
   1982   Appendix. Ceramic Chronology for the Cuicatlán Cañada. In *The
          Cuicatlán Cañada and Monte Albán,* ed. C. S. Spencer, pp. 261–307.
          Academic Press, New York.

1997   *Archaeology of the Cañada de Cuicatlán, Oaxaca.* American Museum of Natural History, New York.

2001   The Chronology of Conquest: Implications of New Radiocarbon Analyses from the Cañada de Cuicatlán, Oaxaca. *Latin American Antiquity* 12:182–202.

Spinden, Herbert J.

1916   Portraiture in Central American Art. In *Holmes Anniversary Volume: Anthropological Essays,* pp. 434–50. Smithsonian Institution, Washington, D.C.

Spores, Ronald

1967   *The Mixtec Kings and Their People.* University of Oklahoma Press, Norman.

1972   *An Archaeological Settlement Survey of the Nochixtlán Valley, Oaxaca.* Vanderbilt University Publications in Anthropology No. 1, Nashville.

1993   Tututepec: A Postclassic-Period Mixtec Conquest State. *Ancient Mesoamerica* 4:167–74.

Stanislawski, Dan

1947   Tarascan Political Geography. *American Anthropologist* 47:46–55.

Stanton, Travis W.

1998   *Shifting Patterns of Classic Maya Warfare: Evidence from the Northern Lowlands.* Paper presented at the First Annual Graduate Symposium at the University of Pennsylvania, Philadelphia.

1999   *From Cetelac to the Coast: The Archaeology of Itzá Expansion.* Paper presented at the 64th annual meeting of the Society for American Archaeology.

Stanton, Travis W., and Tomás Gallareta N.

2001   Warfare, Ceramic Economy, and the Itzá: A Reconsideration of the Itzá Polity in Ancient Yucatan. *Ancient Mesoamerica* 12:229–46.

Stanton, Travis W., and Jonathan B. Pagliaro

1997   *Garbage of the Gods? Termination versus Trash Disposal.* Paper presented at the 62nd annual meeting of the Society for American Archaeology.

Stark, Barbara L.

1990   The Gulf Coast and the Central Highlands of Mexico: Alternative Models for Interaction. *Research in Economic Anthropology* 12:243–85.

Stein, Gil J.

1999   *Rethinking World-Systems.* University of Arizona Press, Tucson.

Stirling, Mathew W.

1940   Great Stone Faces of the Mexican Jungle. *National Geographic* 78:309–34.

1955   Stone Monuments of the Rio Chiquito, Veracruz, Mexico. *Bureau of American Ethnology, Bulletin 157, Anthropological Papers* 43:1–23.

Stone, Andrea J.

1989   Disconnection, Foreign Insignia, and Political Expansion: Teotihuacan and the Warrior Stelae of Piedras Negras. In *Mesoamerica after the Decline of Teotihuacan*, A.D. 700–900, ed. R. A. Diehl and J. C. Berlo, pp. 153–72. Dumbarton Oaks Research Library and Collection, Washington, D.C.

1995 *Images from the Underworld: Naj Tunich and the Tradition of Maya Cave Painting*. University of Texas Press, Austin.

Stross, Brian

1998 Seven Ingredients in Mesoamerican Ensoulments: Dedication and Termination in Tenejapa. In *The Sowing and the Dawning: Termination, Dedication, and Transformation in the Archaeological and Ethnographic Record of Mesoamerica*, ed. S. B. Mock, pp. 31–39. University of New Mexico Press, Albuquerque.

Stuart, David

1985 The "Count-of-Captives" Epithet in Classic Maya Writing. In *Fifth Palenque Round Table, 1983*, ed. M. Greene Robertson and V. M. Fields, pp. 97–101. Pre-Columbian Art Research Institute, San Francisco.

1987 *Ten Phonetic Syllables*. Research Reports on Ancient Maya Writing 14, Center for Maya Research, Washington, D.C.

1988 Blood Symbolism in Maya Iconography. In *Maya Iconography*, ed. E. P. Benson and G. Griffin, pp. 175–221. Princeton University Press, Princeton, N.J.

1993 Historical Inscriptions and the Maya Collapse. In *Lowland Maya Civilization in the Eighth Century* A.D., ed. J. A. Sabloff and J. S. Henderson, pp. 321–54. Dumbarton Oaks Research Library and Collection, Washington, D.C.

1997 The Hills Are Alive: Sacred Mountains in the Maya Cosmos. *Symbols* (Spring 1997):13–17.

1998a Una Guerra entre Yaxchilan y Piedras Negras. In *Proyecto Arqueologico Piedras Negras: Informe Preliminar No. 2, Segunda Temporada 1998*, ed. H. L. Escobedo and S. D. Houston, pp. 389–92. Proyecto Arqueologico Piedras Negras, Guatemala City.

1998b "The Fire Enters His House": Architecture and Ritual in Classic Maya Texts. In *Functions and Meaning in Classic Maya Architecture*, ed. S. D. Houston, pp. 373–425, Dumbarton Oaks Research Library and Collection, Washington, D.C.

1998c "*The Arrival of Strangers*": Teotihuacan and Tollan in Classic Maya History. Paper prepared for "The Classic Heritage: From Teotihuacan to the Templo Mayor" symposium, Princeton University, Princeton, N.J. (manuscript in possession of author).

1999 The Arrival of Strangers: Teotihuacan and Tollan in Classic Maya History. In *Mesoamerica's Classic Heritage: Teotihuacan to the Aztecs*, ed. D. Carrasco, L. Jones, and S. Sessions, pp. 465–513. University Press of Colorado, Niwot, Colo.

Stuart, George E.
  1992 Mural Masterpieces of Ancient Cacaxtla. *National Geographic* 182(3):120–36.
Suárez C., Sergio
  1985 *Un Entierro del Clásico Superior en Cholula, Puebla.* Cuaderno de Trabajo 6, Centro Regional de Puebla, INAH, D.F.
Sugiyama, Saburo
  1989 Iconographic Interpretation of the Temple of Quetzalcoatl at Teotihuacan. *Mexicon* 11:68–74.
  1992 Rulership, Warfare, and Human Sacrifice at the Ciudadela: An Iconographic Study of Feathered Serpent Representations. In *Art, Ideology, and the City of Teotihuacan,* ed. J. C. Berlo, pp. 205–30. Dumbarton Oaks Research Library and Collection, Washington, D.C.
  1998 Deliberate Destruction and Looting in Prehispanic Times at the Feathered Serpent Pyramid in Teotihuacan, Mexico. In *The Sowing and the Dawning: Termination, Dedication, and Transformation in the Archaeological and Ethnographic Record of Mesoamerica,* ed. S. B. Mock, pp. 147–64. University of New Mexico Press, Albuquerque.
Suhler, Charles K.
  1996 *Excavations at the North Acropolis, Yaxuná, Yucatán, México.* Unpublished Ph.D. dissertation, Southern Methodist University, Dallas.
Suhler, Charles K., Traci Ardren, and David Johnstone
  1998 The Chronology of Yaxuna: Evidence from Excavation and Ceramics. *Ancient Mesoamerica* 9:176–82.
Suhler, Charles K., and David A. Freidel
  1993 *The Selz Foundation Yaxuna Project: Final Report of the 1992 Field Season.* Manuscript on file, Department of Anthropology, Southern Methodist University, Dallas.
  1995a *Termination Rituals: Implications for Maya War.* Paper presented at the Palenque Mesa Redonda.
  1995b *The Sack of Chichen Itza: Reinterpreting the Early Stratigraphic Excavations.* Paper presented at the 1995 Maya Meetings at Texas.
  1998 Life and Death in a Maya War Zone. *Archaeology* 51(3):28–34.
Taladoire, Eric, and Benoit Colsenet
  1991 "Bois Ton Sang, Beaumanoir": The Political and Conflictual Aspects of the Ballgame in the Northern Chiapas Area. In *The Mesoamerican Ballgame,* ed. V. Scarborough and D. Wilcox, pp. 161–74. University of Arizona Press, Tucson.
Tambiah, Stanley J.
  1977 The Galactic Polity: The Structure of Traditional Kingdoms in Southeast Asia. *Annuals of the New York Academy of Sciences* 293:69–97.
Tarlow, Sarah
  1997 The Dread of Something after Death: Violation and Desecration on the Isle of Man in the Tenth Century. In *Material Harm: Archaeological*

Studies of War and Violence, ed. J. Carman, pp. 133–42. Cruithne Press, Glasgow.

Tate, Carolyn E.

1995　Art in Olmec Culture. In *The Olmec World: Ritual and Rulership,* pp. 47–67. The Art Museum, Princeton University, Princeton, N.J.

Taube, Karl

1983　The Teotihuacan Spider Woman. *Journal of Latin American Lore* 9:107–89.

1988　A Study of Classic Maya Scaffold Sacrifice. In *Maya Iconography,* ed. E. P. Benson and G. Griffin, pp. 331–51. Princeton University Press, Princeton, N.J.

1989　Ritual Humor in Classic Maya Religion. In *Word and Image in Maya Culture: Explorations in Language, Writing, and Representation,* ed. W. F. Hanks and D. S. Rice, pp. 351–82. University of Utah Press, Salt Lake City.

1992a　The Temple of Quetzalcoatl and the Cult of Sacred War at Teotihuacan. *RES* 21:53–87.

1992b　*The Major Gods of Ancient Yucatan.* Dumbarton Oaks Research Library and Collection, Washington, D.C.

1995　The Rains Makers: The Olmec and Their Contributions to Mesoamerican Belief and Ritual. In *The Olmec World: Ritual and Rulership,* pp. 83–103. The Art Museum, Princeton University, Princeton, N.J.

1996　The Olmec Maize God: The Face of Corn in Formative Mesoamerica. *RES* 29/30:39–81.

1998　*The Turquoise Hearth: Fire, Sacrifice, and the Central Mexican Cult of War.* Paper prepared for "The Classic Heritage: From Teotihuacan to the Templo Mayor" symposium, Princeton University, Princeton, N.J. (manuscript in possession of author).

Tedlock, Dennis (trans.)

1985　*Popol Vuh: The Mayan Book of the Dawn of Life.* 1st Edition, Simon & Schuster, New York.

1996　*Popol Vuh: The Mayan Book of the Dawn of Life.* 2nd Edition, Simon & Schuster, New York.

Tedlock, Dennis, and Barbara Tedlock

1975　*Teachings for the American Earth: Indian Religion and Philosophy.* Liveright Publishing, New York.

Thompson, J. Eric

1954　*The Rise and Fall of Maya Civilization.* 1st Edition, University of Oklahoma Press, Norman.

1966　*The Rise and Fall of Maya Civilization.* 2nd Edition, University of Oklahoma Press, Norman.

1970　*Maya History and Religion.* University of Oklahoma Press, Norman.

Thompson, J. E. S., H. E. D. Pollock, and Jean Charlot

1932　*A Preliminary Study of the Ruins of Coba, Quintana Roo, Mexico.* Carnegie Institution of Washington, Publication 424, Washington, D.C.

Tomka, Steve A.
1993   Site Abandonment Behavior among Transhumant Agropastoralists: The Effects of Delayed Curation on Assemblage Composition. In *Abandonments of Settlements and Regions: Ethnoarchaeological and Archaeological Approaches*, ed. C. A. Cameron and S. A. Tomka, pp. 11–24. Cambridge University Press, Cambridge,U.K.

Torquemada, Fray Juan de
1975–1983   *Monarquía Indiana*. Coord. M. Leon-Portilla. Instituto de Investigaciones Historicas, Universidad Nacional Autonoma de México, D.F.

Toscano, Salvador
1954   Los Murales Prehispanicos. *Artes de México* 3:30–38.

Tourtellot, Gair, III
1990   *Burials: A Cultural Analysis*. Excavations at Seibal, Memoirs of the Peabody Museum of Archaeology and Ethnology, Vol. 16, No. 2, Harvard University, Cambridge, Mass.

Townsend, Richard
1992   *The Aztecs*. Thames and Hudson, New York.

Tozzer, Alfred M.
1957   *Chichen Itza and Its Cenote of Sacrifice*. Memoirs of the Peabody Museum of Archaeology and Ethnology, Volumes 1 and 12, Harvard University, Cambridge, Mass.

Tozzer, Alfred M. (trans.)
1941   *Landa's Relacion de Las Cosas de Yucatan*. Papers of the Peabody Museum of American Archaeology and Ethnology, Paper 18, Harvard University, Cambridge, Mass.

Turner, Christy G., II, and Jacqueline A. Turner
1999   *Man Corn: Cannibalism and Violence in the Prehistoric American Southwest*. University of Utah Press, Salt Lake City.

Turner, Victor
1969   *The Ritual Process: Structure and Anti-Structure*. Cornell University Press, Ithaca, N.Y.

Upham, Steadman
1982   *Polities and Power: An Economic and Political History of the Western Pueblo*. Academic Press, New York.

Urcid, Javier
1993   The Pacific Coast of Oaxaca and Guerrero: The Westernmost Extent of Zapotec Script. *Ancient Mesoamerica* 4:141–65.

Valliant, George C.
1941   *Aztecs of Mexico: Origin, Rise, and Fall of the Aztec Nation*. Doubleday, Doran, Garden City, N.Y.

Varela T., Carmen
1998   *El Clasico Medio en el Noroccidente de Yucatán*. Paris Monographs in American Archaeology, No. 2, BAR International Series 739, Oxford, U.K.

1999   *Teotihuacan and the Maya: New Perspectives from the North of Yucatan.*
        Paper presented at the 64th annual meeting of the Society for Ameri-
        can Archaeology.

Villa Rojas, Alfonso
1934   *The Yaxuná-Cobá Causeway.* Contributions to American Archaeology
        No. 9, Carnegie Institution of Washington, Publication 436, Wash-
        ington, D.C.

Villela, Kristaan D.
1993   *The Classic Maya Secondary Tier: Power and Prestige at Three Polities.*
        Unpublished master's thesis, University of Texas, Austin.

Vivian, R. Gwinn
1990   *The Chacoan Prehistory of the San Juan Basin.* Academic Press, San
        Diego.

Vogt, Evon Z.
1993   *Tortillas for the Gods: A Symbolic Analysis of Zinacanteco Rituals.* Uni-
        versity of Oklahoma Press, Norman.

Von Winning, Hasso
1947   Representations of Temple Buildings as Decorative Patterns on Teo-
        tihuacan Pottery and Figurines. *Carnegie Institution of Washington
        Notes* 83:170–77.
1948   The Teotihuacan Owl-and-Weapon Symbol and Its Association with
        "Serpent Head X" at Kaminaljuyu. *American Antiquity* 14:129–32.
1979   Representaciones de Fachadas de Templos en Ceramica de Teotihua-
        can. In *Las Representaciones de Arquitectura en la Arqueología de
        America, Vol. I, Mesoamerica,* ed. D. Schávelzon, pp. 319–27. UNAM,
        México.
1987   *La Iconografía de Teotihuacan: Los Dioses y los Signos.* UNAM, México.

Walker, Debra S.
1998   Smashed Pots and Shattered Dreams: The Material Evidence for an
        Early Classic Maya Site Termination at Cerros, Belize. In *The Sowing
        and the Dawning: Termination, Dedication, and Transformation in the
        Archaeological and Ethnographic Record of Mesoamerica,* ed. S. B. Mock,
        pp. 81–99. University of New Mexico Press, Albuquerque.

Wagner, Henry R.
1944   *The Rise of Fernando Cortés.* The Cortés Society, Fox Printing, Los
        Angeles.

Wauchope, Robert
1948   *Excavations at Zacualpa, Guatemala.* Middle American Research Insti-
        tute, Publication 14, Tulane University, New Orleans.

Weaver, Muriel P.
1972   *The Aztec, Maya, and Their Predecessors: Archaeology of Mesoamerica.*
        Seminar Press, New York.

Webster, David L.
1975   Warfare and the Evolution of the State. *American Antiquity*
        40:464–70.

1976a *Defensive Earthworks at Becan, Campeche, Mexico: Implications for Maya Warfare.* Middle American Research Institute, Publication 41, Tulane University, New Orleans.

1976b *Warfare and the Evolution of the State: A Perspective from the Maya Lowlands.* Museum of Anthropology Miscellaneous Series No. 19, Pennsylvania State University, State College.

1976c Lowland Maya Fortifications. *Proceedings of the American Philosophical Society* 120:361–72.

1977 Warfare and the Evolution of Maya Civilization. In *The Origins of Maya Civilization,* ed. R. E. W. Adams, pp. 335–71. University of New Mexico Press, Albuquerque.

1979 *Cuca, Chacchob, Dzonote Ake: Three Walled Northern Maya Centers.* Occasional Papers in Anthropology, Department of Anthropology, Pennsylvania State University, No. 11, University Park.

1980 Spatial Bounding and Settlement History at Three Walled Northern Maya Centers. *American Antiquity* 45:834–44.

1993 The Study of Maya Warfare: What It Tells Us about the Maya and What It Tells Us about Maya Archaeology. In *Lowland Maya Civilization in the Eighth Century A.D.,* ed. J. A. Sabloff and J. S. Henderson, pp. 415–44. Dumbarton Oaks Research Library and Collection, Washington, D.C.

1998 Warfare and Status Rivalry: Lowland Maya and Polynesian Comparisons. In *Archaic States,* ed. G. M. Feinman and J. Marcus, pp. 311–51. School of American Research, Santa Fe, N.M.

2000 The Not So Peaceful Civilization: A Review of Maya War. *Journal of World Prehistory* 14:65–119.

Webster, David L. (ed.)

1989 *The House of the Bacabs, Copan, Honduras.* Dumbarton Oaks Research Library and Collection, Washington, D.C.

Whitecotton, Joseph W.

1977 *The Zapotecs: Princes, Priests, and Peasants.* University of Oklahoma Press, Norman.

Whittaker, G.

1980 *The Hieroglyphics of Monte Albán.* Ph.D. dissertation, Department of Anthropology, Yale University, New Haven, Conn. University Microfilms, Ann Arbor, Mich.

Wilcox, David R.

1979 The Warfare Implications of Dry-Laid Masonry Walls on Tumamoc Hill. *The Kiva* 45:15–38.

1989 Hohokam Warfare. In *Cultures in Conflict: Current Archaeological Perspectives,* ed. D. C. Tkaczuk and B. C. Vivian, pp. 163–72. Proceedings of the 20th Chacmool Conference, Department of Anthropology, University of Calgary, Calgary.

1993 The Evolution of the Chaco Polity. In *The Chimney Rock Archaeological Symposium*, ed. J. McKim Malville and G. Matlock, pp. 76–90. Rocky Mountain Forest and Range Experiment Station, USDA Forest Service, General Technical Report RM-227, U.S. Department of Agriculture, Fort Collins, Colo.

Wilcox, David R., and Jonathan Haas
1994 The Scream of the Butterfly: Competition and Conflict in the Prehistoric Southwest. In *Themes in Southwest Prehistory*, ed. G. J. Gumerman, pp. 211–38. School of American Research Press, Santa Fe, N.M.

Willey, Gordon R.
1974 The Classic Maya Hiatus: A Rehearsal for the Collapse? In *Mesoamerican Archaeology: New Approaches*, ed. N. Hammond, pp. 417–30. University of Texas Press, Austin.
1990 *General Summary and Conclusions.* Excavations at Seibal, Memoirs of the Peabody Museum of Archaeology and Ethnology, Vol. 17, No. 4, Harvard University, Cambridge, Mass.

Willey, G. R., W. R. Bullard Jr., J. B. Glass, and J. C. Gifford
1965 *Prehistoric Maya Settlements in the Belize Valley.* Papers of the Peabody Museum of Archaeology and Ethnology, Vol. 54, Harvard University, Cambridge, Mass.

Wills, W. H.
1988 *Early Prehistoric Agriculture in the American Southwest.* School of American Research Press, Santa Fe, N.M.

Winter, Marcus C.
1984 Exchange in Formative Highland Oaxaca. In *Trade and Exchange in Early Mesoamerica*, ed. K. G. Hirth, pp. 179–214. University of New Mexico Press, Albuquerque.
1989 *Oaxaca: The Archaeological Record.* Minutiae Mexicana, México.

Wolf, Eric R.
1999 *Envisioning Power: Ideologies of Dominance and Crisis.* University of California Press, Los Angeles.

Wolfman, Daniel
1968 *Preliminary Report on Excavations at UA-1.* Report submitted to the Departmento de Monumentos Prehispanicos, manuscript on file at the Department of Anthropology, Universidad de las Américas, Santa Catarina Martir, Puebla, Mexico.

Woodson, Michael K.
1995 *The Goat Hill Site: A Western Anasazi Pueblo in the Safford Valley of Southeastern Arizona.* Unpublished master's thesis, University of Texas, Austin.

Workinger, A. G.
2002 *Understanding Coastal/Highland Interaction in Prehispanic Oaxaca, Mexico: The Perspective from San Francisco de Arriba.* Unpublished Ph.D. dissertation, Department of Anthropology, Vanderbilt University, Nashville.

Workinger, A. G., and C. Colby
  1997 *El Proyecto Arqueológico San Francisco de Arriba.* Final report submitted to the Consejo de Arqueología and the Centro INAH Oaxaca, Instituto Nacional de Antropología e Historia, México.

Yarborough, C. M.
  1992 *Teotihuacan and the Gulf Coast: Ceramic Evidence for Contact and Interaction.* Ph.D. dissertation, Department of Anthropology, University of Arizona, Tucson. University Microfilms, Ann Arbor, Mich.

Yoffee, Norman
  1993 Too Many Chiefs? (or, Safe Texts for the '90s). In *Archaeological Theory: Who Sets the Agenda?*, ed. N. Yoffee and A. Sherratt, pp. 60–78. Cambridge University Press, Cambridge, U.K.

  1994 Memorandum to Murray Gell-Mann Concerning: The Complications of Complexity in the Prehistoric Southwest. In *Understanding Complexity on the Prehistoric Southwest*, ed. G. J. Gumerman and M. Gell-Mann, pp. 15–24. Proceedings Volume XVI, Santa Fe Institute Studies in the Sciences of Complexity, Addison-Wesley Publishing, Reading, Mass.

Zeitlin, Robert N.
  1979 *Prehistoric Long-Distance Exchange on the Southern Isthmus of Tehuantepec, Mexico.* Ph.D. dissertation, Department of Anthropology, Yale University, New Haven, Conn. University Microfilms, Ann Arbor, Mich.

  1982 Toward a More Comprehensive Model of Interregional Commodity Distribution: Political Variables and Prehistoric Obsidian Procurement in Mesoamerica. *American Antiquity* 47:260–75.

  1990 The Isthmus and the Valley of Oaxaca: Questions about Zapotec Imperialism in Formative Period Mesoamerica. *American Antiquity* 55:250–61.

  1993 Pacific Coastal Laguna Zope: A Regional Center in the Terminal Formative Hinterlands of Monte Albán. *Ancient Mesoamerica* 4:85–101.

Zeitlin, Robert N., and Arthur A. Joyce
  1999 The Zapotec Imperialism Argument: Insights from the Oaxaca Coast. *Current Anthropology* 40:383–92.

Index

About the Contributors

Jim Ambrosino is a staff archaeologist for Panamerican Consultants, Inc., in Tampa, Florida, where he oversees CRM projects throughout the southeastern United States. He received an M.A. degree from the University of Iowa, where his thesis was an assessment of Classic Maya political organization based on epigraphic data. He is currently finishing his Ph.D. dissertation, titled "Warfare and Destruction in the Maya Lowlands: Pattern and Process in the Archaeological Record of Yaxuna, Yucatan, Mexico," at Southern Methodist University. His publications have focused on Maya warfare, termination rituals, and world systems approaches. He is currently expanding his interest in Geographic Information Systems to include applications within Maya archaeology in addition to CRM applications within Florida and the southeastern United States.

Traci Ardren was codirector of the Selz Foundation Yaxuna Archaeological Project from 1992 to 1997. Her research focuses on gender, iconography, architecture, and other forms of symbolic representation in the archaeological record. She is currently assistant professor of anthropology at the University of Miami.

George Bey is the associate dean of sciences at Millsaps College. He has worked extensively in both the Tula region of Central Mexico and the Maya area at the site of Ek Balam. He presently codirects the Labna-Kiuic Regional Archaeological Project, carrying out excavations at the site of Kiuic. He is the coeditor of *Ceramic Production and*

Distribution: An Integrated Approach and La Tinaja, a newsletter of archaeological ceramics, as well as the author of a number of publications on Maya archaeology in the northern Maya lowlands.

M. Kathryn Brown received an M.A. from the University of Texas at San Antonio in 1995 and a Ph.D. from Southern Methodist University in 2003. She is currently assistant professor at the University of Texas at Arlington. She has been conducting research in the Belize River valley at the site of Blackman Eddy, focusing on the origin and function of early public architecture and associated ritual behavior. In 2003, she received a grant from the Foundation for Advancement of Mesoamerican Studies, Inc., to examine early ceramics from several sites in the Belize River valley.

Arlen F. Chase is the interim director of Latin American Studies, the anthropology coordinator, and a professor of anthropology at the University of Central Florida. He received his B.A. from the University of Pennsylvania in 1975 and his Ph.D. from the same institution in 1983 ("A Contextual Consideration of the Tayasal-Paxcaman Zone, El Peten, Guatemala"). His research interests focus on archaeological method and theory in the Maya area with particular emphasis on urbanism and ethnicity, hieroglyphic interpretation, settlement patterns, and ceramic and contextual analysis. After working in Mexico and Guatemala, he began archaeological research in Belize in 1978; since 1985, he has codirected research at the Classic period site of Caracol in the country on an annual basis. He has published numerous articles and a half dozen monographs and books, many with Diane Z. Chase, to whom he has been married for twenty-seven years. He is currently working on a book being coauthored with D. Z. Chase called *Maya Archaeology.*

Diane Z. Chase is the university coordinator for interdisciplinary studies, the director of Maya studies, and a professor of anthropology at the University of Central Florida. She received her B.A. from the University of Pennsylvania in 1975 and her Ph.D. from the same institution in 1982 ("Spatial and Temporal Variability in Postclassic Northern Belize"). Her research interests focus on archaeological method and theory in the Maya area with particular emphasis on complex societies and hermeneutics, ethnohistory, and ceramic and mortuary analysis. For the past nineteen years, she has codirected excavations at

Caracol, Belize; before that, she directed a seven-year project at Santa Rita Corozal in the same country. She has authored scores of articles as well as *Investigations at the Classic Maya City of Caracol, Belize* (1987; with A. F. Chase), *A Postclassic Perspective* (1988; with A. F. Chase), *Meso-american Elites: An Archaeological Assessment* (1992, 1994; edited with A. F. Chase), and *Studies in the Archaeology of Caracol, Belize* (1994; with A. F. Chase).

David Freidel is University Distinguished Professor at Southern Methodist University. He has investigated the archaeological contexts of warfare at the site of Yaxuna in Yucatan, Mexico, and is initiating research at the site of Waka' (El Peru) in Peten, Guatemala, where he anticipates discovery of additional archaeological evidence of warfare. He is completing a book manuscript on pre-Columbian Maya warfare in the lowlands.

James F. Garber is currently professor of anthropology at Southwest Texas State University (Ph.D., Southern Methodist University, 1981). He has been active in Maya archaeology for the past twenty-five years. Research interests include the investigation of the role of trade in sociopolitical development, reconstructing ritual, and the rise of complex society. He has conducted research at several sites in Belize and is the author of numerous publications.

Charles Golden is a research associate in the American Section of the University of Pennsylvania Museum. He has conducted fieldwork in Belize, Honduras, and most recently at the site of Piedras Negras, Guatemala, where he completed his doctoral research. He is currently the director of the Sierra del Lacandon Regional Archaeology Project, an archaeological survey along the Usumacinta River exploring the development of political frontiers between the Classic period centers of Piedras Negras and Yaxchilan.

Annabeth Headrick (B.A., Colorado College; M.A., Ph.D., University of Texas) specializes in the cultures of Mesoamerica, including the Olmec, Maya, and Aztec. Her articles include "The Street of the Dead . . . It Really Was: Mortuary Bundles at Teotihuacan" in *Ancient Mesoamerica* and "Merging Myth and Politics: The Three Temple Complex at Teotihuacan" in a book titled *Landscape and Power in Ancient Mesoamerica*, which she coedited. She is currently working on a book concerning the sociopolitical structure of Teotihuacan. She has served as the lab director on several archaeological projects in Belize, including excavations organized by Boston University, the University of Texas, and Pacific Lutheran University.

Steven A. LeBlanc is director of collections at the Peabody Museum of Archaeology and Ethnology, Harvard University. His long-term research interest has been the American Southwest, especially the Mimbres culture, resulting in *The Mimbres People: Ancient Painters of the American Southwest, The Galaz Ruin: A Prehistoric Mimbres Village in Southwestern New Mexico,* and *Short-Term Sedentism in the American Southwest: The Mimbres Valley Salado.* Recently, he has focused on warfare in the Southwest, publishing *Prehistoric Warfare in the American Southwest, Deadly Landscapes: Case Studies in Prehistoric Southwestern Warfare,* and a worldwide perspective in *Constant Battles: The Myth of the Peaceful, Noble Savage.*

Arthur A. Joyce (Ph.D., Rutgers University, 1991) is assistant professor of anthropology at the University of Colorado at Boulder. His research focuses on pre-Columbian states in Mesoamerica using theories of practice, power, ideology, and interregional interaction. He is also interested in the social and ecological effects of human impact on pre-Columbian landscapes. For the past fifteen years, he has directed an interdisciplinary archaeological project in the lower Río Verde valley, Oaxaca, Mexico. His publications include (with R. N. Zeitlin) "The Zapotec-Imperialism Argument: Insights from the Oaxaca Coast" (*Current Anthropology* 40[3]:383–92), "The Founding of Monte Albán: Sacred Propositions and Social Practices" (in *Agency in Archaeology,* edited by M. Dobres and J. Robb [London: Routledge], 71–91), and (with L. Arnaud Bustamante and M. N. Levine) "Commoner Power: A Case Study from the Classic Period Collapse on the Oaxaca Coast" (*Journal of Archaeological Method and Theory* 8[4]:343–85).

Geoff McCafferty is associate professor of archaeology at the University of Calgary. His interest in the ancient center of Cholula began when he was a graduate student at the University of the Americas, located in Cholula, in the early 1980s, studying with Michael Lind, David Peterson, and Wigberto Jimenez Moreno. Since then, he has worked closely with Arqlgo. Sergio Suarez Cruz of the INAH center in Puebla, and he has published numerous articles on various aspects of Cholula and a book on the Postclassic ceramics from the site. His current research is in Pacific Nicaragua, where, according to ethnohistorical sources, migrants from Cholula settled in the Postclassic period. Thus, he continues to research Cholula archaeology but in a warmer climate.

Barbara MacLeod received her Ph.D. from the University of Texas at Austin specializing in linguistic anthropology. Her research has focused on linguistic approaches to Maya hieroglyph decipherments and Mayan languages. She currently manages a flight school and teaches both primary and aerobatic flying.

Shirley Boteler Mock is a researcher/curator with the University of Texas at San Antonio, Institute of Texas Cultures. She received her Ph.D. in anthropology from the University of Texas at Austin with a specialty in archaeology. Her focus is complex societies, in particular those of Mesoamerica. Her dissertation covered several years of archaeological fieldwork in coastal Belize examining Maya salt-making and trading sites. Her other area of specialization is ceramic analysis and iconography, and she has papers in peer-reviewed journals on the topic and is currently coediting a volume titled *New Horizons in Ceramic Analysis* for the University of Press of Florida. She also recently published an edited volume titled *Sowing and Dawning*, which focuses on the interpretation of the material culture record.

Jonathan Pagliaro received his B.A. from the University of California, Davis, and is currently a student in the Ph.D. program at Southern Methodist University. He has conducted fieldwork in California, Mexico, and Belize. Currently working in the field in the Belize River valley, he is studying the nature and variability of termination ritual deposits among the Classic Maya.

Frank Kent Reilly III holds a Ph.D. and an M.A. from the University of Texas at Austin and a B.A. from the University of West Florida. His dissertation is "Visions to Another World: Art, Shamanism and Political Power in Middle Formative Mesoamerica." Currently, he is an associate professor of anthropology at Southwest Texas State University in San Marcos. In 1995, he was a senior curator and a catalog contributor to the Princeton University exhibition "The Olmec World: Art, Ritual, and Rulership." His published works include articles on the ecological origin of Olmec symbols, the influence of Olmec symbols on the iconography of Maya rulership, and the origin and function of the Olmec symbol system. Since 1992, he has organized and currently directs the only conference in the United States specifically focused on the art and iconography of the prehistoric, Native American, Mississippian period. Currently, the University of Texas Press has accepted the written results of this conference, for which he is coeditor and a chapter contributor, for publication as *Studies in Mississippian Iconography, Vol. I.* His current interests include the art and iconography of the prehistoric Mississippian period of the southeastern United States and the development of an instructional program through which to teach the ancient American past in secondary schools.

Payson Sheets received a Ph.D. from the University of Pennsylvania. He has worked on Tikal and Chalchuapa projects and has focused on the effects of explosive volcanism on egalitarian, ranked, and stratified societies from Panama to Mexico. Currently, he is a professor of anthropology at the University of Colorado, Boulder.

Charles Suhler received his M.A. from the University of Texas at San Antonio. In 1996, he graduated with a doctorate from Southern Methodist University. He has worked extensively throughout the Maya lowlands in Guatemala, Belize, and Mexico and was the codirector of the Selz Foundation Yaxuna Project. His interests include Maya ritual and politics, including the role of termination rituals in Maya warfare.

Travis W. Stanton, currently working in Yucatan, Mexico, has also conducted field research in New York State and Bolivia. He received his B.A. from Binghamton University and his M.A. and Ph.D. from Southern Methodist University. He has taught at Jamestown Community College and the State University of New York at Fredonia.